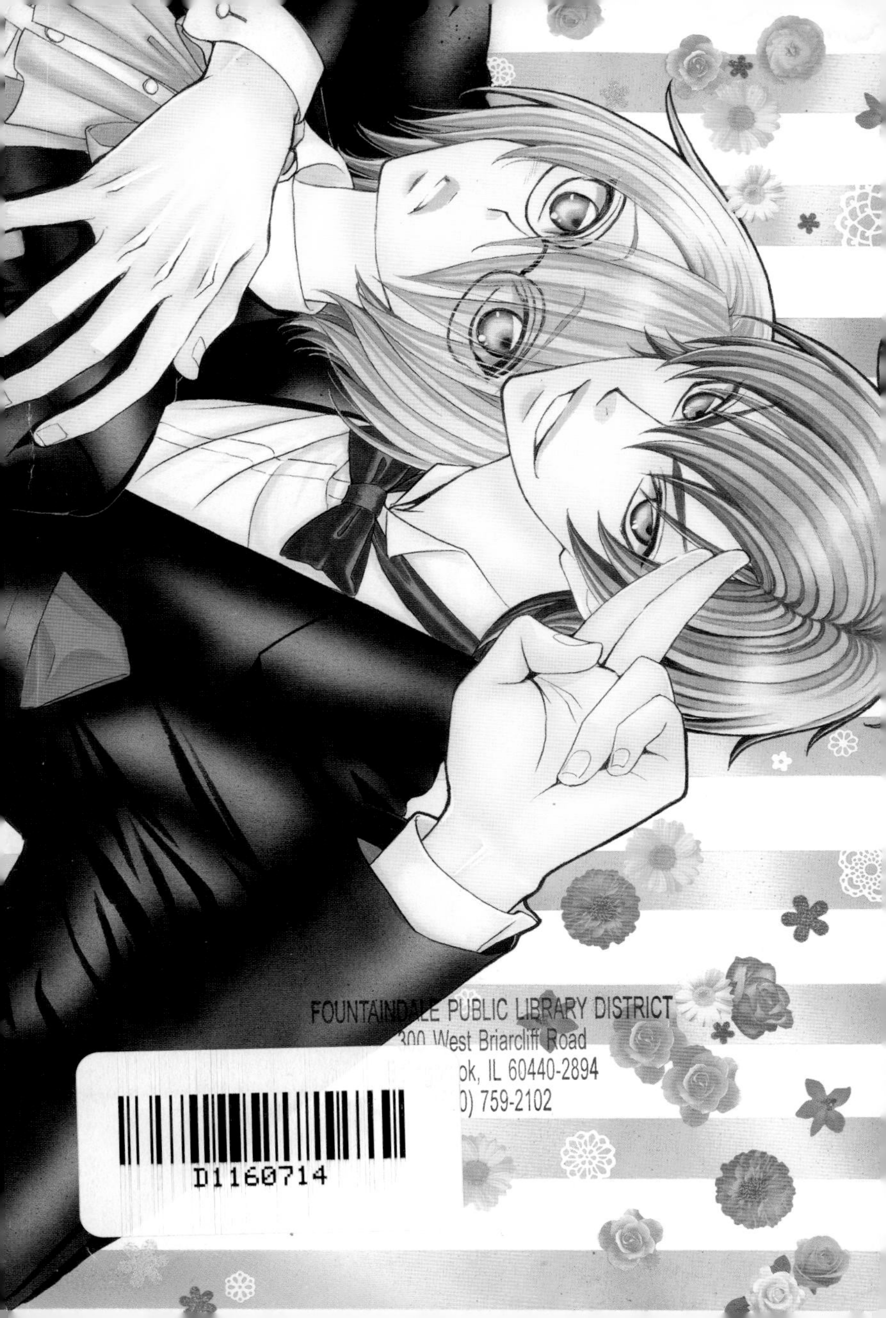

Love Stage!!

Story by **Eiki Eiki,** Art by **Taishi Zaou**   volume **2**

CONTENTS

SUBLIME
SuBLime Manga Edition

Can someone be *too* shy for love?

Awkward Silence

Story & Art by Hinako TAKANAGA

Satoru is an introvert with a longtime crush on Keigo, a popular boy on the baseball team. But much to his surprise, Keigo comes up to him and asks him out! Satoru is so overcome he can't respond. Will Satoru be able to get past his shyness, or will he lose his chance with the boy he loves?

Bukiyou na Silent 1 © 2008 Hinako Takanaga/Libre Publishing

Your Toys Love Boys' Love

Own your SuBLime book as a convenient PDF document that is downloadable to the following devices:

- ♥ Computer
- ♥ Kindle™
- ♥ NOOK™
- ♥ iPad™, iPhone™, and iPod Touch™
- ♥ Any device capable of reading a PDF document

www.SuBLimeManga.com

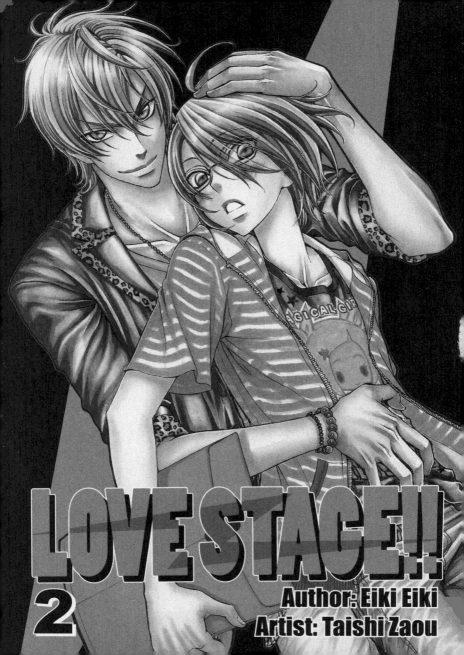

LOVE STAGE!!

2

Author: Eiki Eiki

Artist: Taishi Zaou

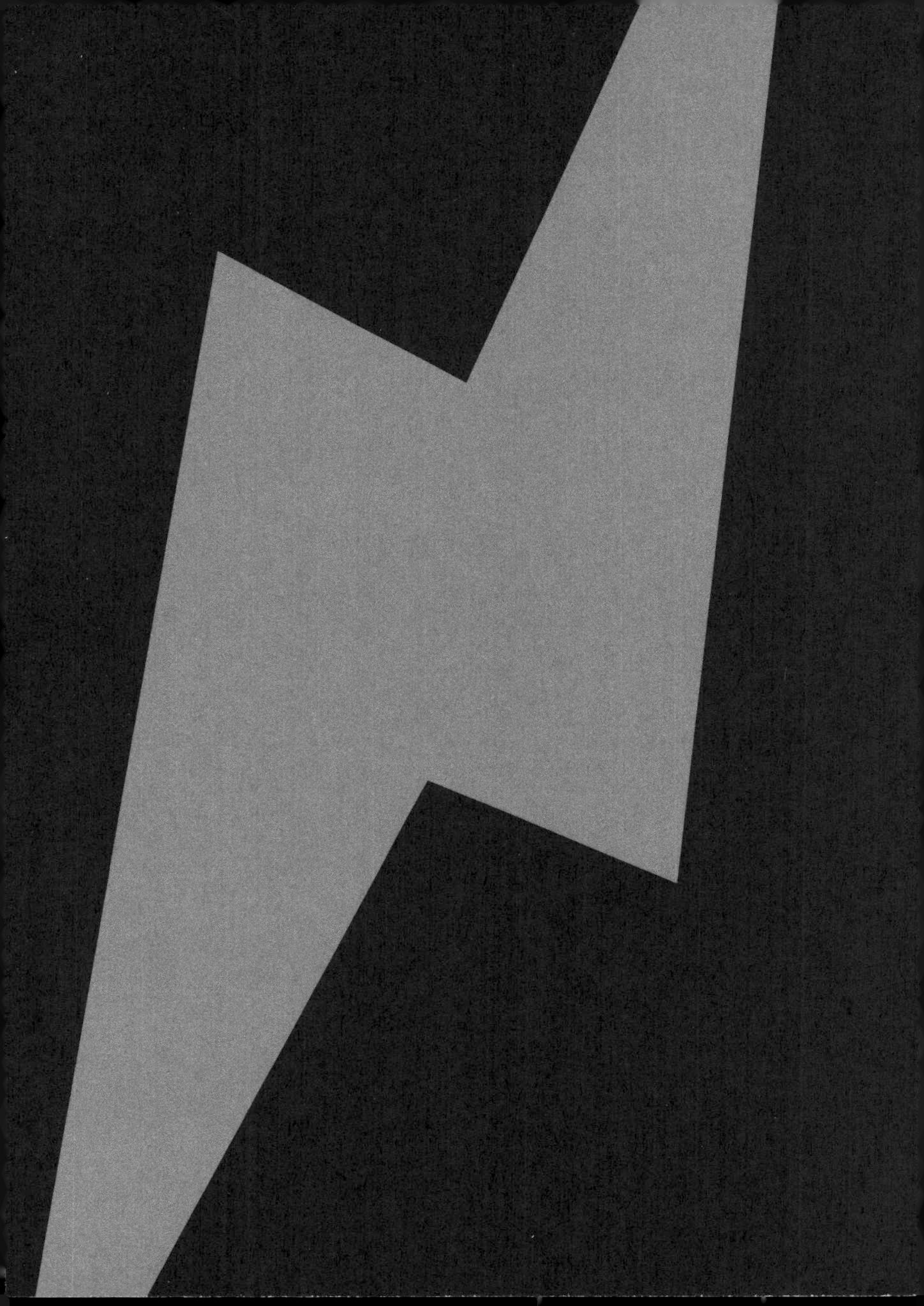

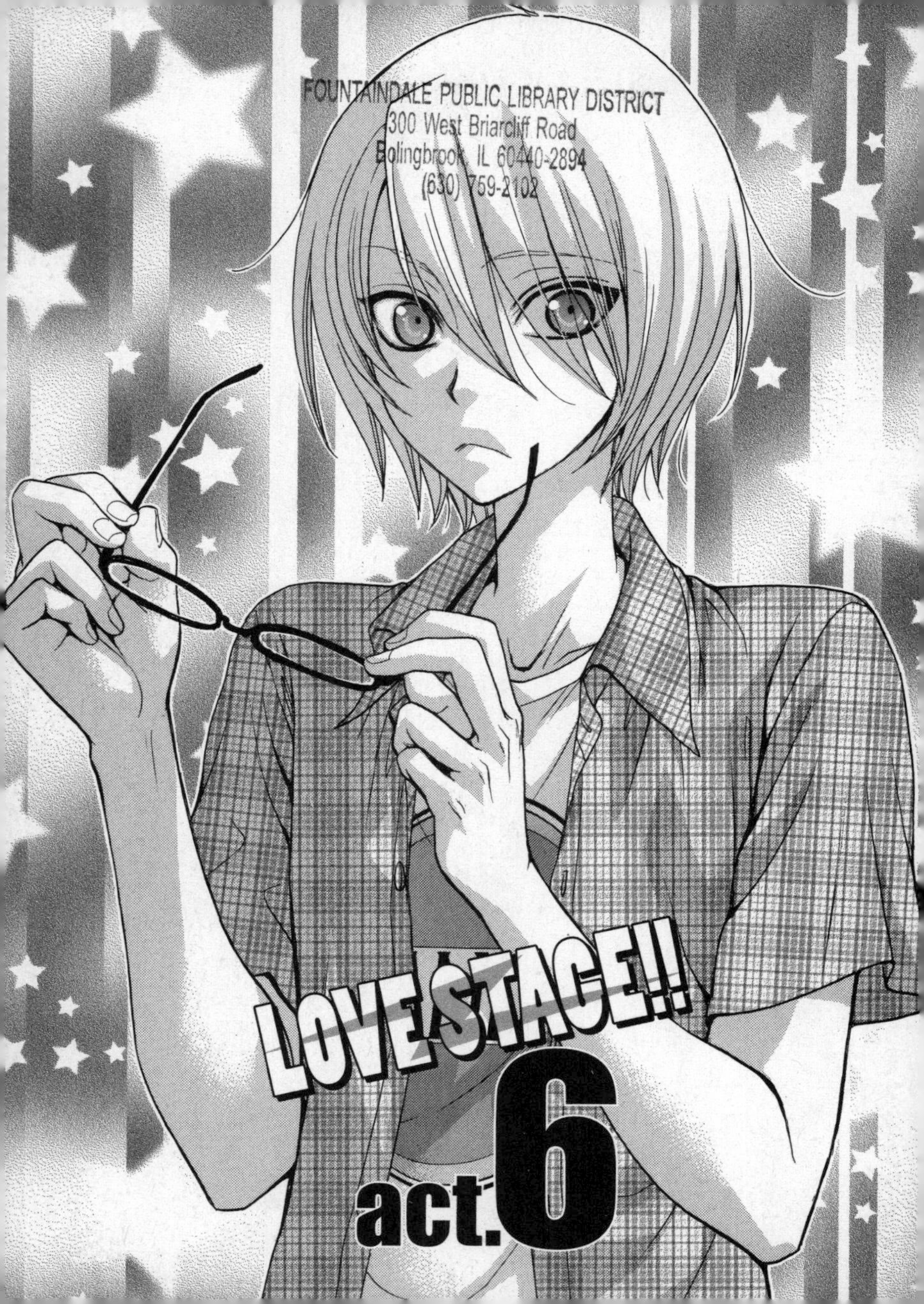
LOVE STAGE!!
act.6

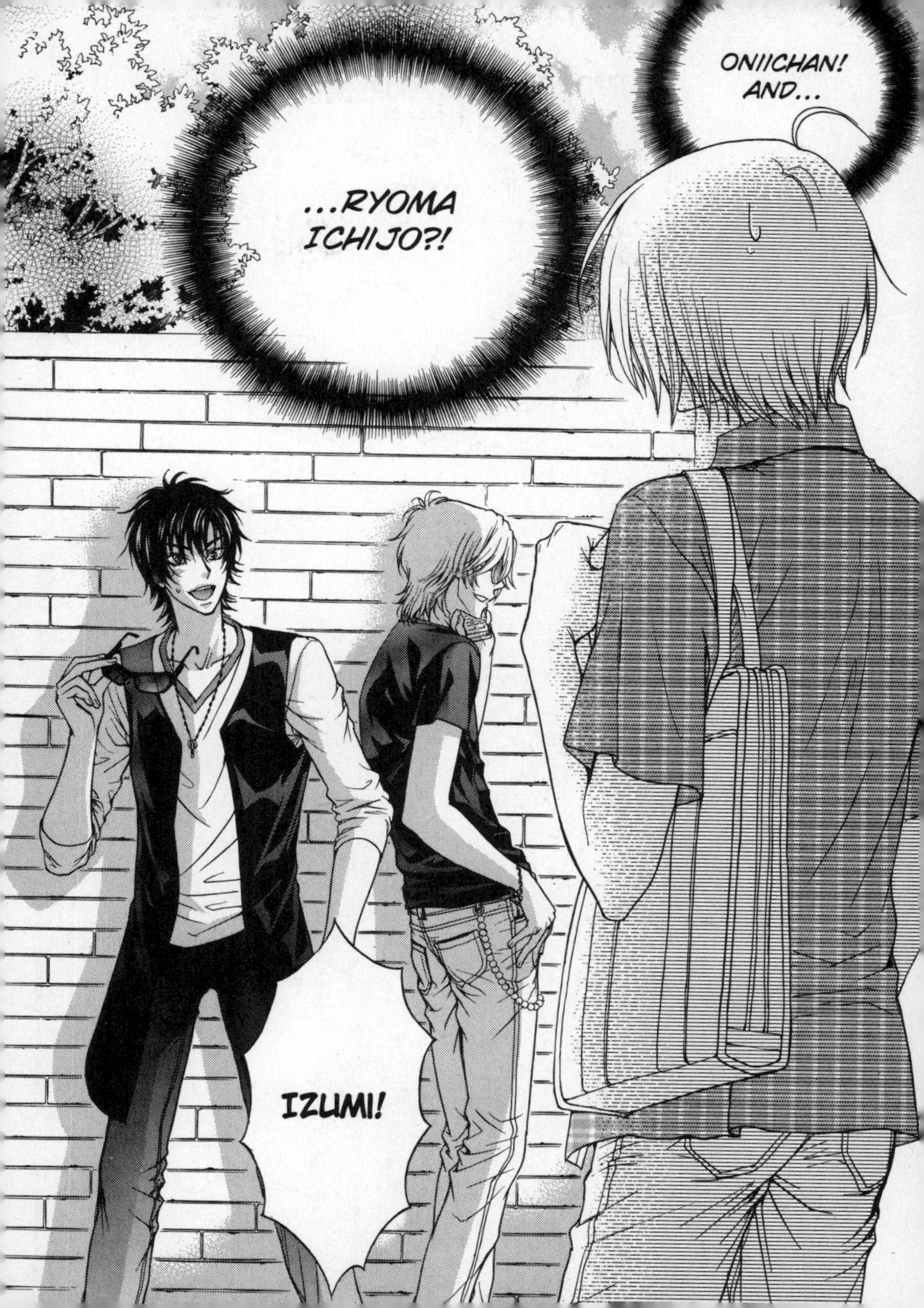
ONIICHAN! AND...
...RYOMA ICHIJO?!
IZUMI!

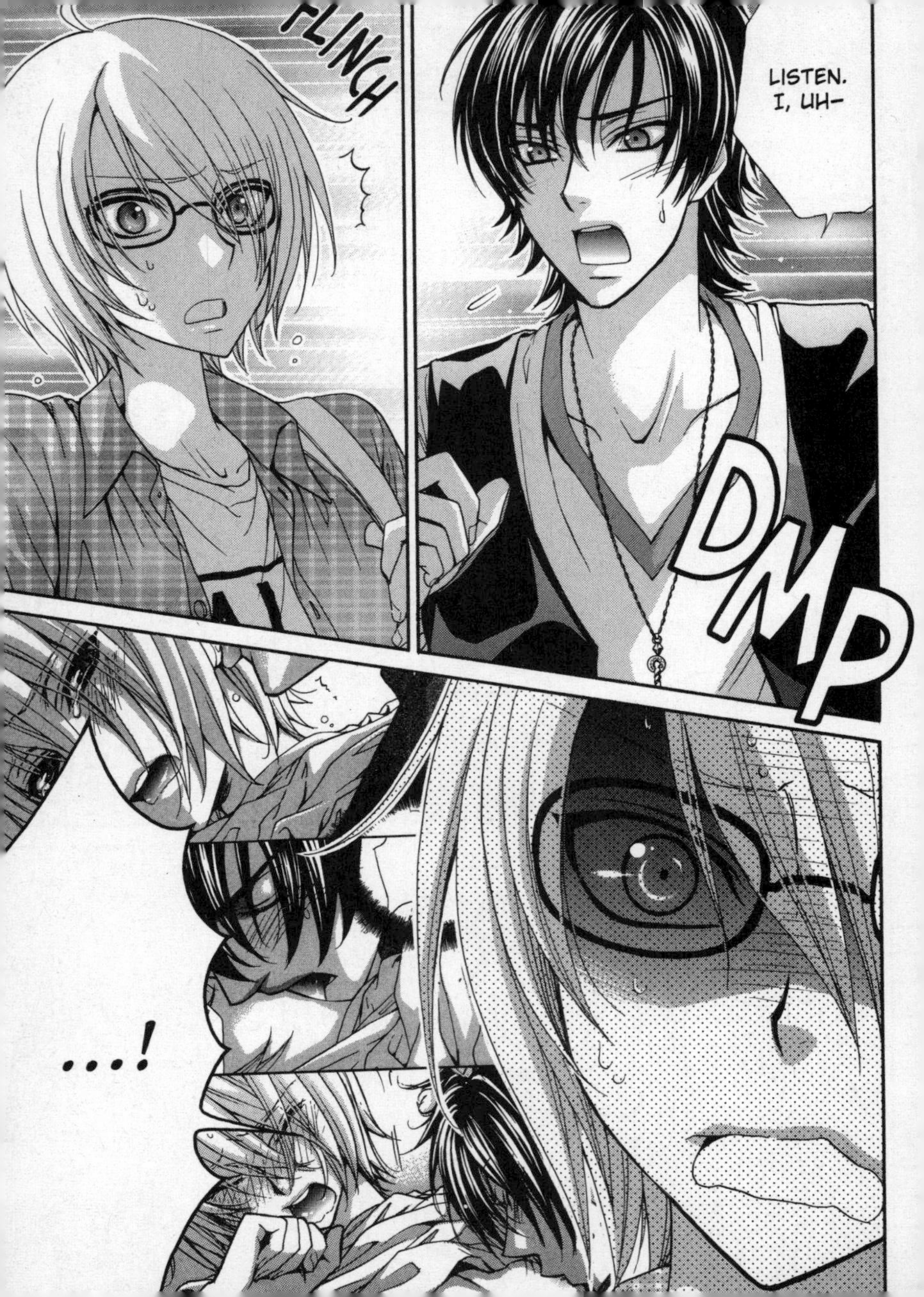
LISTEN. I, UH–
DMP
FLINCH
...!

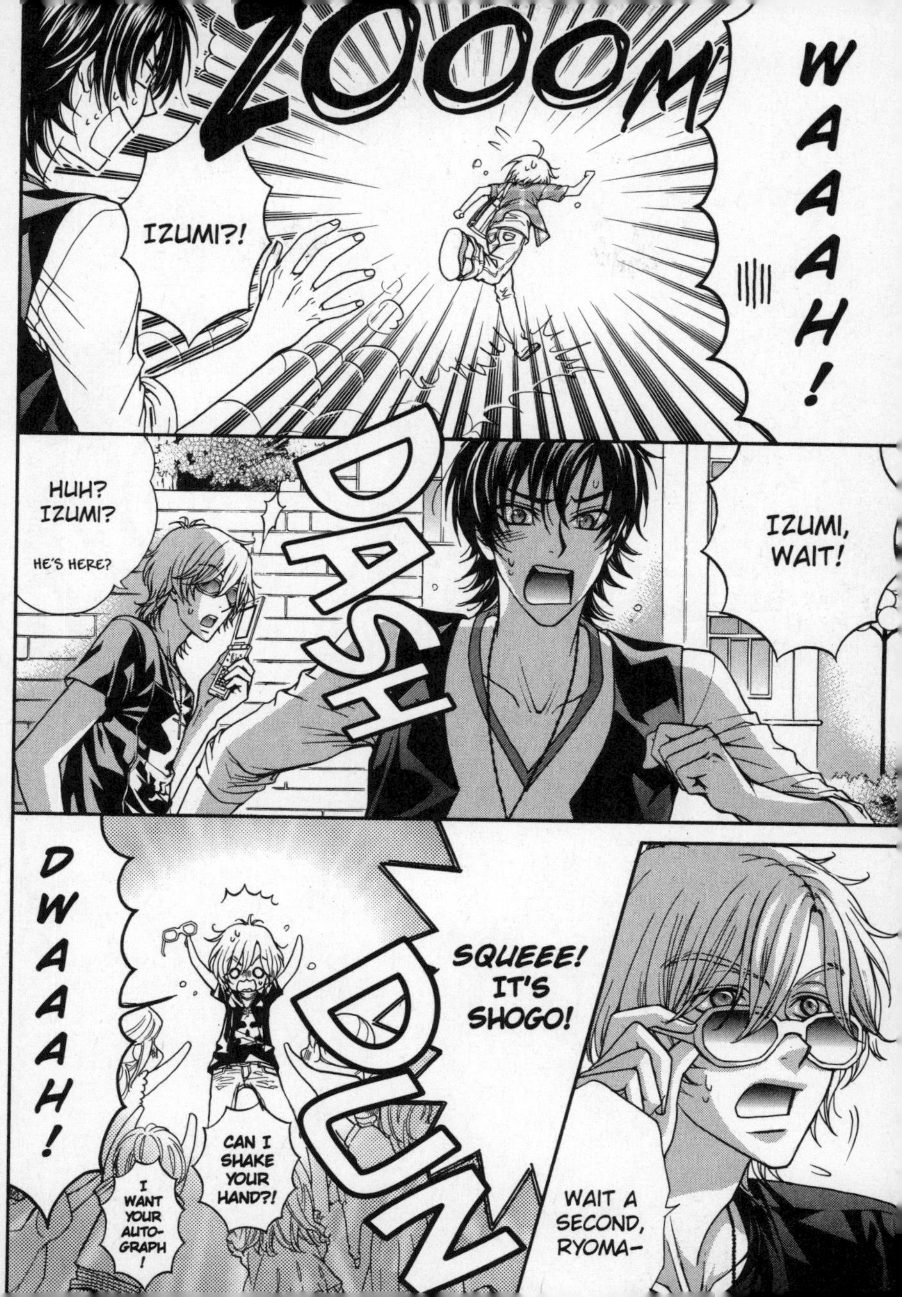
WAAAAH!
ZOOOM
IZUMI?!
IZUMI, WAIT!
DASH
HUH? IZUMI?
HE'S HERE?
WAIT A SECOND, RYOMA-
SQUEEE! IT'S SHOGO!
DUN
CAN I SHAKE YOUR HAND?!
I WANT YOUR AUTO-GRAPH!
DWAAAAH!

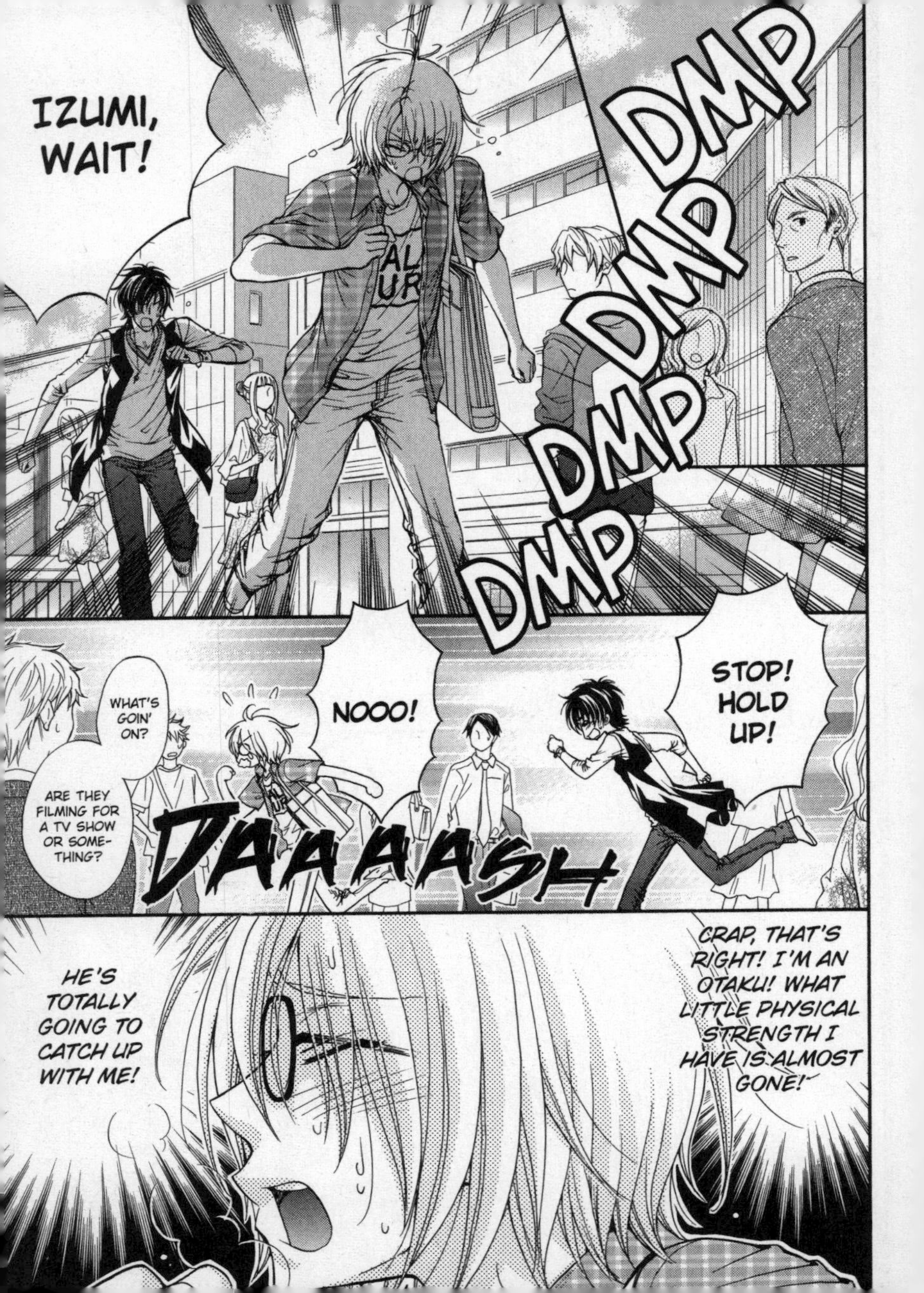
DMP DMP DMP DMP DMP
IZUMI, WAIT!
STOP! HOLD UP!
NOOO!
DAAAASH
WHAT'S GOIN' ON?
ARE THEY FILMING FOR A TV SHOW OR SOME-THING?
CRAP, THAT'S RIGHT! I'M AN OTAKU! WHAT LITTLE PHYSICAL STRENGTH I HAVE IS ALMOST GONE!
HE'S TOTALLY GOING TO CATCH UP WITH ME!

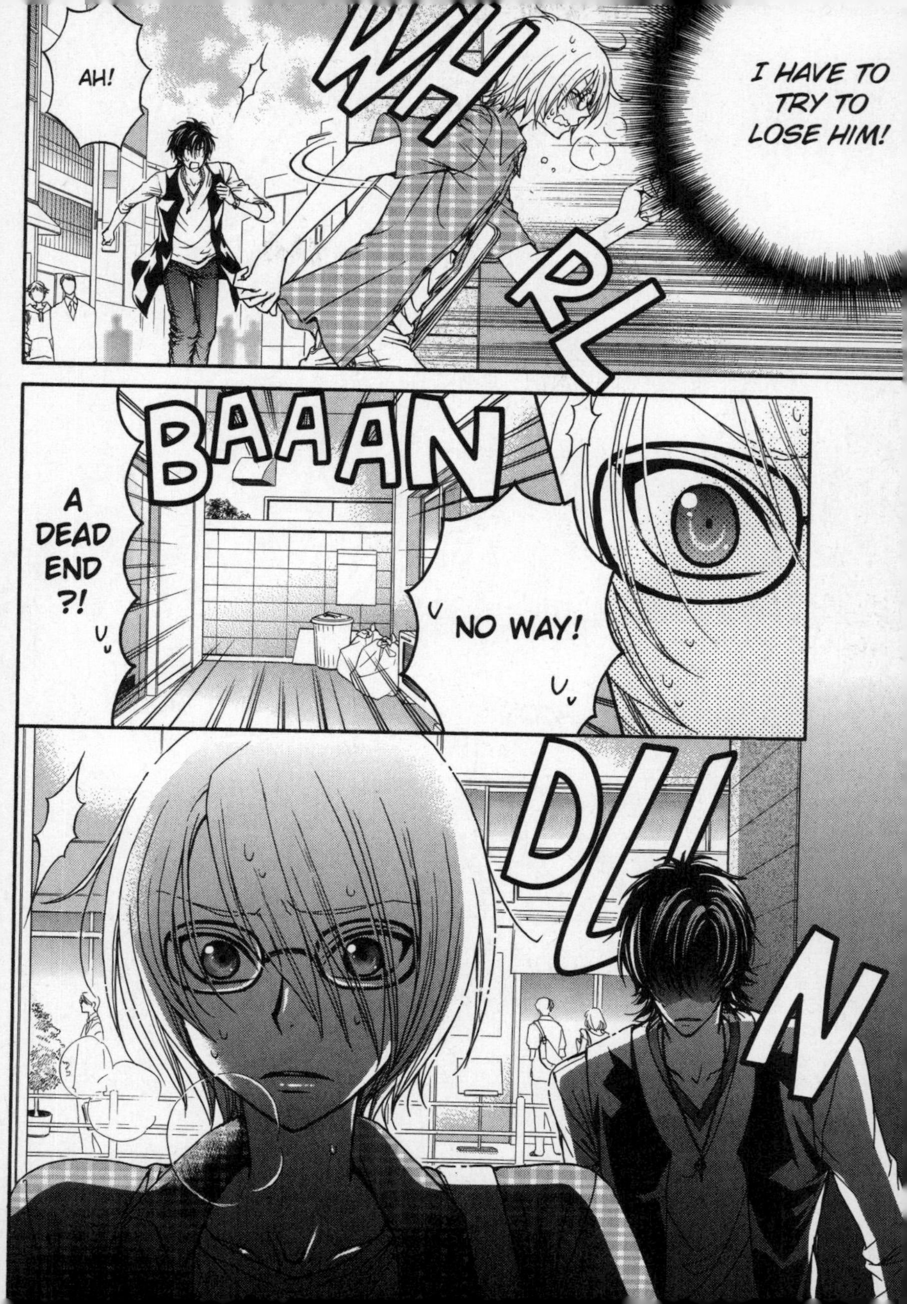
I HAVE TO TRY TO LOSE HIM!
WHRL
AH!
BAAAN
NO WAY!
A DEAD END?!
DUN

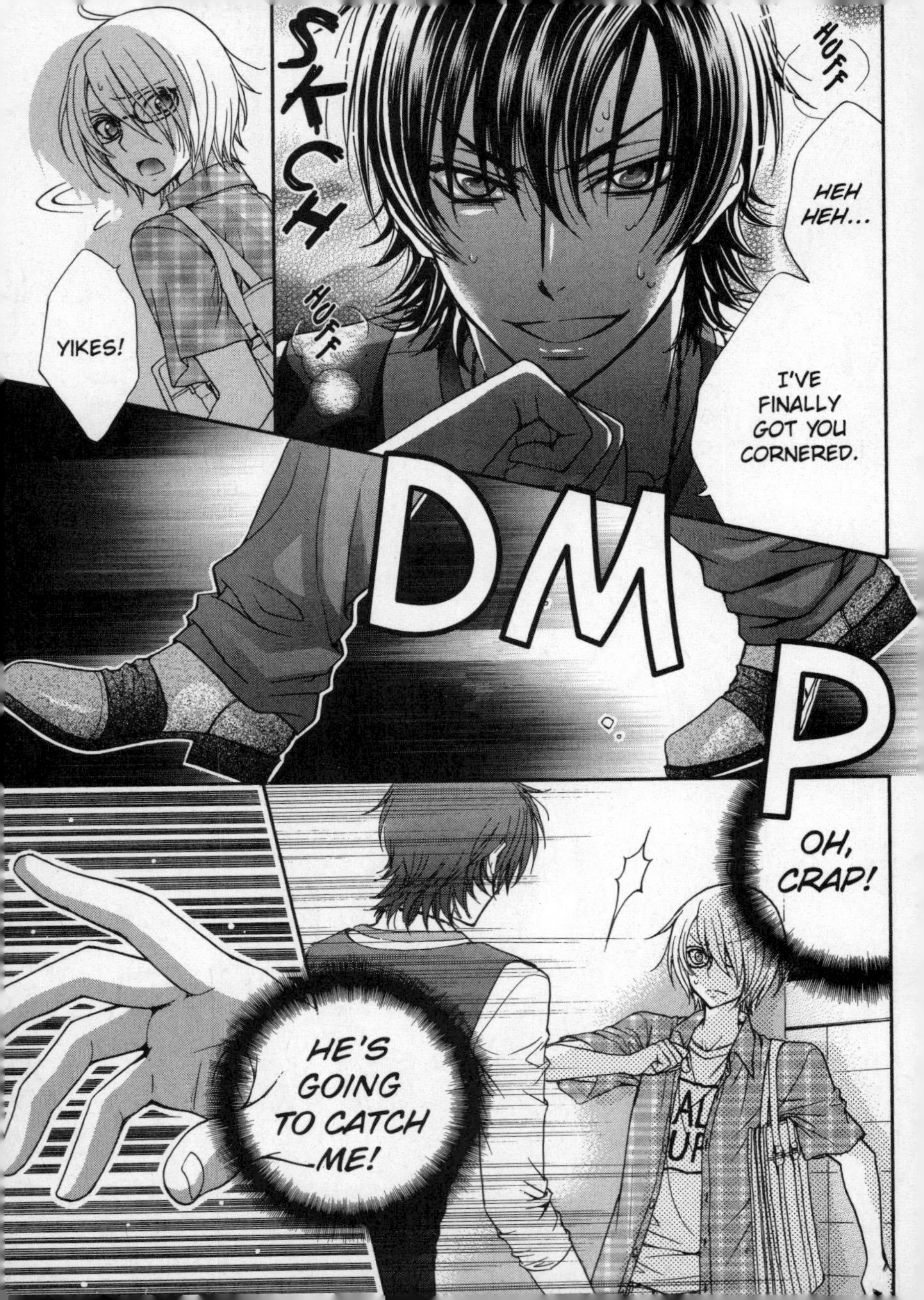
HUFF HUFF
HEH HEH...
I'VE FINALLY GOT YOU CORNERED.
SKCH
HUFF HUFF
YIKES!
DMP
OH, CRAP!
HE'S GOING TO CATCH ME!

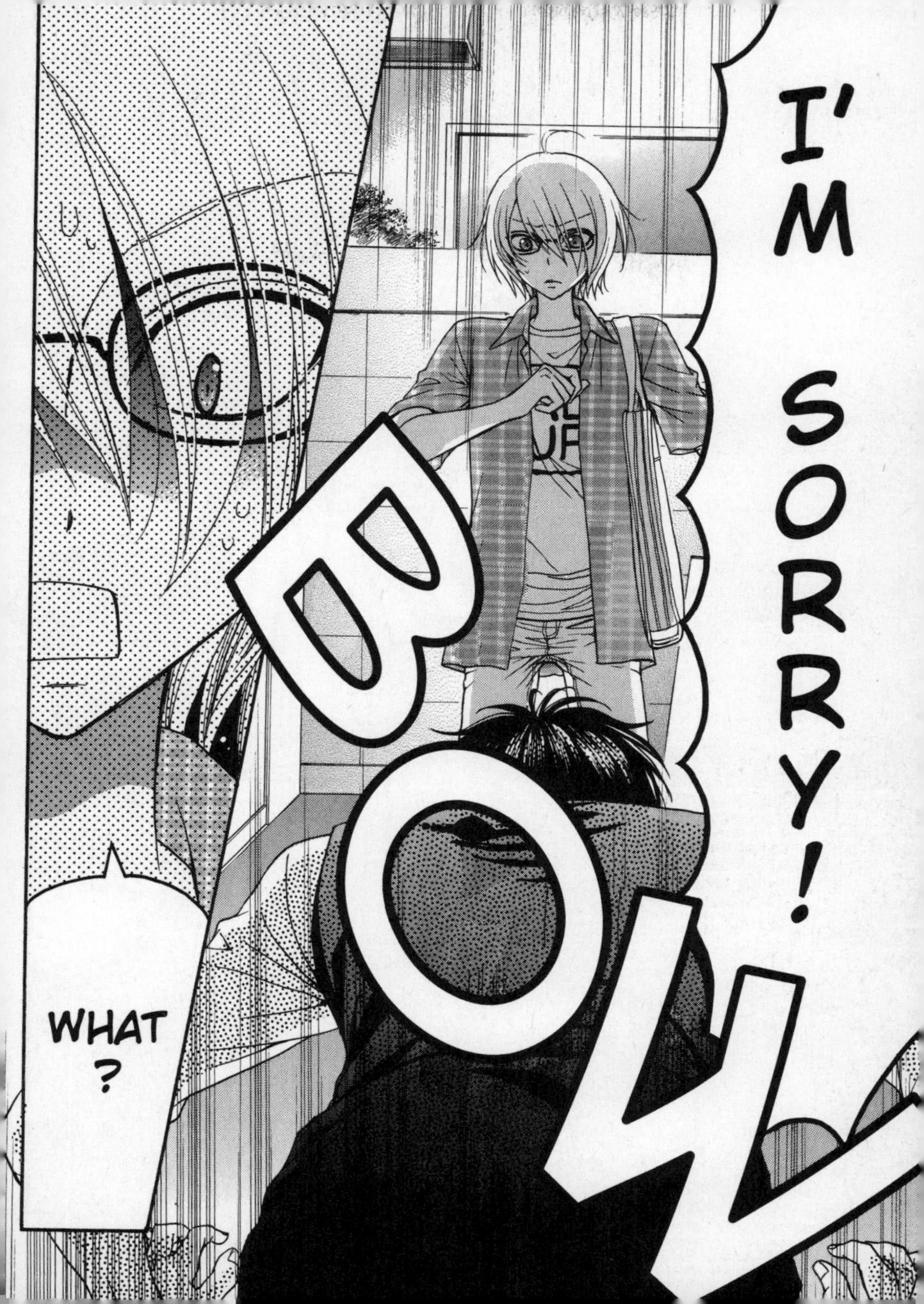
I'M SORRY!
BOW
WHAT?

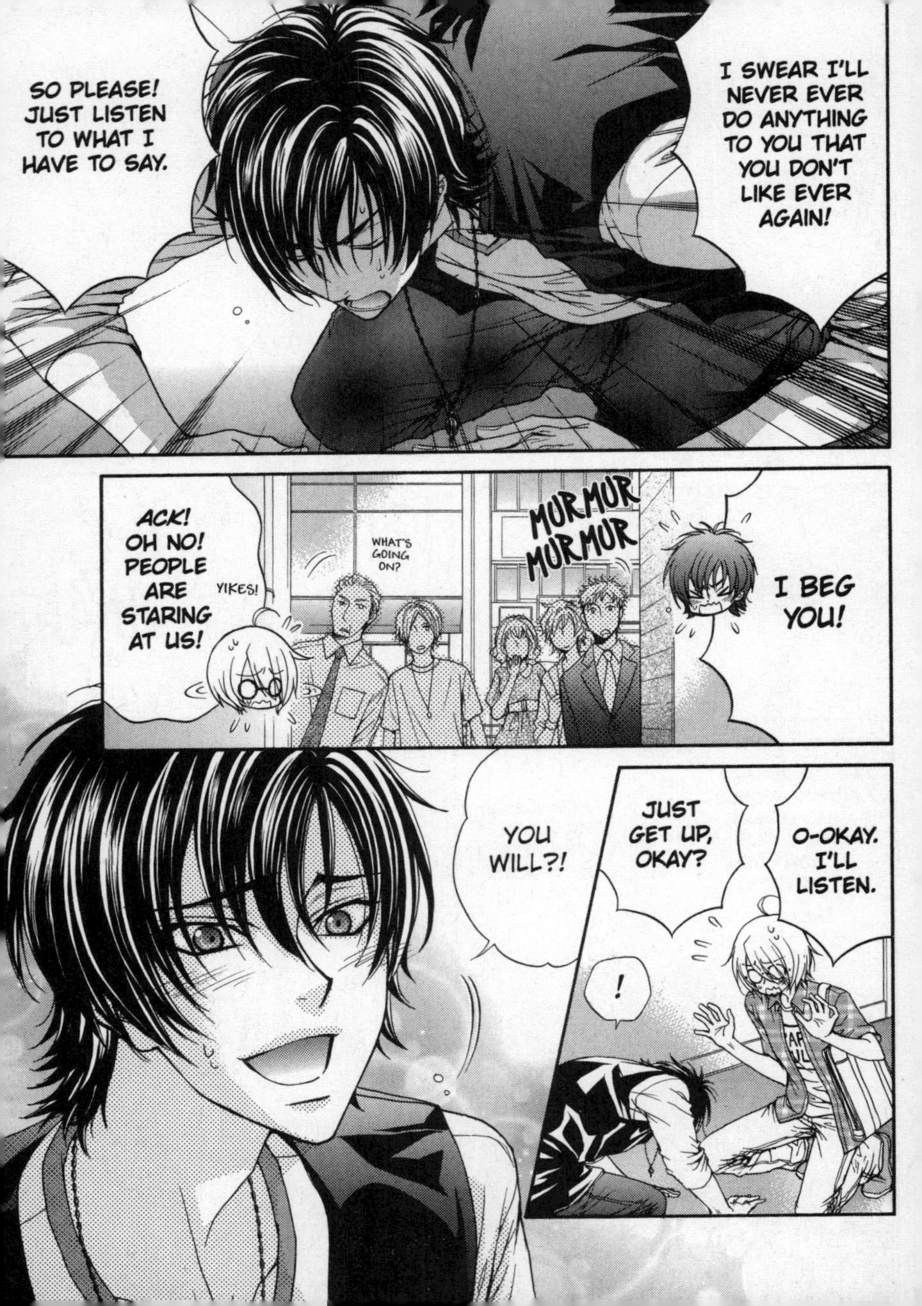

I SWEAR I'LL NEVER EVER DO ANYTHING TO YOU THAT YOU DON'T LIKE EVER AGAIN!
SO PLEASE! JUST LISTEN TO WHAT I HAVE TO SAY.
I BEG YOU!
MURMUR MURMUR
WHAT'S GOING ON?
ACK! OH NO! PEOPLE ARE STARING AT US!
YIKES!
O-OKAY. I'LL LISTEN.
JUST GET UP, OKAY?
!
YOU WILL?!

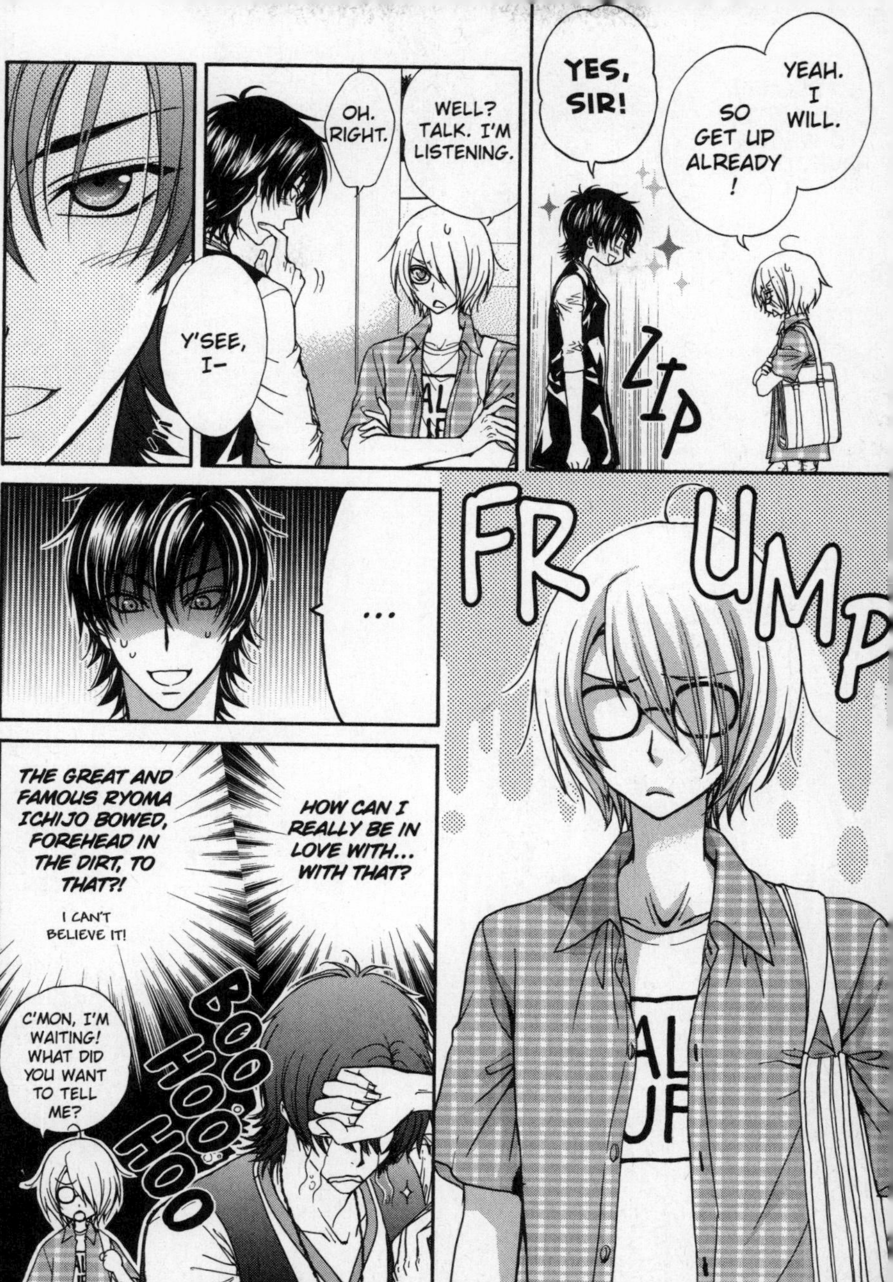
YEAH. I WILL. SO GET UP ALREADY!
YES, SIR!
ZIP
WELL? TALK. I'M LISTENING.
OH. RIGHT.
Y'SEE, I–
FRUMP
...
HOW CAN I REALLY BE IN LOVE WITH... WITH THAT?
THE GREAT AND FAMOUS RYOMA ICHIJO BOWED, FOREHEAD IN THE DIRT, TO THAT?!
I CAN'T BELIEVE IT!
BOO HOO HOO
C'MON, I'M WAITING! WHAT DID YOU WANT TO TELL ME?

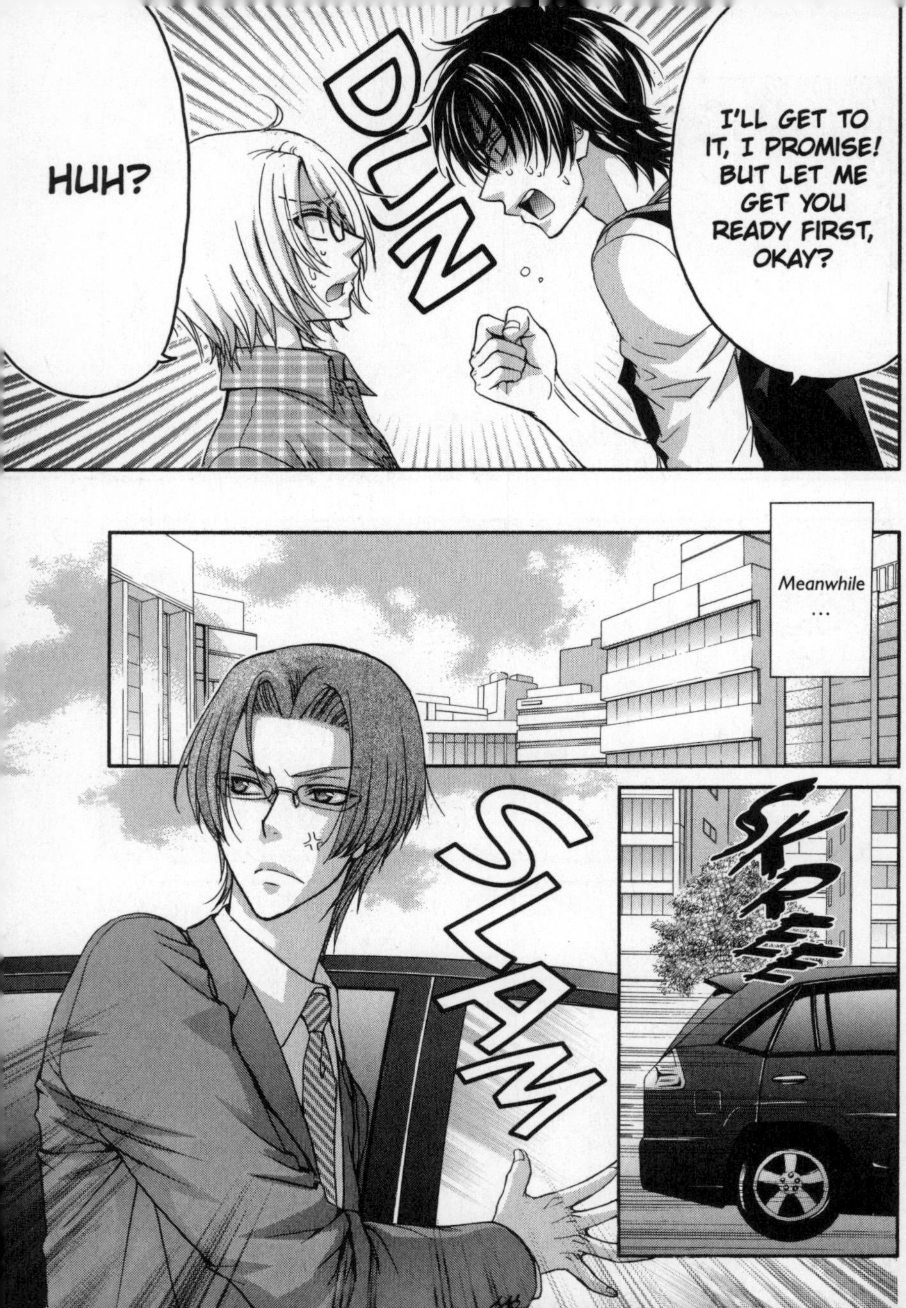
I'LL GET TO IT, I PROMISE! BUT LET ME GET YOU READY FIRST, OKAY?
DUN
HUH?
Meanwhile . . .
SKREE
SLAM

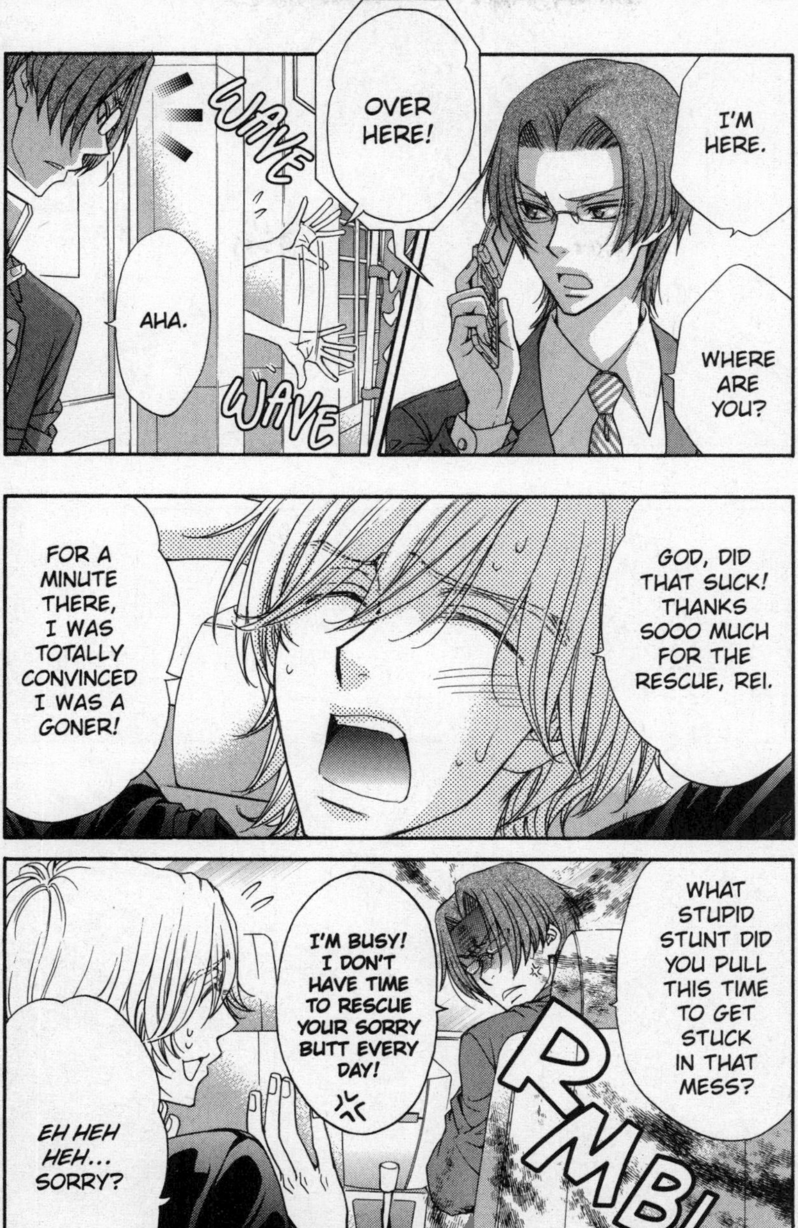
I'M HERE.
WHERE ARE YOU?
OVER HERE!
WAVE
WAVE
AHA.
GOD, DID THAT SUCK! THANKS SOOO MUCH FOR THE RESCUE, REI.
FOR A MINUTE THERE, I WAS TOTALLY CONVINCED I WAS A GONER!
WHAT STUPID STUNT DID YOU PULL THIS TIME TO GET STUCK IN THAT MESS?
RMBL
I'M BUSY! I DON'T HAVE TIME TO RESCUE YOUR SORRY BUTT EVERY DAY!
EH HEH HEH... SORRY?

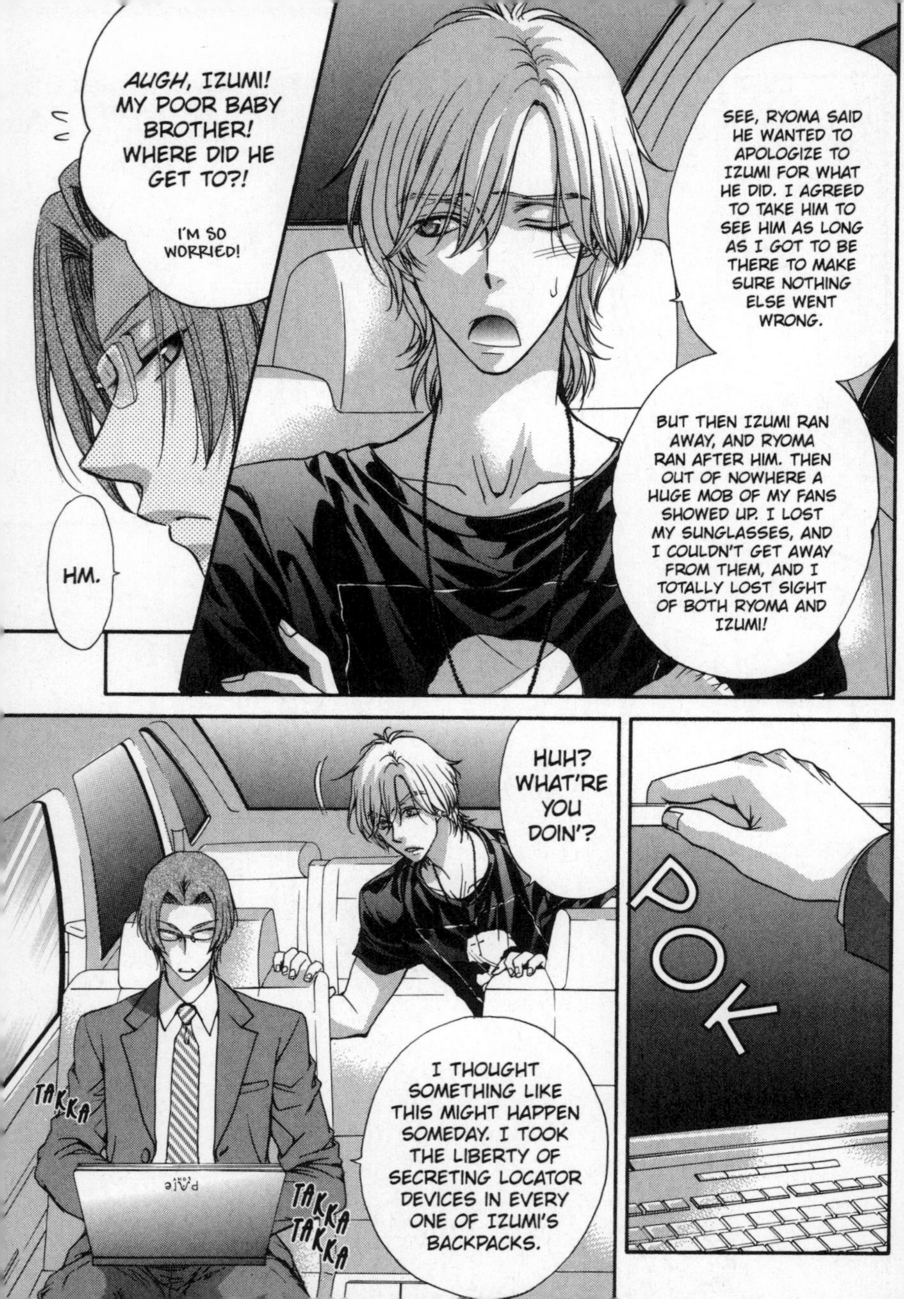
SEE, RYOMA SAID HE WANTED TO APOLOGIZE TO IZUMI FOR WHAT HE DID. I AGREED TO TAKE HIM TO SEE HIM AS LONG AS I GOT TO BE THERE TO MAKE SURE NOTHING ELSE WENT WRONG.
BUT THEN IZUMI RAN AWAY, AND RYOMA RAN AFTER HIM. THEN OUT OF NOWHERE A HUGE MOB OF MY FANS SHOWED UP. I LOST MY SUNGLASSES, AND I COULDN'T GET AWAY FROM THEM, AND I TOTALLY LOST SIGHT OF BOTH RYOMA AND IZUMI!
AUGH, IZUMI! MY POOR BABY BROTHER! WHERE DID HE GET TO?!
I'M SO WORRIED!
HM.
POK
HUH? WHAT'RE YOU DOIN'?
I THOUGHT SOMETHING LIKE THIS MIGHT HAPPEN SOMEDAY. I TOOK THE LIBERTY OF SECRETING LOCATOR DEVICES IN EVERY ONE OF IZUMI'S BACKPACKS.
TAKKA
TAKKA TAKKA
TAKKA

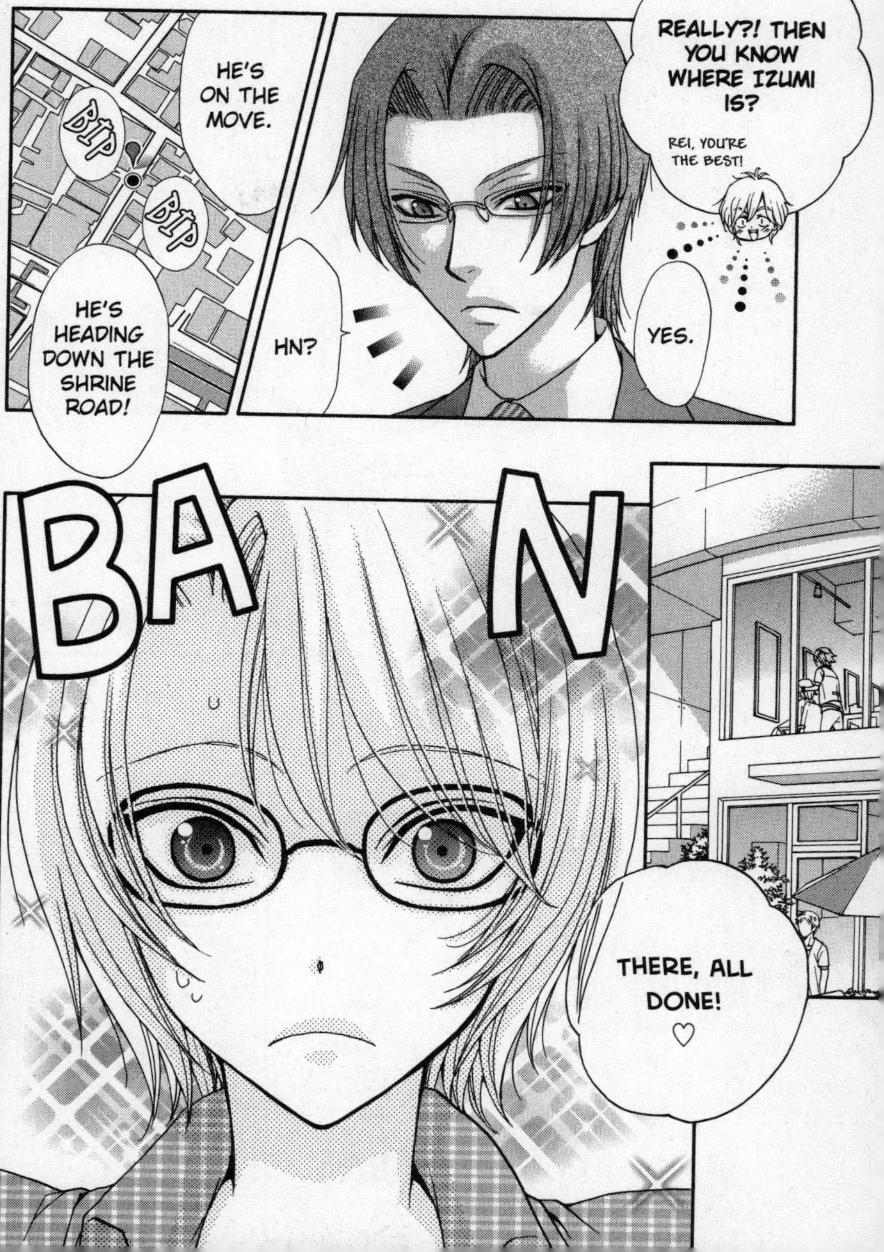
REALLY?! THEN YOU KNOW WHERE IZUMI IS?
REI, YOU'RE THE BEST!
YES.
HN?
HE'S ON THE MOVE.
BIP
BIP
HE'S HEADING DOWN THE SHRINE ROAD!
THERE, ALL DONE! ♡
BAN

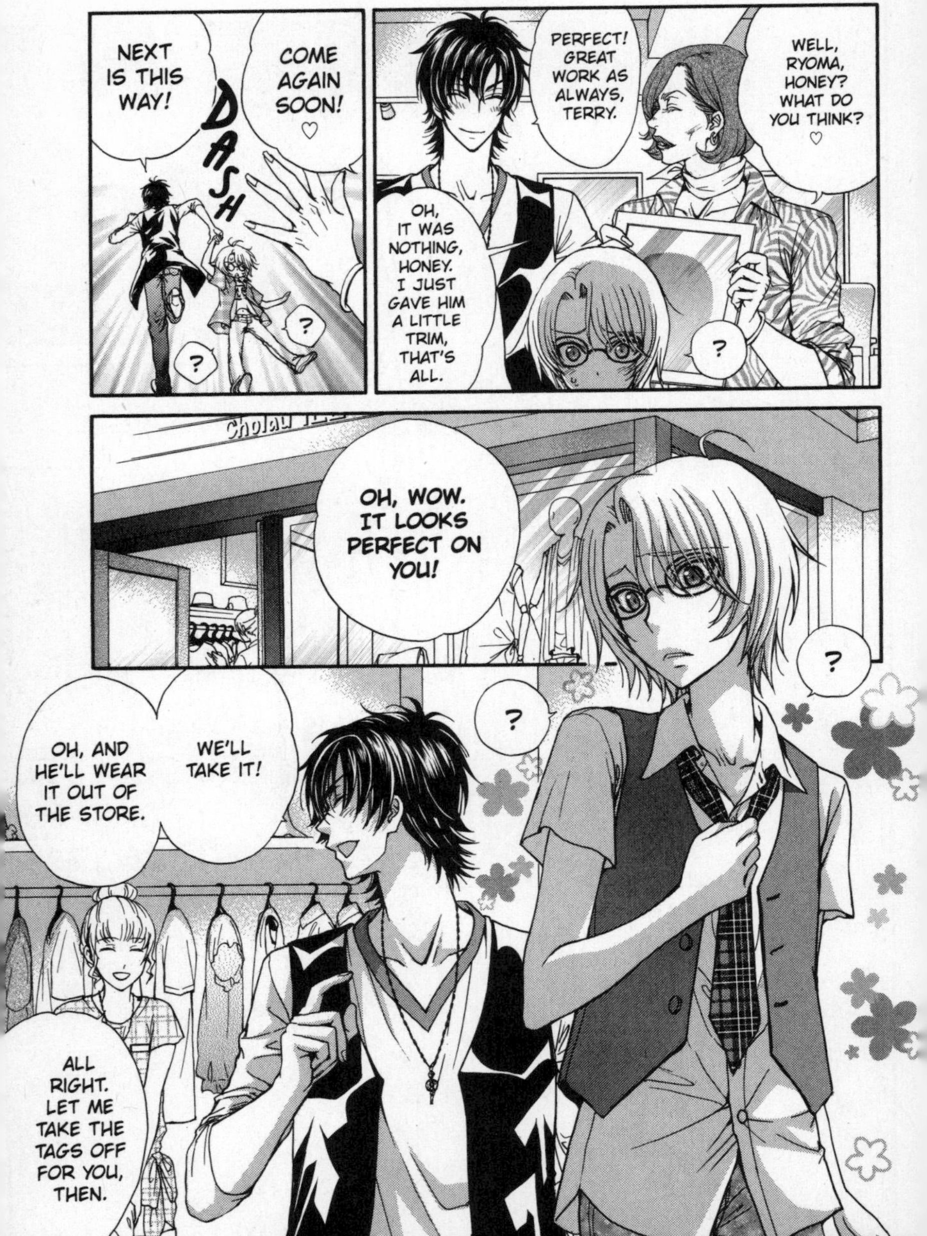

WELL, RYOMA, HONEY? WHAT DO YOU THINK? ♡
PERFECT! GREAT WORK AS ALWAYS, TERRY.
?
OH, IT WAS NOTHING, HONEY. I JUST GAVE HIM A LITTLE TRIM, THAT'S ALL.
COME AGAIN SOON! ♡
NEXT IS THIS WAY!
DASH
?
?
OH, WOW. IT LOOKS PERFECT ON YOU!
?
?
WE'LL TAKE IT!
OH, AND HE'LL WEAR IT OUT OF THE STORE.
ALL RIGHT. LET ME TAKE THE TAGS OFF FOR YOU, THEN.

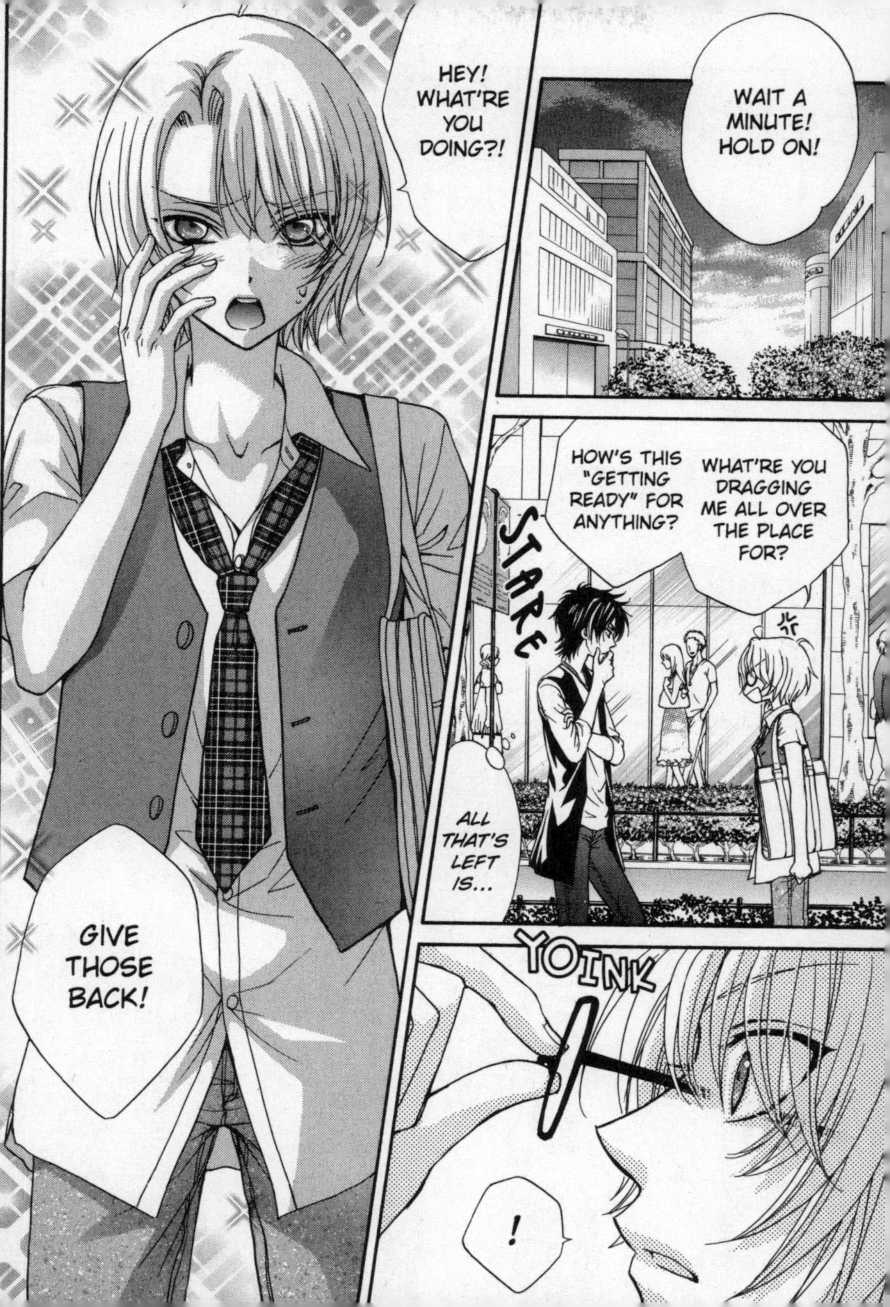

WAIT A MINUTE! HOLD ON!
WHAT'RE YOU DRAGGING ME ALL OVER THE PLACE FOR?
HOW'S THIS "GETTING READY" FOR ANYTHING?
STARE
ALL THAT'S LEFT IS...
YOINK
!
HEY! WHAT'RE YOU DOING?!
GIVE THOSE BACK!

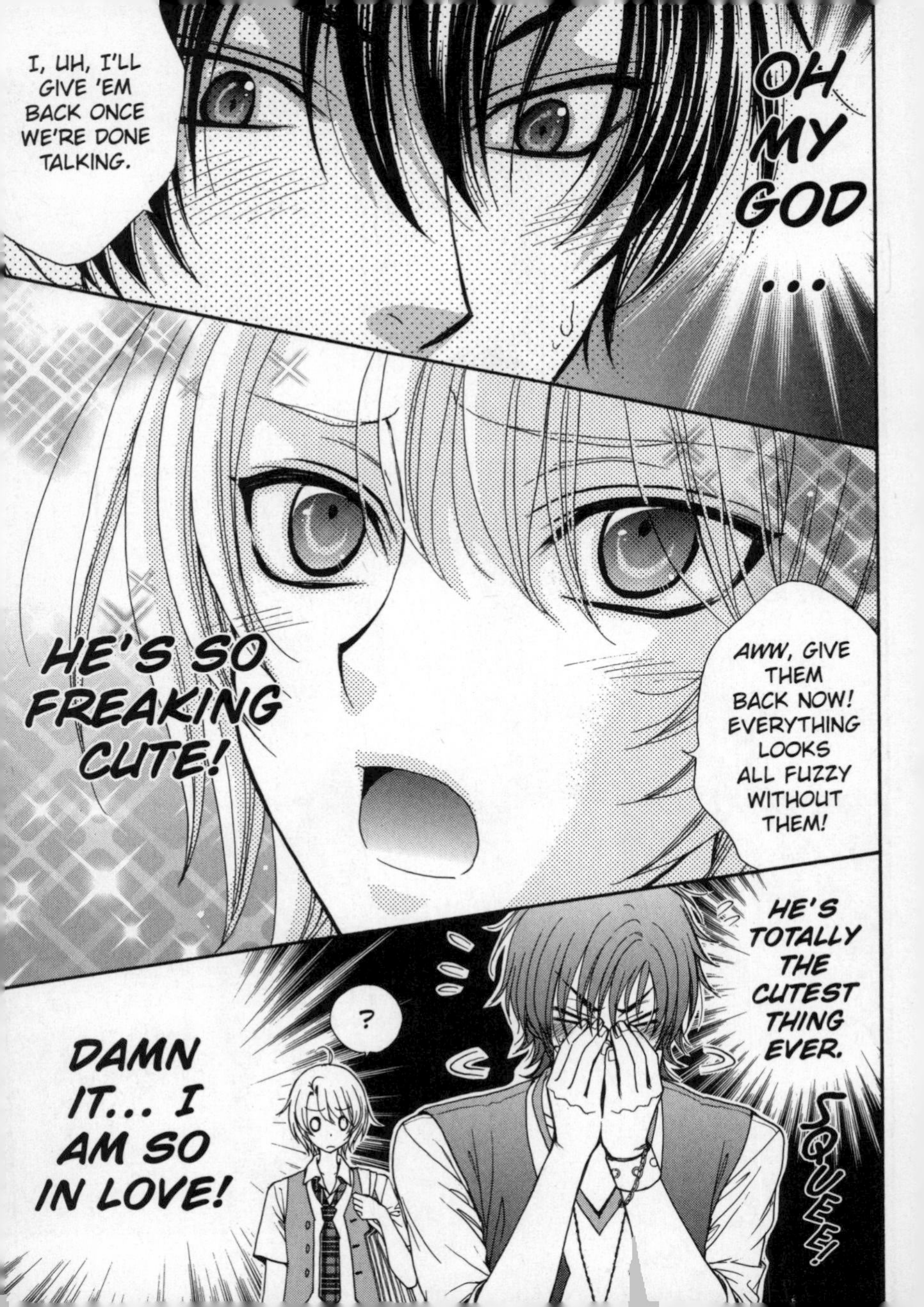
OH MY GOD...
I, UH, I'LL GIVE 'EM BACK ONCE WE'RE DONE TALKING.
AWW, GIVE THEM BACK NOW! EVERYTHING LOOKS ALL FUZZY WITHOUT THEM!
HE'S SO FREAKING CUTE!
HE'S TOTALLY THE CUTEST THING EVER.
SQUEE!
?
DAMN IT... I AM SO IN LOVE!

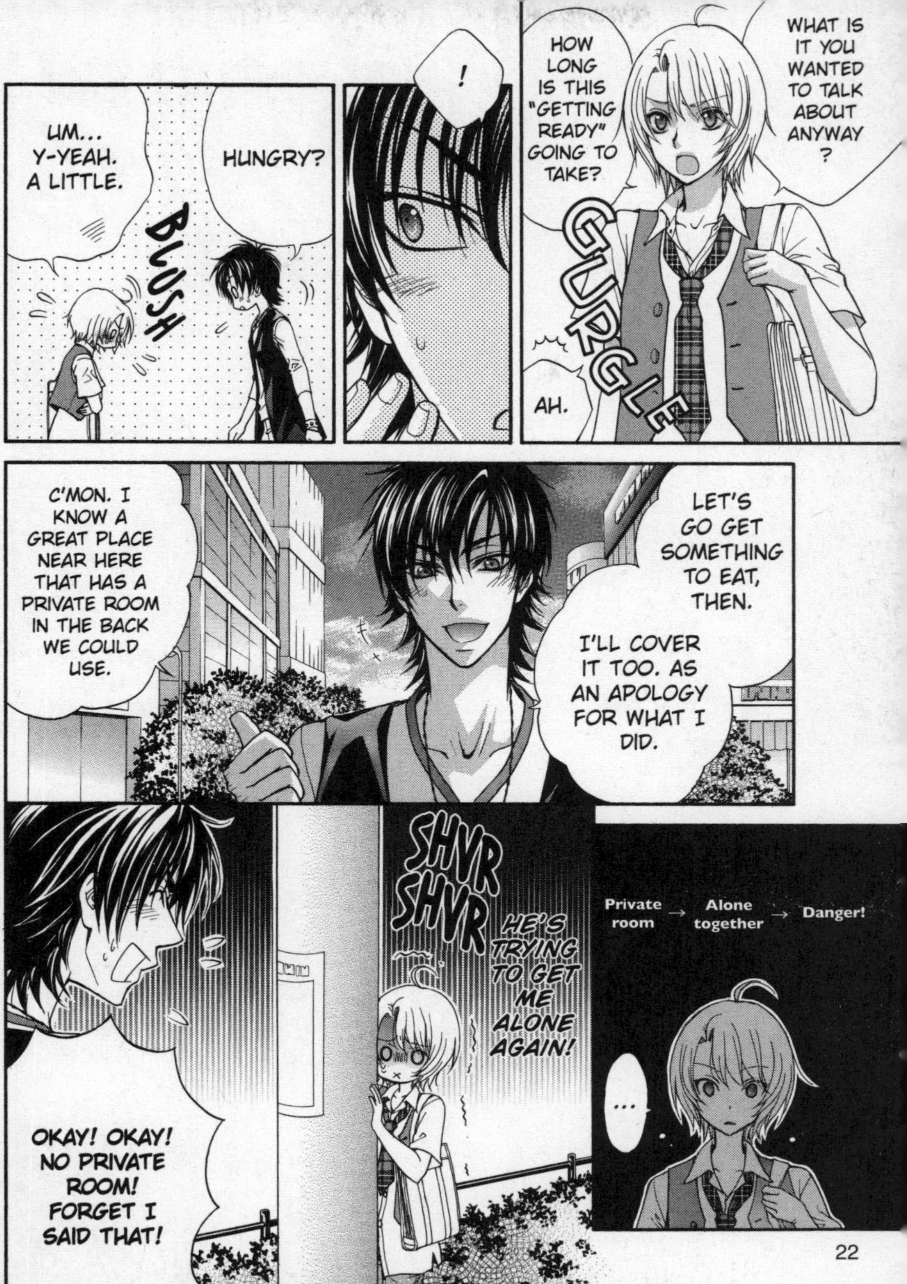
WHAT IS IT YOU WANTED TO TALK ABOUT ANYWAY?
HOW LONG IS THIS "GETTING READY" GOING TO TAKE?
GURGLE
AH.
!
HUNGRY?
UM... Y-YEAH. A LITTLE.
BLUSH
LET'S GO GET SOMETHING TO EAT, THEN.
I'LL COVER IT TOO. AS AN APOLOGY FOR WHAT I DID.
C'MON. I KNOW A GREAT PLACE NEAR HERE THAT HAS A PRIVATE ROOM IN THE BACK WE COULD USE.
Private room → Alone together → Danger!
...
SHVR SHVR
HE'S TRYING TO GET ME ALONE AGAIN!
OKAY! OKAY! NO PRIVATE ROOM! FORGET I SAID THAT!

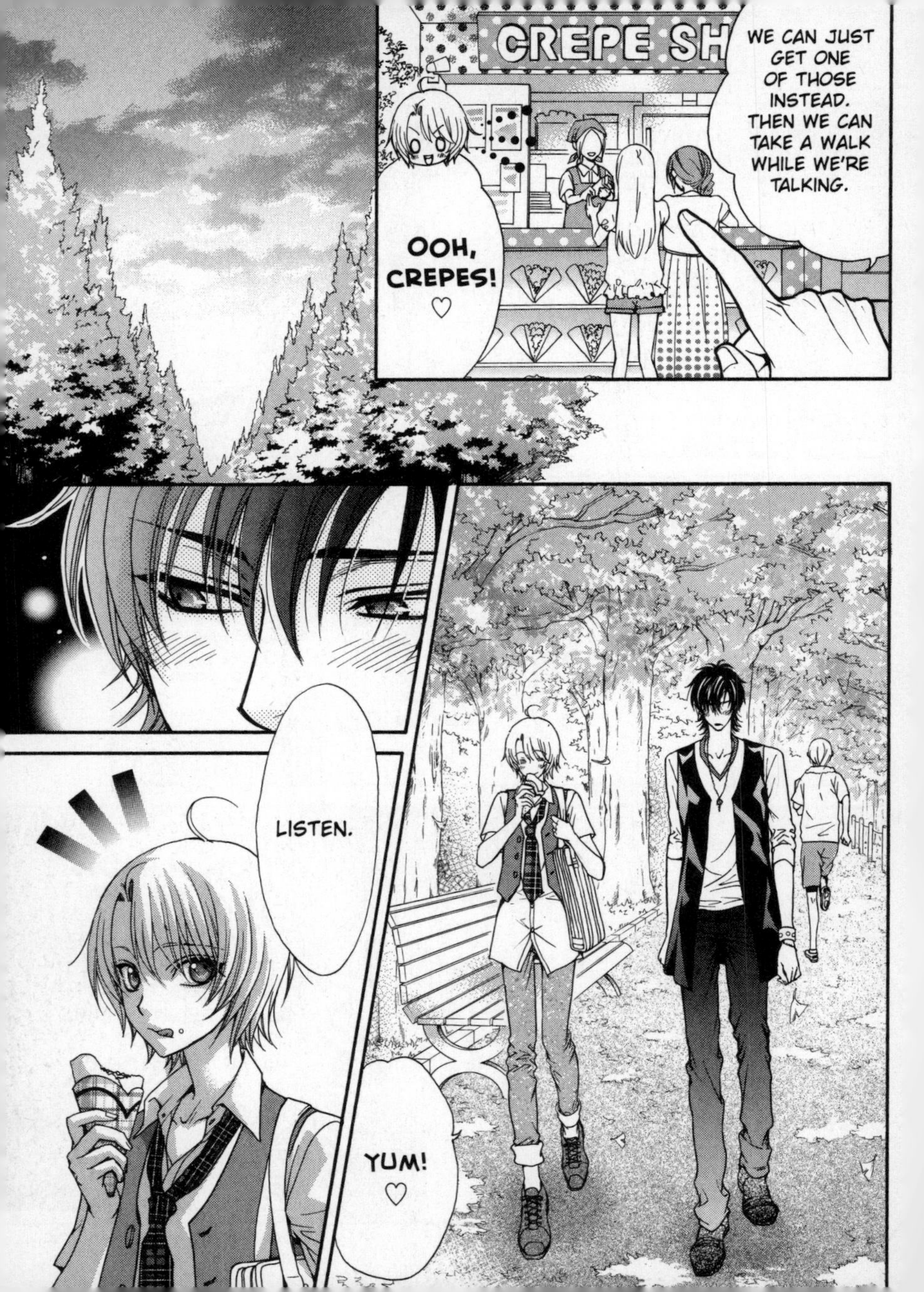

CREPE SH
WE CAN JUST GET ONE OF THOSE INSTEAD. THEN WE CAN TAKE A WALK WHILE WE'RE TALKING.
OOH, CREPES! ♡
YUM! ♡
LISTEN.

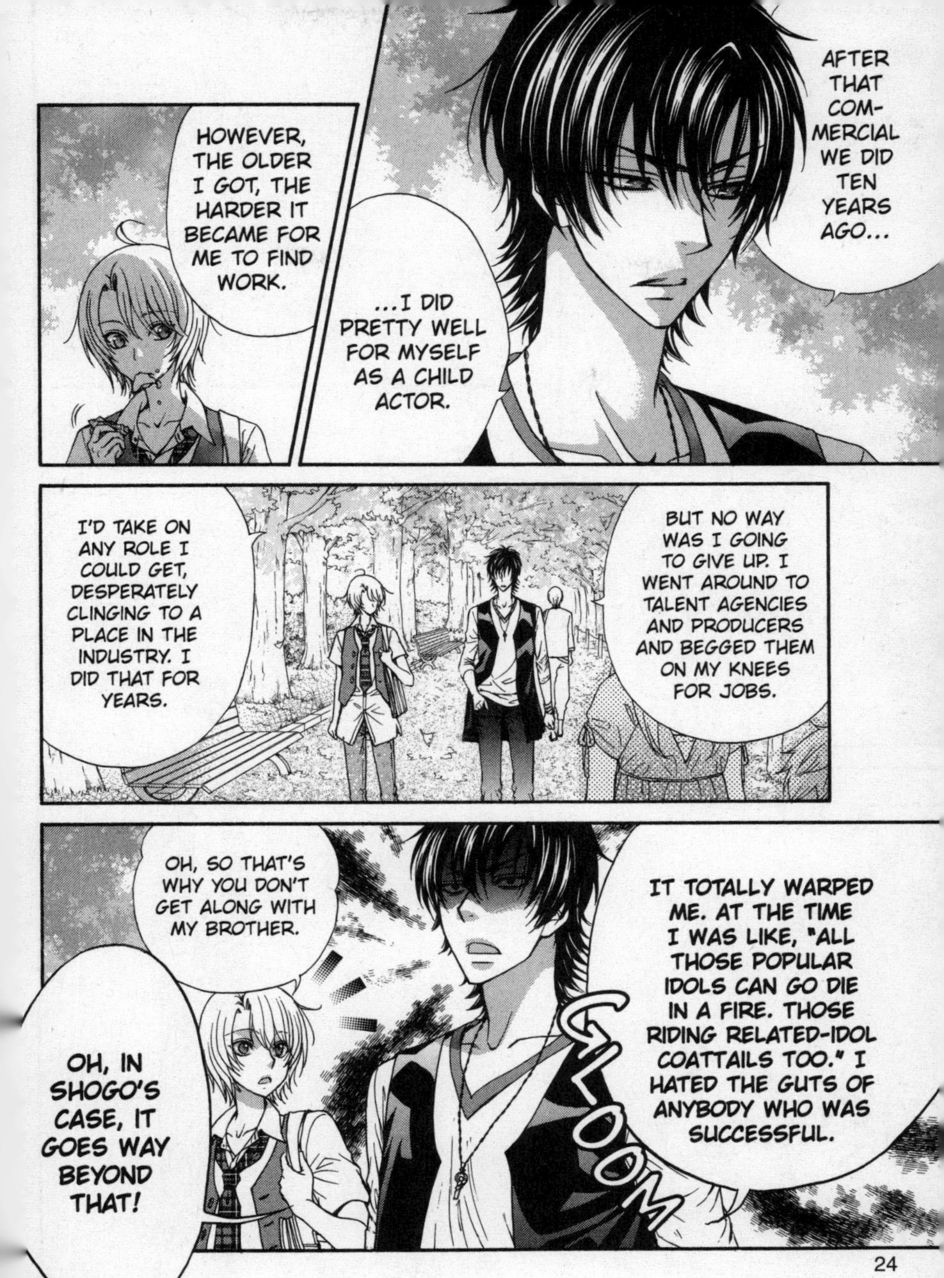
AFTER THAT COM- MERCIAL WE DID TEN YEARS AGO...
...I DID PRETTY WELL FOR MYSELF AS A CHILD ACTOR.
HOWEVER, THE OLDER I GOT, THE HARDER IT BECAME FOR ME TO FIND WORK.
BUT NO WAY WAS I GOING TO GIVE UP. I WENT AROUND TO TALENT AGENCIES AND PRODUCERS AND BEGGED THEM ON MY KNEES FOR JOBS.
I'D TAKE ON ANY ROLE I COULD GET, DESPERATELY CLINGING TO A PLACE IN THE INDUSTRY. I DID THAT FOR YEARS.
IT TOTALLY WARPED ME. AT THE TIME I WAS LIKE, "ALL THOSE POPULAR IDOLS CAN GO DIE IN A FIRE. THOSE RIDING RELATED-IDOL COATTAILS TOO." I HATED THE GUTS OF ANYBODY WHO WAS SUCCESSFUL.
GLOOM
OH, SO THAT'S WHY YOU DON'T GET ALONG WITH MY BROTHER.
OH, IN SHOGO'S CASE, IT GOES WAY BEYOND THAT!

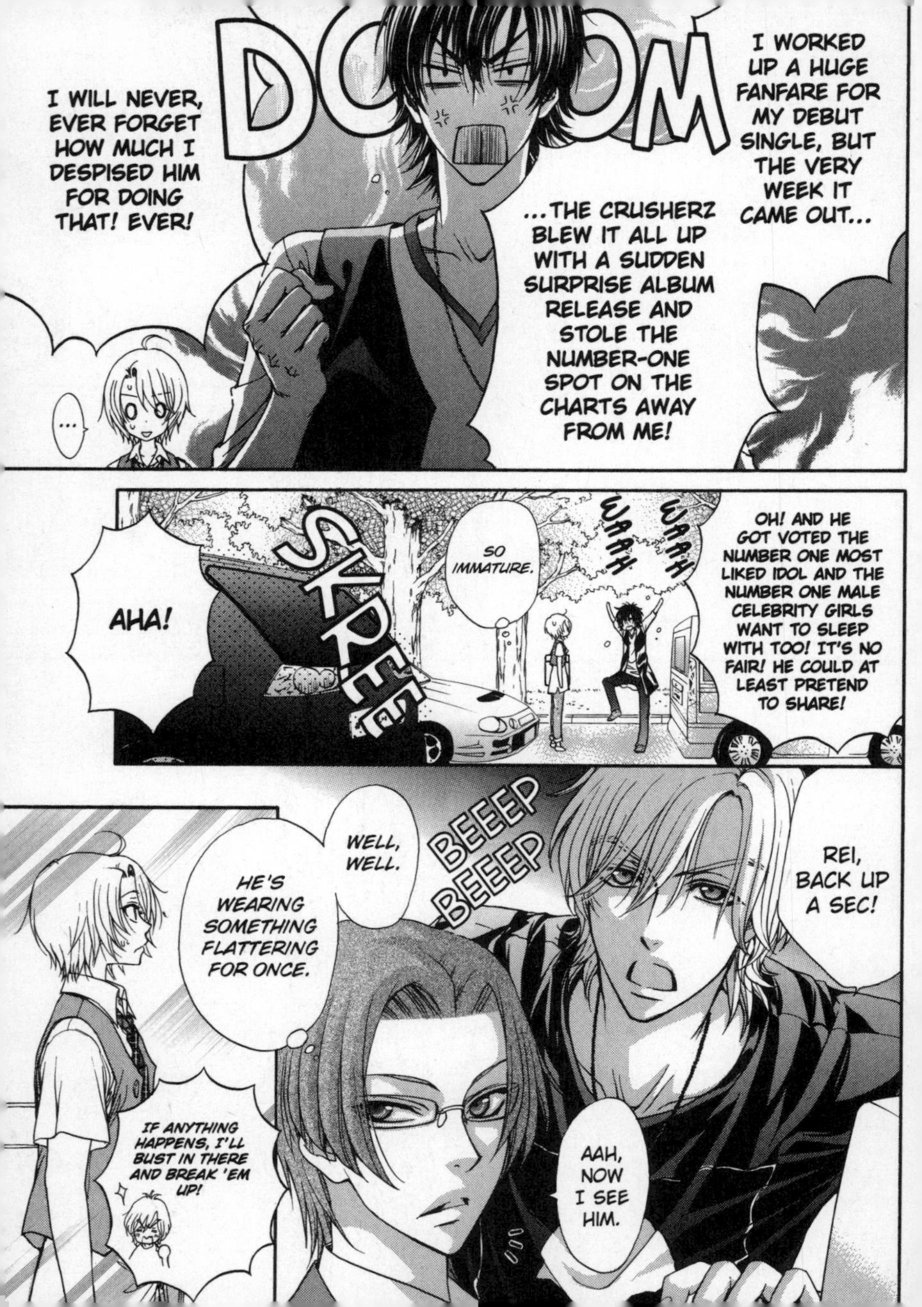

I WORKED UP A HUGE FANFARE FOR MY DEBUT SINGLE, BUT THE VERY WEEK IT CAME OUT...
...THE CRUSHERZ BLEW IT ALL UP WITH A SUDDEN SURPRISE ALBUM RELEASE AND STOLE THE NUMBER-ONE SPOT ON THE CHARTS AWAY FROM ME!
DOOM
I WILL NEVER, EVER FORGET HOW MUCH I DESPISED HIM FOR DOING THAT! EVER!
....
OH! AND HE GOT VOTED THE NUMBER ONE MOST LIKED IDOL AND THE NUMBER ONE MALE CELEBRITY GIRLS WANT TO SLEEP WITH TOO! IT'S NO FAIR! HE COULD AT LEAST PRETEND TO SHARE!
WAAAH
WAAAH
SO IMMATURE.
SKREEE
AHA!
REI, BACK UP A SEC!
BEEEP
BEEEP
WELL, WELL.
HE'S WEARING SOMETHING FLATTERING FOR ONCE.
AAH, NOW I SEE HIM.
IF ANYTHING HAPPENS, I'LL BUST IN THERE AND BREAK 'EM UP!

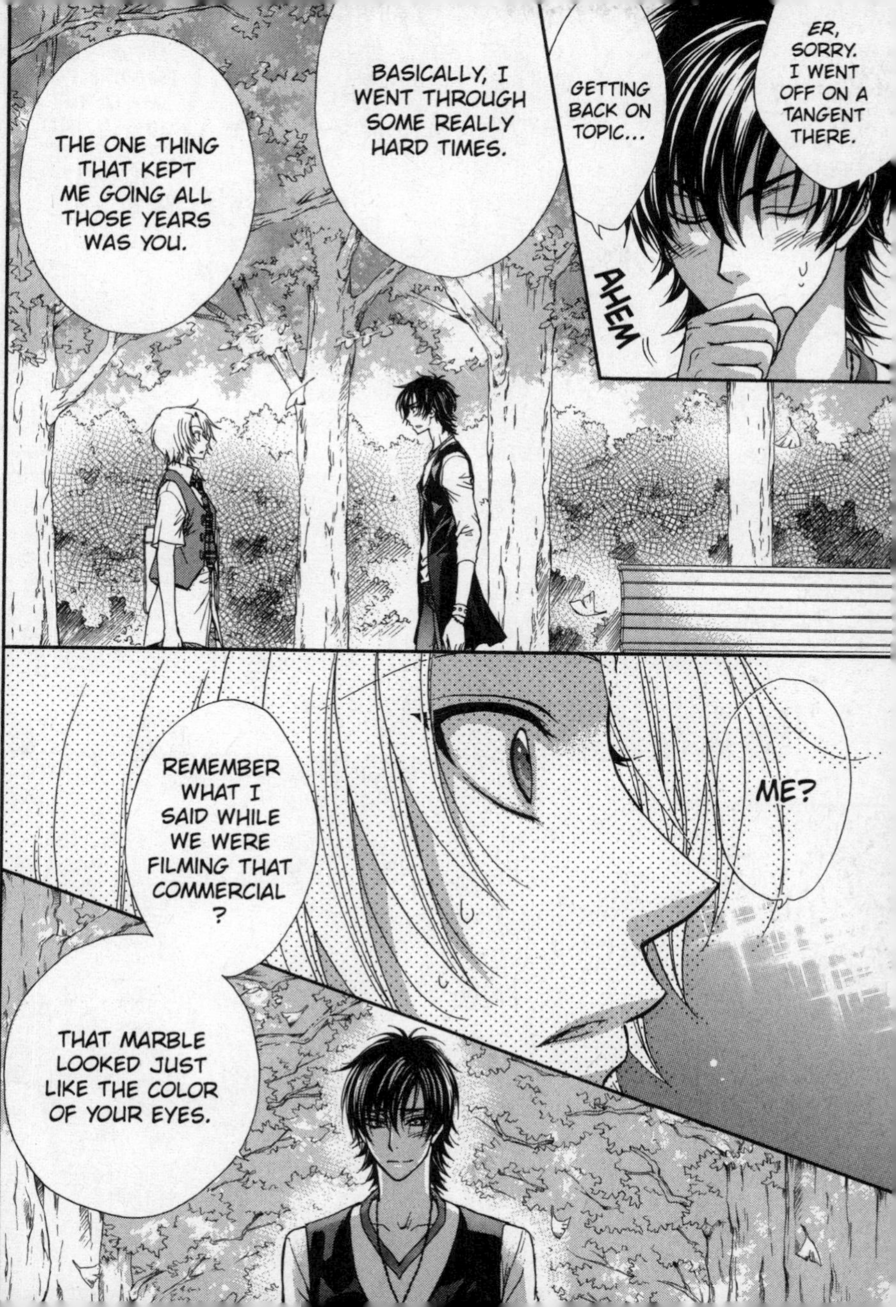
ER, SORRY. I WENT OFF ON A TANGENT THERE.
AHEM
GETTING BACK ON TOPIC...
BASICALLY, I WENT THROUGH SOME REALLY HARD TIMES.
THE ONE THING THAT KEPT ME GOING ALL THOSE YEARS WAS YOU.
ME?
REMEMBER WHAT I SAID WHILE WE WERE FILMING THAT COMMERCIAL?
THAT MARBLE LOOKED JUST LIKE THE COLOR OF YOUR EYES.

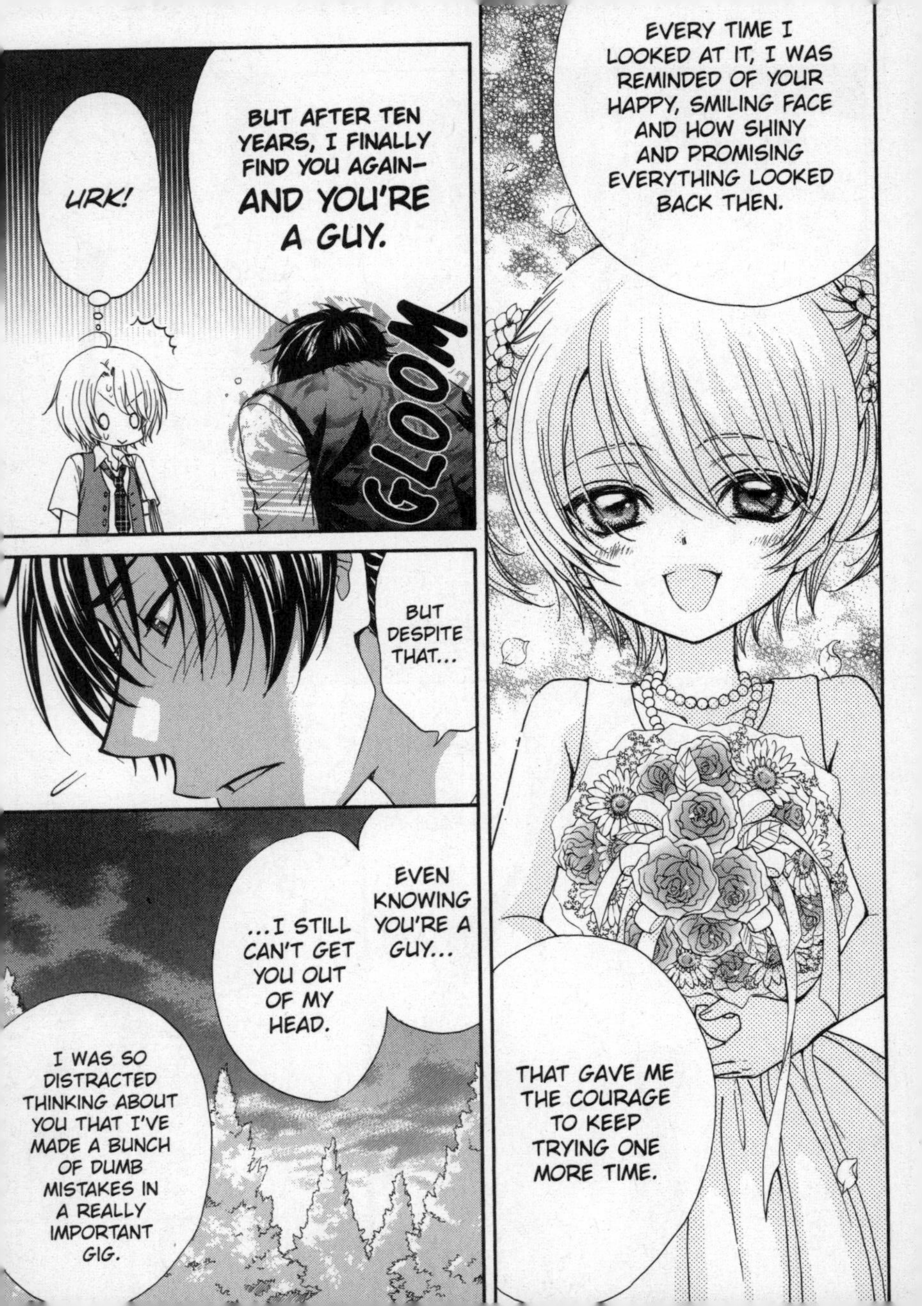
EVERY TIME I LOOKED AT IT, I WAS REMINDED OF YOUR HAPPY, SMILING FACE AND HOW SHINY AND PROMISING EVERYTHING LOOKED BACK THEN.
THAT GAVE ME THE COURAGE TO KEEP TRYING ONE MORE TIME.
BUT AFTER TEN YEARS, I FINALLY FIND YOU AGAIN- AND YOU'RE A GUY.
URK!
GLOOM
BUT DESPITE THAT...
EVEN KNOWING YOU'RE A GUY...
...I STILL CAN'T GET YOU OUT OF MY HEAD.
I WAS SO DISTRACTED THINKING ABOUT YOU THAT I'VE MADE A BUNCH OF DUMB MISTAKES IN A REALLY IMPORTANT GIG.

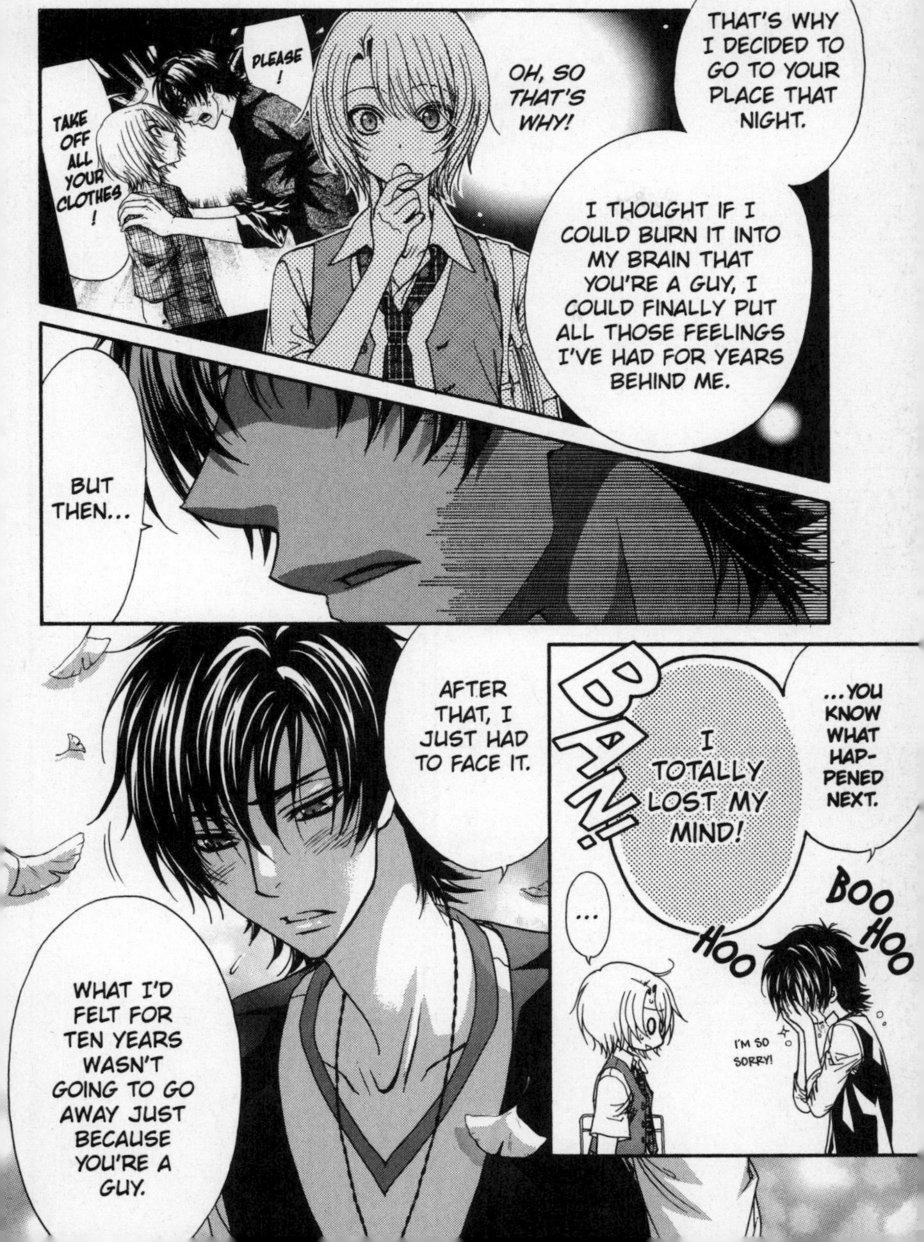
THAT'S WHY I DECIDED TO GO TO YOUR PLACE THAT NIGHT.
OH, SO THAT'S WHY!
PLEASE!
TAKE OFF ALL YOUR CLOTHES!
I THOUGHT IF I COULD BURN IT INTO MY BRAIN THAT YOU'RE A GUY, I COULD FINALLY PUT ALL THOSE FEELINGS I'VE HAD FOR YEARS BEHIND ME.
BUT THEN...
...YOU KNOW WHAT HAP-PENED NEXT.
I TOTALLY LOST MY MIND!
BAN!
BOO HOO HOO
I'M SO SORRY!
...
AFTER THAT, I JUST HAD TO FACE IT.
WHAT I'D FELT FOR TEN YEARS WASN'T GOING TO GO AWAY JUST BECAUSE YOU'RE A GUY.

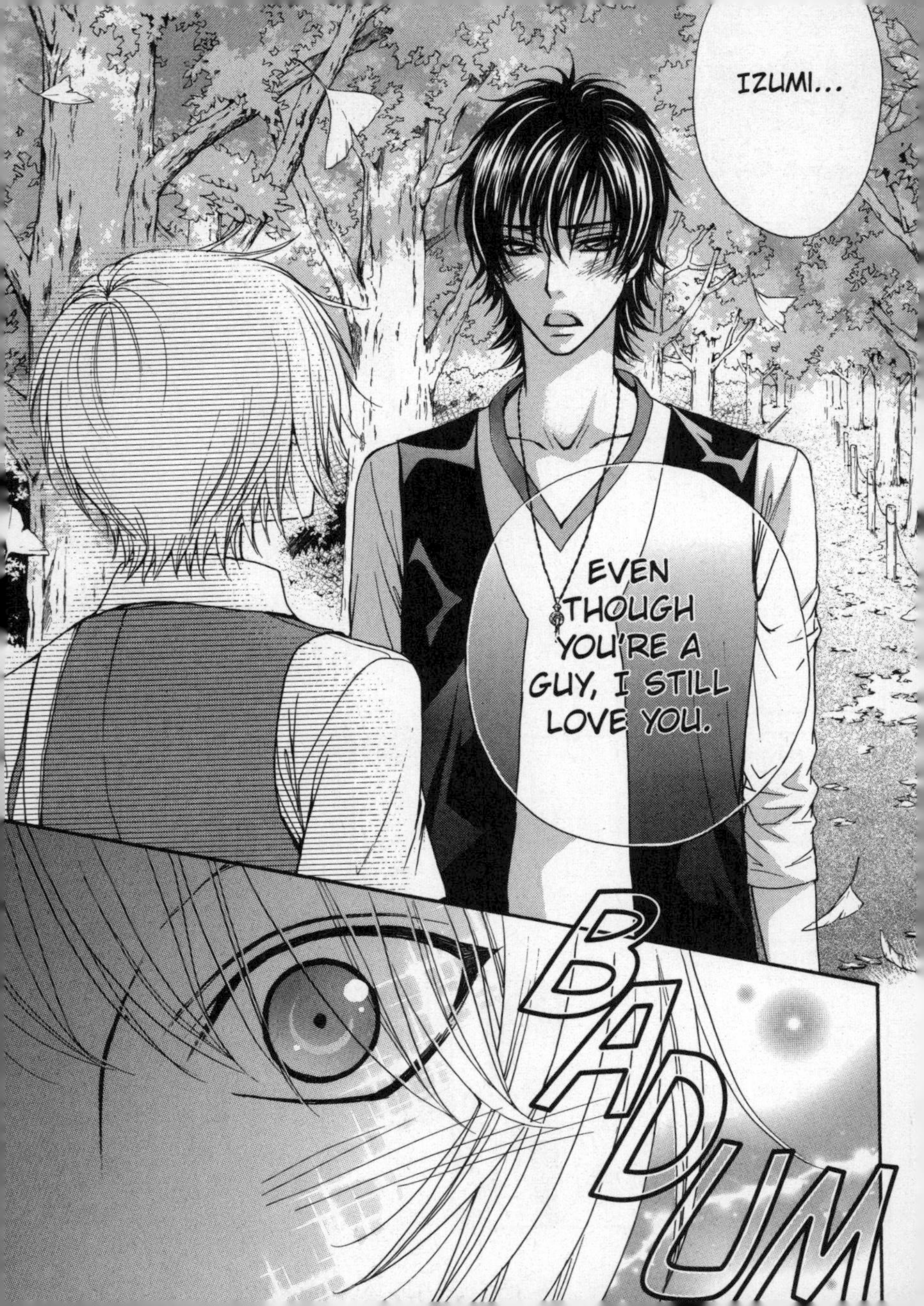
IZUMI...
EVEN THOUGH YOU'RE A GUY, I STILL LOVE YOU.
BADUM

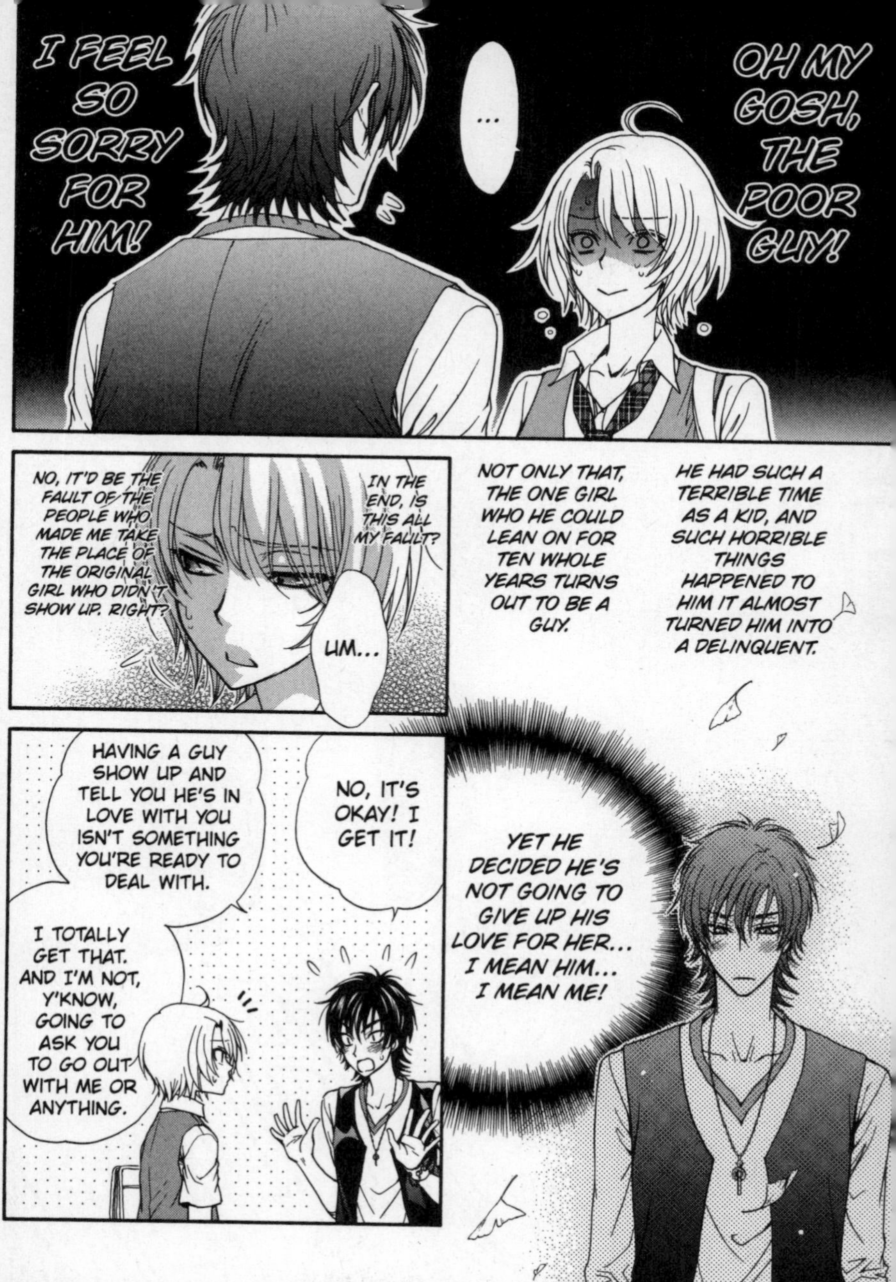
OH MY GOSH, THE POOR GUY!
...
I FEEL SO SORRY FOR HIM!
HE HAD SUCH A TERRIBLE TIME AS A KID, AND SUCH HORRIBLE THINGS HAPPENED TO HIM IT ALMOST TURNED HIM INTO A DELINQUENT.
NOT ONLY THAT, THE ONE GIRL WHO HE COULD LEAN ON FOR TEN WHOLE YEARS TURNS OUT TO BE A GUY.
YET HE DECIDED HE'S NOT GOING TO GIVE UP HIS LOVE FOR HER... I MEAN HIM... I MEAN ME!
IN THE END, IS THIS ALL MY FAULT?
NO, IT'D BE THE FAULT OF THE PEOPLE WHO MADE ME TAKE THE PLACE OF THE ORIGINAL GIRL WHO DIDN'T SHOW UP. RIGHT?
UM...
NO, IT'S OKAY! I GET IT!
HAVING A GUY SHOW UP AND TELL YOU HE'S IN LOVE WITH YOU ISN'T SOMETHING YOU'RE READY TO DEAL WITH.
I TOTALLY GET THAT. AND I'M NOT, Y'KNOW, GOING TO ASK YOU TO GO OUT WITH ME OR ANYTHING.

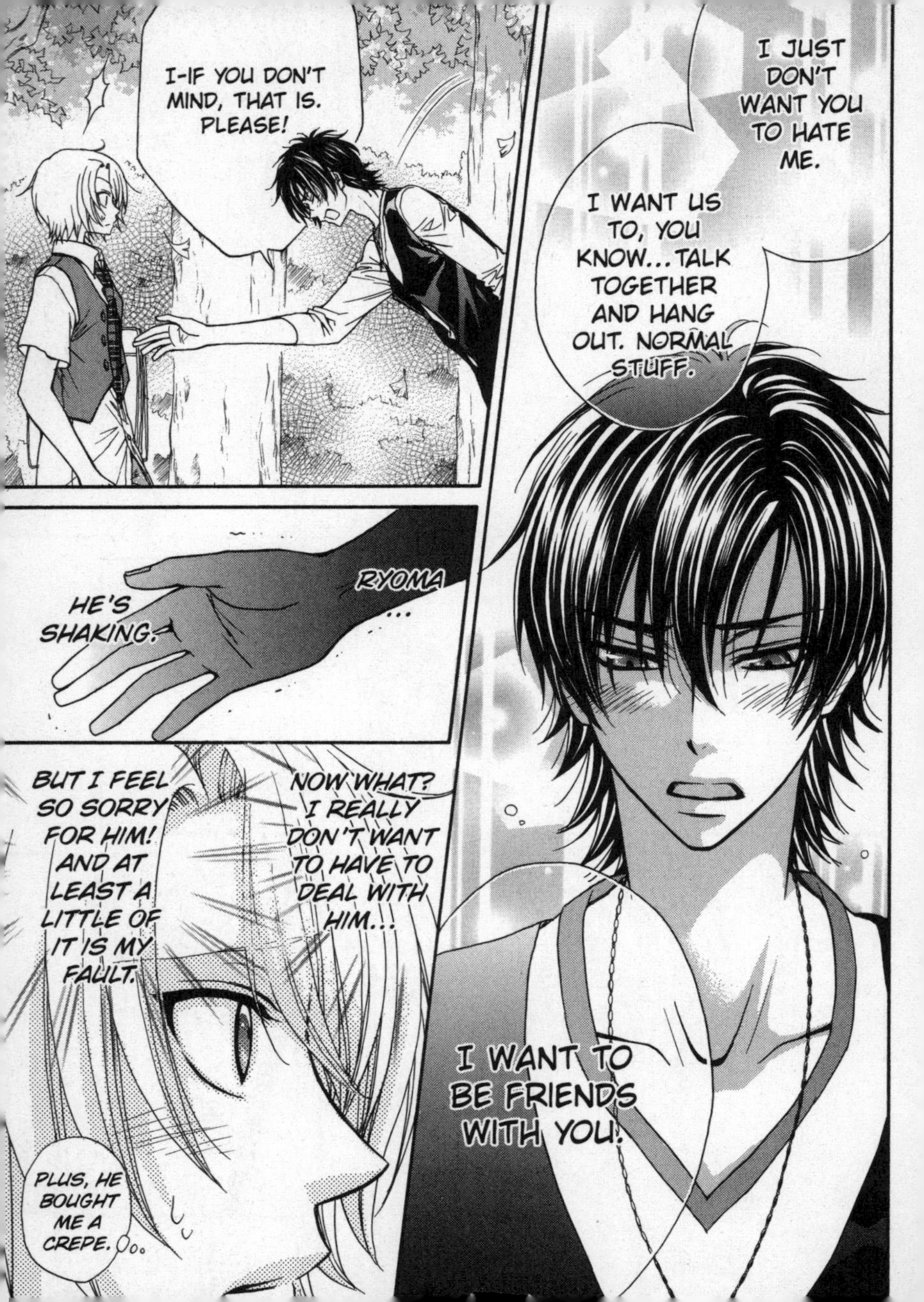
I JUST DON'T WANT YOU TO HATE ME.
I WANT US TO, YOU KNOW... TALK TOGETHER AND HANG OUT. NORMAL STUFF.
I WANT TO BE FRIENDS WITH YOU.
I-IF YOU DON'T MIND, THAT IS. PLEASE!
RYOMA...
HE'S SHAKING.
NOW WHAT? I REALLY DON'T WANT TO HAVE TO DEAL WITH HIM...
BUT I FEEL SO SORRY FOR HIM! AND AT LEAST A LITTLE OF IT IS MY FAULT.
PLUS, HE BOUGHT ME A CREPE.

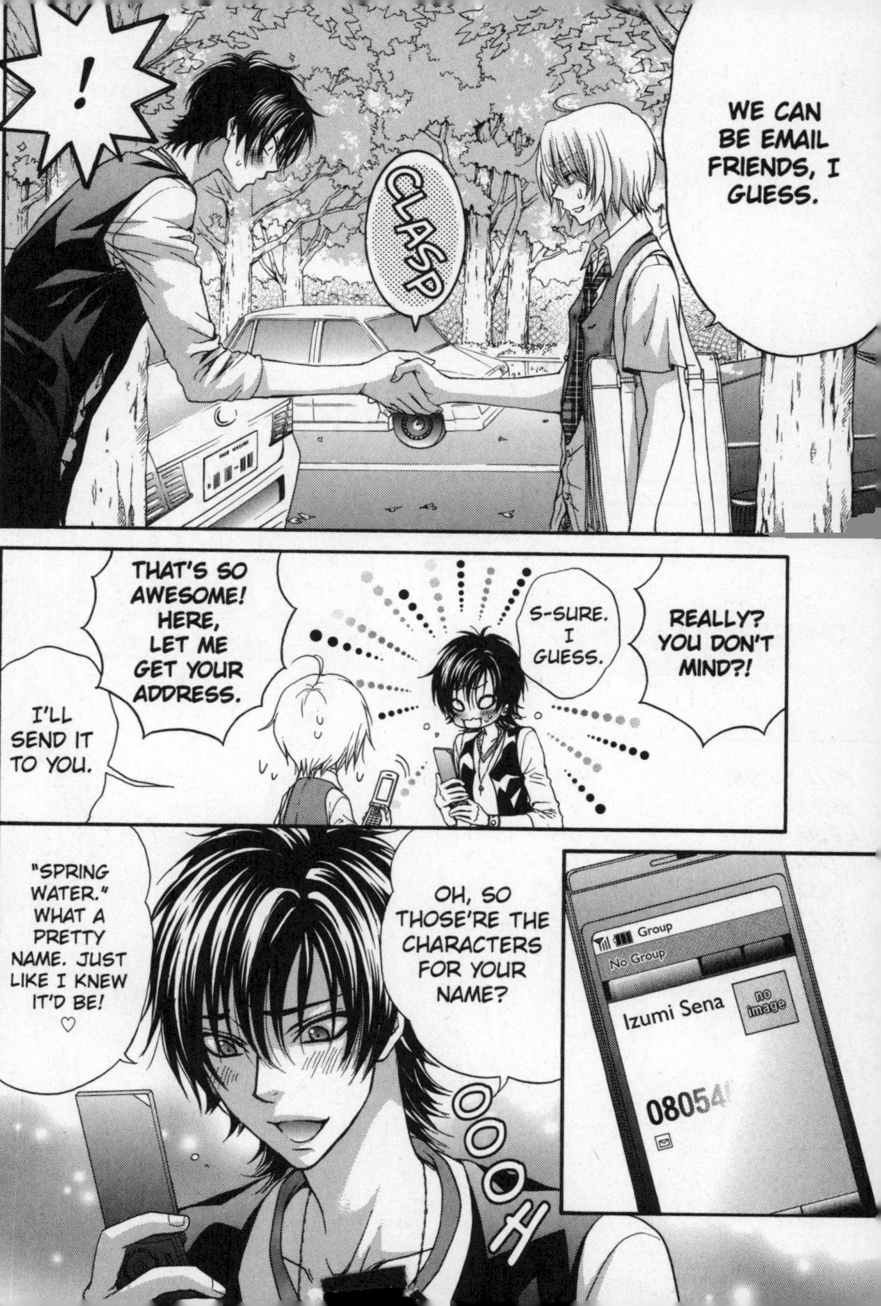
WE CAN BE EMAIL FRIENDS, I GUESS.
CLASP
!
REALLY? YOU DON'T MIND?!
S-SURE. I GUESS.
THAT'S SO AWESOME! HERE, LET ME GET YOUR ADDRESS.
I'LL SEND IT TO YOU.
Group
No Group
Izumi Sena
no image
08054
OH, SO THOSE'RE THE CHARACTERS FOR YOUR NAME?
OOOOH
"SPRING WATER." WHAT A PRETTY NAME. JUST LIKE I KNEW IT'D BE! ♡

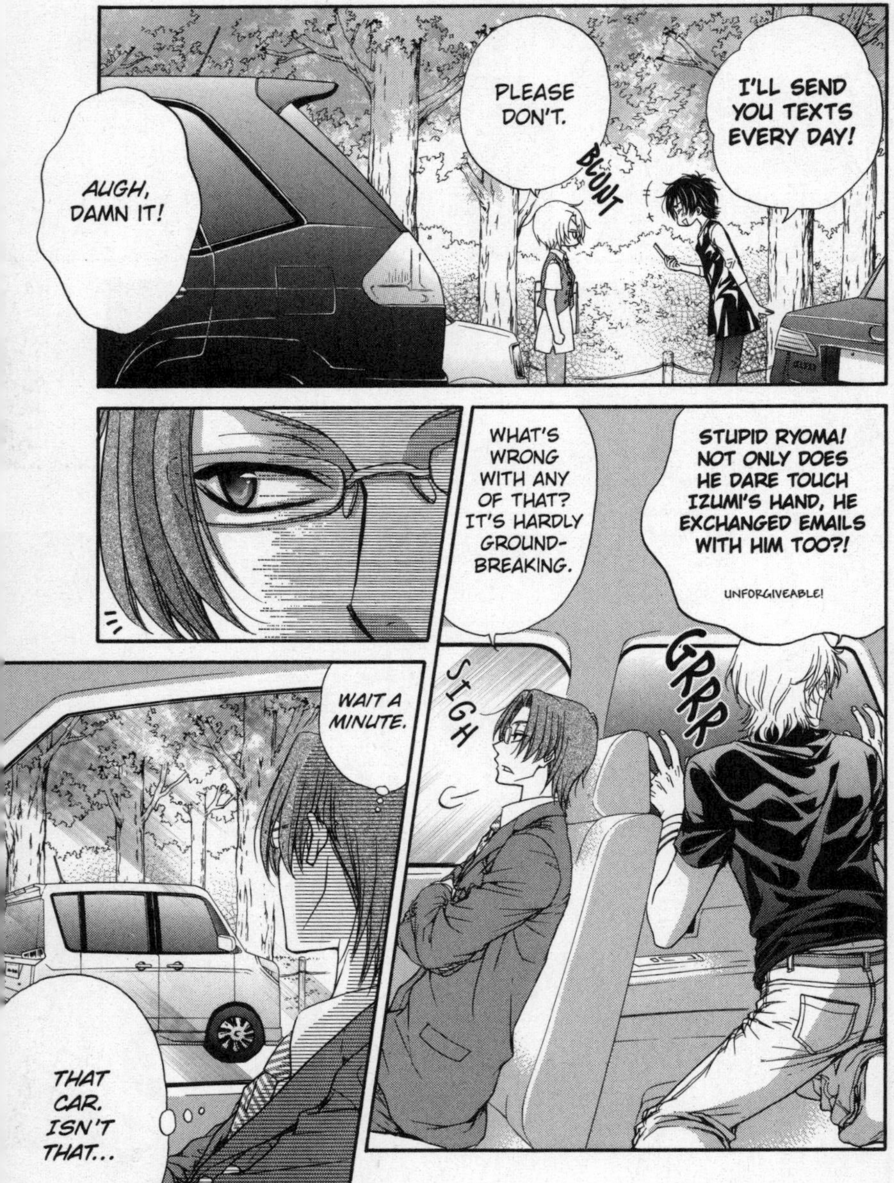
I'LL SEND YOU TEXTS EVERY DAY!
PLEASE DON'T.
BLUNT
AUGH, DAMN IT!
STUPID RYOMA! NOT ONLY DOES HE DARE TOUCH IZUMI'S HAND, HE EXCHANGED EMAILS WITH HIM TOO?!
UNFORGIVEABLE!
GRRR
WHAT'S WRONG WITH ANY OF THAT? IT'S HARDLY GROUND-BREAKING.
SIGH
WAIT A MINUTE.
THAT CAR. ISN'T THAT...

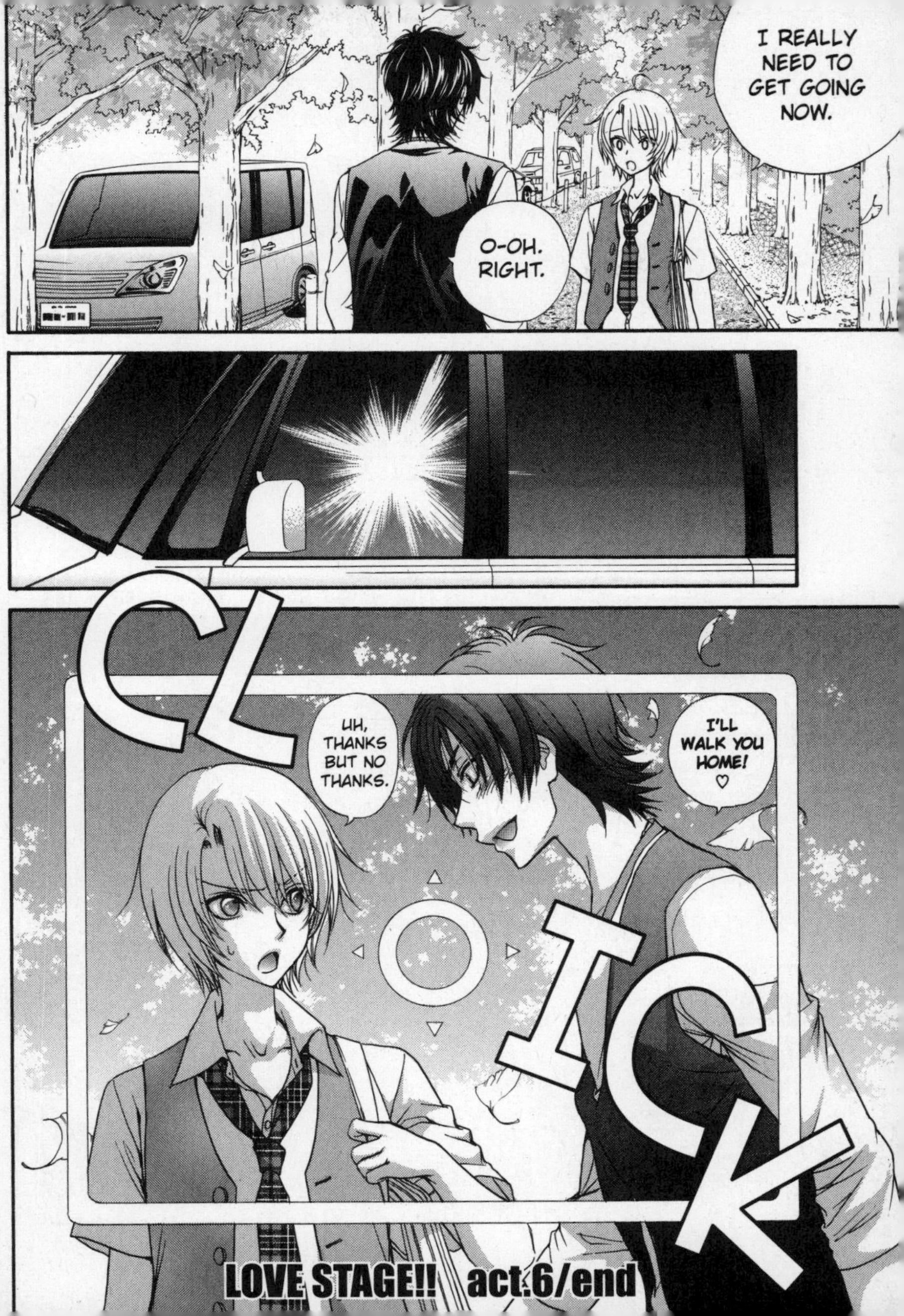
I REALLY NEED TO GET GOING NOW.
O-OH. RIGHT.
CLICK
I'LL WALK YOU HOME! ♡
UH, THANKS BUT NO THANKS.
LOVE STAGE!! act.6/end

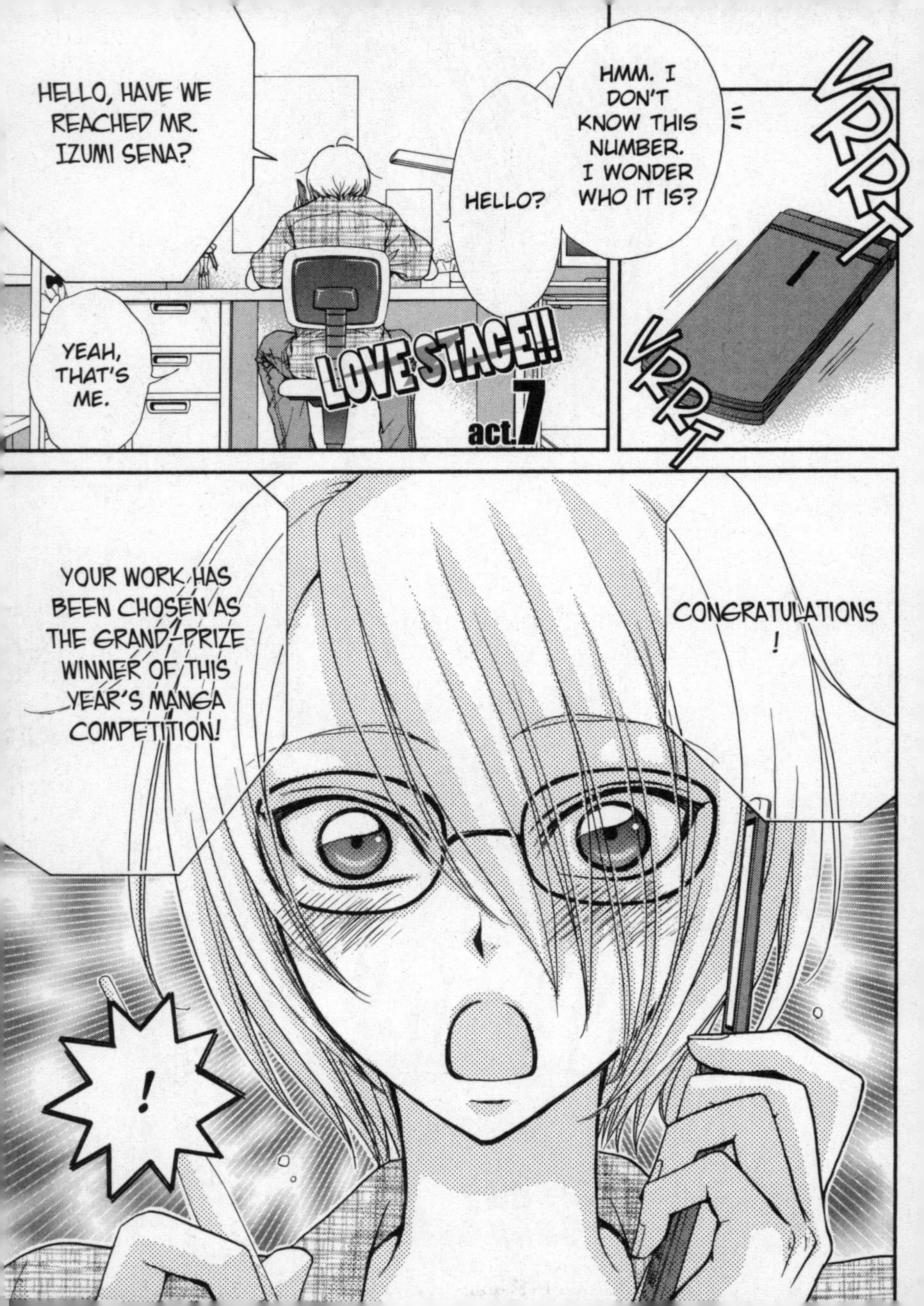
VRRT
VRRT
HMM. I DON'T KNOW THIS NUMBER. I WONDER WHO IT IS?
HELLO?
HELLO, HAVE WE REACHED MR. IZUMI SENA?
YEAH, THAT'S ME.
LOVE STAGE!!
act.7
CONGRATULATIONS!
YOUR WORK HAS BEEN CHOSEN AS THE GRAND-PRIZE WINNER OF THIS YEAR'S MANGA COMPETITION!
!

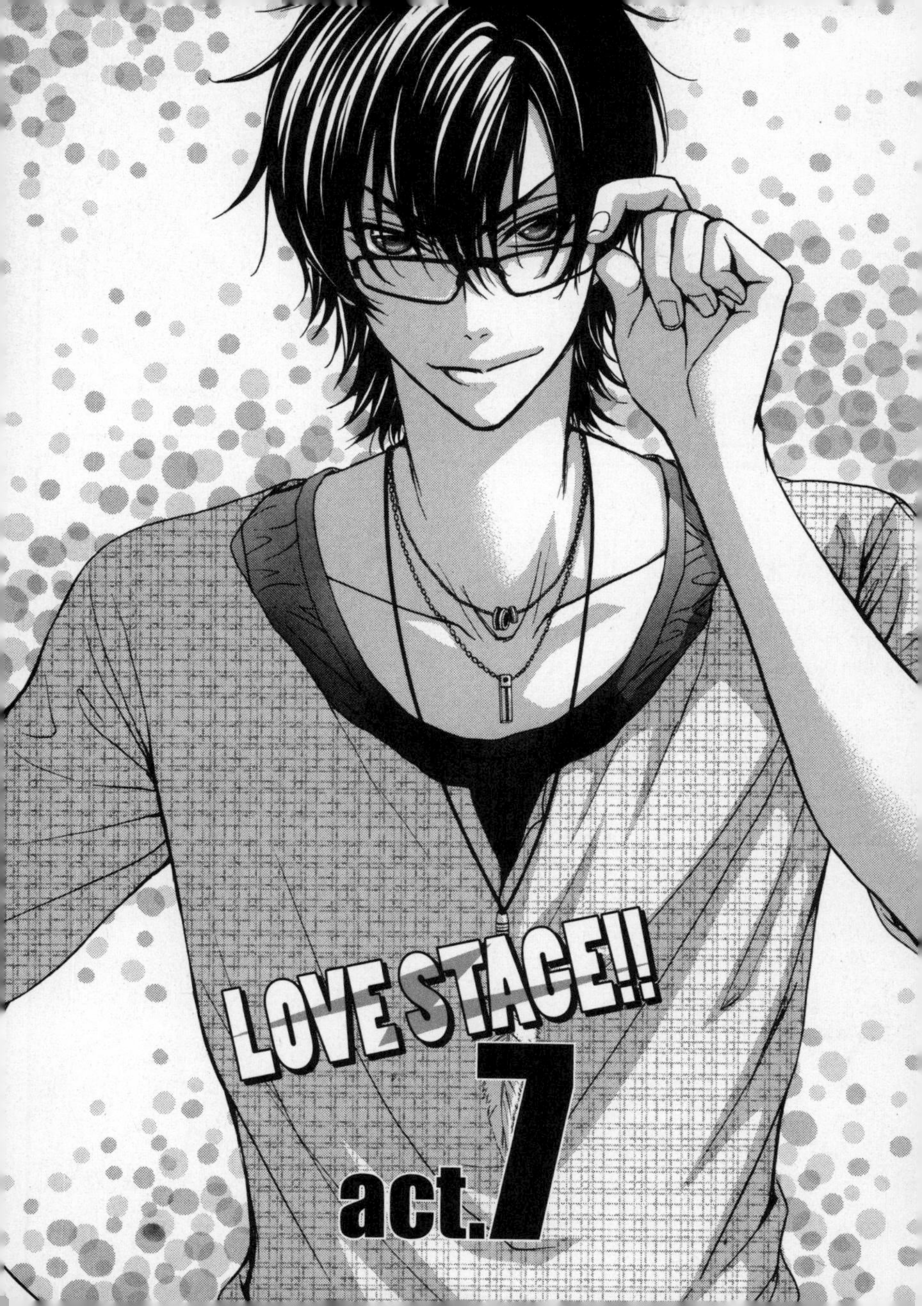
LOVE STAGE!!
act.7

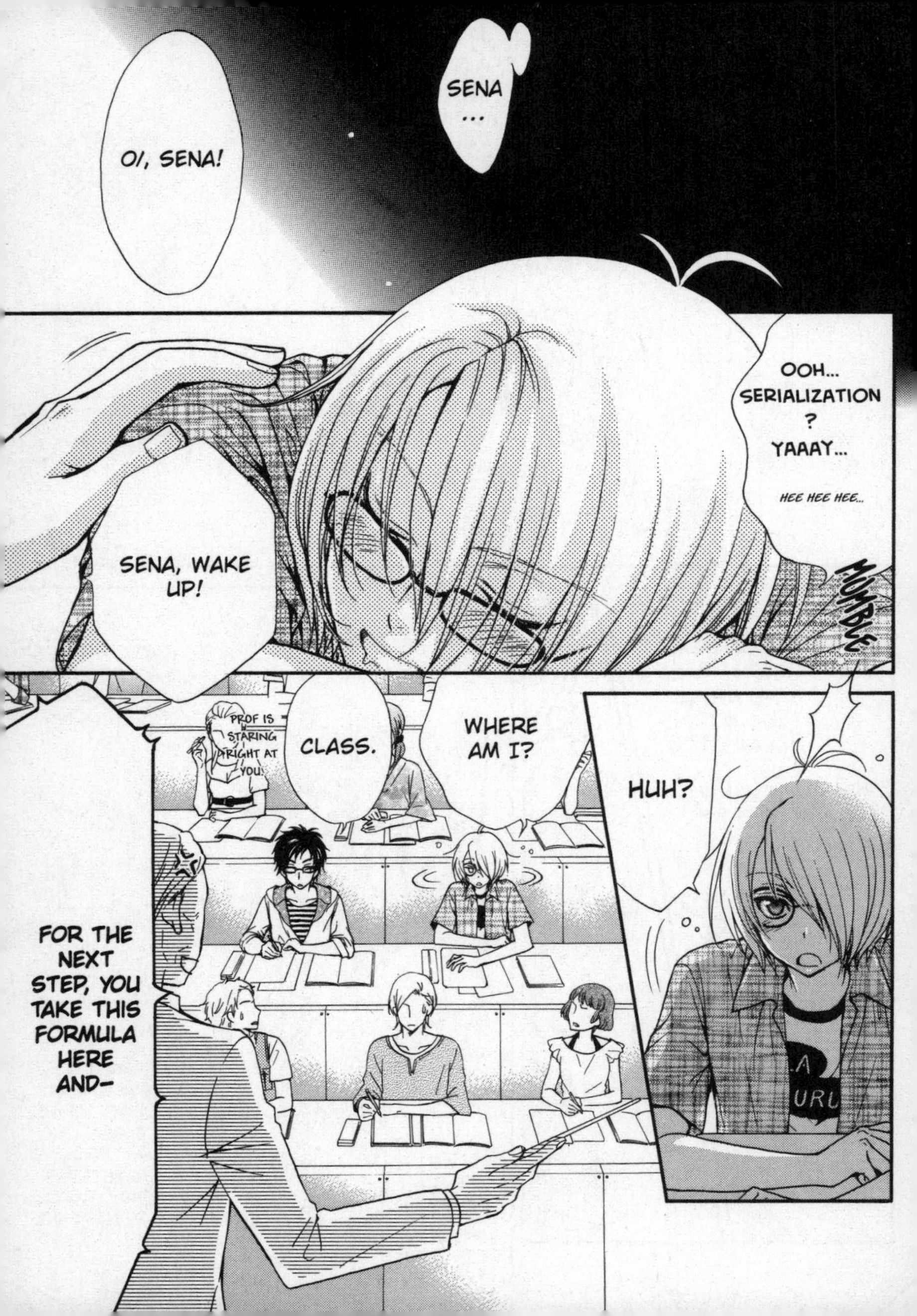
SENA...
OI, SENA!
OOH... SERIALIZATION? YAAAY...
HEE HEE HEE...
MUMBLE
SENA, WAKE UP!
HUH?
WHERE AM I?
CLASS.
PROF IS STARING RIGHT AT YOU!
FOR THE NEXT STEP, YOU TAKE THIS FORMULA HERE AND-

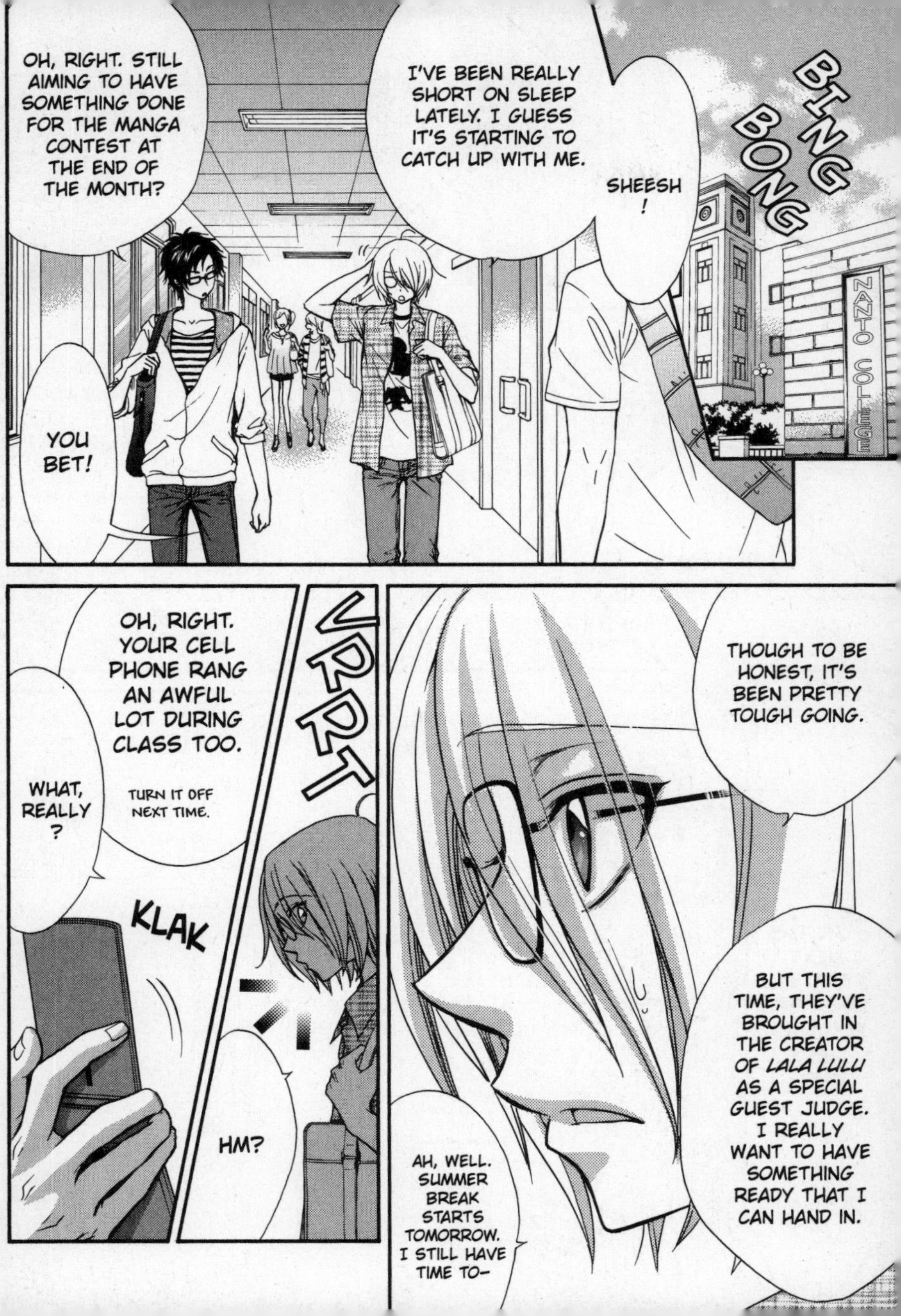
BING BONG
NANTO COLLEGE
I'VE BEEN REALLY SHORT ON SLEEP LATELY. I GUESS IT'S STARTING TO CATCH UP WITH ME.
SHEESH!
OH, RIGHT. STILL AIMING TO HAVE SOMETHING DONE FOR THE MANGA CONTEST AT THE END OF THE MONTH?
YOU BET!
THOUGH TO BE HONEST, IT'S BEEN PRETTY TOUGH GOING.
BUT THIS TIME, THEY'VE BROUGHT IN THE CREATOR OF *LALA LULU* AS A SPECIAL GUEST JUDGE. I REALLY WANT TO HAVE SOMETHING READY THAT I CAN HAND IN.
AH, WELL. SUMMER BREAK STARTS TOMORROW. I STILL HAVE TIME TO–
VRRT
HM?
OH, RIGHT. YOUR CELL PHONE RANG AN AWFUL LOT DURING CLASS TOO.
WHAT, REALLY?
TURN IT OFF NEXT TIME.
KLAK

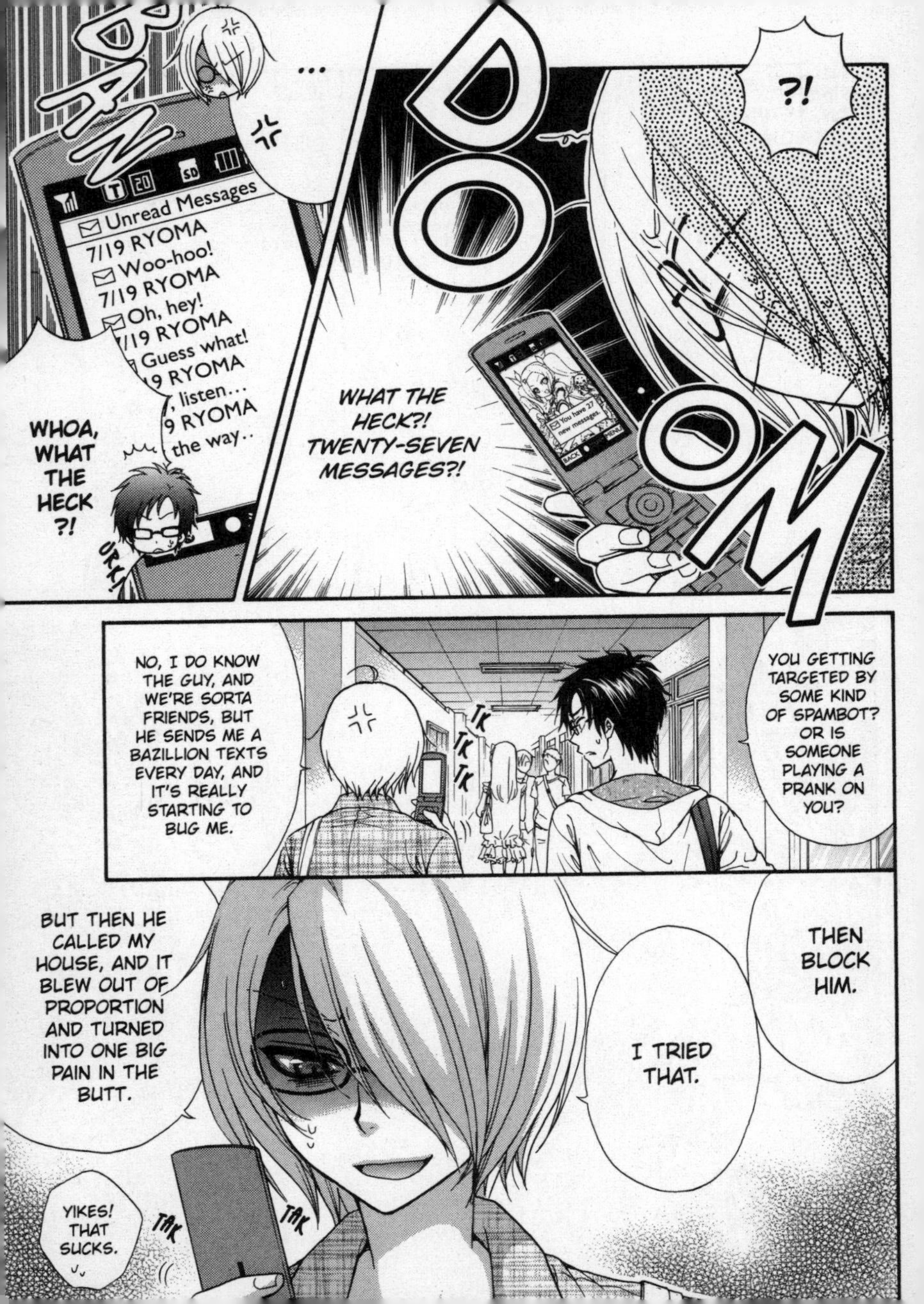
?!
DOOM
You have 27 new messages.
WHAT THE HECK?! TWENTY-SEVEN MESSAGES?!
BAM
...
Unread Messages
7/19 RYOMA
Woo-hoo!
7/19 RYOMA
Oh, hey!
7/19 RYOMA
Guess what!
WHOA, WHAT THE HECK?!
URK!
YOU GETTING TARGETED BY SOME KIND OF SPAMBOT? OR IS SOMEONE PLAYING A PRANK ON YOU?
NO, I DO KNOW THE GUY, AND WE'RE SORTA FRIENDS, BUT HE SENDS ME A BAZILLION TEXTS EVERY DAY, AND IT'S REALLY STARTING TO BUG ME.
TK TK TK
THEN BLOCK HIM.
I TRIED THAT.
BUT THEN HE CALLED MY HOUSE, AND IT BLEW OUT OF PROPORTION AND TURNED INTO ONE BIG PAIN IN THE BUTT.
TAK
TAK
YIKES! THAT SUCKS.

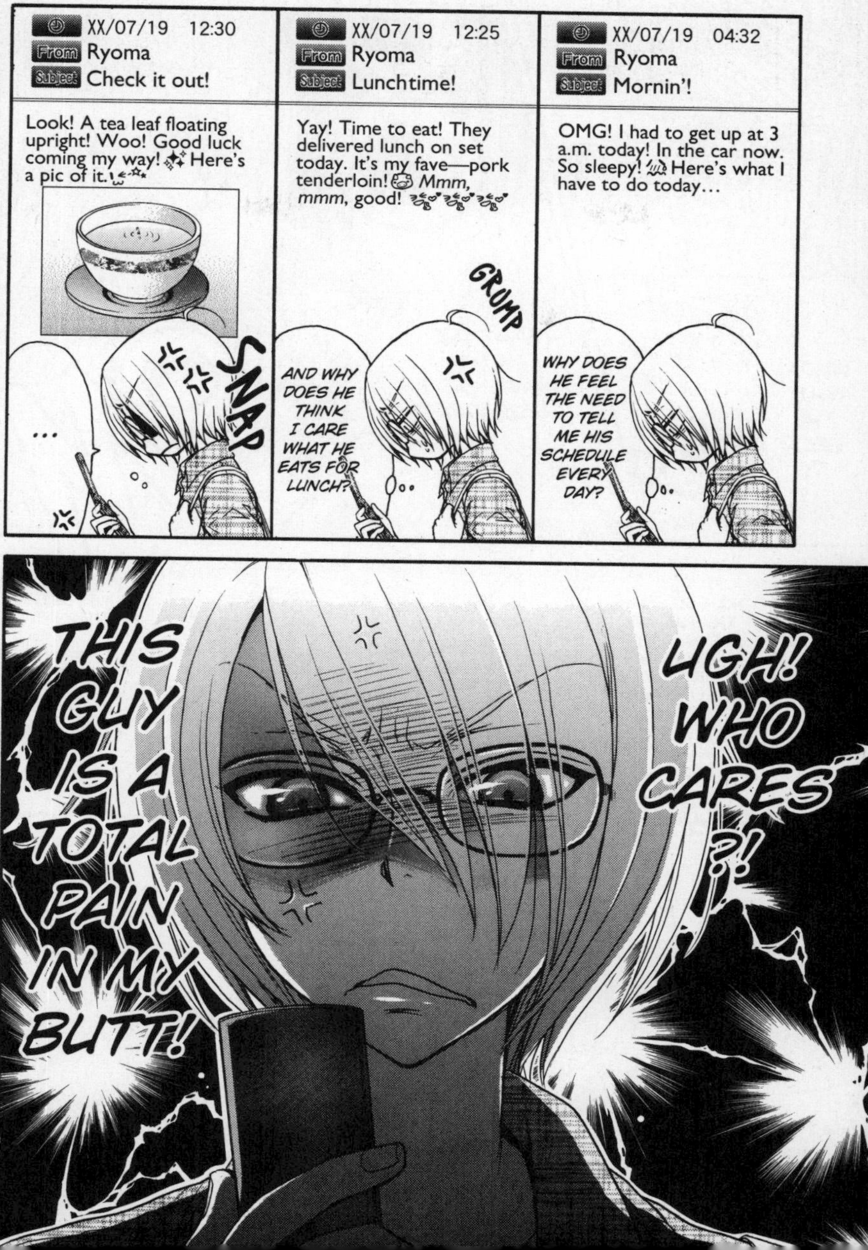
XX/07/19 04:32
From Ryoma
Subject Mornin'!
OMG! I had to get up at 3 a.m. today! In the car now. So sleepy! Here's what I have to do today...
WHY DOES HE FEEL THE NEED TO TELL ME HIS SCHEDULE EVERY DAY?
XX/07/19 12:25
From Ryoma
Subject Lunchtime!
Yay! Time to eat! They delivered lunch on set today. It's my fave—pork tenderloin! Mmm, mmm, good!
GRUMP
AND WHY DOES HE THINK I CARE WHAT HE EATS FOR LUNCH?
XX/07/19 12:30
From Ryoma
Subject Check it out!
Look! A tea leaf floating upright! Woo! Good luck coming my way! Here's a pic of it.
SNAP
...
UGH! WHO CARES?!
THIS GUY IS A TOTAL PAIN IN MY BUTT!

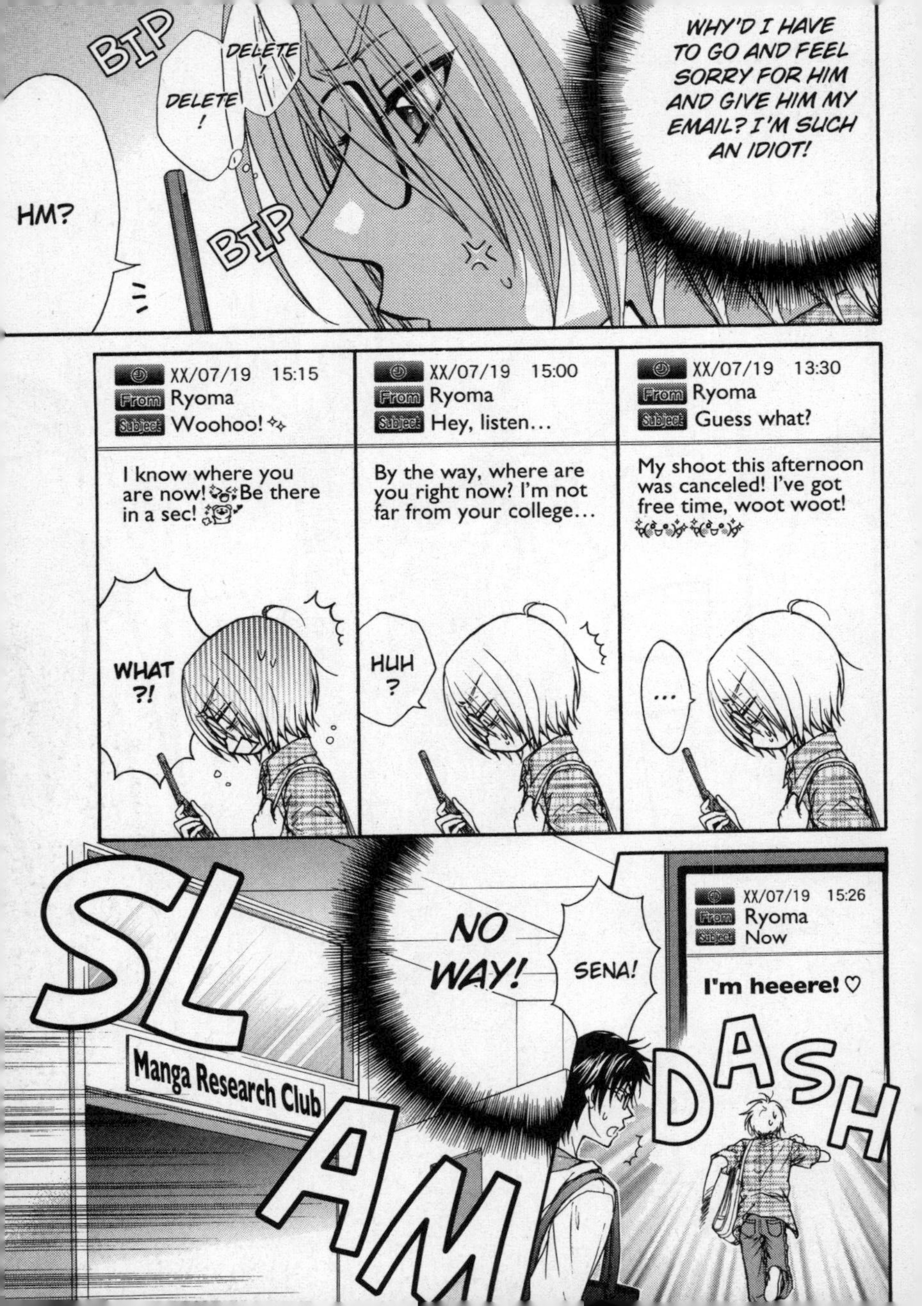
WHY'D I HAVE TO GO AND FEEL SORRY FOR HIM AND GIVE HIM MY EMAIL? I'M SUCH AN IDIOT!
BIP
DELETE!
DELETE!
BIP
HM?
XX/07/19 13:30
From Ryoma
Subject Guess what?
My shoot this afternoon was canceled! I've got free time, woot woot!
...
XX/07/19 15:00
From Ryoma
Subject Hey, listen...
By the way, where are you right now? I'm not far from your college...
HUH?
XX/07/19 15:15
From Ryoma
Subject Woohoo!
I know where you are now! Be there in a sec!
WHAT?!
XX/07/19 15:26
From Ryoma
Subject Now
I'm heeere! ♡
SENA!
NO WAY!
SLAM
DASH
Manga Research Club

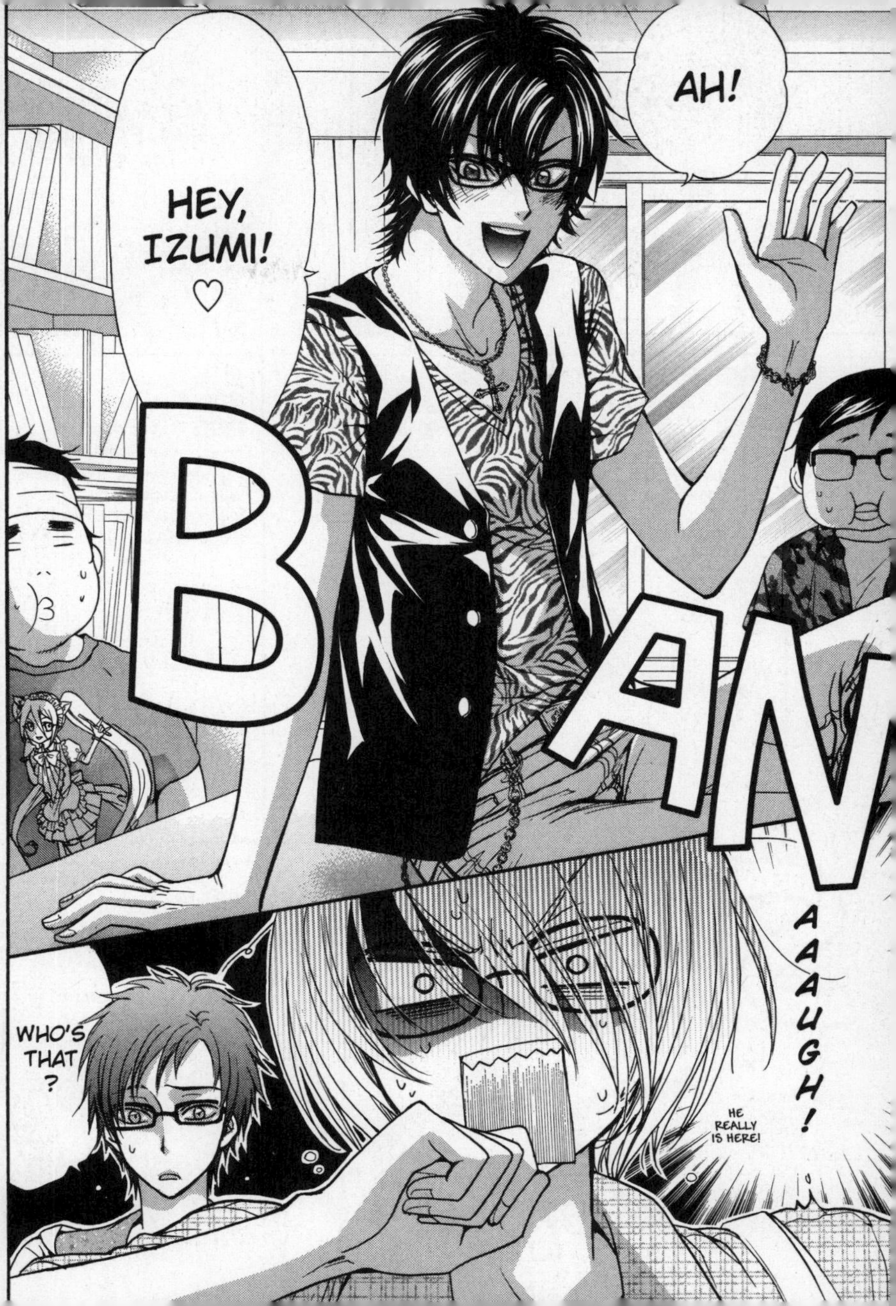
AH!
HEY, IZUMI! ♡
BAN
AAAAUGH!
HE REALLY IS HERE!
WHO'S THAT?

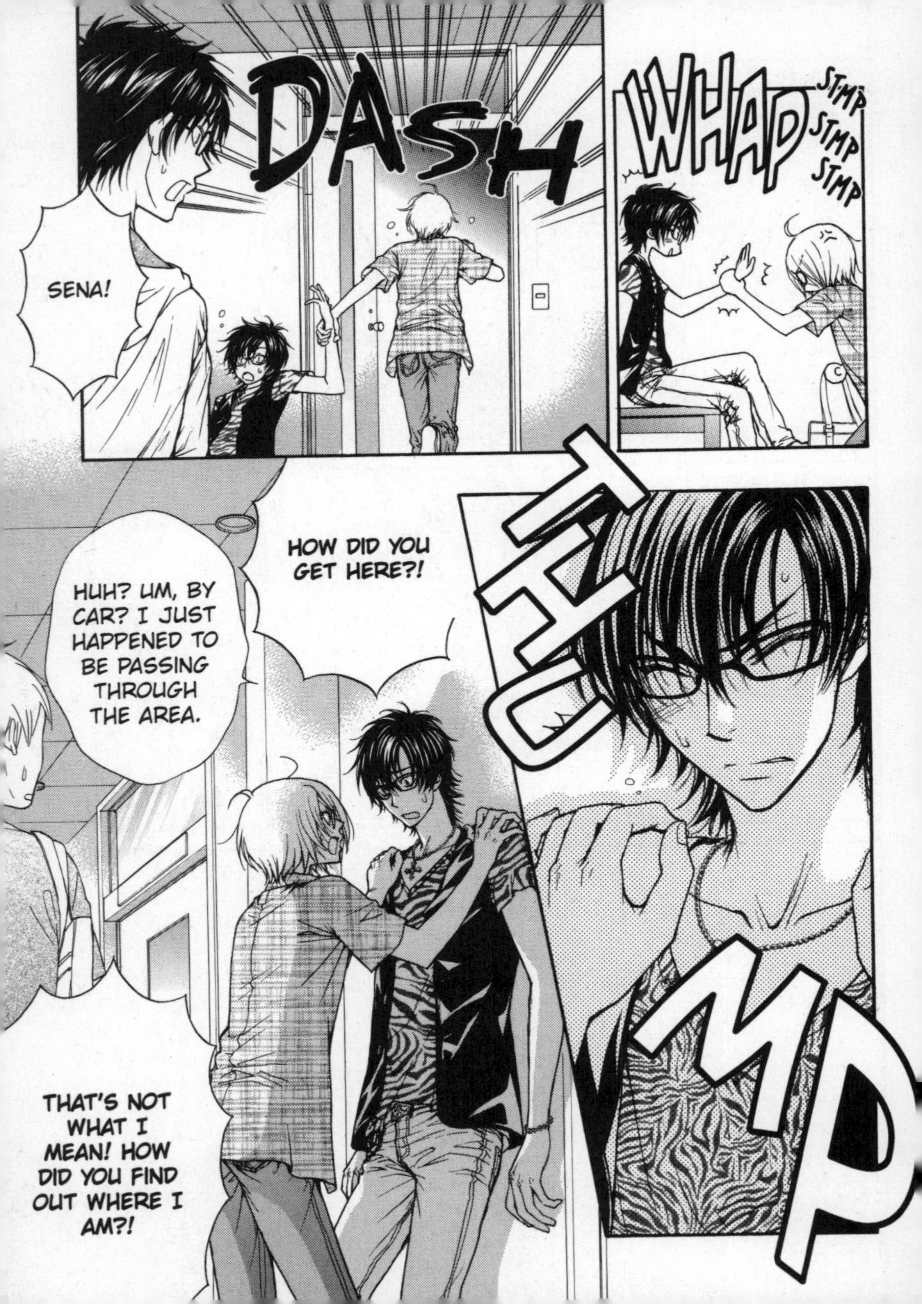
WHAP
STMP STMP STMP
DASH
SENA!
THUMP
HOW DID YOU GET HERE?!
HUH? UM, BY CAR? I JUST HAPPENED TO BE PASSING THROUGH THE AREA.
THAT'S NOT WHAT I MEAN! HOW DID YOU FIND OUT WHERE I AM?!

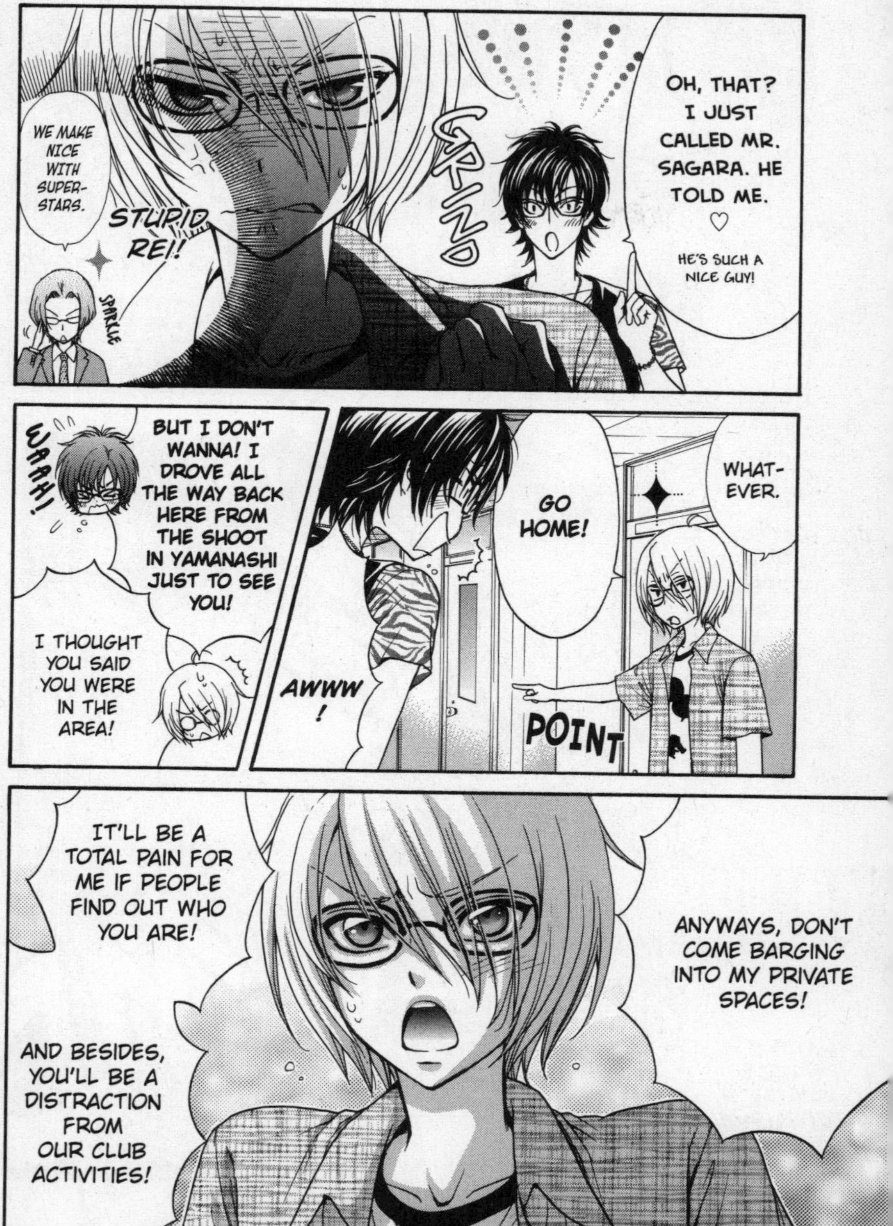
OH, THAT? I JUST CALLED MR. SAGARA. HE TOLD ME. ♡
HE'S SUCH A NICE GUY!
GRIND
STUPID REI!
WE MAKE NICE WITH SUPER-STARS.
SPARKLE
WHAT-EVER.
GO HOME!
POINT
AWWW!
BUT I DON'T WANNA! I DROVE ALL THE WAY BACK HERE FROM THE SHOOT IN YAMANASHI JUST TO SEE YOU!
WAAAH!
I THOUGHT YOU SAID YOU WERE IN THE AREA!
ANYWAYS, DON'T COME BARGING INTO MY PRIVATE SPACES!
IT'LL BE A TOTAL PAIN FOR ME IF PEOPLE FIND OUT WHO YOU ARE!
AND BESIDES, YOU'LL BE A DISTRACTION FROM OUR CLUB ACTIVITIES!

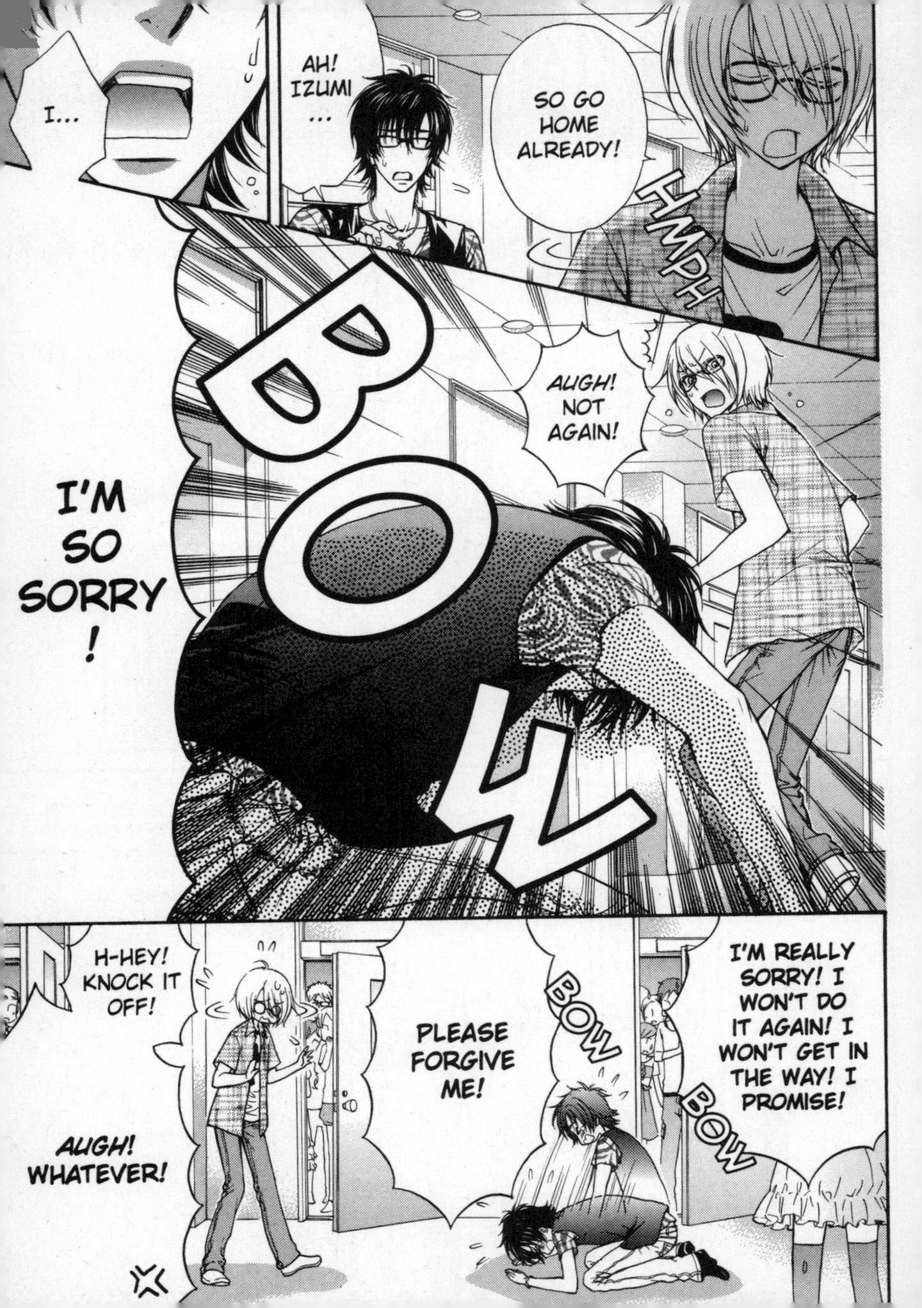

SO GO HOME ALREADY!
HMPH
AH! IZUMI ...
I...
AUGH! NOT AGAIN!
BOW
I'M SO SORRY!
I'M REALLY SORRY! I WON'T DO IT AGAIN! I WON'T GET IN THE WAY! I PROMISE!
BOW
BOW
PLEASE FORGIVE ME!
H-HEY! KNOCK IT OFF!
AUGH! WHATEVER!

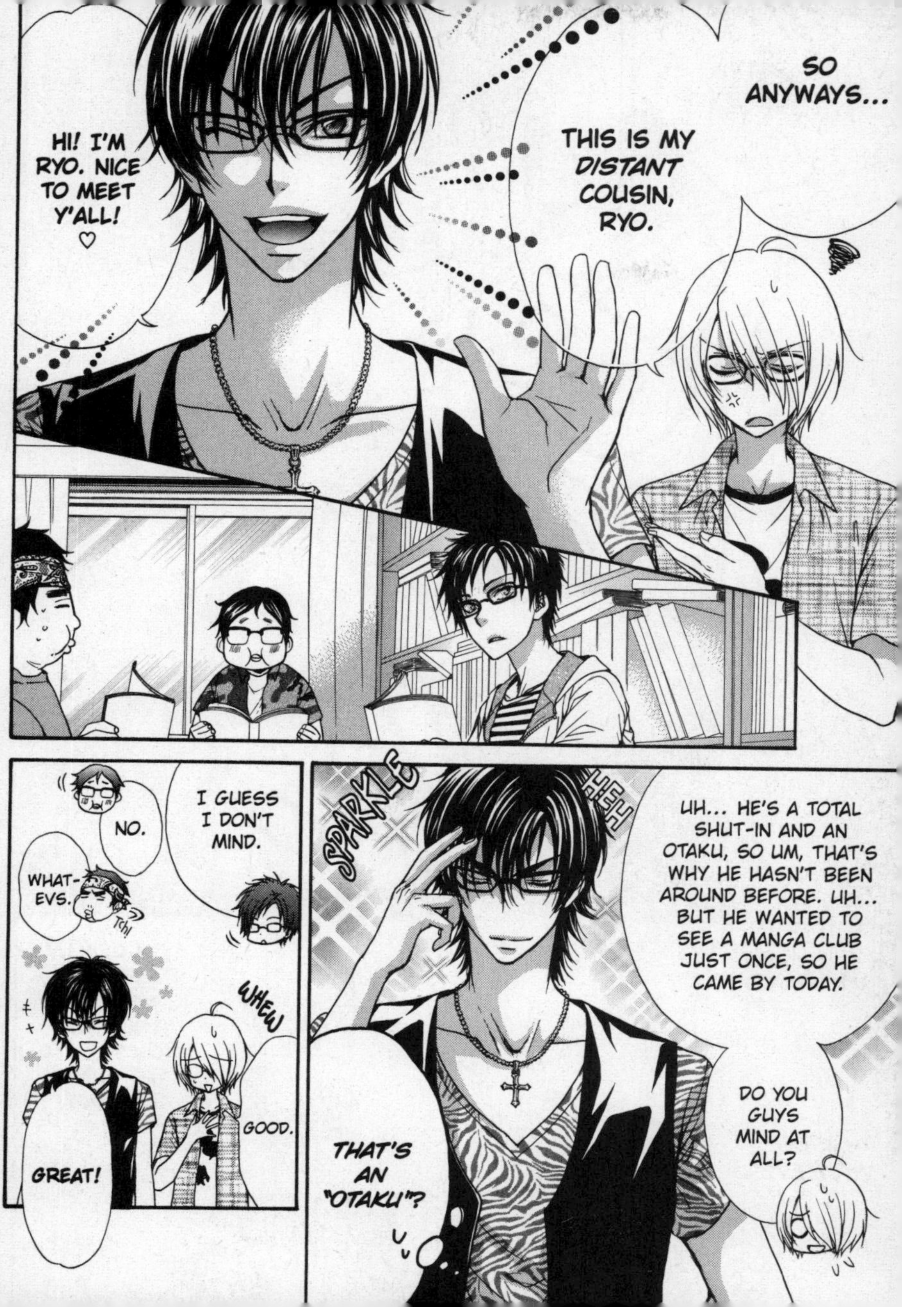
SO ANYWAYS...
THIS IS MY DISTANT COUSIN, RYO.
HI! I'M RYO. NICE TO MEET Y'ALL! ♡
HEH
UH... HE'S A TOTAL SHUT-IN AND AN OTAKU, SO UM, THAT'S WHY HE HASN'T BEEN AROUND BEFORE. UH... BUT HE WANTED TO SEE A MANGA CLUB JUST ONCE, SO HE CAME BY TODAY.
SPARKLE
DO YOU GUYS MIND AT ALL?
THAT'S AN "OTAKU"?
I GUESS I DON'T MIND.
NO.
WHAT-EVS.
Tch!
WHEW
GOOD.
GREAT!

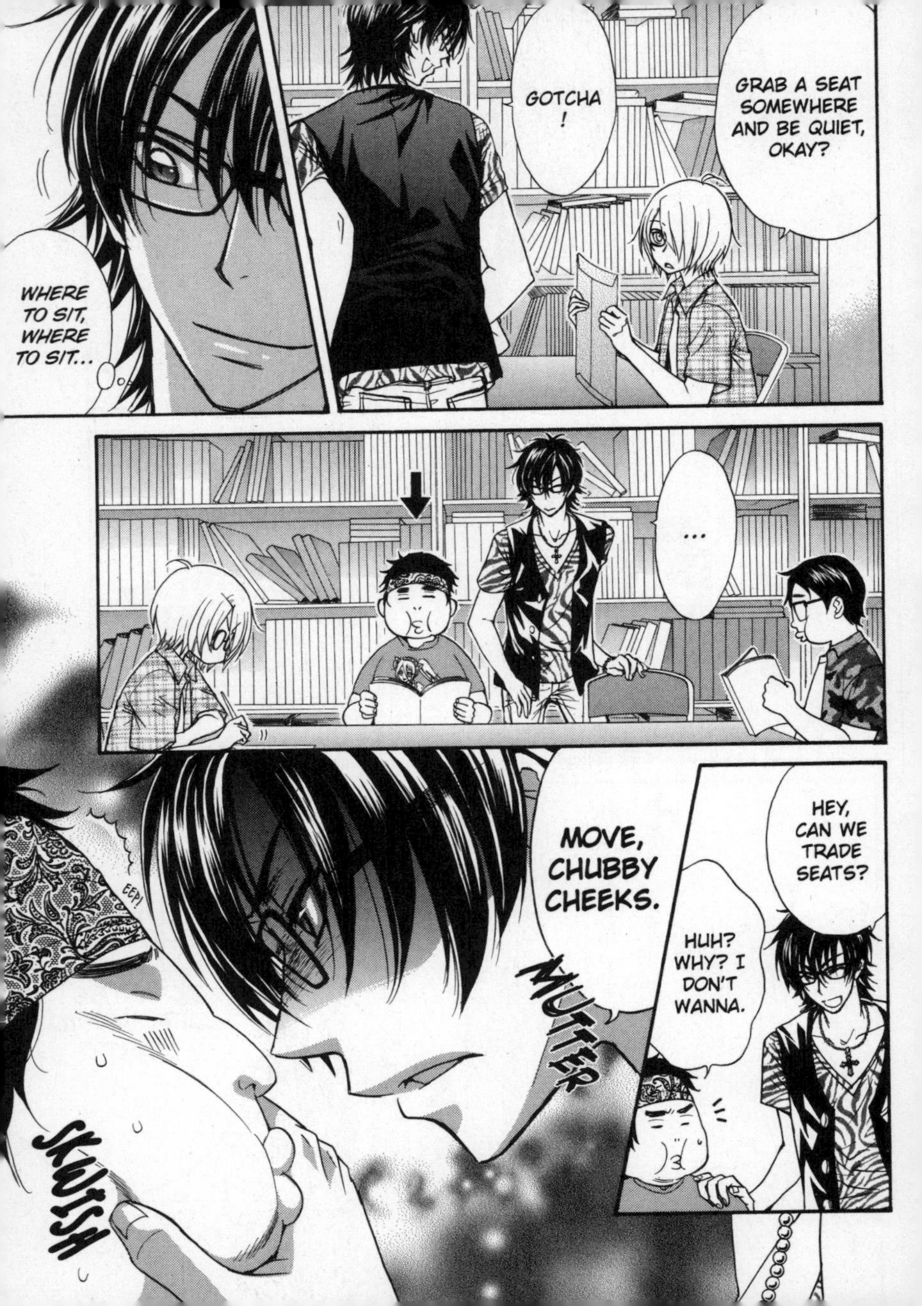
GRAB A SEAT SOMEWHERE AND BE QUIET, OKAY?
GOTCHA!
WHERE TO SIT, WHERE TO SIT...
...
HEY, CAN WE TRADE SEATS?
HUH? WHY? I DON'T WANNA.
MOVE, CHUBBY CHEEKS.
MUTTER
EEP!
SKWISH

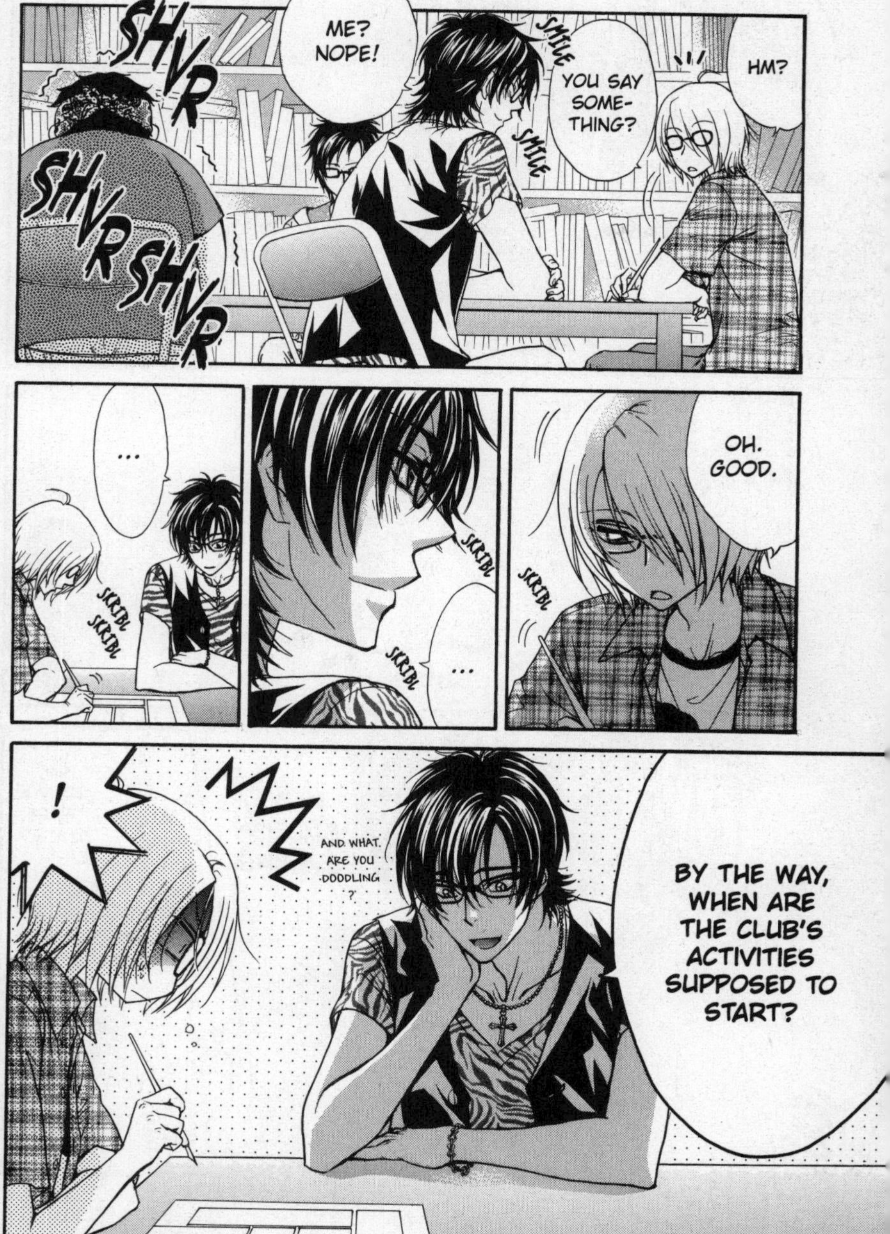
HM?
YOU SAY SOME-THING?
SMILE
SMILE
ME? NOPE!
SHVR
SHVR
SHVR
SHVR
OH. GOOD.
SKRIBL
SKRIBL
...
...
SKRIBL
SKRIBL
BY THE WAY, WHEN ARE THE CLUB'S ACTIVITIES SUPPOSED TO START?
AND WHAT ARE YOU DOODLING?
!

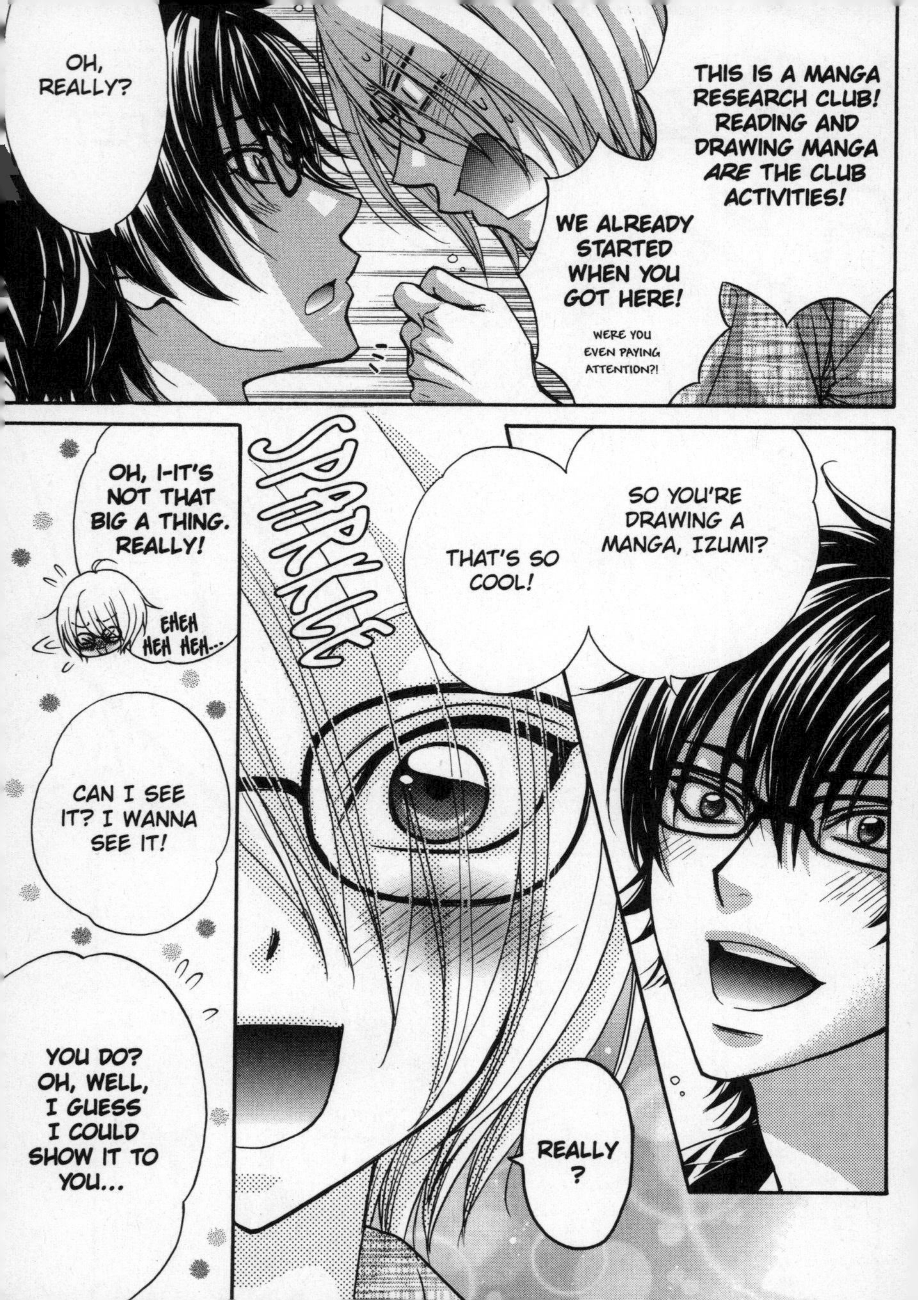
THIS IS A MANGA RESEARCH CLUB! READING AND DRAWING MANGA ARE THE CLUB ACTIVITIES!
WE ALREADY STARTED WHEN YOU GOT HERE!
WERE YOU EVEN PAYING ATTENTION?!
OH, REALLY?
SO YOU'RE DRAWING A MANGA, IZUMI?
THAT'S SO COOL!
SPARKLE
REALLY?
OH, I-IT'S NOT THAT BIG A THING. REALLY!
EHEH HEH HEH...
CAN I SEE IT? I WANNA SEE IT!
YOU DO? OH, WELL, I GUESS I COULD SHOW IT TO YOU...

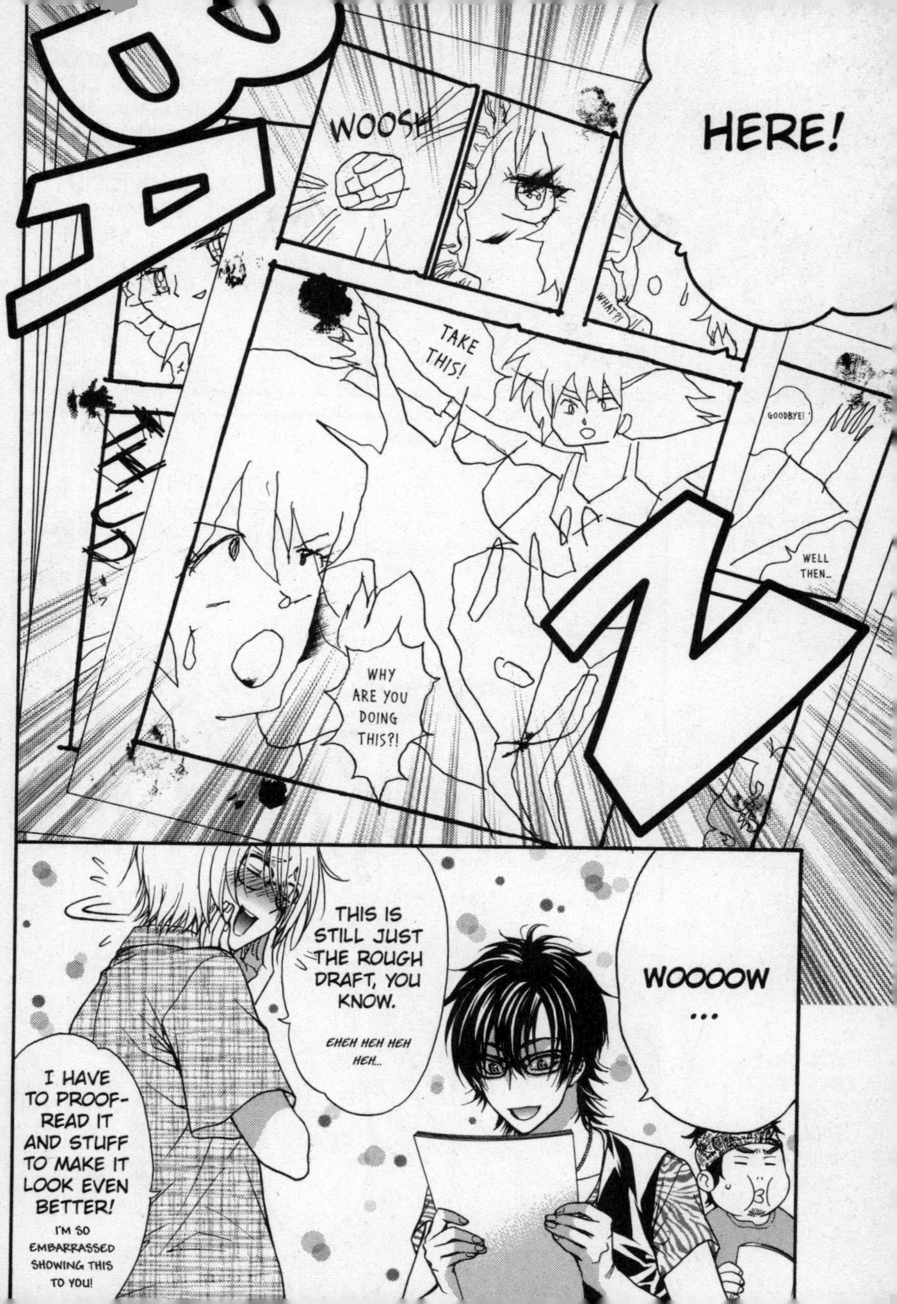
HERE!
WHAT?!
WOOSH
GOODBYE!
WELL THEN...
TAKE THIS!
WHY ARE YOU DOING THIS?!
THUD
WOOOOW...
THIS IS STILL JUST THE ROUGH DRAFT, YOU KNOW.
EHEH HEH HEH HEH...
I HAVE TO PROOF-READ IT AND STUFF TO MAKE IT LOOK EVEN BETTER!
I'M SO EMBARRASSED SHOWING THIS TO YOU!

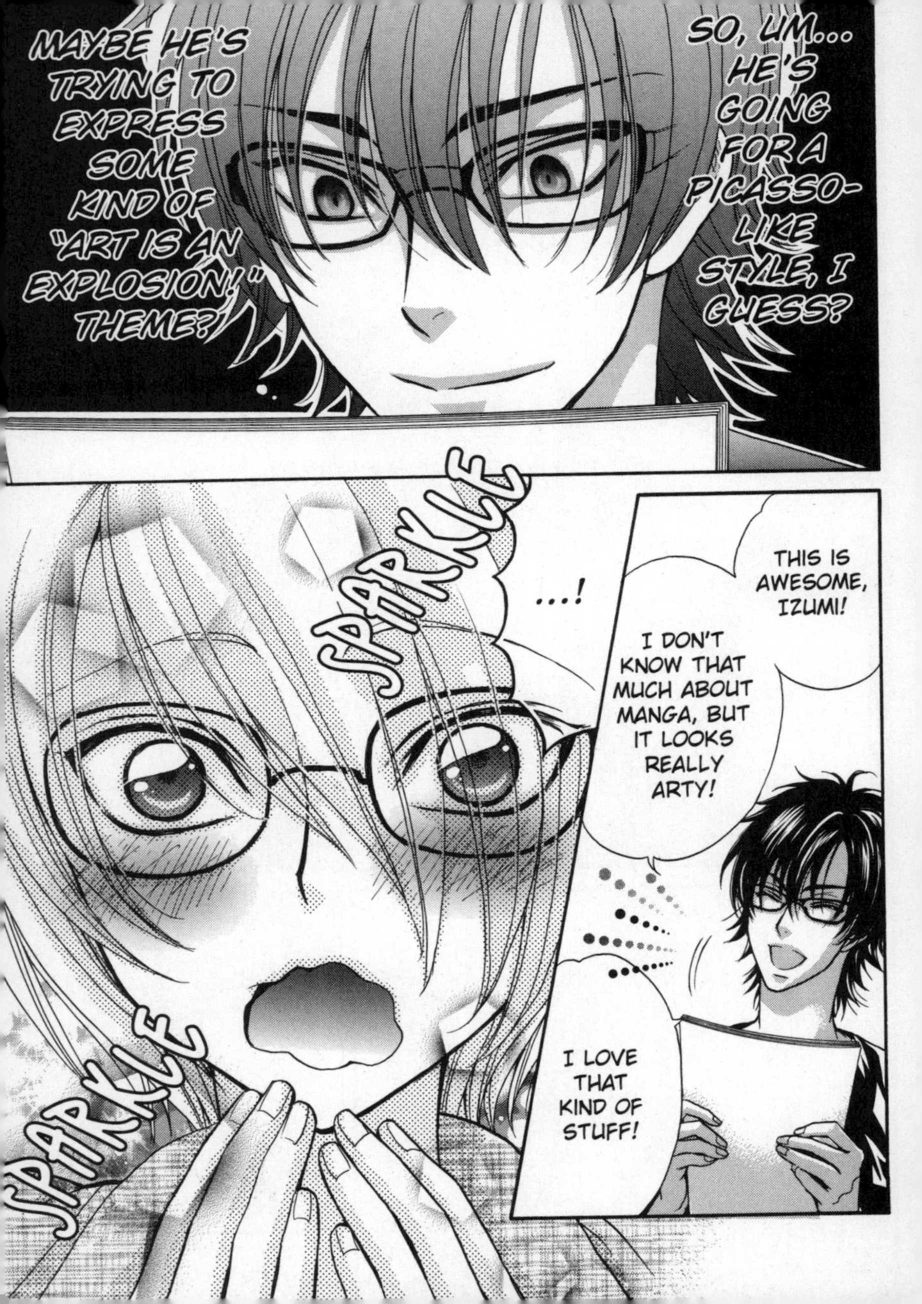
SO, UM... HE'S GOING FOR A PICASSO-LIKE STYLE, I GUESS?
MAYBE HE'S TRYING TO EXPRESS SOME KIND OF "ART IS AN EXPLOSION!" THEME?
THIS IS AWESOME, IZUMI!
I DON'T KNOW THAT MUCH ABOUT MANGA, BUT IT LOOKS REALLY ARTY!
I LOVE THAT KIND OF STUFF!
...!
SPARKLE
SPARKLE

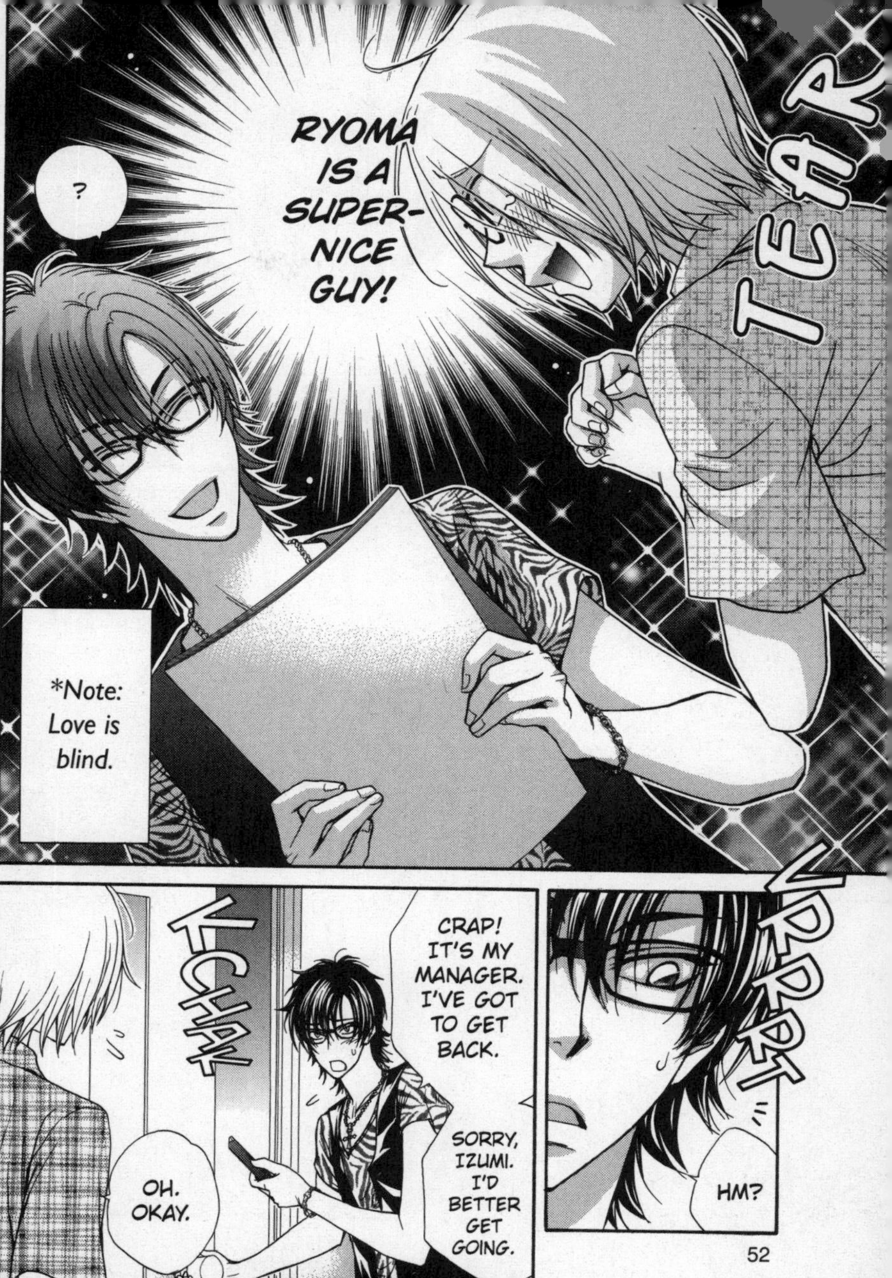
TEAR
RYOMA IS A SUPER-NICE GUY!
?
*Note: Love is blind.
VRRRT
HM?
CRAP! IT'S MY MANAGER. I'VE GOT TO GET BACK.
KCHAK
SORRY, IZUMI. I'D BETTER GET GOING.
OH. OKAY.

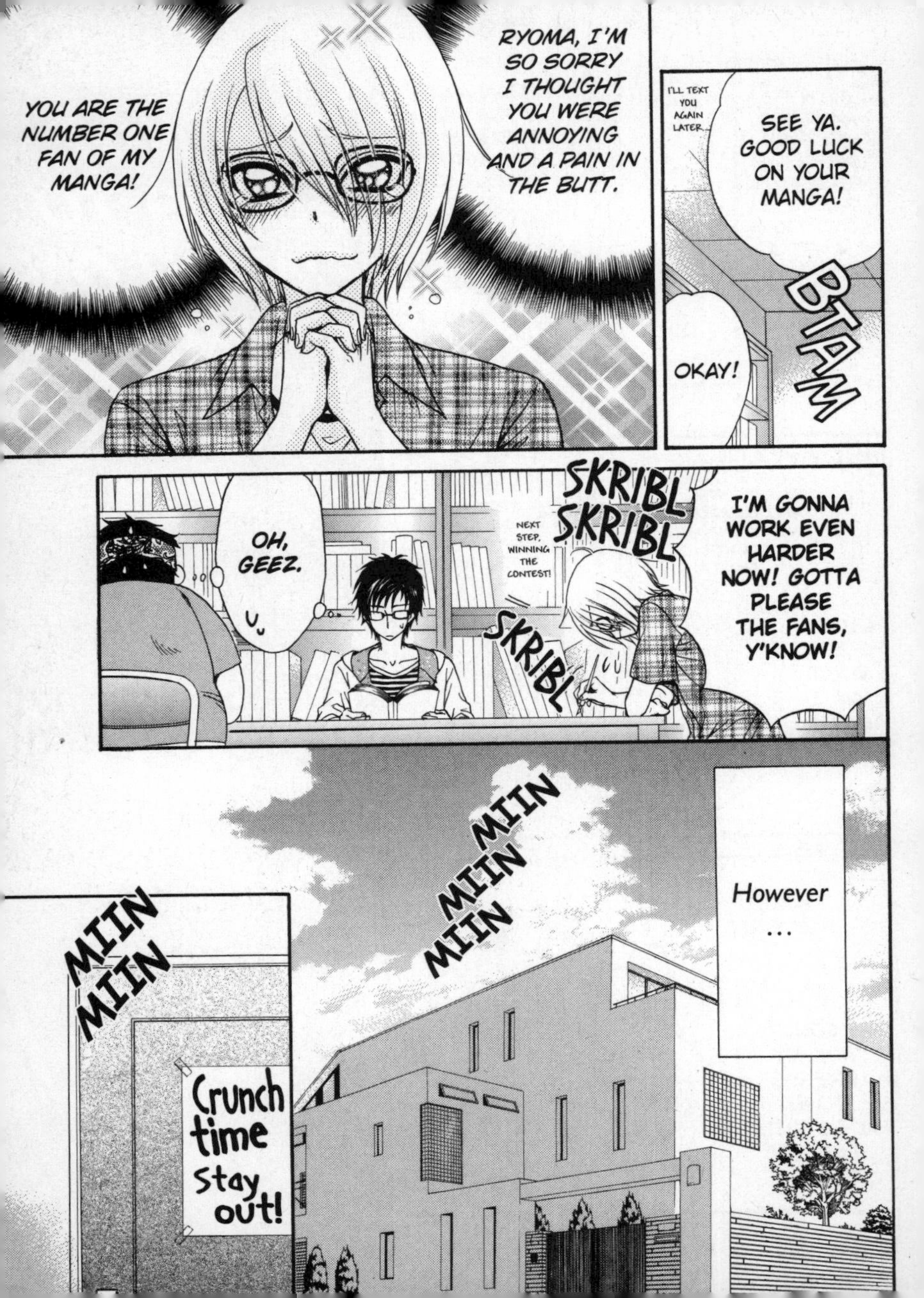
I'LL TEXT YOU AGAIN LATER.
SEE YA. GOOD LUCK ON YOUR MANGA!
BTAM
OKAY!
RYOMA, I'M SO SORRY I THOUGHT YOU WERE ANNOYING AND A PAIN IN THE BUTT.
YOU ARE THE NUMBER ONE FAN OF MY MANGA!
I'M GONNA WORK EVEN HARDER NOW! GOTTA PLEASE THE FANS, Y'KNOW!
SKRIBL SKRIBL
SKRIBL
NEXT STEP, WINNING THE CONTEST!
OH, GEEZ.
However ...
MIIN MIIN
MIIN MIIN
Crunch time Stay out!

EVEN IF I HAND IT IN TO THEIR OFFICES IN PERSON ON THE 31ST, I ONLY HAVE A LITTLE UNDER TWO DAYS LEFT.

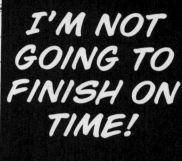

7	20XX JULY				
Sunday	Monday				Thursday
1	2		THE DUE DATE FOR THE CONTEST IS JULY 31ST, AND IT'S ALREADY JULY 29TH!		
8	9				2
15	16	17	18	19	
22	23	24	25	26	
29	30	(31)	MANGA CONTEST DEADLINE!		

I'M NOT GOING TO FINISH ON TIME!

EVEN IF I PULLED TWO ALL-NIGHTERS AND WORKED STRAIGHT THROUGH FROM NOW UNTIL THE DEADLINE, I STILL WOULDN'T MAKE IT.

THERE'RE FIVE PAGES LEFT TO INK AND ALL THE FINISHING TOUCHES ON IT!

OH MY GOSH, WHAT AM I GOING TO DO!

GLOOOM

WAIT, THAT'S IT!

I COULD ASK MY FRIENDS TO BE ASSISTANTS FOR ME!

AH!

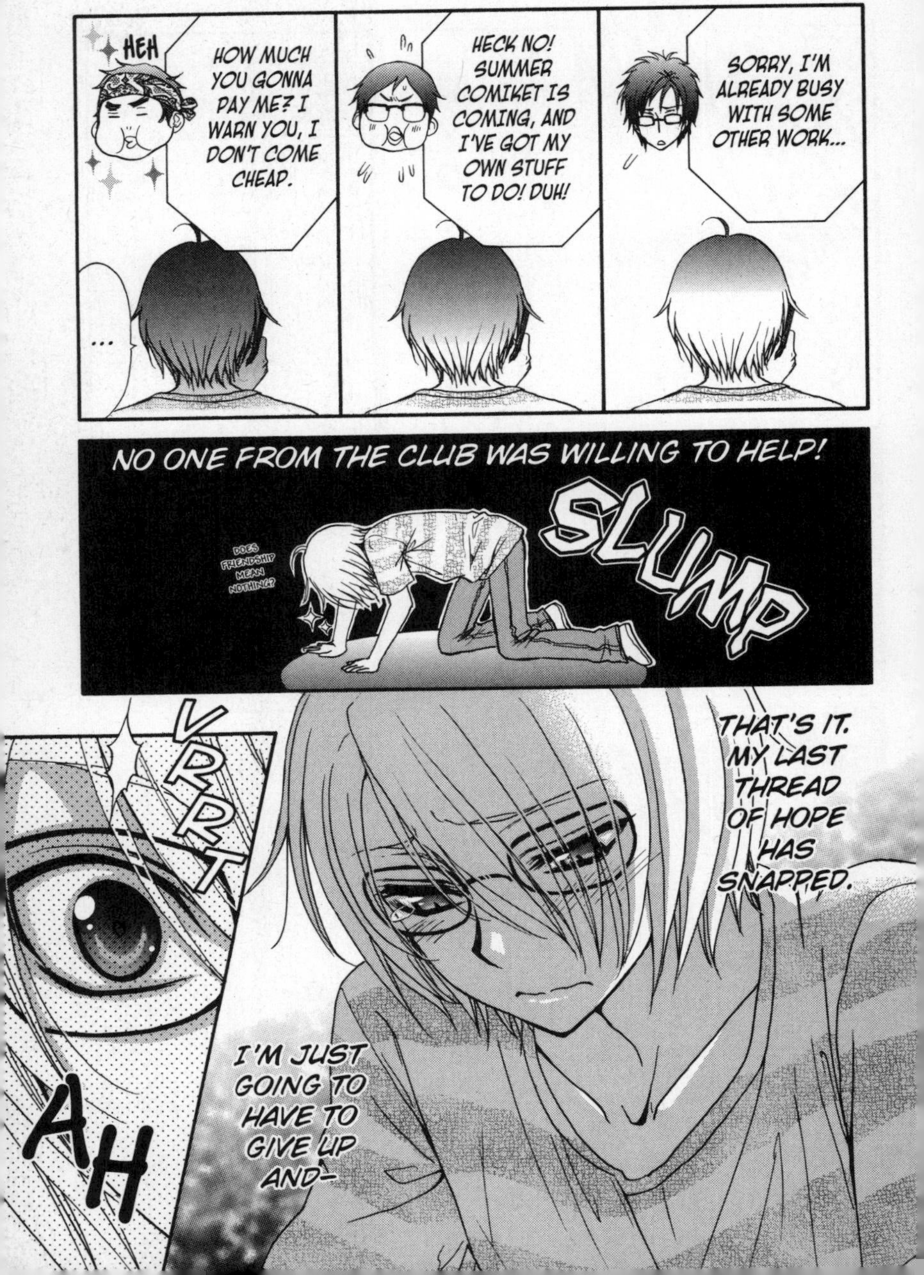
SORRY, I'M ALREADY BUSY WITH SOME OTHER WORK...
HECK NO! SUMMER COMIKET IS COMING, AND I'VE GOT MY OWN STUFF TO DO! DUH!
HEH
HOW MUCH YOU GONNA PAY ME? I WARN YOU, I DON'T COME CHEAP.
...
NO ONE FROM THE CLUB WAS WILLING TO HELP!
SLUMP
DOES FRIENDSHIP MEAN NOTHING?
THAT'S IT. MY LAST THREAD OF HOPE HAS SNAPPED.
I'M JUST GOING TO HAVE TO GIVE UP AND-
VRRT
AH

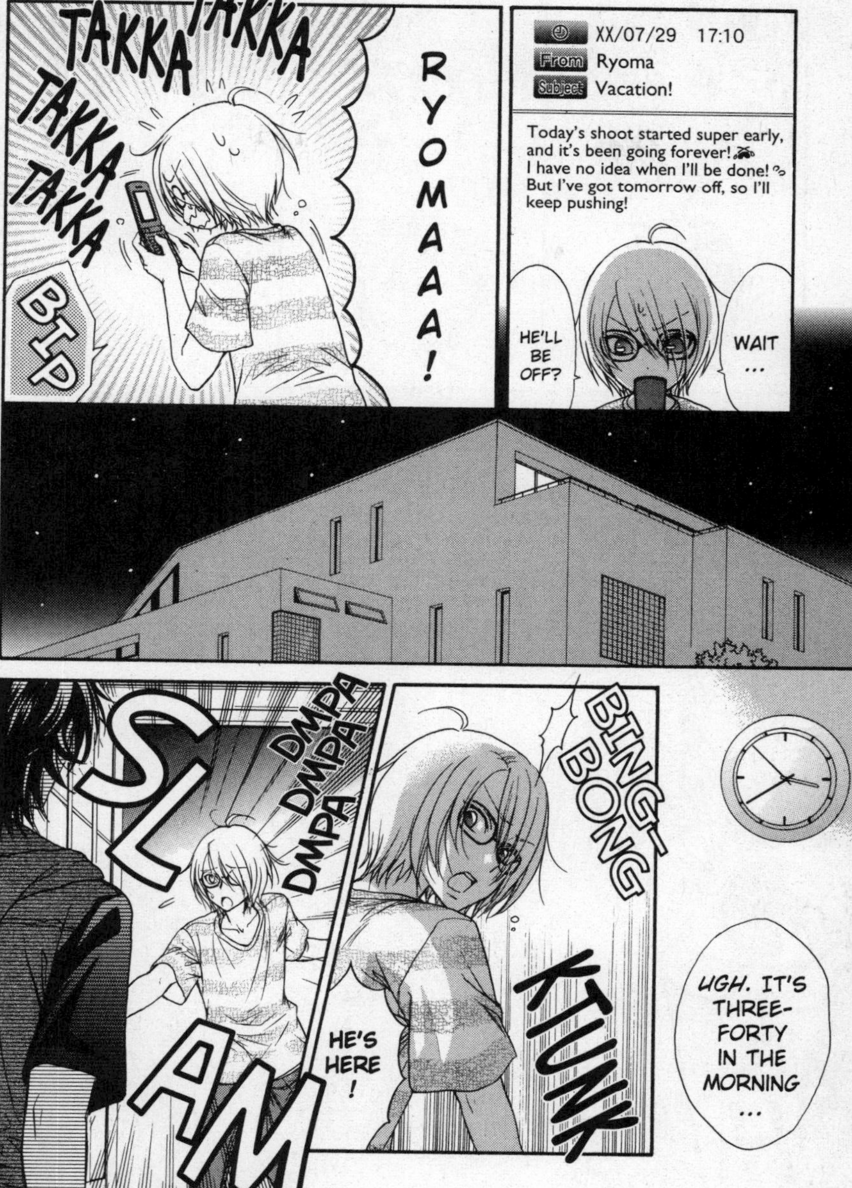
XX/07/29 17:10
From Ryoma
Subject Vacation!
Today's shoot started super early, and it's been going forever! I have no idea when I'll be done! But I've got tomorrow off, so I'll keep pushing!
WAIT ...
HE'LL BE OFF?
TAKKA TAKKA TAKKA TAKKA TAKKA TAKKA
RYOMAAAA!
BIP
UGH. IT'S THREE-FORTY IN THE MORNING ...
BING-BONG
KTUNK
HE'S HERE!
DMPA DMPA DMPA DMPA
SLAM

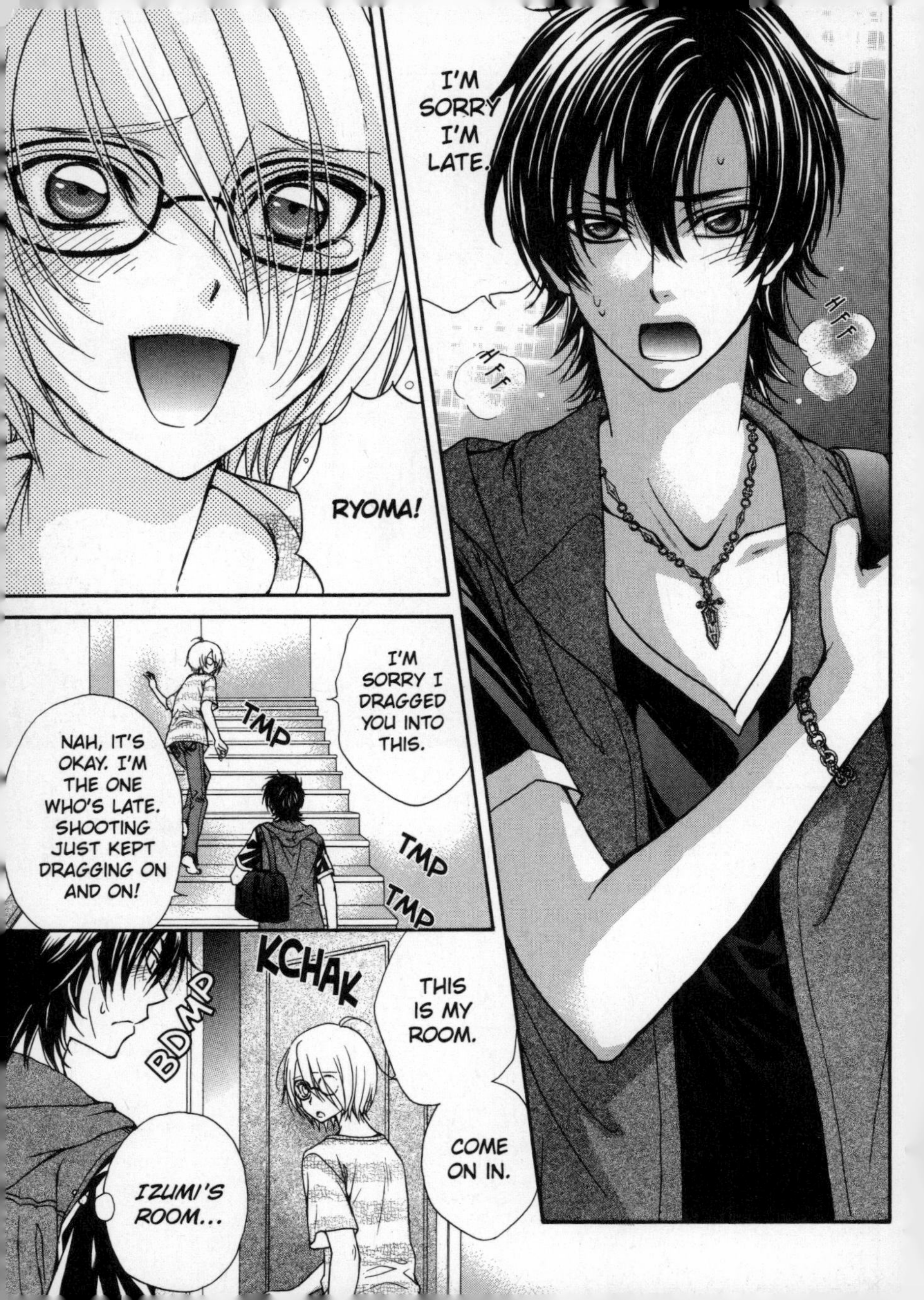
I'M SORRY I'M LATE.
HFF
HFF
RYOMA!
I'M SORRY I DRAGGED YOU INTO THIS.
TMP
NAH, IT'S OKAY. I'M THE ONE WHO'S LATE. SHOOTING JUST KEPT DRAGGING ON AND ON!
TMP
TMP
KCHAK
THIS IS MY ROOM.
COME ON IN.
BDMP
IZUMI'S ROOM...

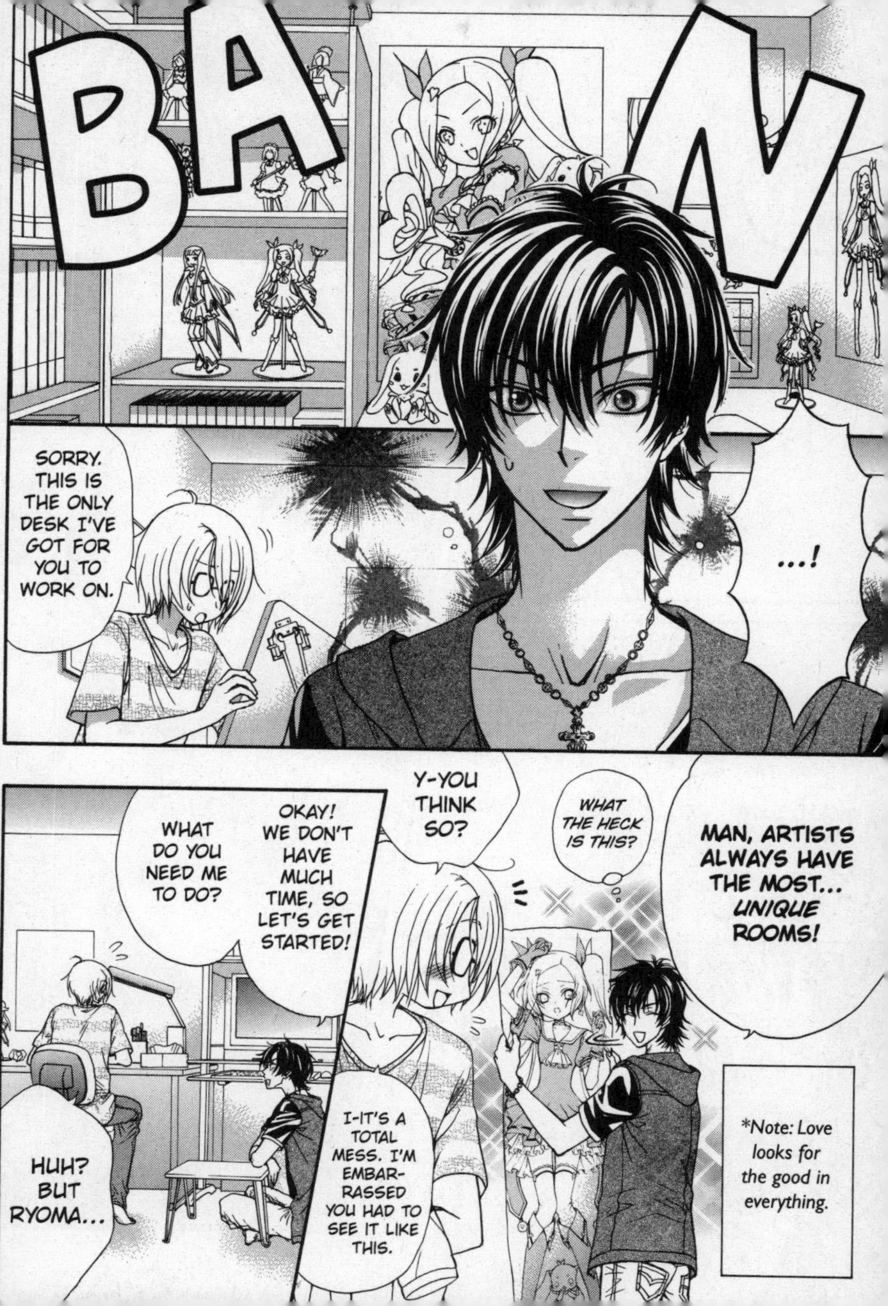
BAM
...!
SORRY. THIS IS THE ONLY DESK I'VE GOT FOR YOU TO WORK ON.
MAN, ARTISTS ALWAYS HAVE THE MOST... *UNIQUE* ROOMS!
WHAT THE HECK IS THIS?
Y-YOU THINK SO?
I-IT'S A TOTAL MESS. I'M EMBAR-RASSED YOU HAD TO SEE IT LIKE THIS.
*Note: Love looks for the good in everything.
OKAY! WE DON'T HAVE MUCH TIME, SO LET'S GET STARTED!
WHAT DO YOU NEED ME TO DO?
HUH? BUT RYOMA...

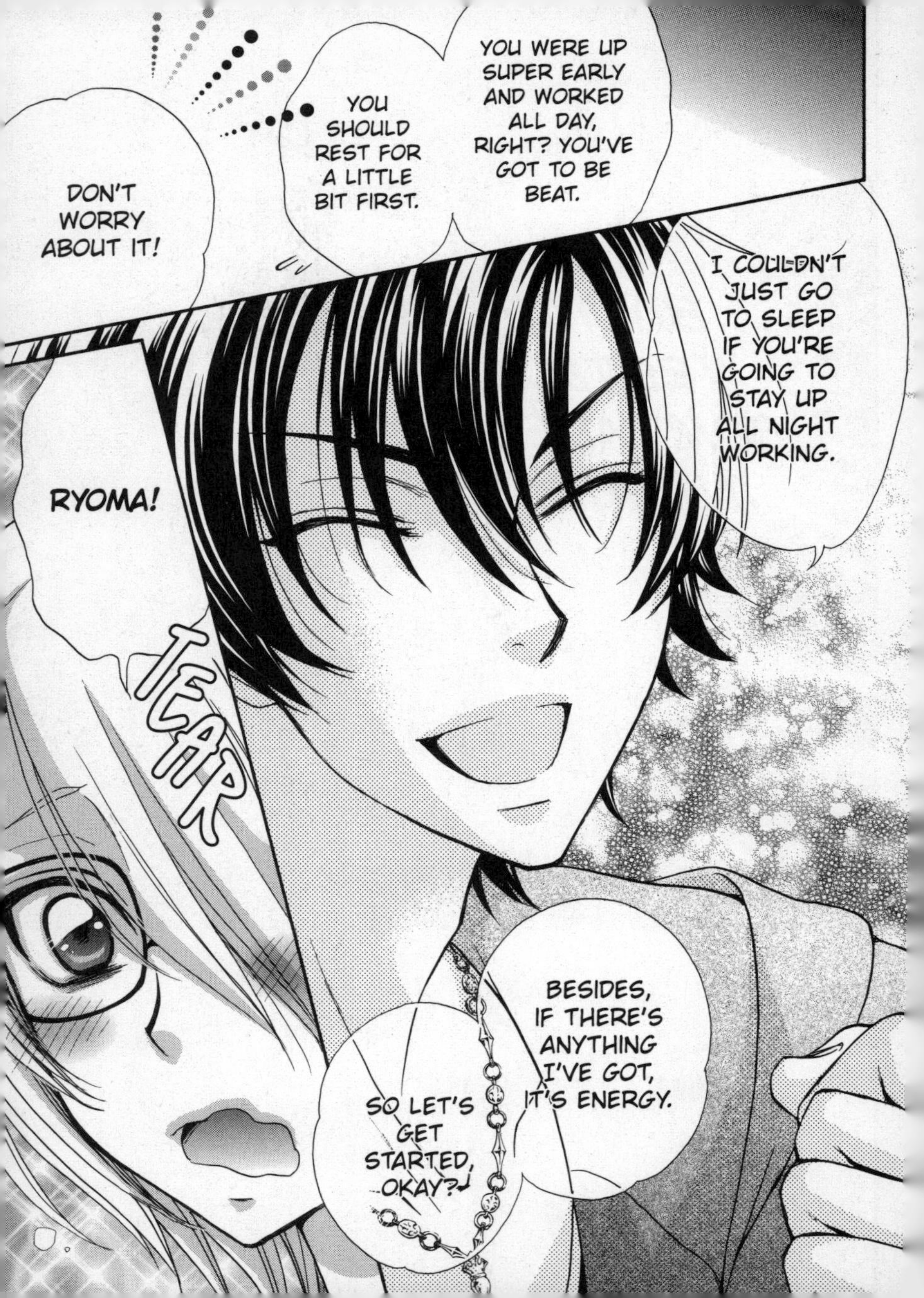
YOU WERE UP SUPER EARLY AND WORKED ALL DAY, RIGHT? YOU'VE GOT TO BE BEAT.
YOU SHOULD REST FOR A LITTLE BIT FIRST.
DON'T WORRY ABOUT IT!
I COULDN'T JUST GO TO SLEEP IF YOU'RE GOING TO STAY UP ALL NIGHT WORKING.
RYOMA!
TEAR
BESIDES, IF THERE'S ANYTHING I'VE GOT, IT'S ENERGY.
SO LET'S GET STARTED, OKAY?

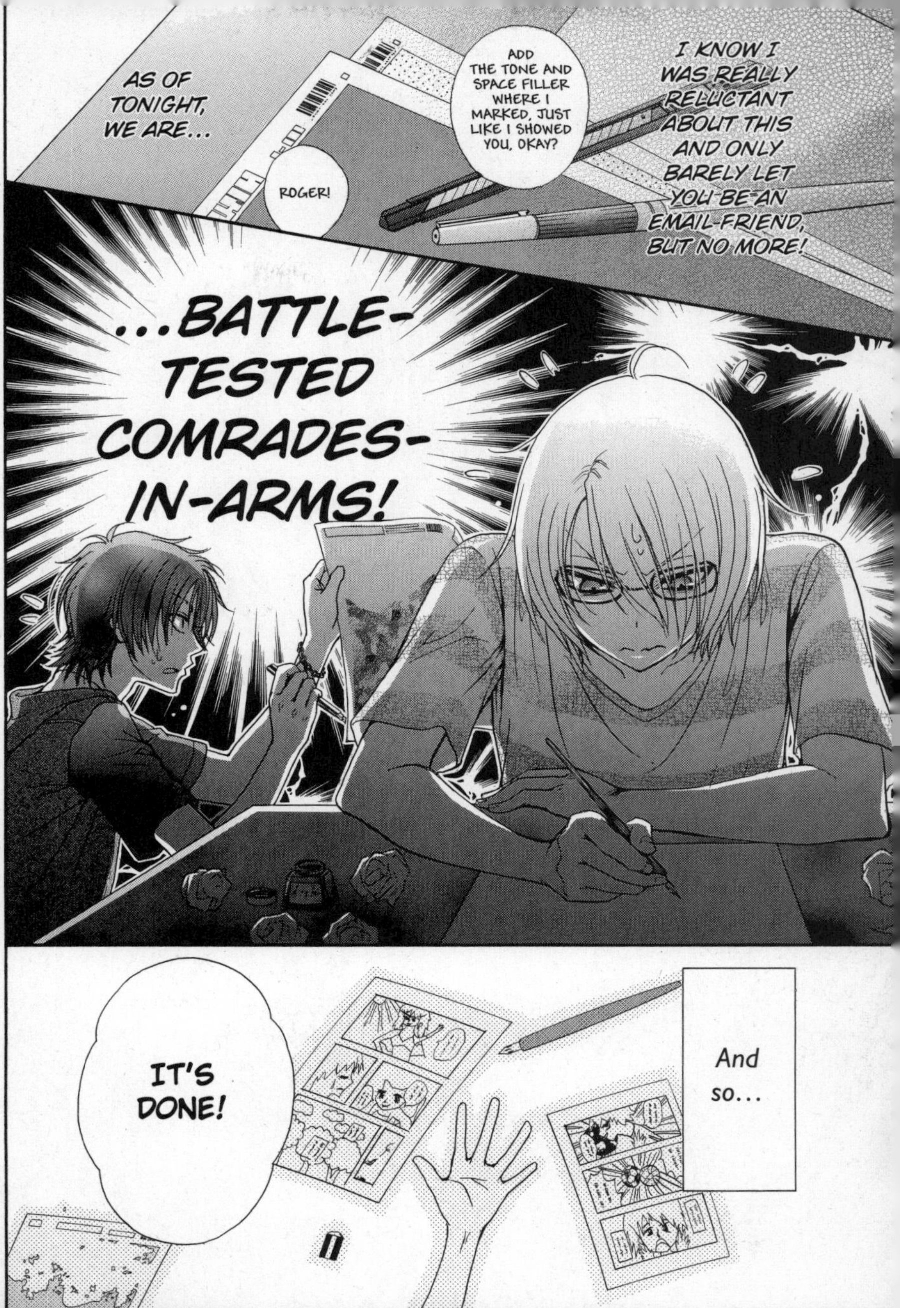
I KNOW I WAS REALLY RELUCTANT ABOUT THIS AND ONLY BARELY LET YOU BE AN EMAIL-FRIEND, BUT NO MORE!
ADD THE TONE AND SPACE FILLER WHERE I MARKED, JUST LIKE I SHOWED YOU, OKAY?
ROGER!
AS OF TONIGHT, WE ARE...
...BATTLE-TESTED COMRADES-IN-ARMS!
And so...
IT'S DONE!

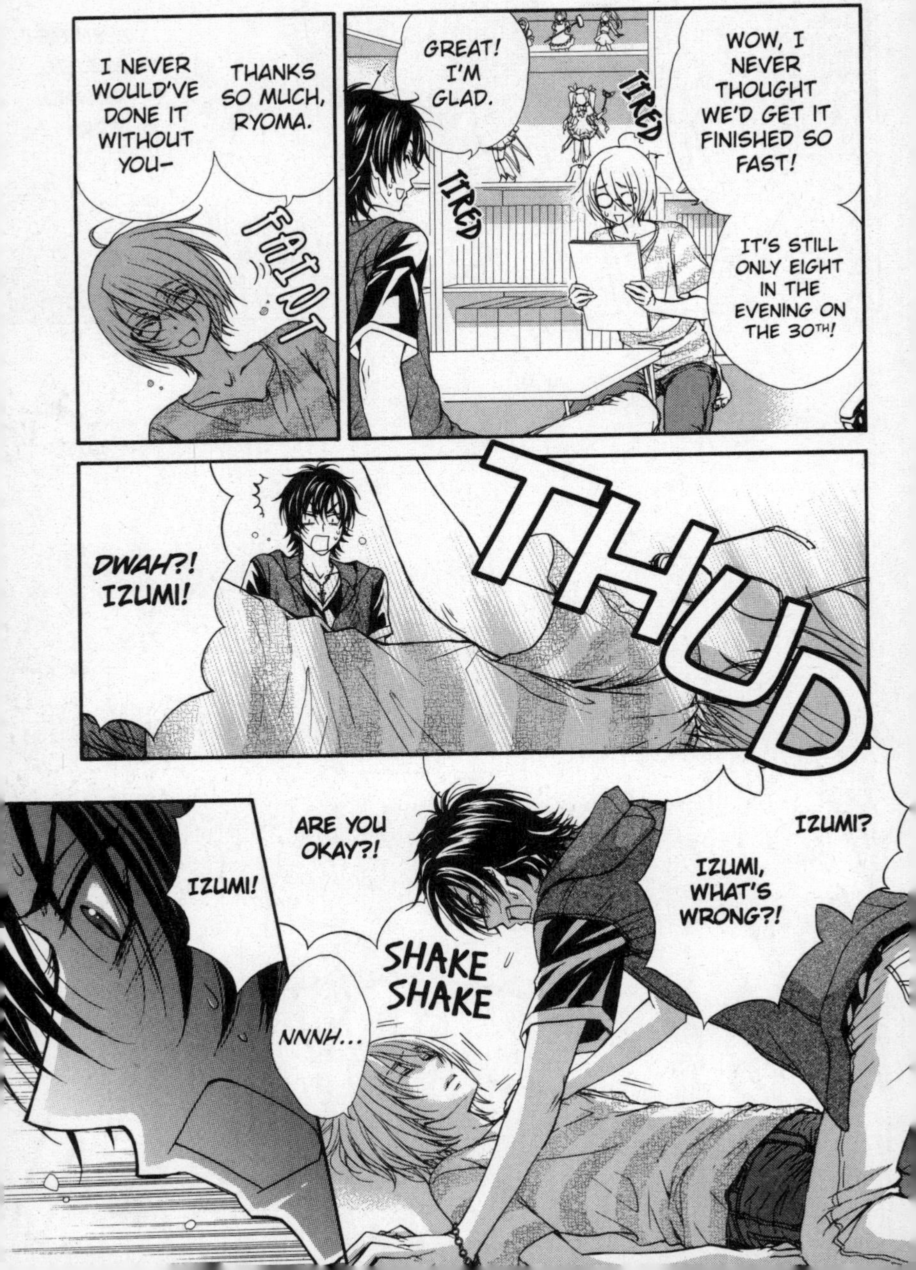
WOW, I NEVER THOUGHT WE'D GET IT FINISHED SO FAST!
IT'S STILL ONLY EIGHT IN THE EVENING ON THE 30TH!
TIRED
GREAT! I'M GLAD.
TIRED
THANKS SO MUCH, RYOMA.
I NEVER WOULD'VE DONE IT WITHOUT YOU-
FAINT
THUD
DWAH?! IZUMI!
IZUMI?
IZUMI, WHAT'S WRONG?!
ARE YOU OKAY?!
SHAKE SHAKE
IZUMI!
NNNH...

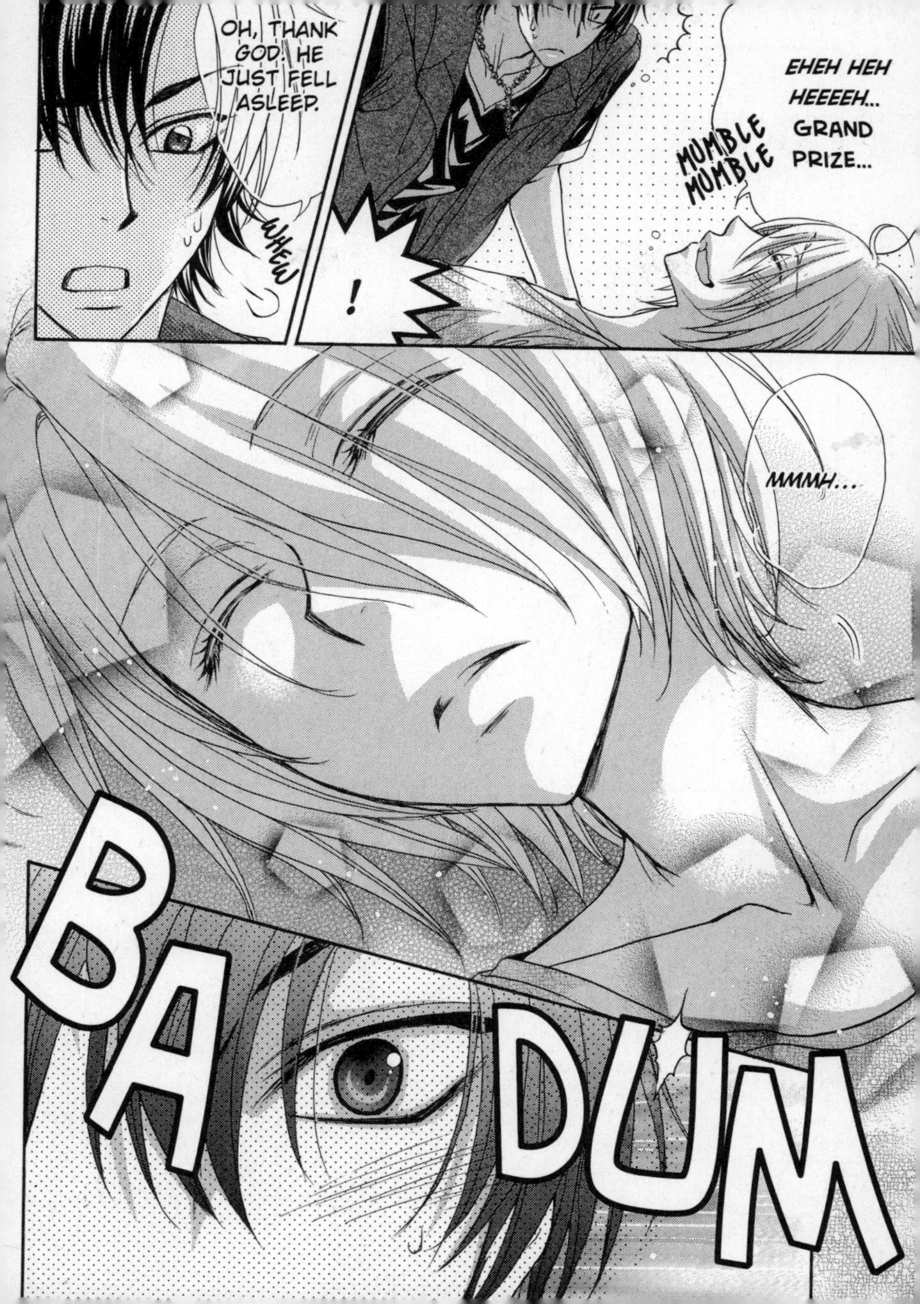
EHEH HEH HEEEEH... GRAND PRIZE...
MUMBLE MUMBLE
!
OH, THANK GOD. HE JUST FELL ASLEEP.
WHEW
MMMH...
BA DUM

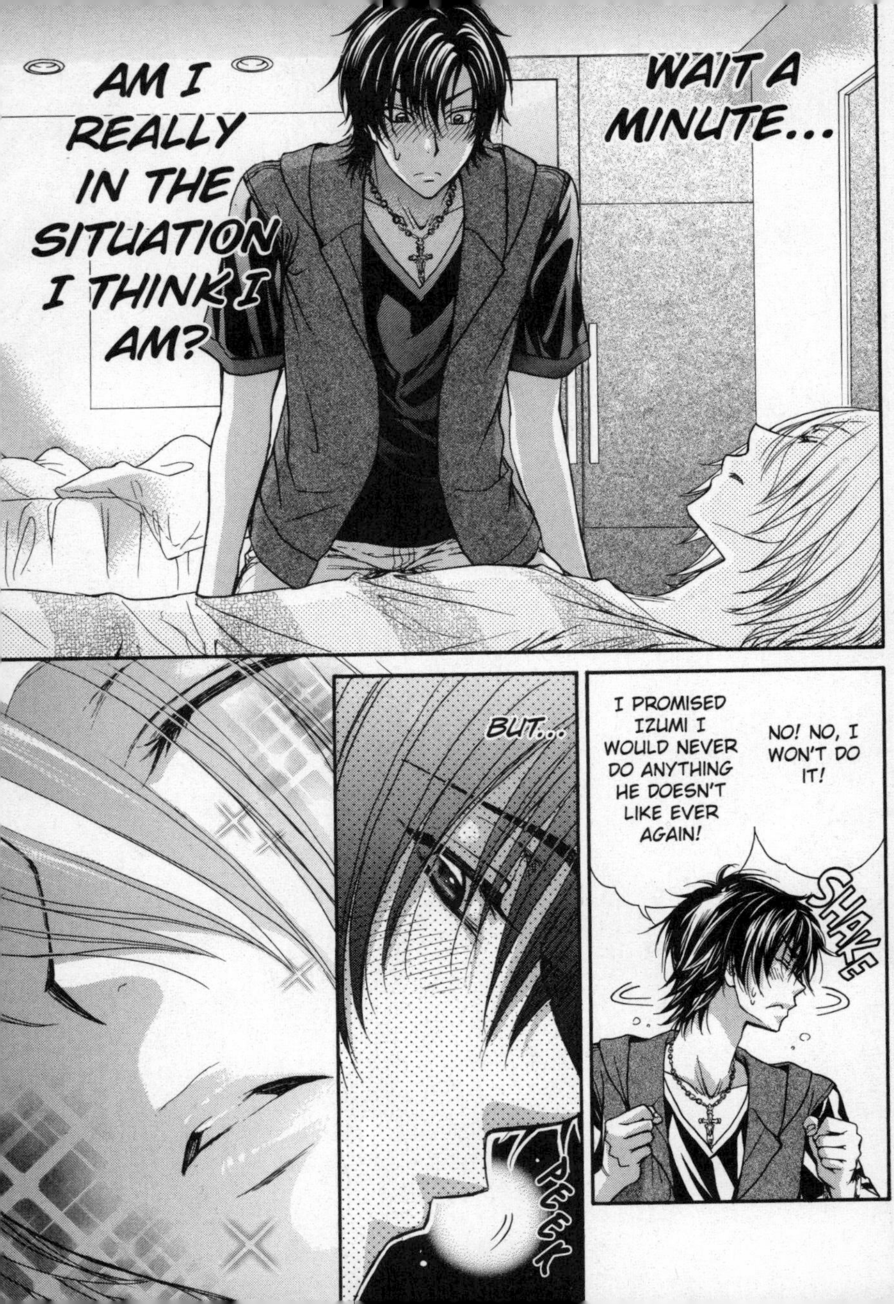
WAIT A MINUTE...
AM I REALLY IN THE SITUATION I THINK I AM?
NO! NO, I WON'T DO IT!
I PROMISED IZUMI I WOULD NEVER DO ANYTHING HE DOESN'T LIKE EVER AGAIN!
SHAKE
BUT...
PEEK

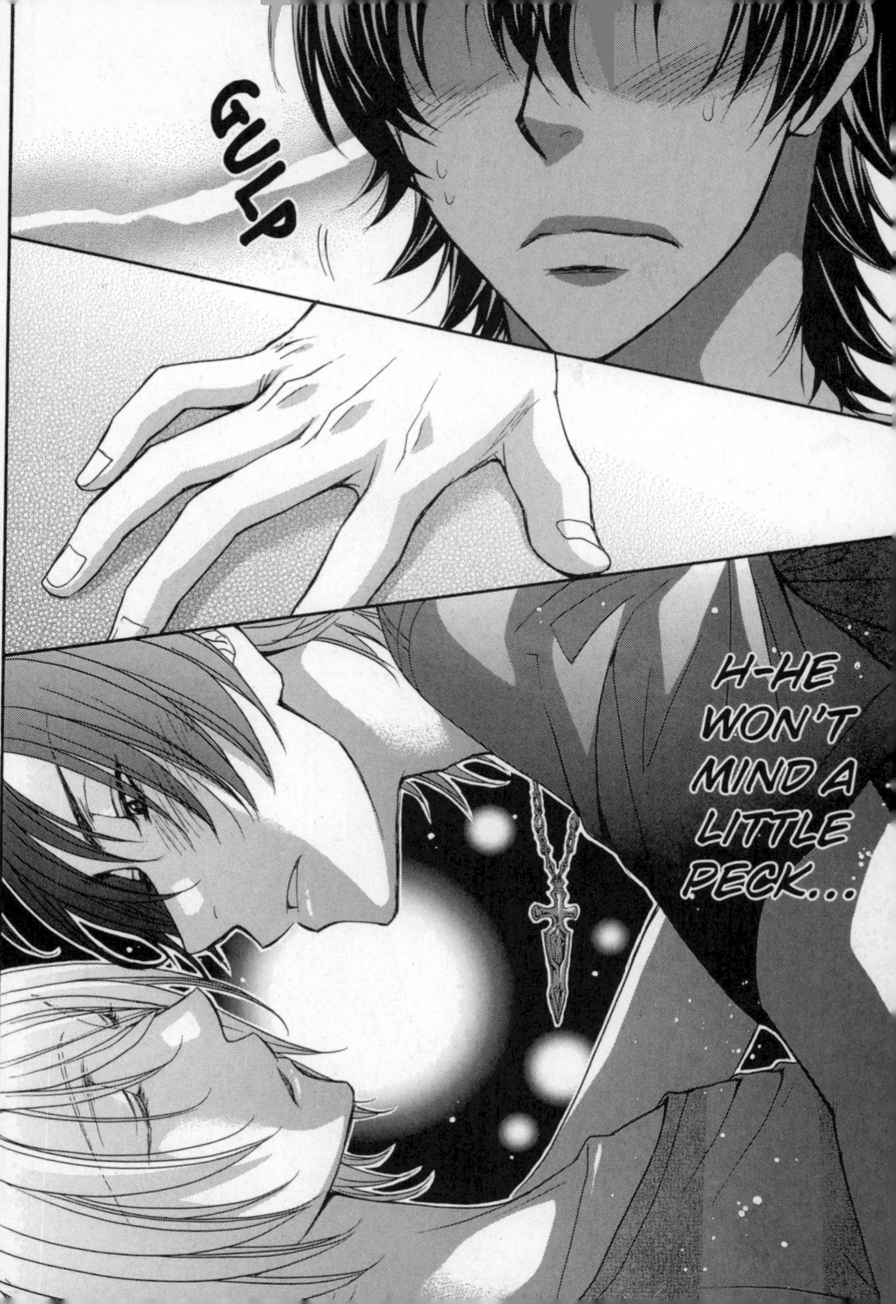
GULP
H-HE WON'T MIND A LITTLE PECK...

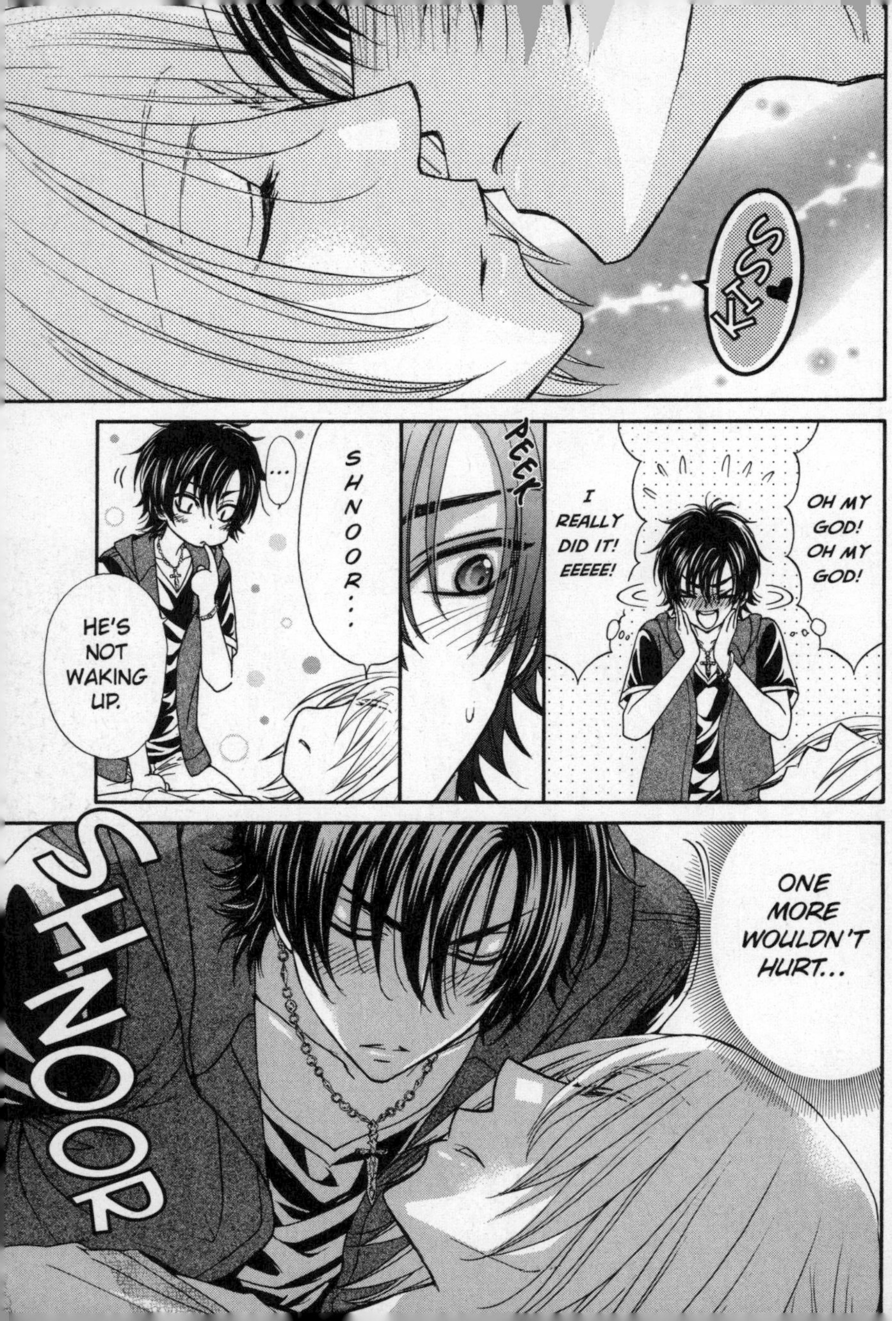
KISS♥
OH MY GOD! OH MY GOD!
I REALLY DID IT! EEEEE!
PEEK
SHNOOR...
...
HE'S NOT WAKING UP.
ONE MORE WOULDN'T HURT...
SHNOOR

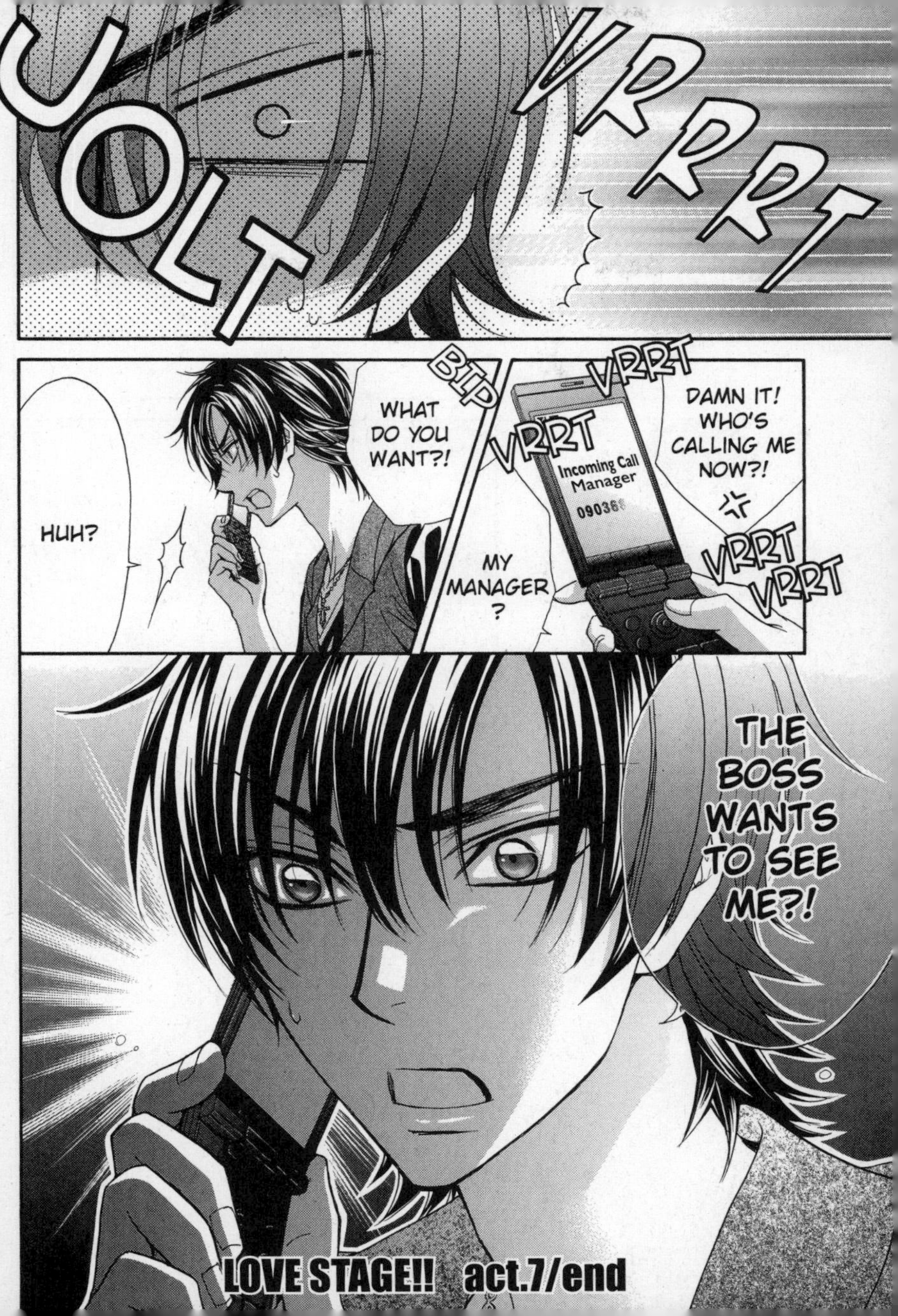
VRRRRT
JOLT
VRRT
DAMN IT! WHO'S CALLING ME NOW?!
VRRT
Incoming Call
Manager
090361
MY MANAGER?
VRRT VRRT
BIP
WHAT DO YOU WANT?!
HUH?
THE BOSS WANTS TO SEE ME?!
LOVE STAGE!! act.7/end

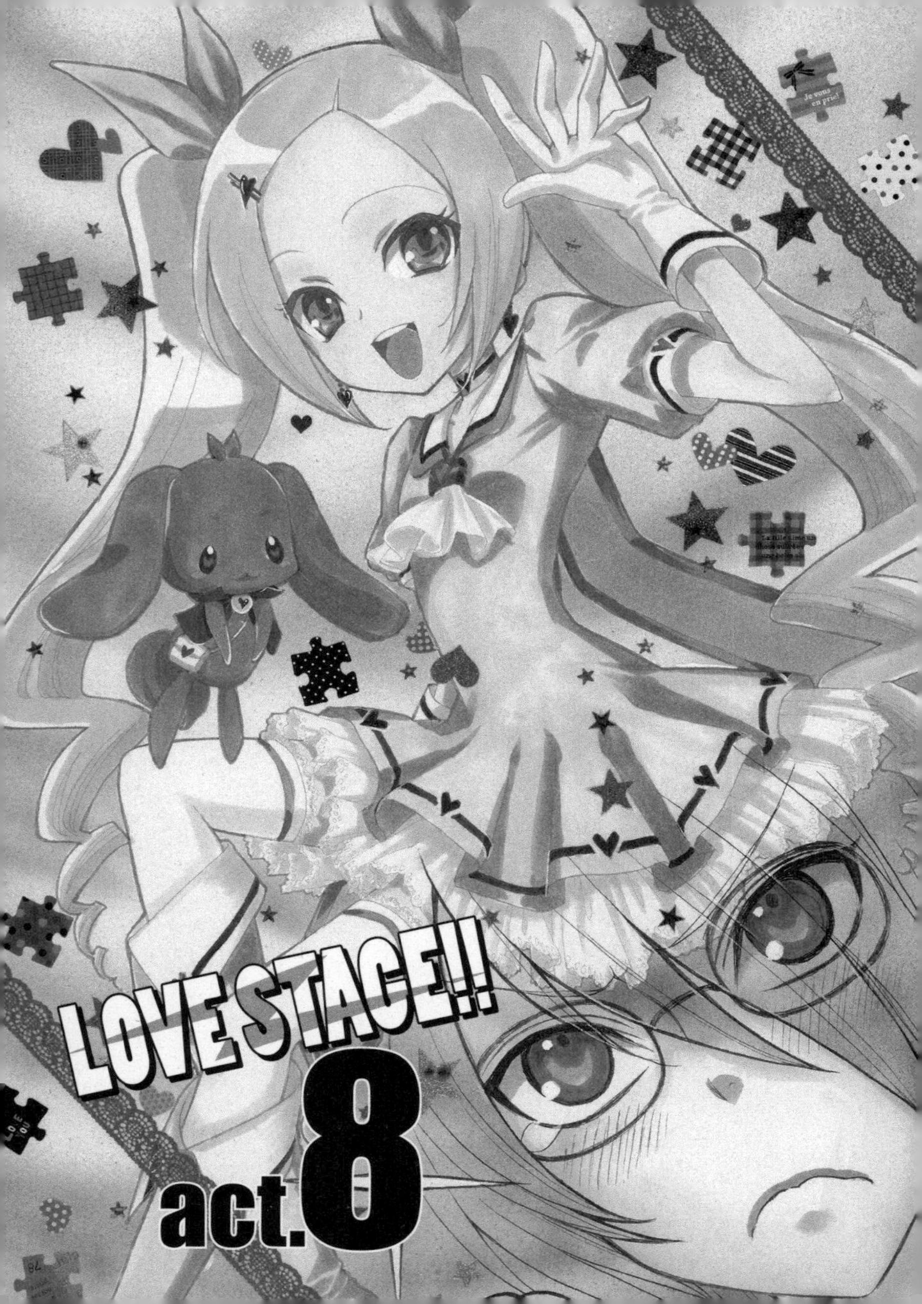
LOVE STAGE!!
act.8
Je vous en prie!

LOVE STAGE!!

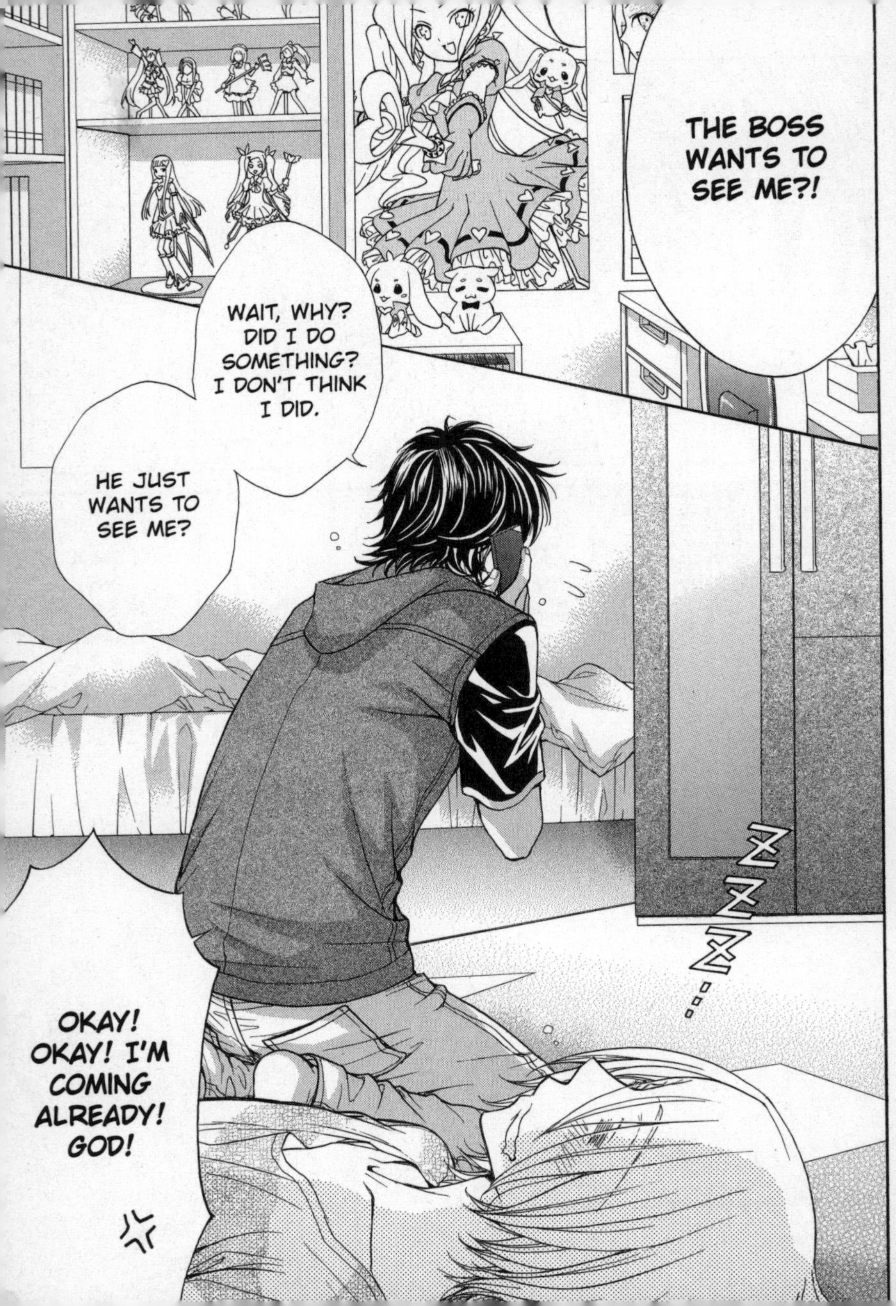
THE BOSS WANTS TO SEE ME?!
WAIT, WHY? DID I DO SOMETHING? I DON'T THINK I DID.
HE JUST WANTS TO SEE ME?
ZZZ...
OKAY! OKAY! I'M COMING ALREADY! GOD!

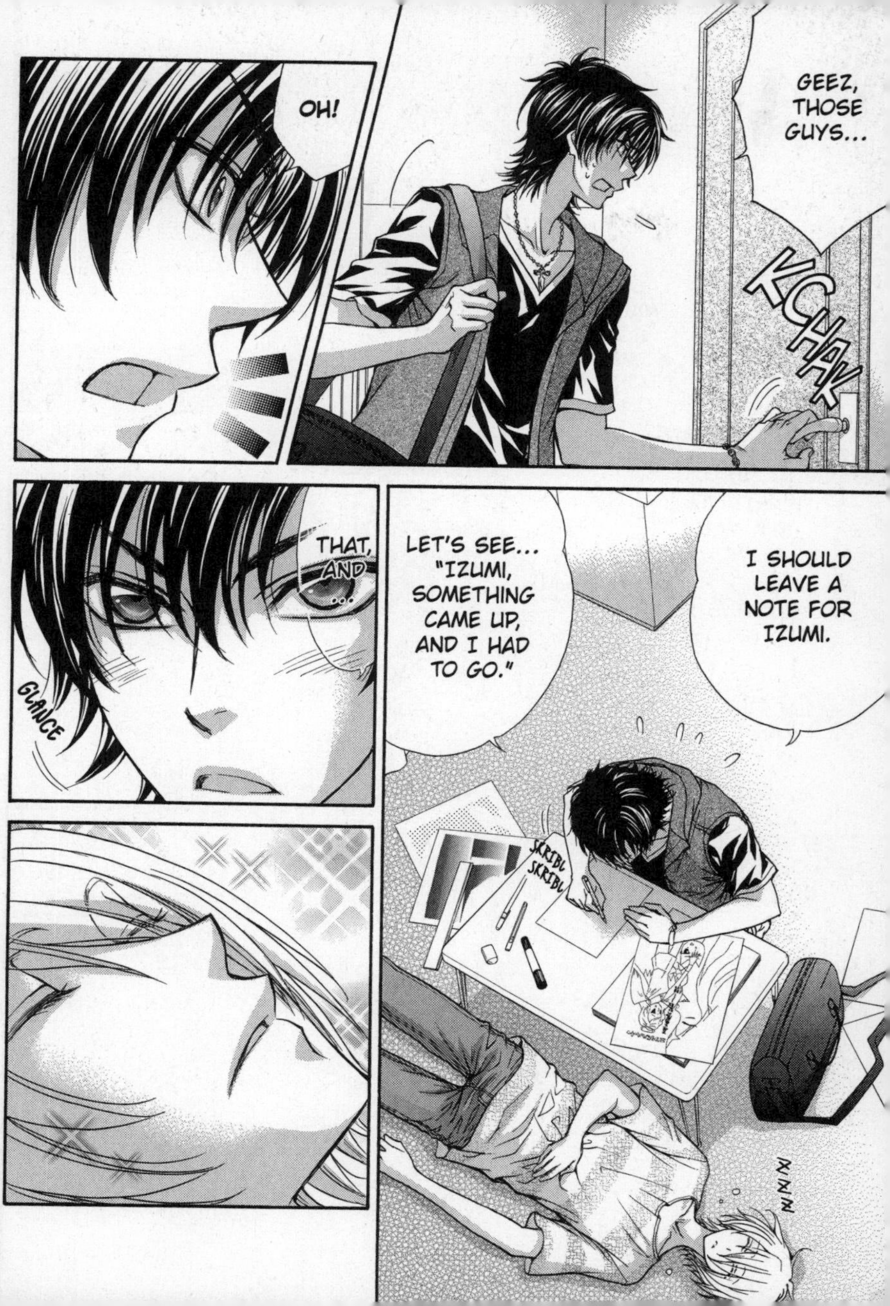
GEEZ, THOSE GUYS...
KCHAK
OH!
I SHOULD LEAVE A NOTE FOR IZUMI.
LET'S SEE... "IZUMI, SOMETHING CAME UP, AND I HAD TO GO."
SKRIBL SKRIBL
ZZZ
THAT, AND...
GLANCE

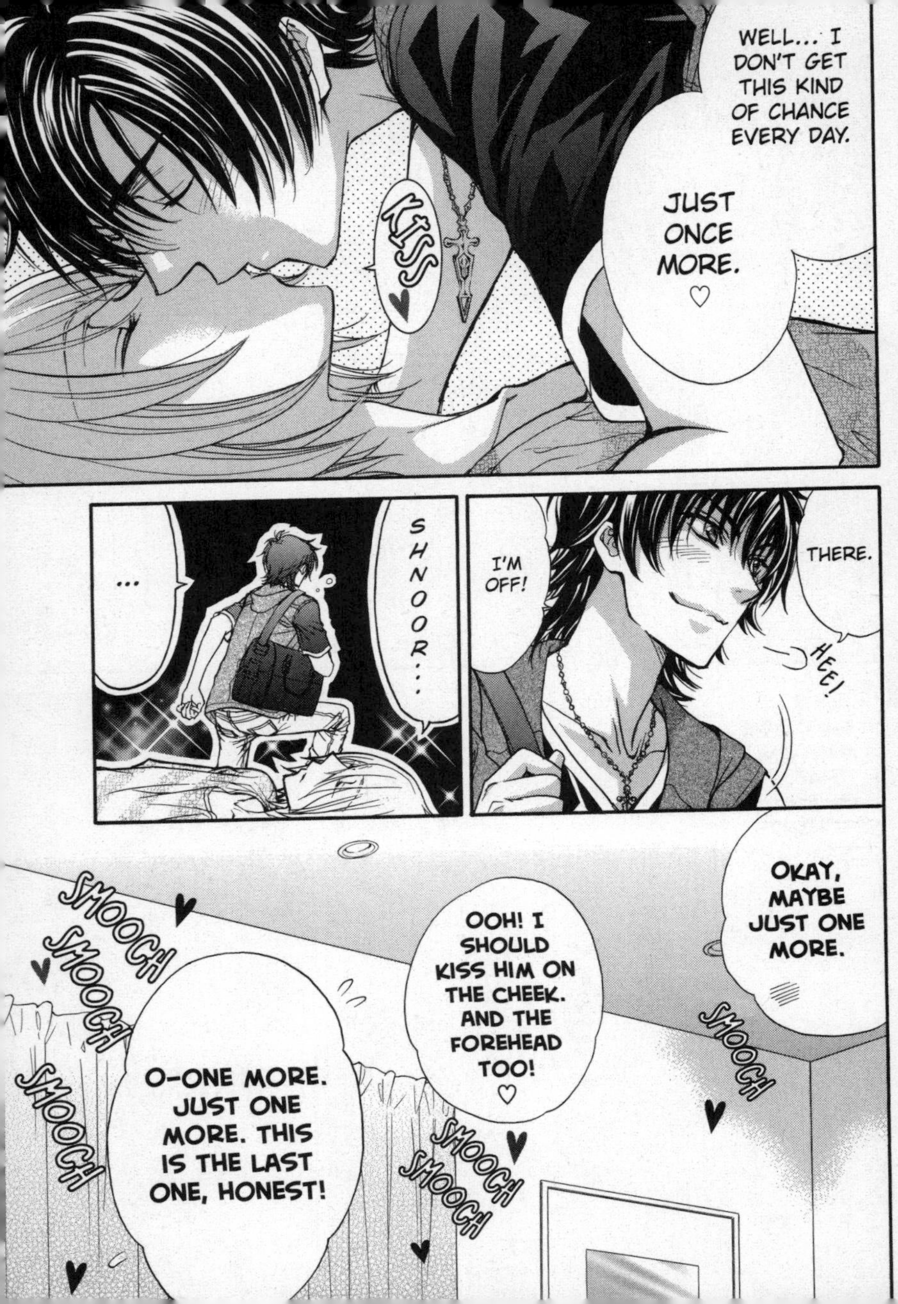
WELL... I DON'T GET THIS KIND OF CHANCE EVERY DAY.
JUST ONCE MORE. ♡
KISS ♥
THERE.
HEE!
I'M OFF!
SHNOOOR...
...
OKAY, MAYBE JUST ONE MORE.
SMOOCH ♥
OOH! I SHOULD KISS HIM ON THE CHEEK. AND THE FOREHEAD TOO! ♡
SMOOCH SMOOCH ♥
O-ONE MORE. JUST ONE MORE. THIS IS THE LAST ONE, HONEST!
SMOOCH ♥ SMOOCH ♥ SMOOCH ♥ SMOOCH ♥ SMOOCH ♥

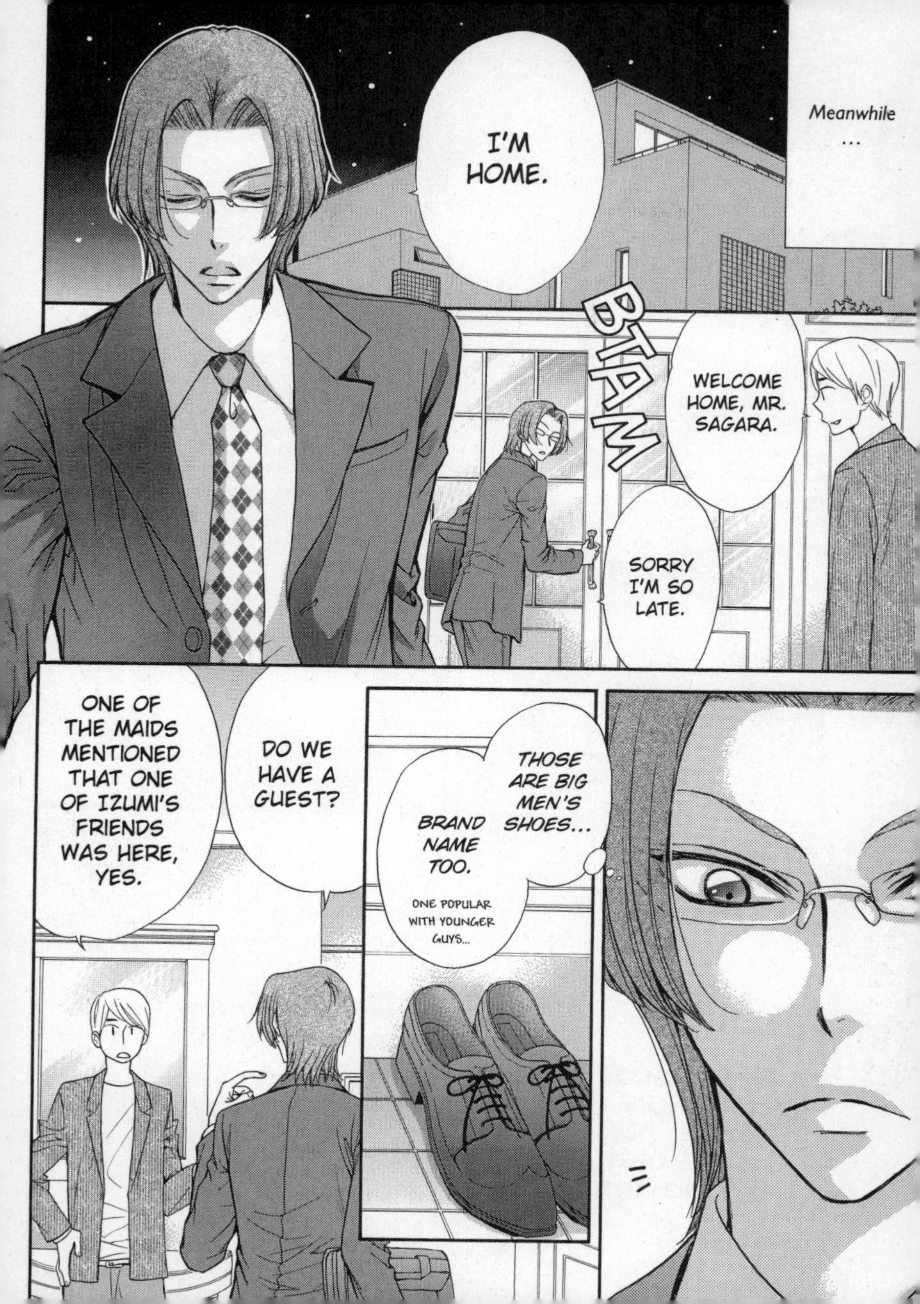
Meanwhile ...
I'M HOME.
BTAM
WELCOME HOME, MR. SAGARA.
SORRY I'M SO LATE.
THOSE ARE BIG MEN'S SHOES...
BRAND NAME TOO.
ONE POPULAR WITH YOUNGER GUYS...
DO WE HAVE A GUEST?
ONE OF THE MAIDS MENTIONED THAT ONE OF IZUMI'S FRIENDS WAS HERE, YES.

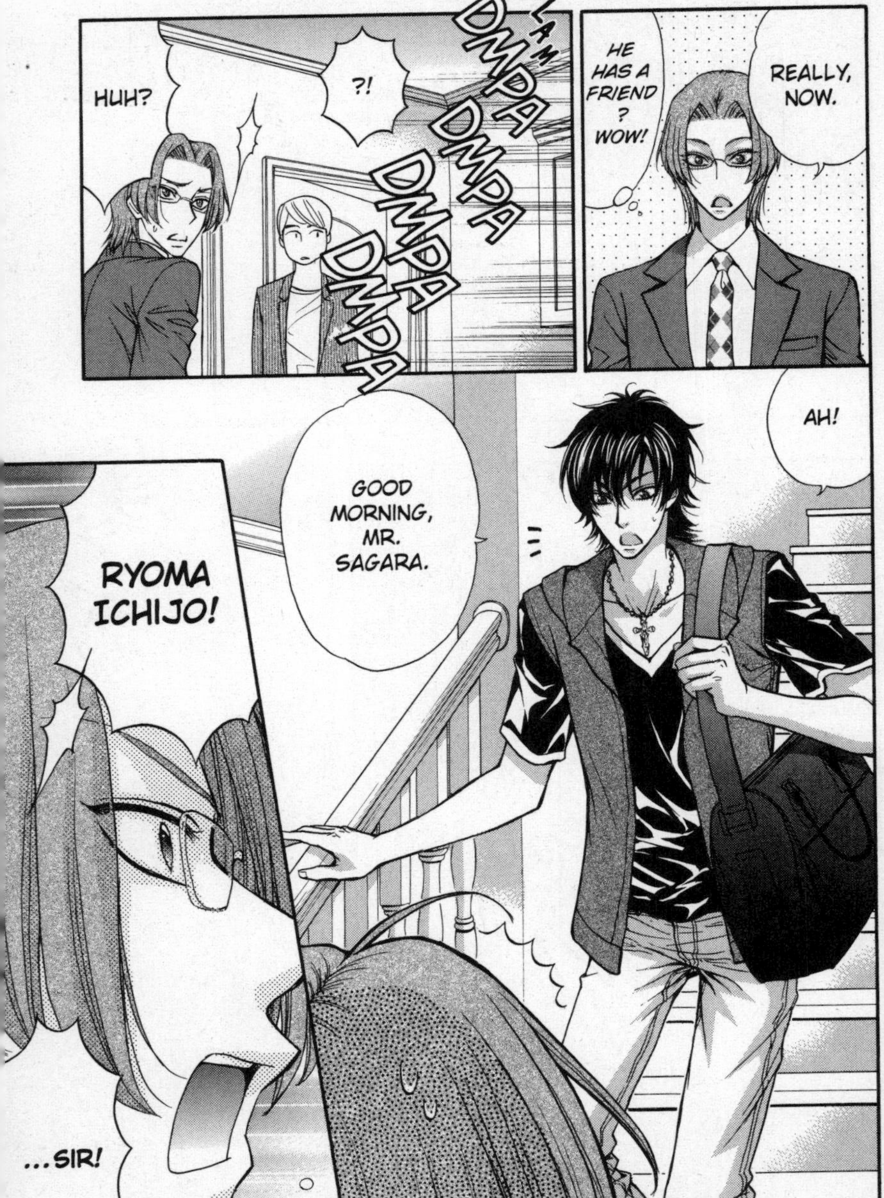
REALLY, NOW.
HE HAS A FRIEND? WOW!
SLAM
DMPA DMPA DMPA DMPA DMPA
?!
HUH?
AH!
GOOD MORNING, MR. SAGARA.
RYOMA ICHIJO!
...SIR!

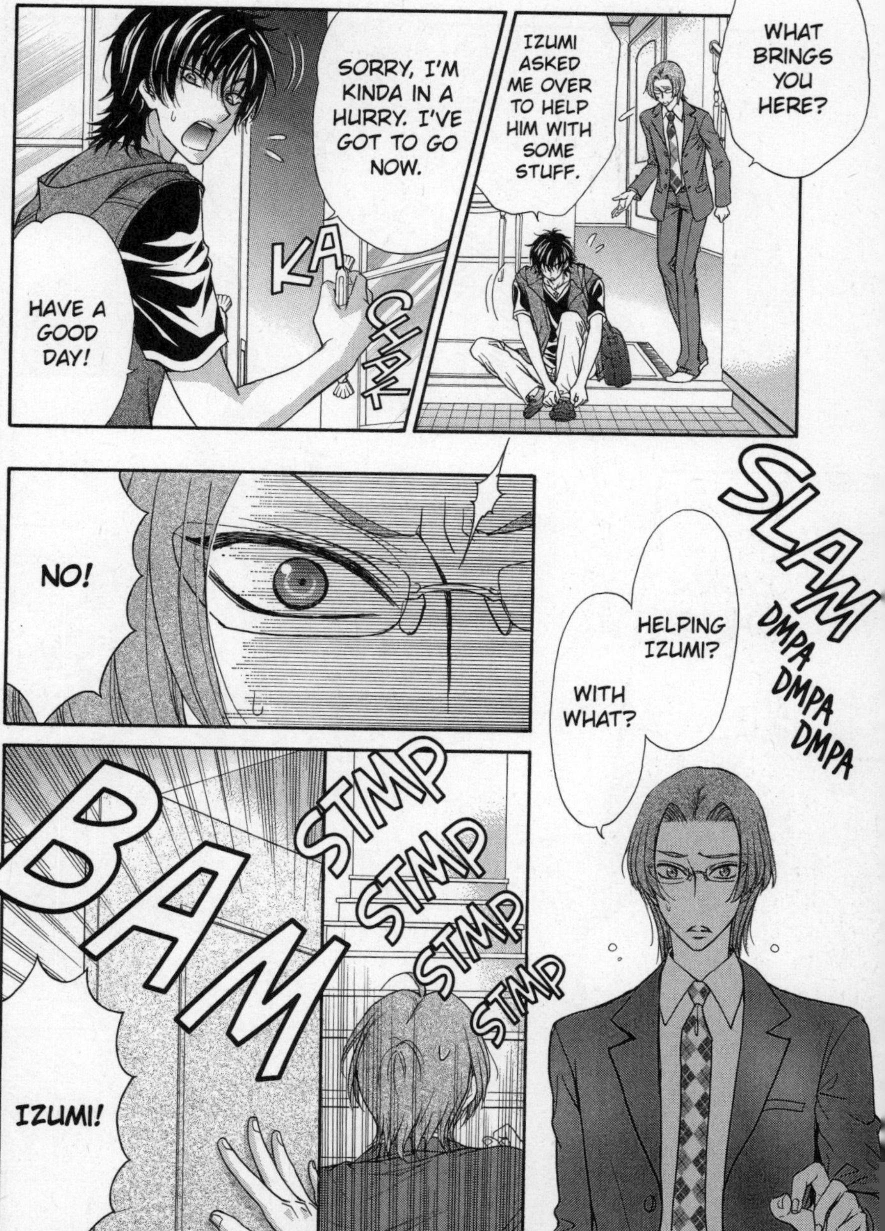
WHAT BRINGS YOU HERE?
IZUMI ASKED ME OVER TO HELP HIM WITH SOME STUFF.
SORRY, I'M KINDA IN A HURRY. I'VE GOT TO GO NOW.
KA CHAK
HAVE A GOOD DAY!
SLAM
DMPA DMPA DMPA DMPA
HELPING IZUMI?
WITH WHAT?
NO!
BAM
STMP STMP STMP STMP
IZUMI!

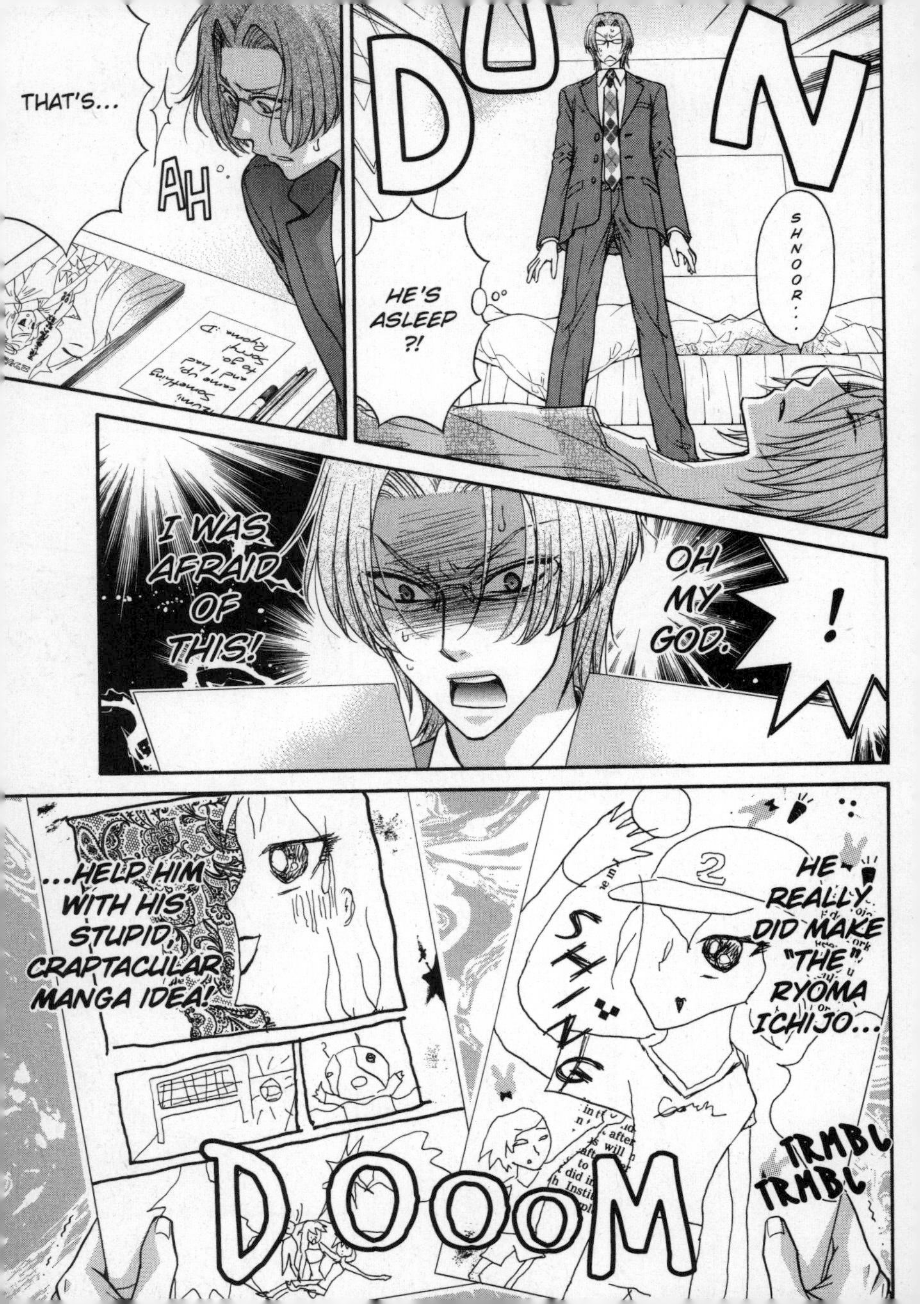
DUN
SHNOOR...
HE'S ASLEEP?!
THAT'S...
AH
Something came up, and I had to go. Sorry! Ryoma :D
OH MY GOD.
!
I WAS AFRAID OF THIS!
HE REALLY DID MAKE "THE" RYOMA ICHIJO...
TRMBL TRMBL
SHING
...HELP HIM WITH HIS STUPID, CRAPTACULAR MANGA IDEA!
DOOOM

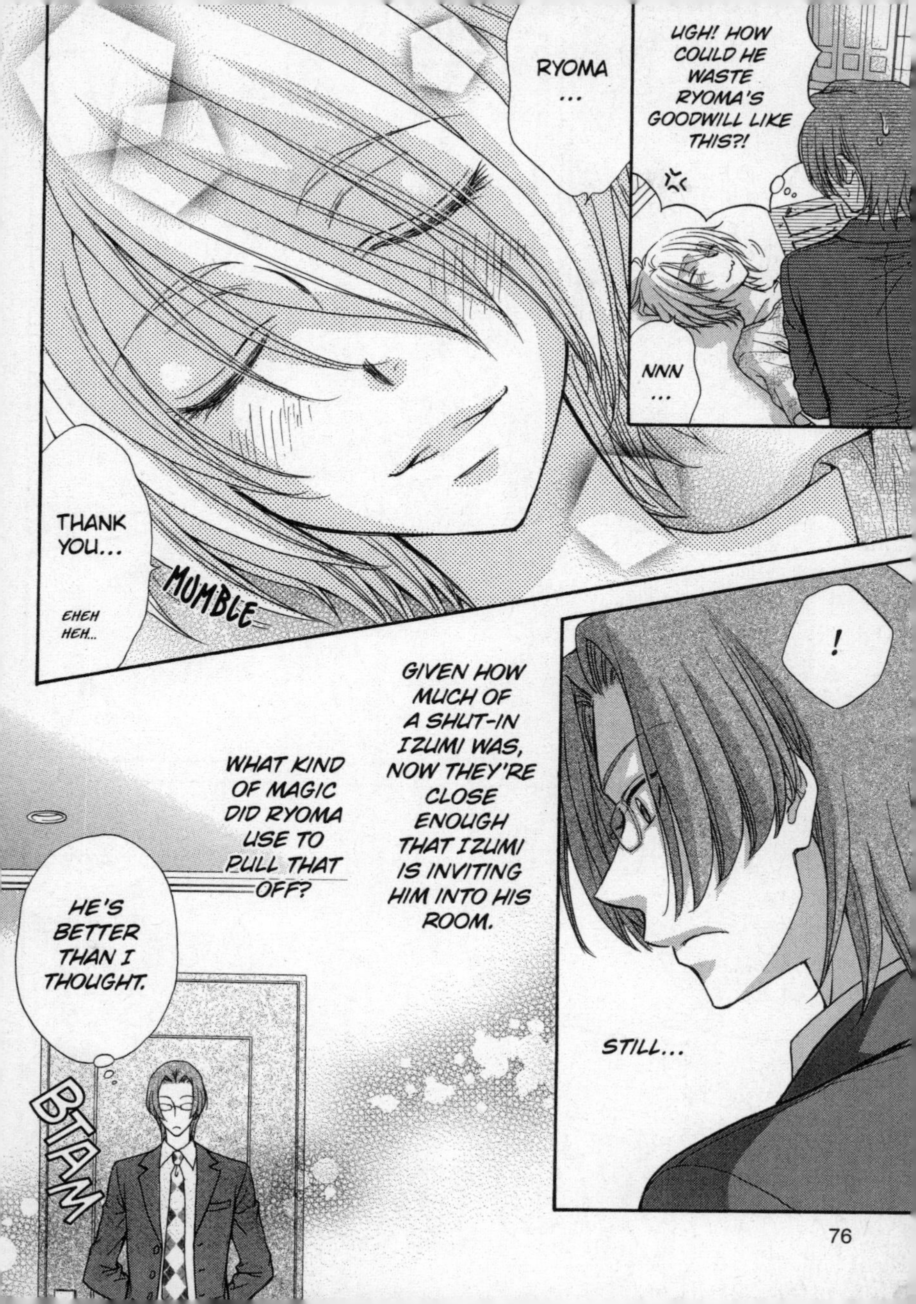
RYOMA ...
UGH! HOW COULD HE WASTE RYOMA'S GOODWILL LIKE THIS?!
NNN ...
THANK YOU...
MUMBLE
EHEH HEH...
!
STILL...
GIVEN HOW MUCH OF A SHUT-IN IZUMI WAS, NOW THEY'RE CLOSE ENOUGH THAT IZUMI IS INVITING HIM INTO HIS ROOM.
WHAT KIND OF MAGIC DID RYOMA USE TO PULL THAT OFF?
HE'S BETTER THAN I THOUGHT.
BTAM

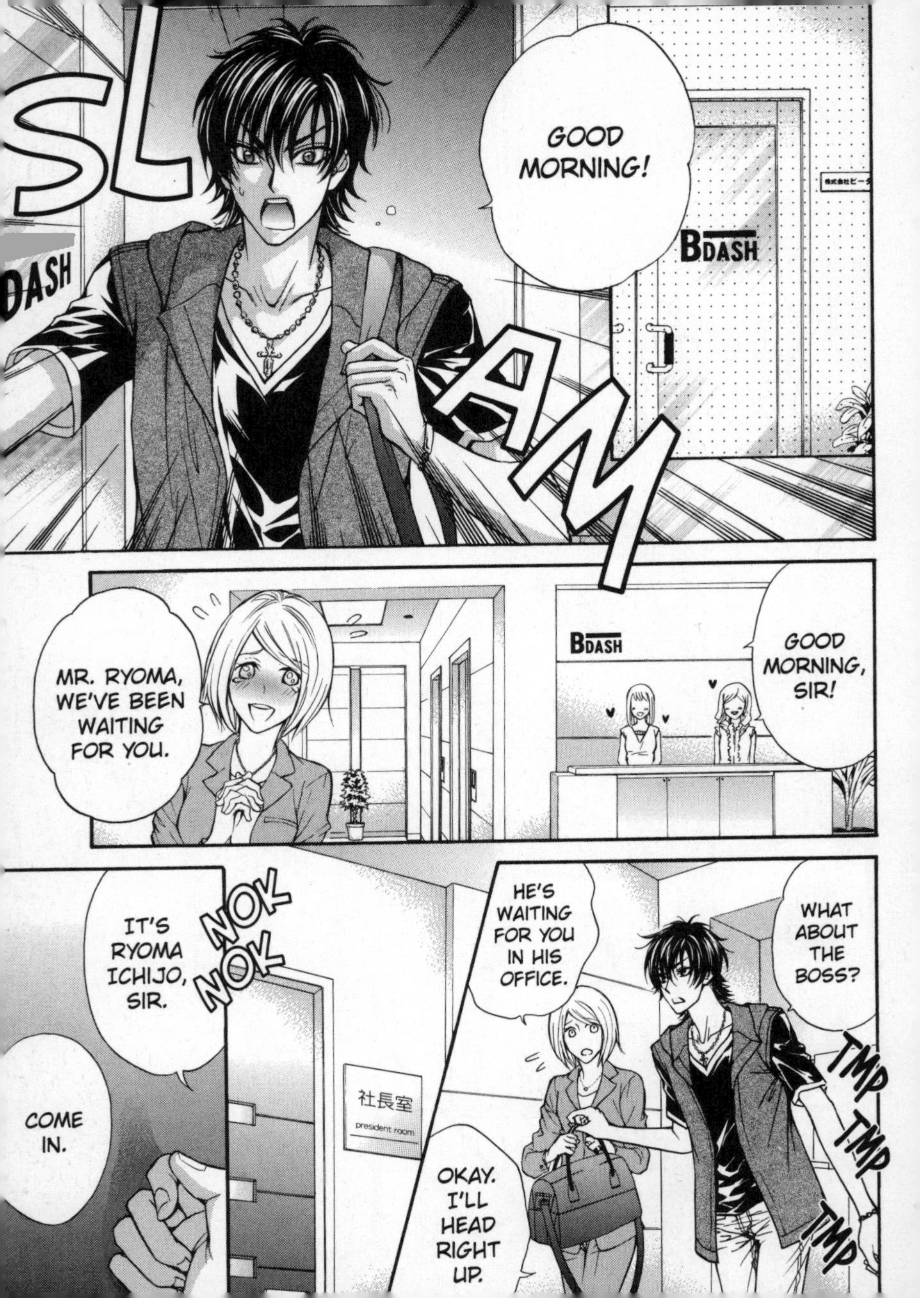
SLAM
GOOD MORNING!
BDASH
GOOD MORNING, SIR!
BDASH
MR. RYOMA, WE'VE BEEN WAITING FOR YOU.
WHAT ABOUT THE BOSS?
HE'S WAITING FOR YOU IN HIS OFFICE.
TMP TMP TMP
OKAY. I'LL HEAD RIGHT UP.
IT'S RYOMA ICHIJO, SIR.
NOK NOK
社長室
president room
COME IN.

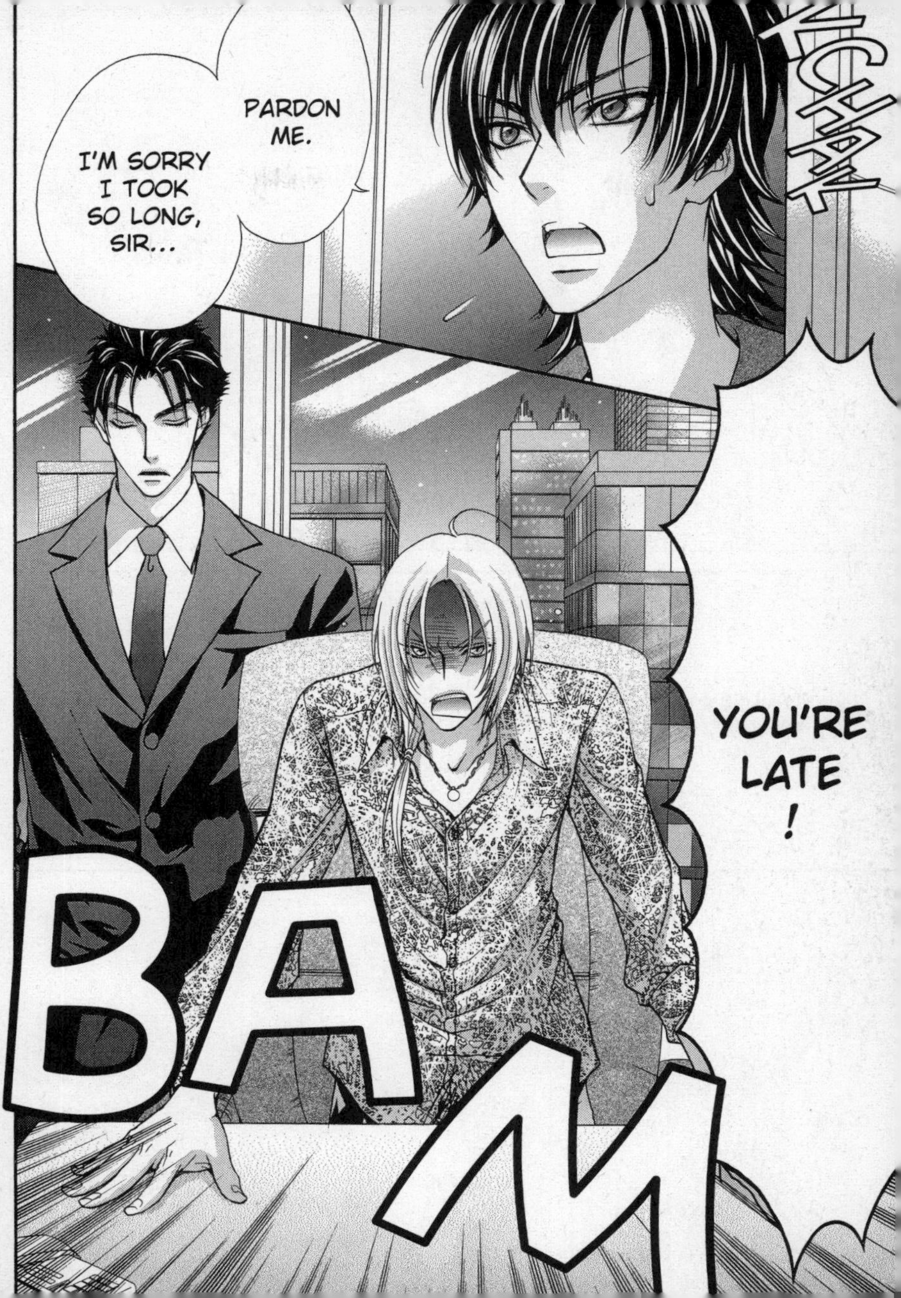
KCHAK
PARDON ME.
I'M SORRY I TOOK SO LONG, SIR...
YOU'RE LATE!
BAM

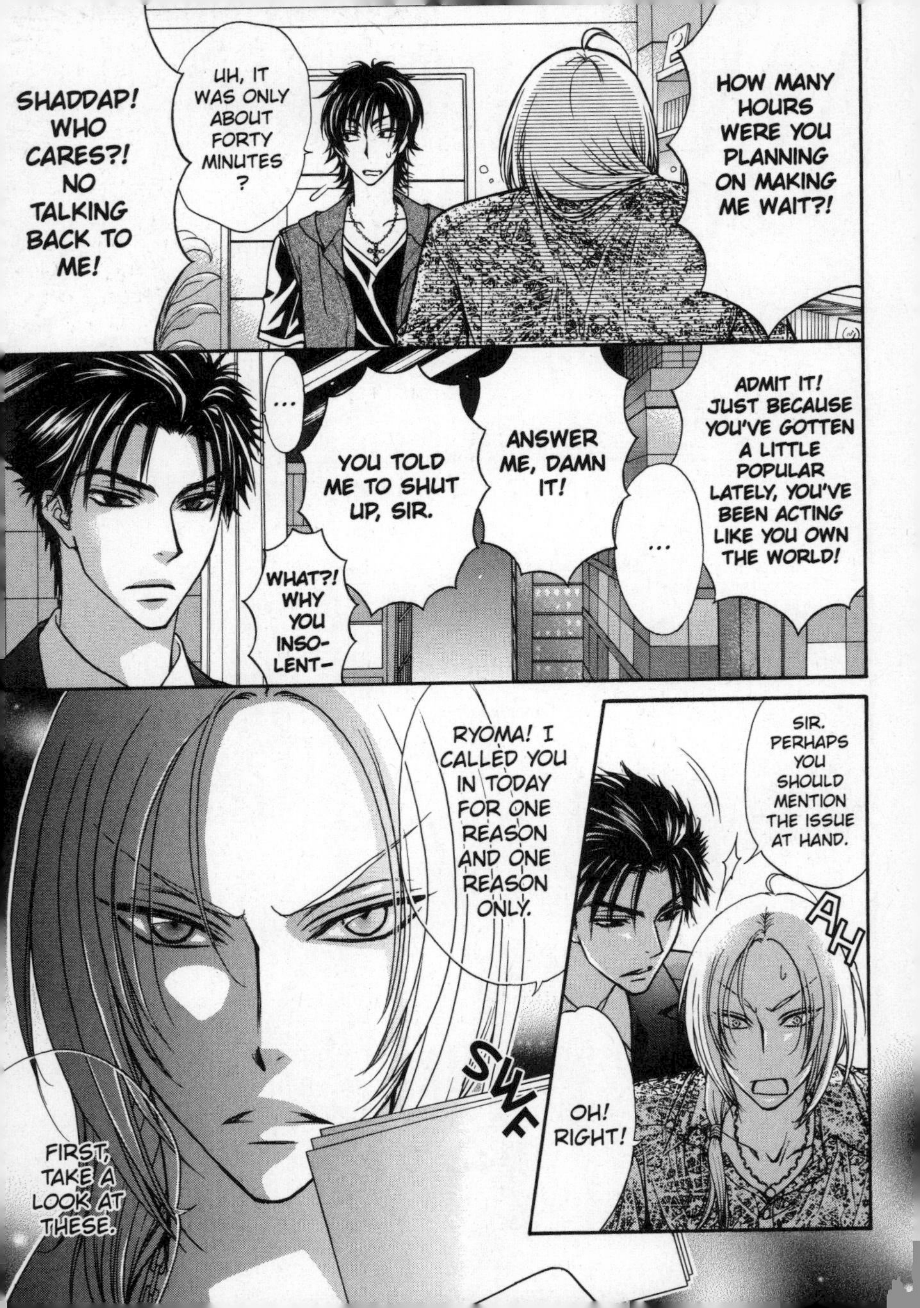
HOW MANY HOURS WERE YOU PLANNING ON MAKING ME WAIT?!
UH, IT WAS ONLY ABOUT FORTY MINUTES ?
SHADDAP! WHO CARES?! NO TALKING BACK TO ME!
ADMIT IT! JUST BECAUSE YOU'VE GOTTEN A LITTLE POPULAR LATELY, YOU'VE BEEN ACTING LIKE YOU OWN THE WORLD!
...
ANSWER ME, DAMN IT!
...
YOU TOLD ME TO SHUT UP, SIR.
WHAT?! WHY YOU INSO-LENT-
SIR. PERHAPS YOU SHOULD MENTION THE ISSUE AT HAND.
AH
OH! RIGHT!
RYOMA! I CALLED YOU IN TODAY FOR ONE REASON AND ONE REASON ONLY.
SWF
FIRST, TAKE A LOOK AT THESE.

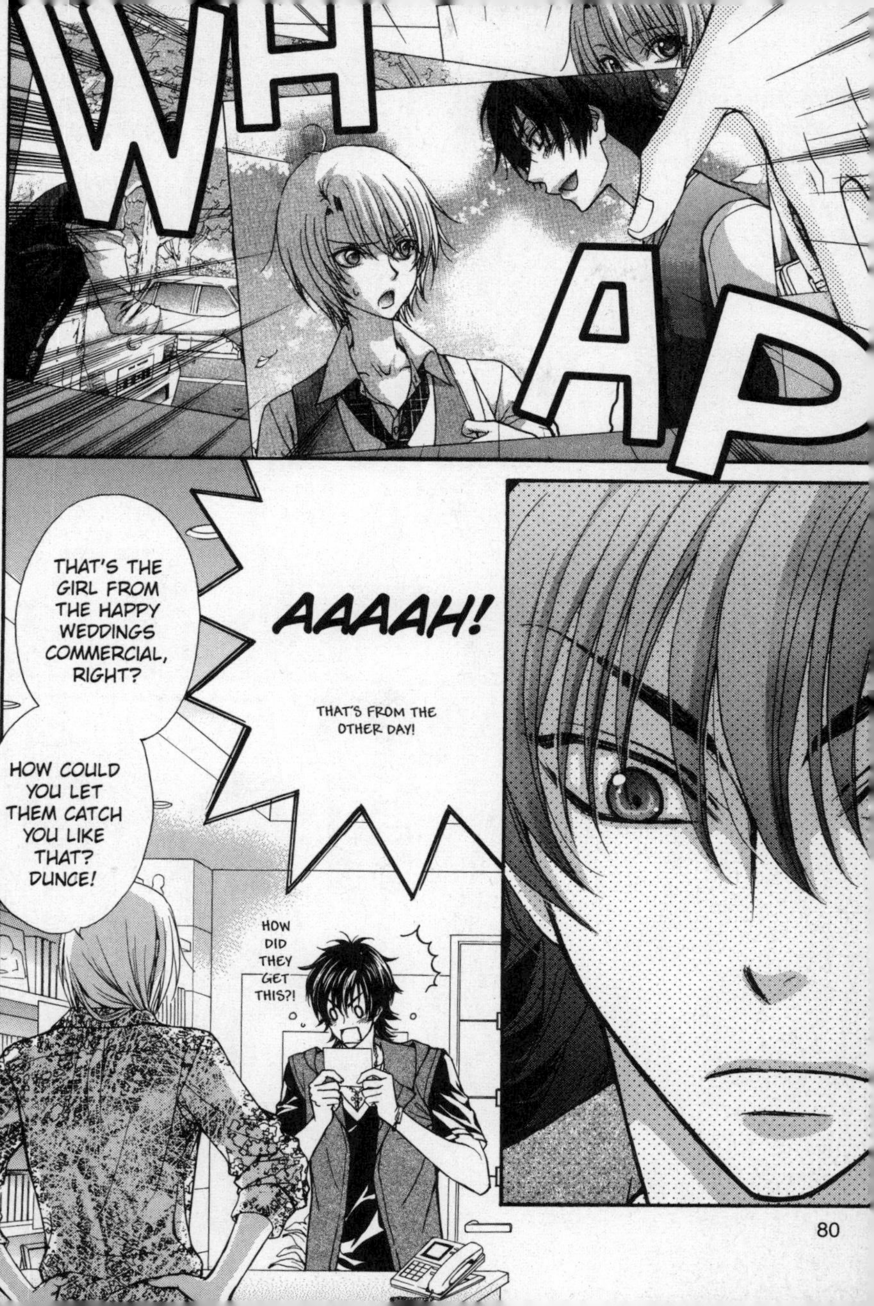
WHAP
AAAAH!
THAT'S FROM THE OTHER DAY!
THAT'S THE GIRL FROM THE HAPPY WEDDINGS COMMERCIAL, RIGHT?
HOW COULD YOU LET THEM CATCH YOU LIKE THAT? DUNCE!
HOW DID THEY GET THIS?!

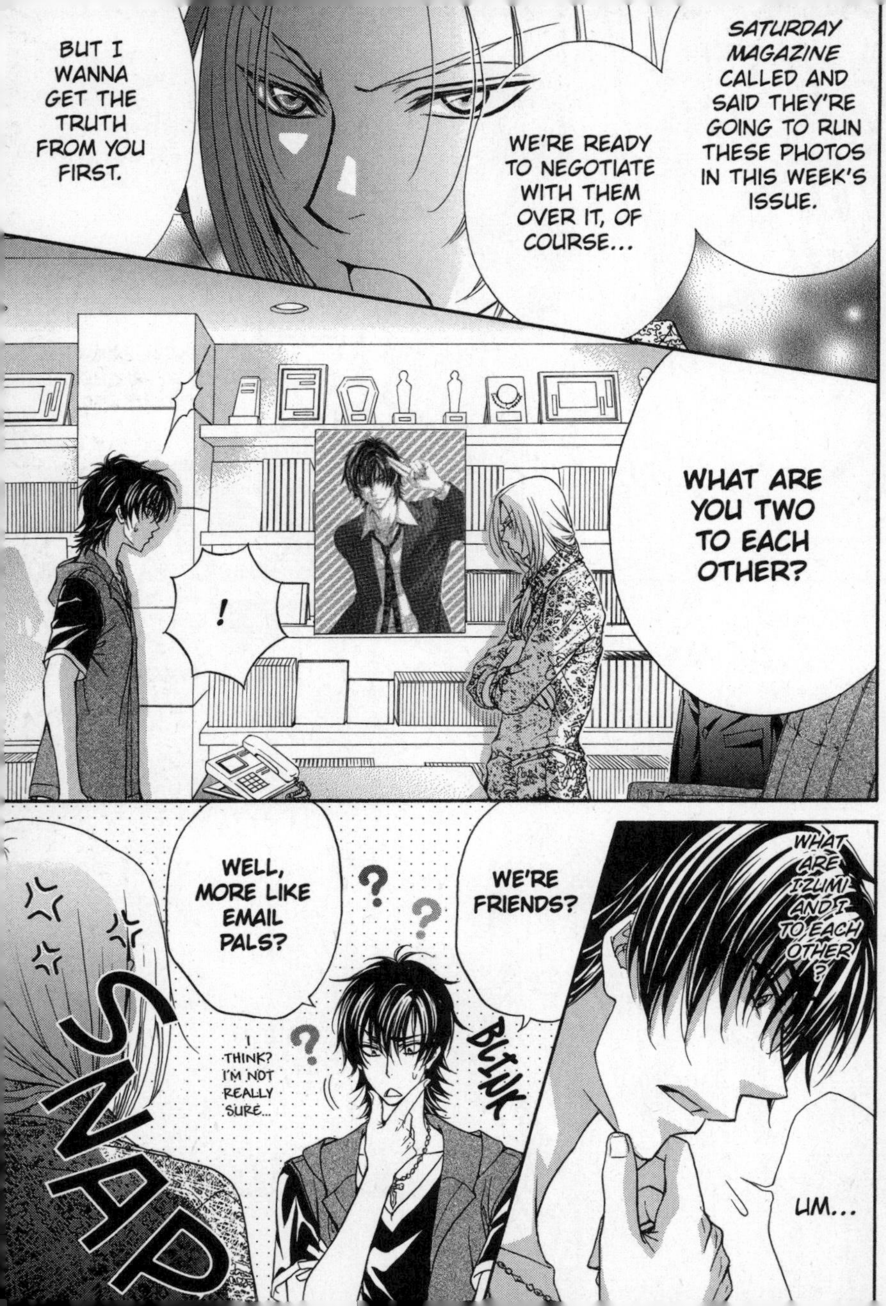
SATURDAY MAGAZINE CALLED AND SAID THEY'RE GOING TO RUN THESE PHOTOS IN THIS WEEK'S ISSUE.
WE'RE READY TO NEGOTIATE WITH THEM OVER IT, OF COURSE...
BUT I WANNA GET THE TRUTH FROM YOU FIRST.
WHAT ARE YOU TWO TO EACH OTHER?
!
WHAT ARE IZUMI AND I TO EACH OTHER?
UM...
WE'RE FRIENDS?
BLINK
WELL, MORE LIKE EMAIL PALS?
I THINK? I'M NOT REALLY SURE...
SNAP

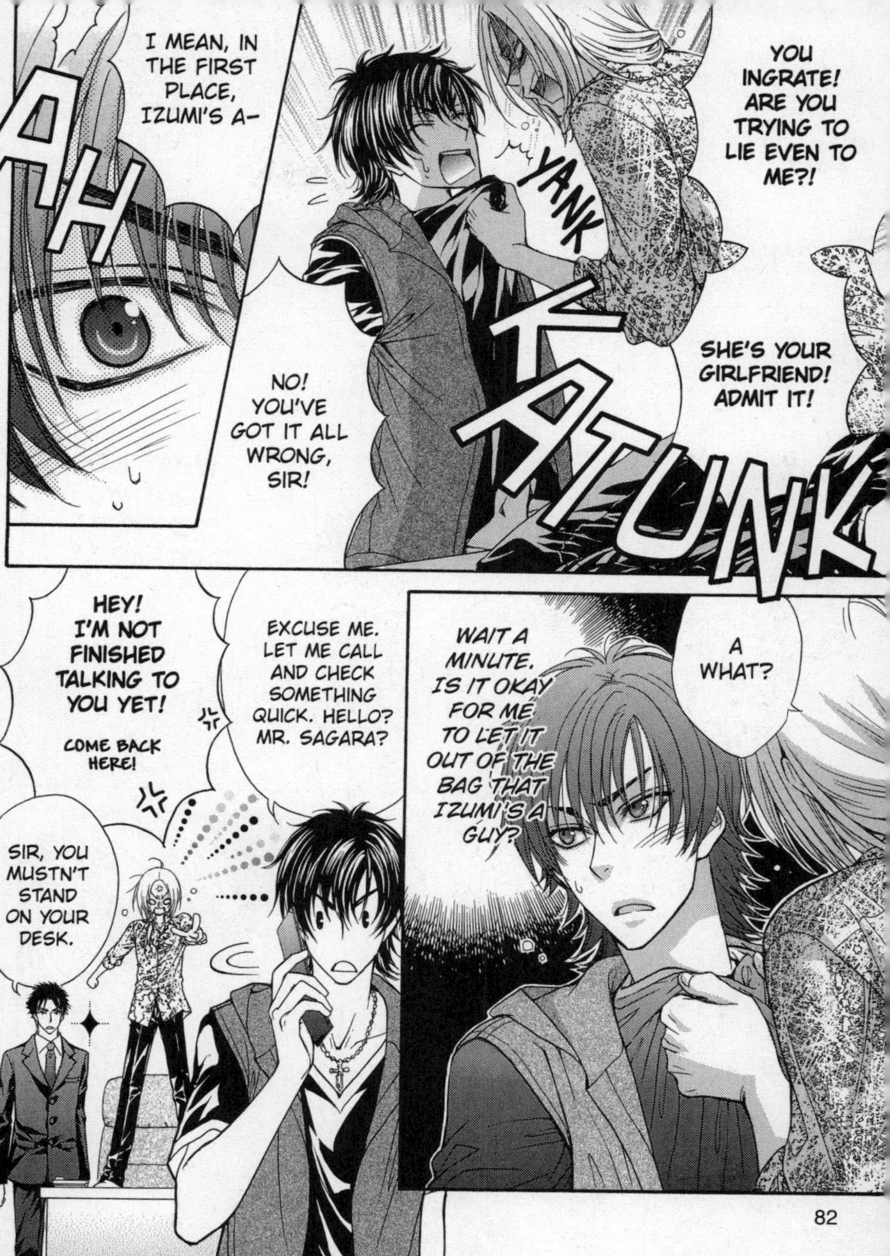
YOU INGRATE! ARE YOU TRYING TO LIE EVEN TO ME?!
SHE'S YOUR GIRLFRIEND! ADMIT IT!
YANK
NO! YOU'VE GOT IT ALL WRONG, SIR!
KATUNK
I MEAN, IN THE FIRST PLACE, IZUMI'S A-
AH
A WHAT?
WAIT A MINUTE. IS IT OKAY FOR ME TO LET IT OUT OF THE BAG THAT IZUMI'S A GUY?
EXCUSE ME. LET ME CALL AND CHECK SOMETHING QUICK. HELLO? MR. SAGARA?
HEY! I'M NOT FINISHED TALKING TO YOU YET!
COME BACK HERE!
SIR, YOU MUSTN'T STAND ON YOUR DESK.

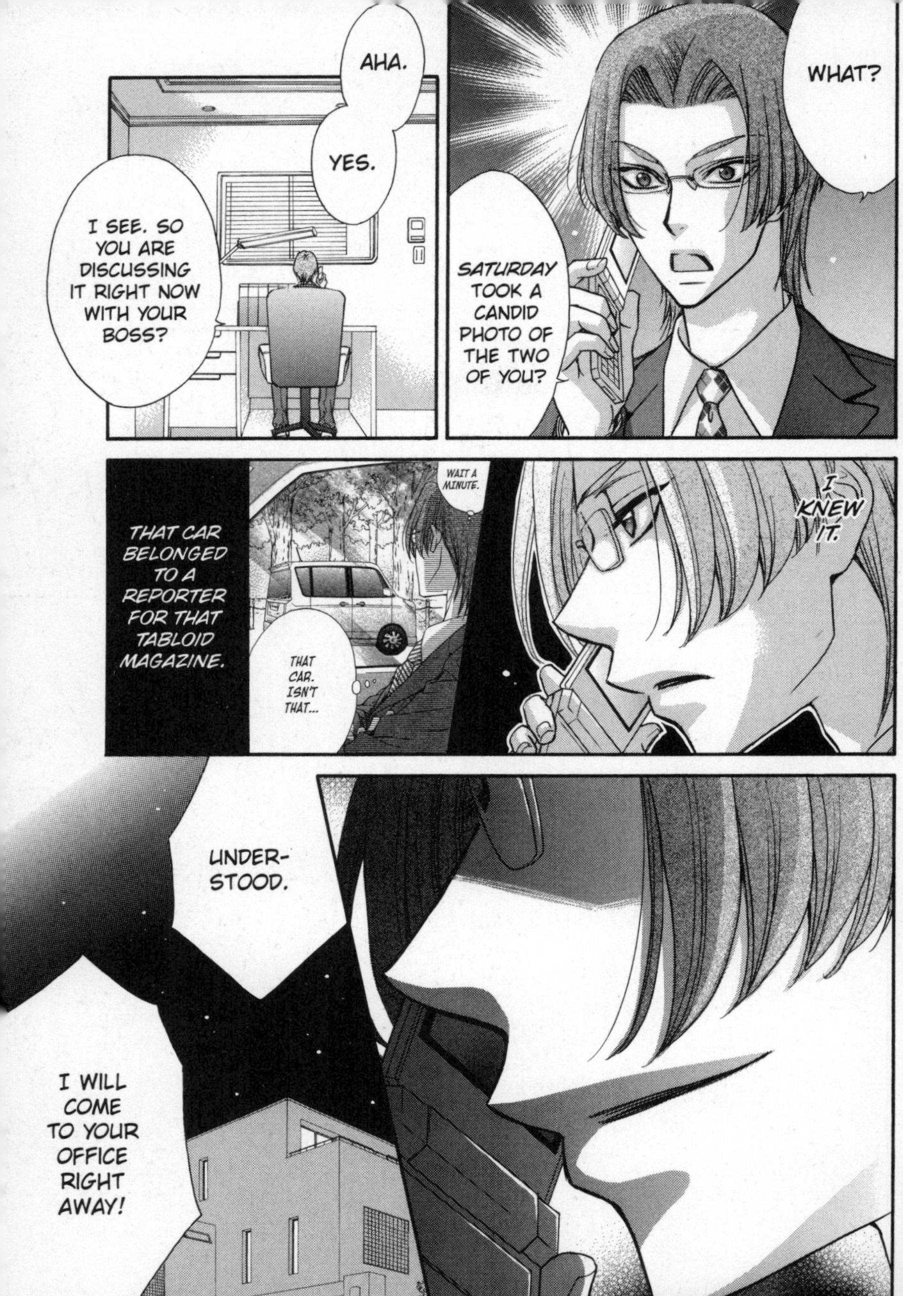
WHAT?
SATURDAY TOOK A CANDID PHOTO OF THE TWO OF YOU?
AHA.
YES.
I SEE. SO YOU ARE DISCUSSING IT RIGHT NOW WITH YOUR BOSS?
I KNEW IT.
WAIT A MINUTE.
THAT CAR. ISN'T THAT...
THAT CAR BELONGED TO A REPORTER FOR THAT TABLOID MAGAZINE.
UNDER-STOOD.
I WILL COME TO YOUR OFFICE RIGHT AWAY!

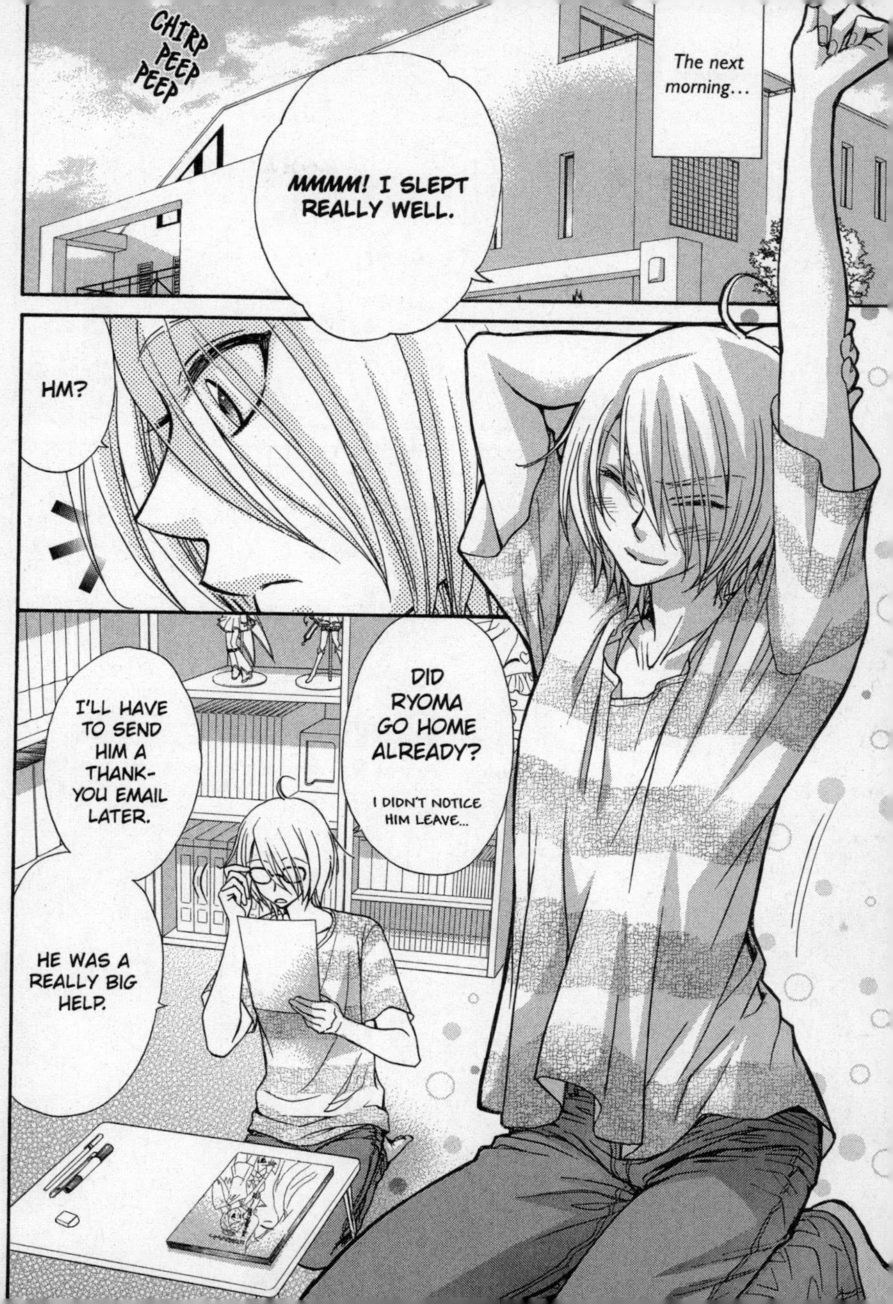
The next morning...
CHIRP PEEP PEEP
MMMM! I SLEPT REALLY WELL.
HM?
DID RYOMA GO HOME ALREADY?
I DIDN'T NOTICE HIM LEAVE...
I'LL HAVE TO SEND HIM A THANK-YOU EMAIL LATER.
HE WAS A REALLY BIG HELP.

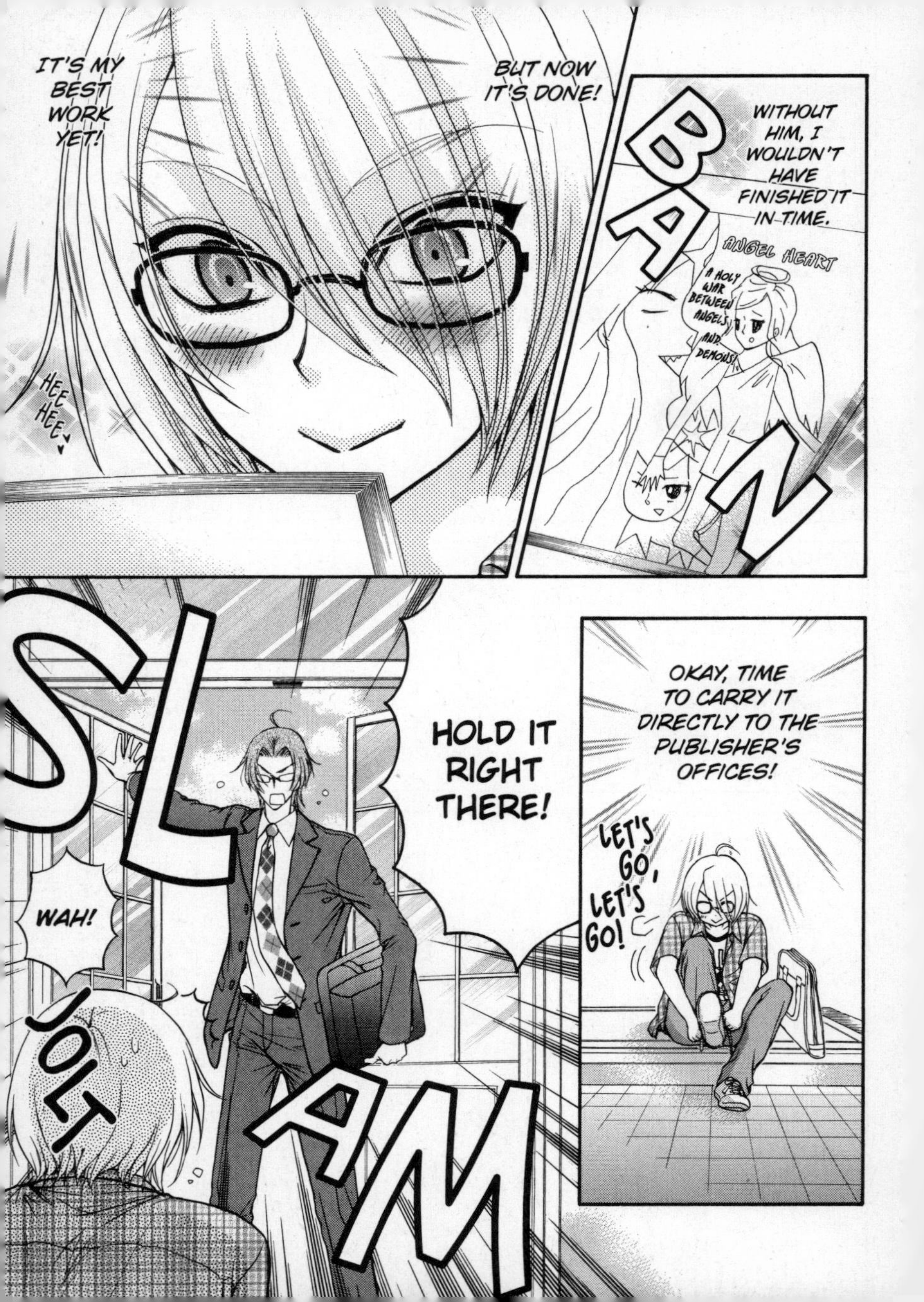
BAN
WITHOUT HIM, I WOULDN'T HAVE FINISHED IT IN TIME.
ANGEL HEART
A HOLY WAR BETWEEN ANGELS AND DEMONS!
BUT NOW IT'S DONE!
IT'S MY BEST WORK YET!
HEE HEE♥
OKAY, TIME TO CARRY IT DIRECTLY TO THE PUBLISHER'S OFFICES!
LET'S GO, LET'S GO!
HOLD IT RIGHT THERE!
SLAM
WAH!
JOLT

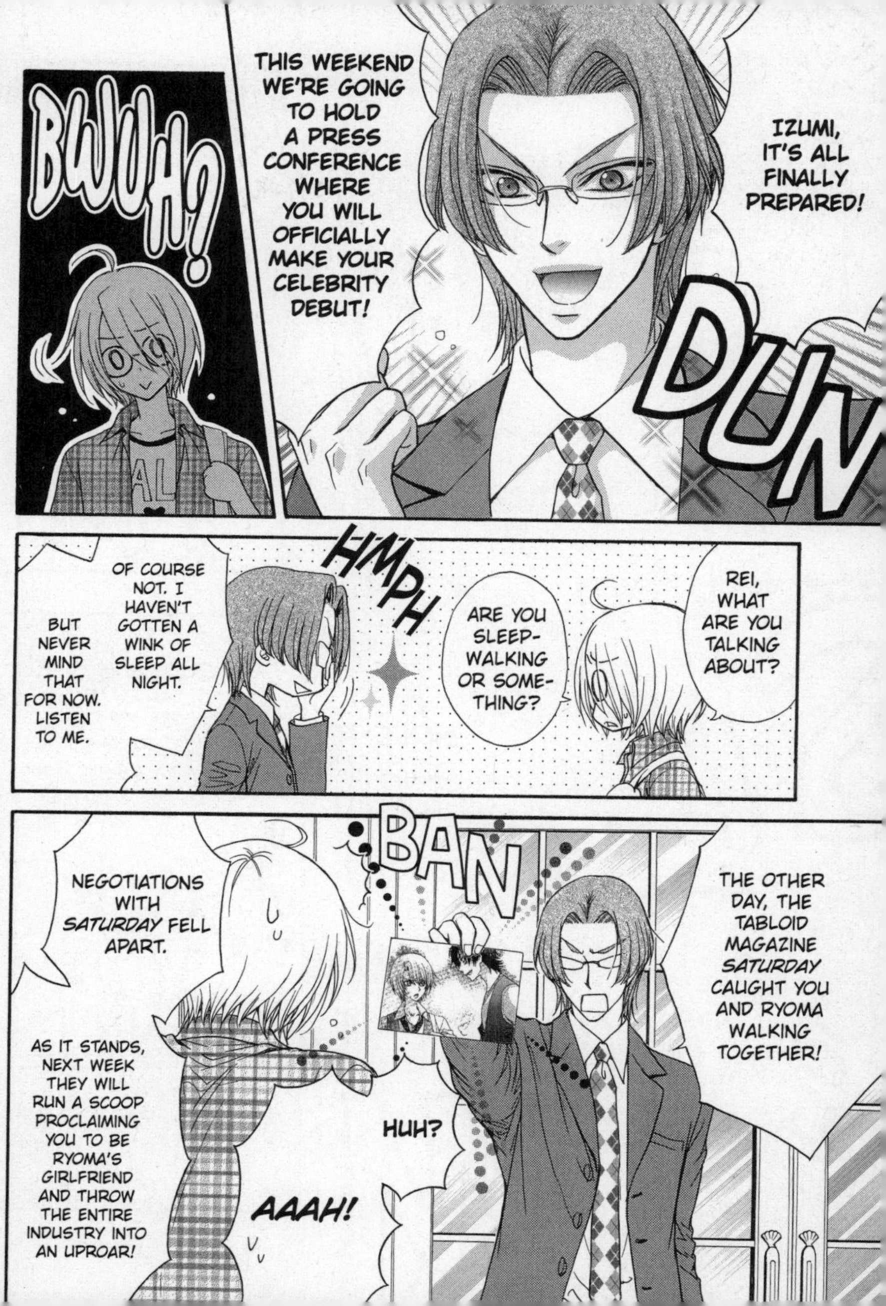
IZUMI, IT'S ALL FINALLY PREPARED!
THIS WEEKEND WE'RE GOING TO HOLD A PRESS CONFERENCE WHERE YOU WILL OFFICIALLY MAKE YOUR CELEBRITY DEBUT!
DUN
BWUH?
REI, WHAT ARE YOU TALKING ABOUT?
ARE YOU SLEEP-WALKING OR SOME-THING?
HMPH
OF COURSE NOT. I HAVEN'T GOTTEN A WINK OF SLEEP ALL NIGHT.
BUT NEVER MIND THAT FOR NOW. LISTEN TO ME.
THE OTHER DAY, THE TABLOID MAGAZINE *SATURDAY* CAUGHT YOU AND RYOMA WALKING TOGETHER!
BAN
NEGOTIATIONS WITH *SATURDAY* FELL APART.
HUH?
AS IT STANDS, NEXT WEEK THEY WILL RUN A SCOOP PROCLAIMING YOU TO BE RYOMA'S GIRLFRIEND AND THROW THE ENTIRE INDUSTRY INTO AN UPROAR!
AAAH!

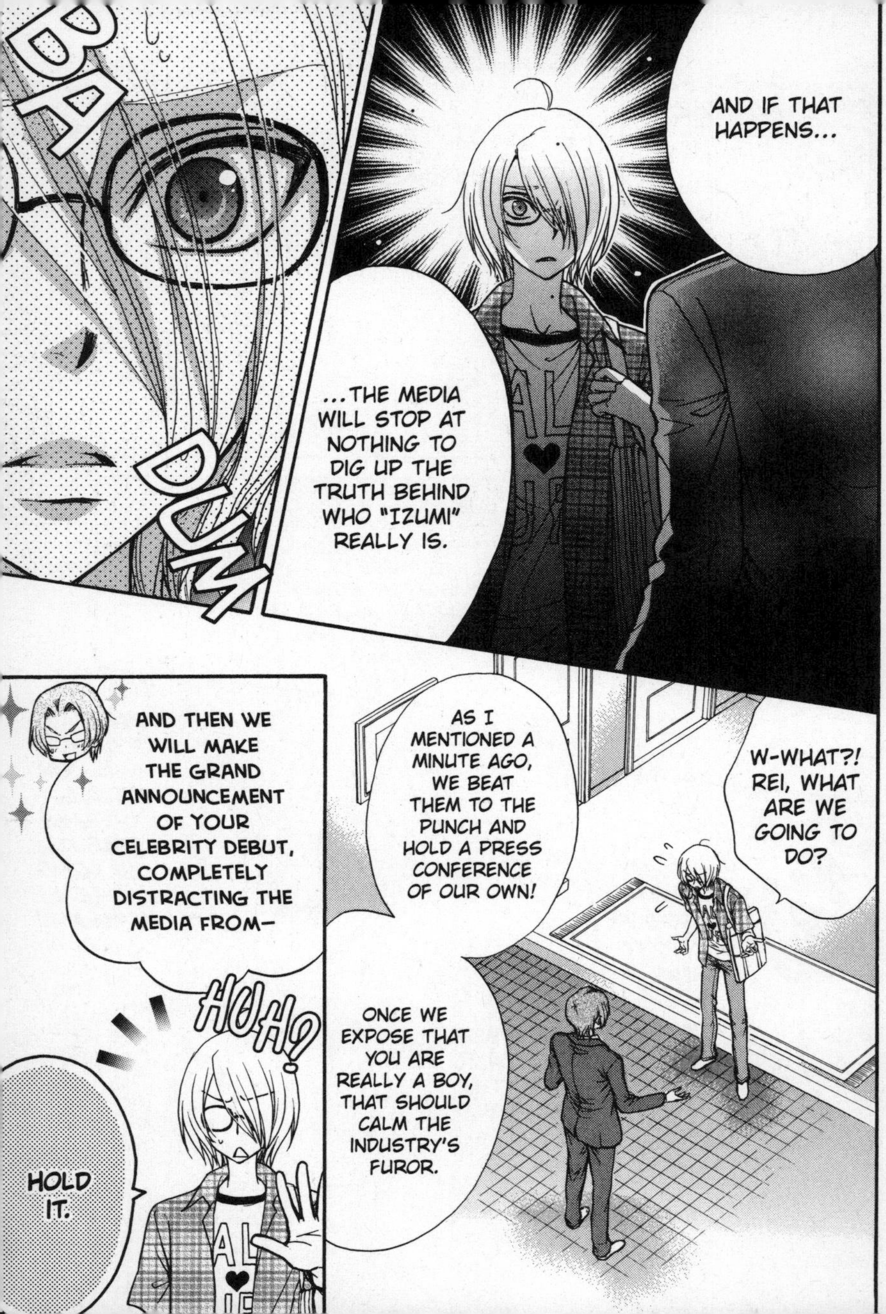
AND IF THAT HAPPENS...
...THE MEDIA WILL STOP AT NOTHING TO DIG UP THE TRUTH BEHIND WHO "IZUMI" REALLY IS.
BA
DUM
W-WHAT?! REI, WHAT ARE WE GOING TO DO?
AS I MENTIONED A MINUTE AGO, WE BEAT THEM TO THE PUNCH AND HOLD A PRESS CONFERENCE OF OUR OWN!
ONCE WE EXPOSE THAT YOU ARE REALLY A BOY, THAT SHOULD CALM THE INDUSTRY'S FUROR.
AND THEN WE WILL MAKE THE GRAND ANNOUNCEMENT OF YOUR CELEBRITY DEBUT, COMPLETELY DISTRACTING THE MEDIA FROM—
HUH?
HOLD IT.

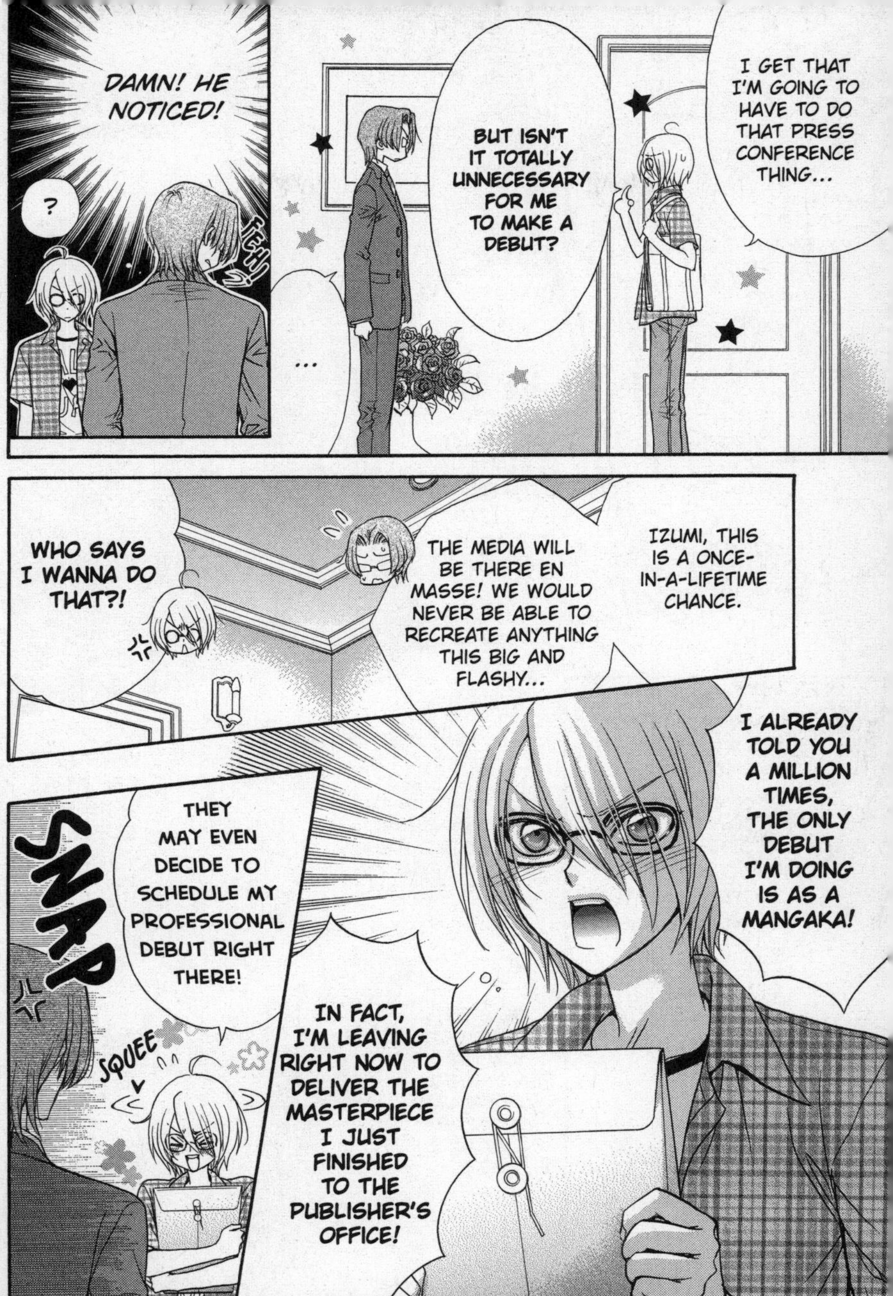
I GET THAT I'M GOING TO HAVE TO DO THAT PRESS CONFERENCE THING...
BUT ISN'T IT TOTALLY UNNECESSARY FOR ME TO MAKE A DEBUT?
...
DAMN! HE NOTICED!
FLCH!
?
IZUMI, THIS IS A ONCE-IN-A-LIFETIME CHANCE.
THE MEDIA WILL BE THERE EN MASSE! WE WOULD NEVER BE ABLE TO RECREATE ANYTHING THIS BIG AND FLASHY...
WHO SAYS I WANNA DO THAT?!
I ALREADY TOLD YOU A MILLION TIMES, THE ONLY DEBUT I'M DOING IS AS A MANGAKA!
IN FACT, I'M LEAVING RIGHT NOW TO DELIVER THE MASTERPIECE I JUST FINISHED TO THE PUBLISHER'S OFFICE!
SNAP
THEY MAY EVEN DECIDE TO SCHEDULE MY PROFESSIONAL DEBUT RIGHT THERE!
SQUEE

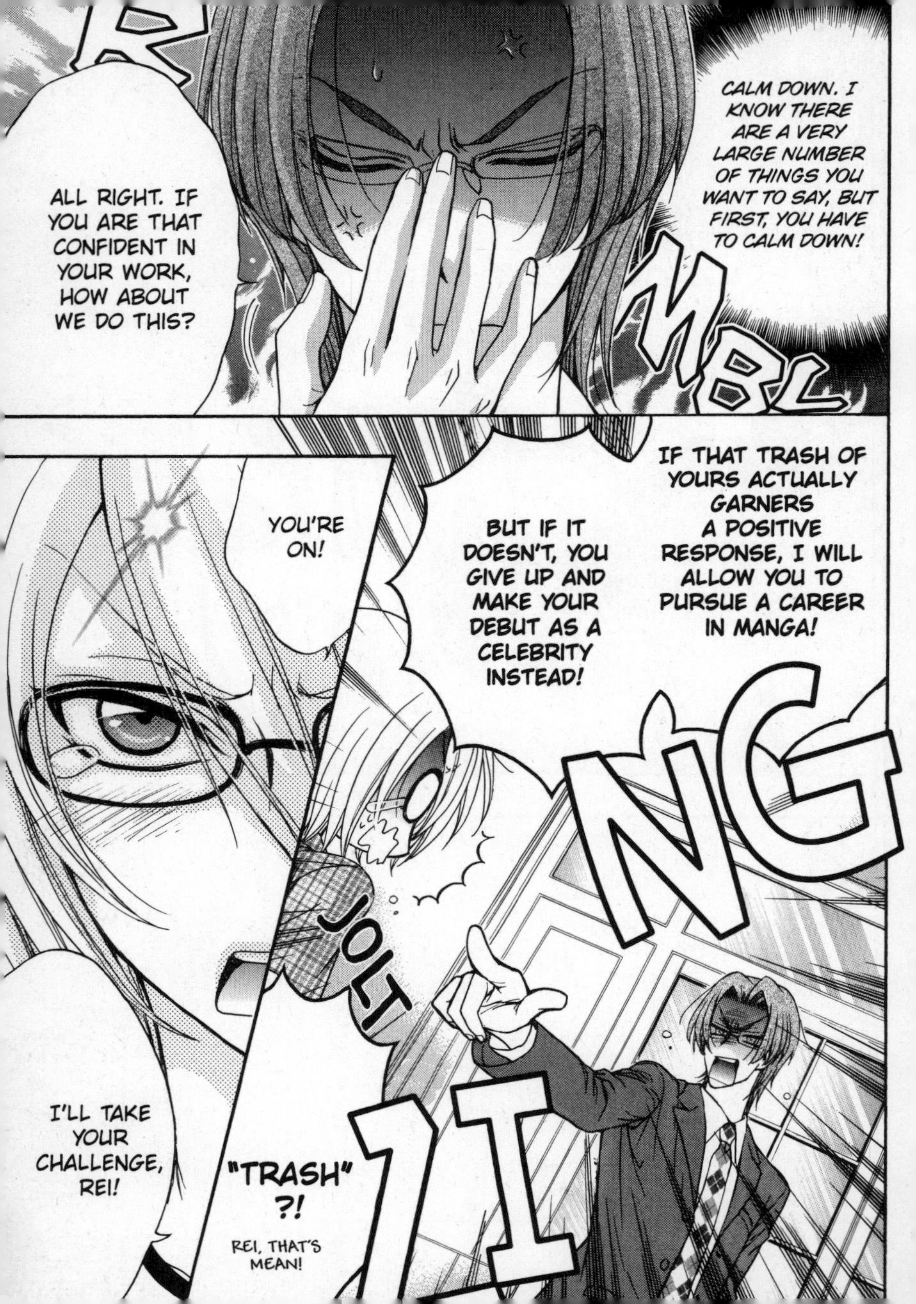
CALM DOWN. I KNOW THERE ARE A VERY LARGE NUMBER OF THINGS YOU WANT TO SAY, BUT FIRST, YOU HAVE TO CALM DOWN!
MBL
ALL RIGHT. IF YOU ARE THAT CONFIDENT IN YOUR WORK, HOW ABOUT WE DO THIS?
IF THAT TRASH OF YOURS ACTUALLY GARNERS A POSITIVE RESPONSE, I WILL ALLOW YOU TO PURSUE A CAREER IN MANGA!
BUT IF IT DOESN'T, YOU GIVE UP AND MAKE YOUR DEBUT AS A CELEBRITY INSTEAD!
YOU'RE ON!
NG
JOLT
I'LL TAKE YOUR CHALLENGE, REI!
"TRASH" ?!
REI, THAT'S MEAN!

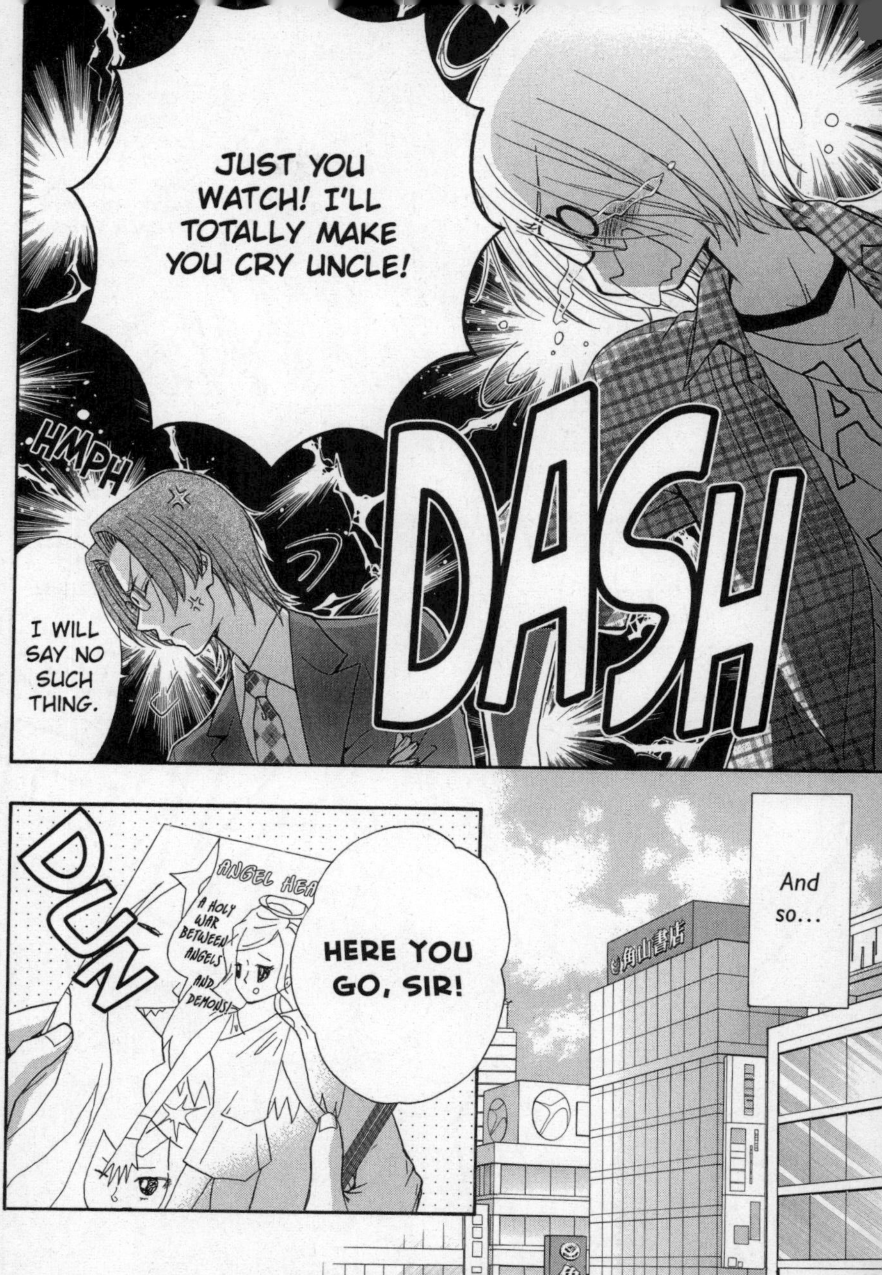
JUST YOU WATCH! I'LL TOTALLY MAKE YOU CRY UNCLE!
DASH
HMPH
I WILL SAY NO SUCH THING.
And so...
角山書店
DUN
ANGEL HEA
A HOLY WAR BETWEEN ANGELS AND DEMONS!
HERE YOU GO, SIR!

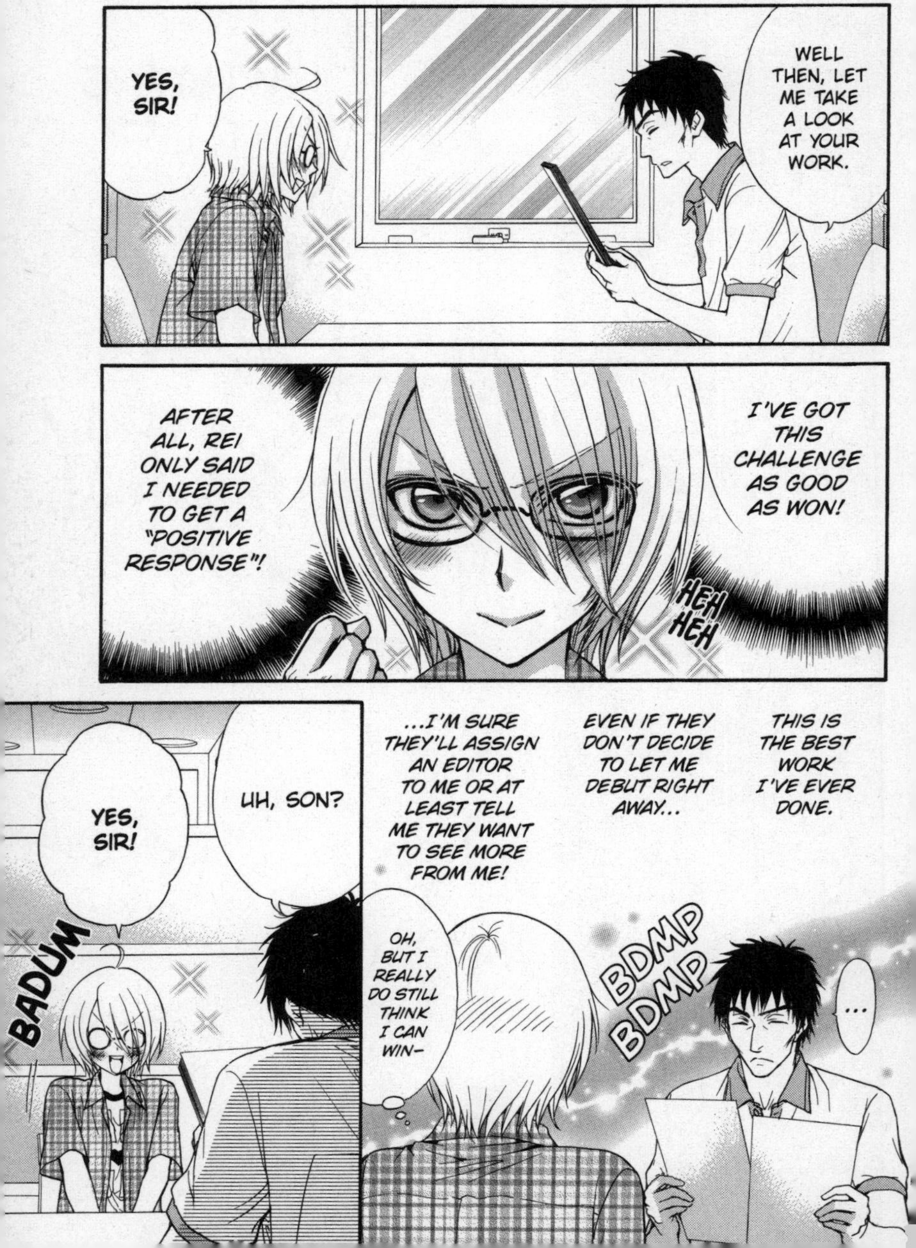
WELL THEN, LET ME TAKE A LOOK AT YOUR WORK.
YES, SIR!
I'VE GOT THIS CHALLENGE AS GOOD AS WON!
AFTER ALL, REI ONLY SAID I NEEDED TO GET A "POSITIVE RESPONSE"!
HEH HEH
THIS IS THE BEST WORK I'VE EVER DONE.
EVEN IF THEY DON'T DECIDE TO LET ME DEBUT RIGHT AWAY...
...I'M SURE THEY'LL ASSIGN AN EDITOR TO ME OR AT LEAST TELL ME THEY WANT TO SEE MORE FROM ME!
...
BDMP BDMP
OH, BUT I REALLY DO STILL THINK I CAN WIN-
UH, SON?
YES, SIR!
BADUM

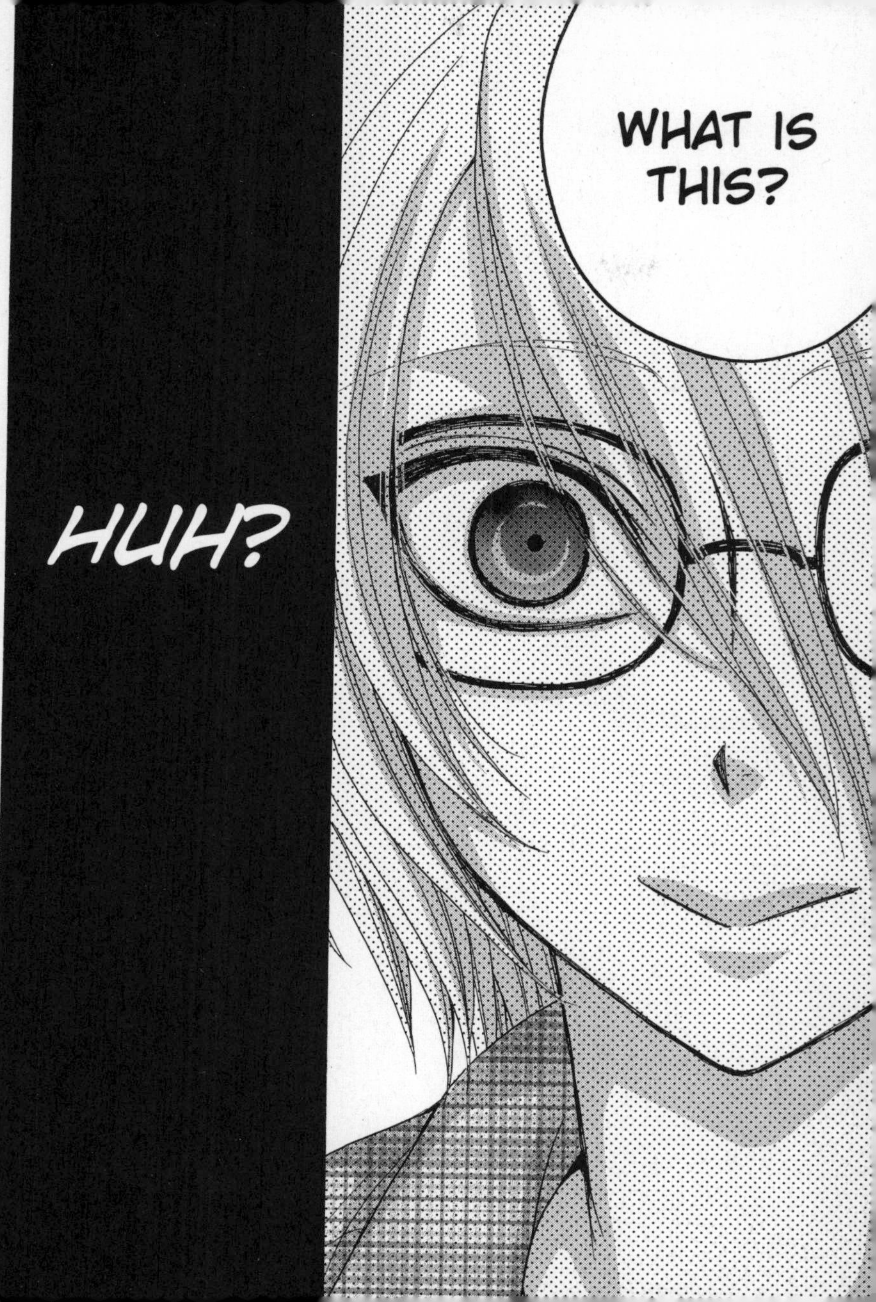
WHAT IS THIS?
HUH?

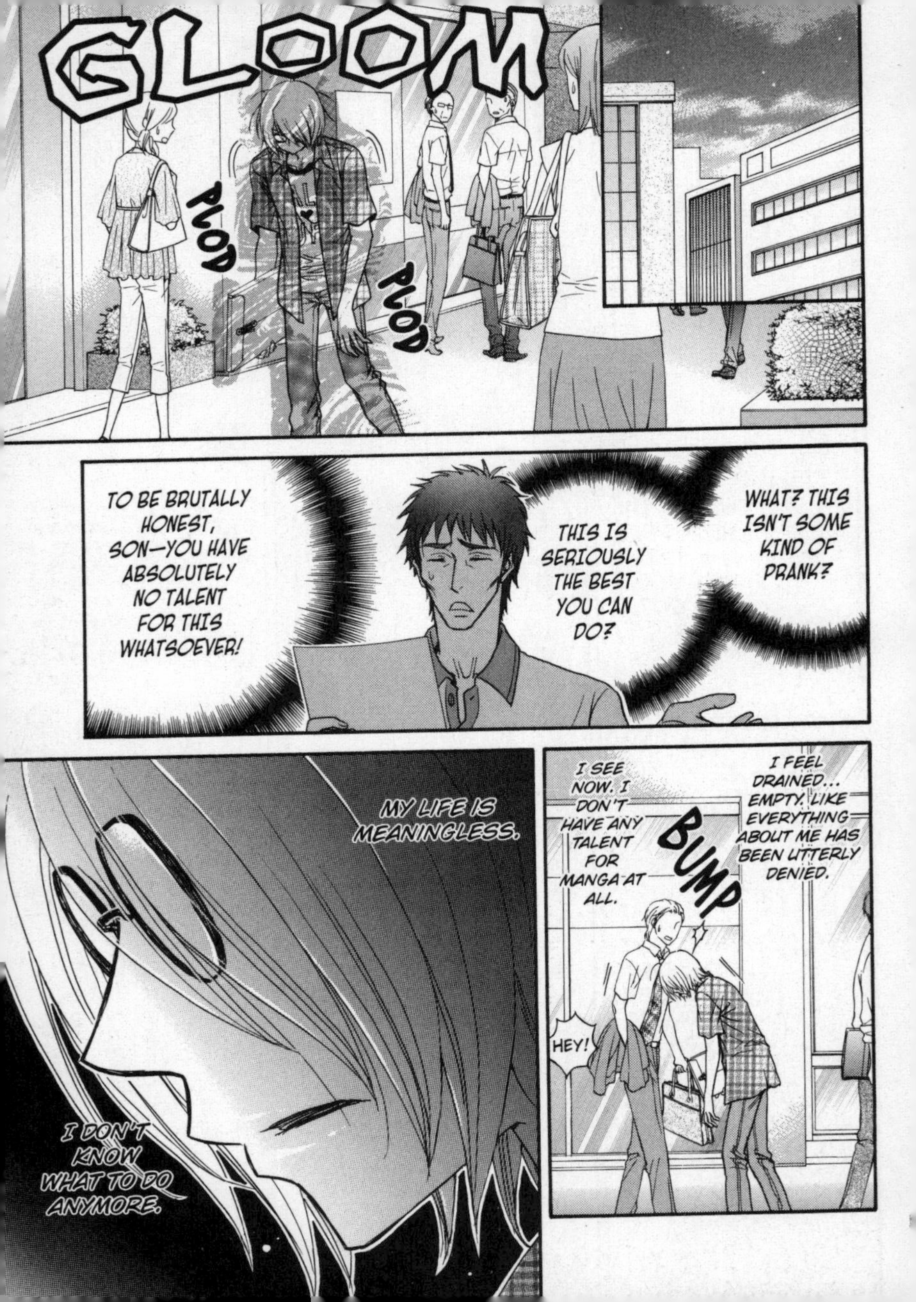
GLOOM
PLOD
PLOD
WHAT? THIS ISN'T SOME KIND OF PRANK?
THIS IS SERIOUSLY THE BEST YOU CAN DO?
TO BE BRUTALLY HONEST, SON—YOU HAVE ABSOLUTELY NO TALENT FOR THIS WHATSOEVER!
I FEEL DRAINED... EMPTY. LIKE EVERYTHING ABOUT ME HAS BEEN UTTERLY DENIED.
I SEE NOW. I DON'T HAVE ANY TALENT FOR MANGA AT ALL.
BUMP
HEY!
MY LIFE IS MEANINGLESS.
I DON'T KNOW WHAT TO DO ANYMORE.

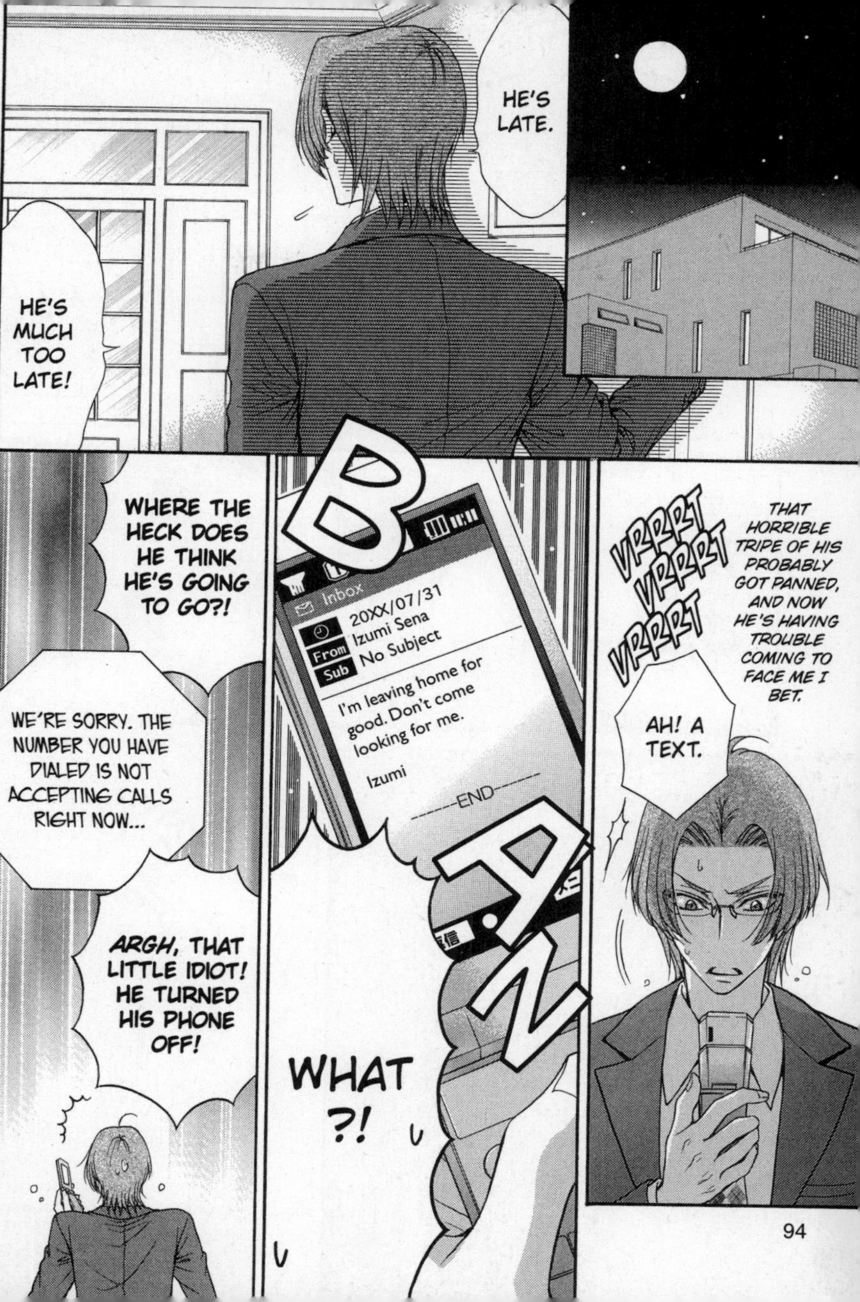
HE'S LATE.
HE'S MUCH TOO LATE!
THAT HORRIBLE TRIPE OF HIS PROBABLY GOT PANNED, AND NOW HE'S HAVING TROUBLE COMING TO FACE ME I BET.
VRRRT VRRRT VRRRT
AH! A TEXT.
BAN
Inbox
20XX/07/31
From Izumi Sena
Sub No Subject
I'm leaving home for good. Don't come looking for me.
Izumi
END
WHAT?!
WHERE THE HECK DOES HE THINK HE'S GOING TO GO?!
WE'RE SORRY. THE NUMBER YOU HAVE DIALED IS NOT ACCEPTING CALLS RIGHT NOW...
ARGH, THAT LITTLE IDIOT! HE TURNED HIS PHONE OFF!

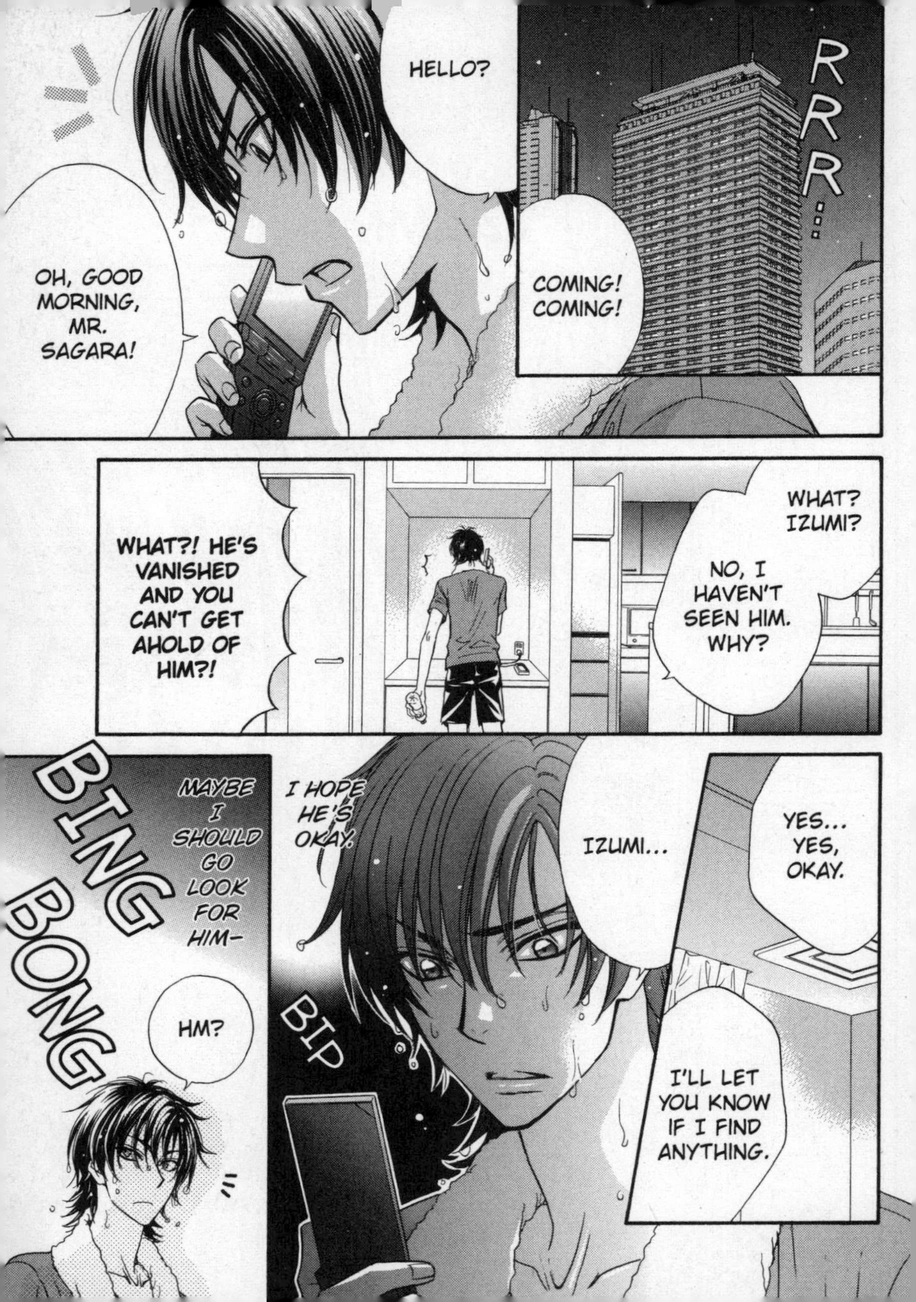
RRR...
COMING! COMING!
HELLO?
OH, GOOD MORNING, MR. SAGARA!
WHAT? IZUMI?
NO, I HAVEN'T SEEN HIM. WHY?
WHAT?! HE'S VANISHED AND YOU CAN'T GET AHOLD OF HIM?!
YES... YES, OKAY.
IZUMI...
I'LL LET YOU KNOW IF I FIND ANYTHING.
BIP
I HOPE HE'S OKAY.
MAYBE I SHOULD GO LOOK FOR HIM-
BING BONG
HM?

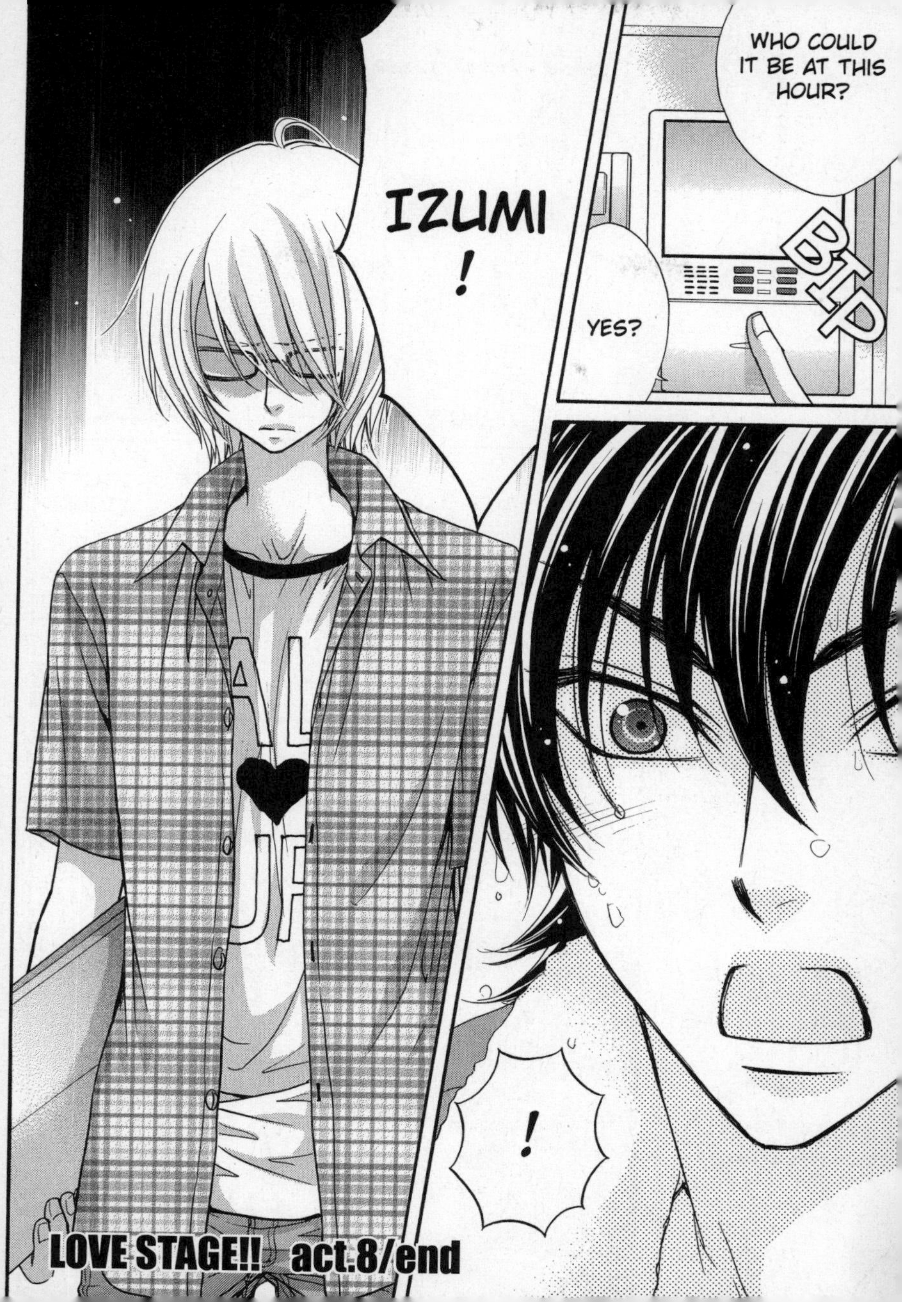
WHO COULD IT BE AT THIS HOUR?
BIP
YES?
!
IZUMI !

LOVE STAGE!! act.8/end

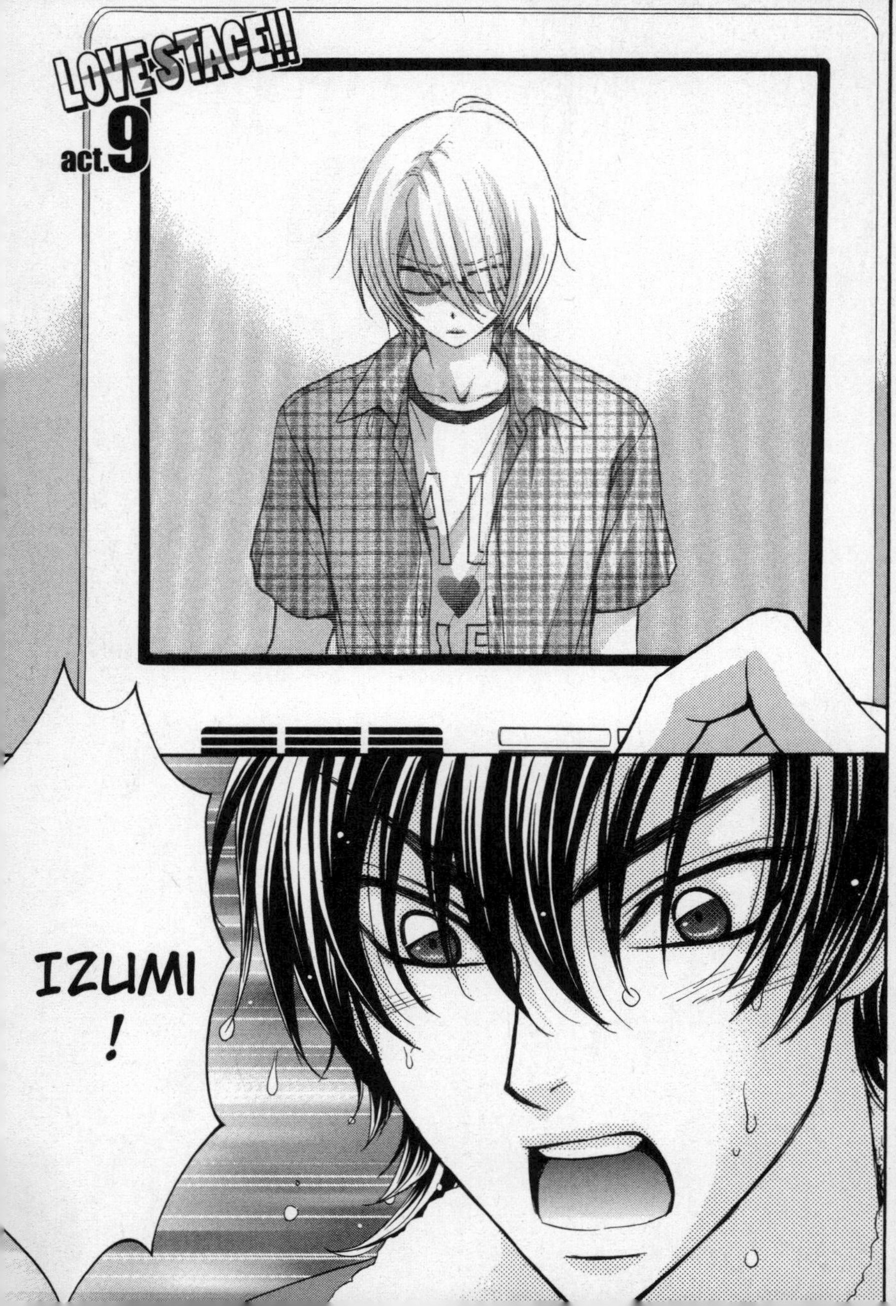
LOVE STAGE!!
act.9
IZUMI
!

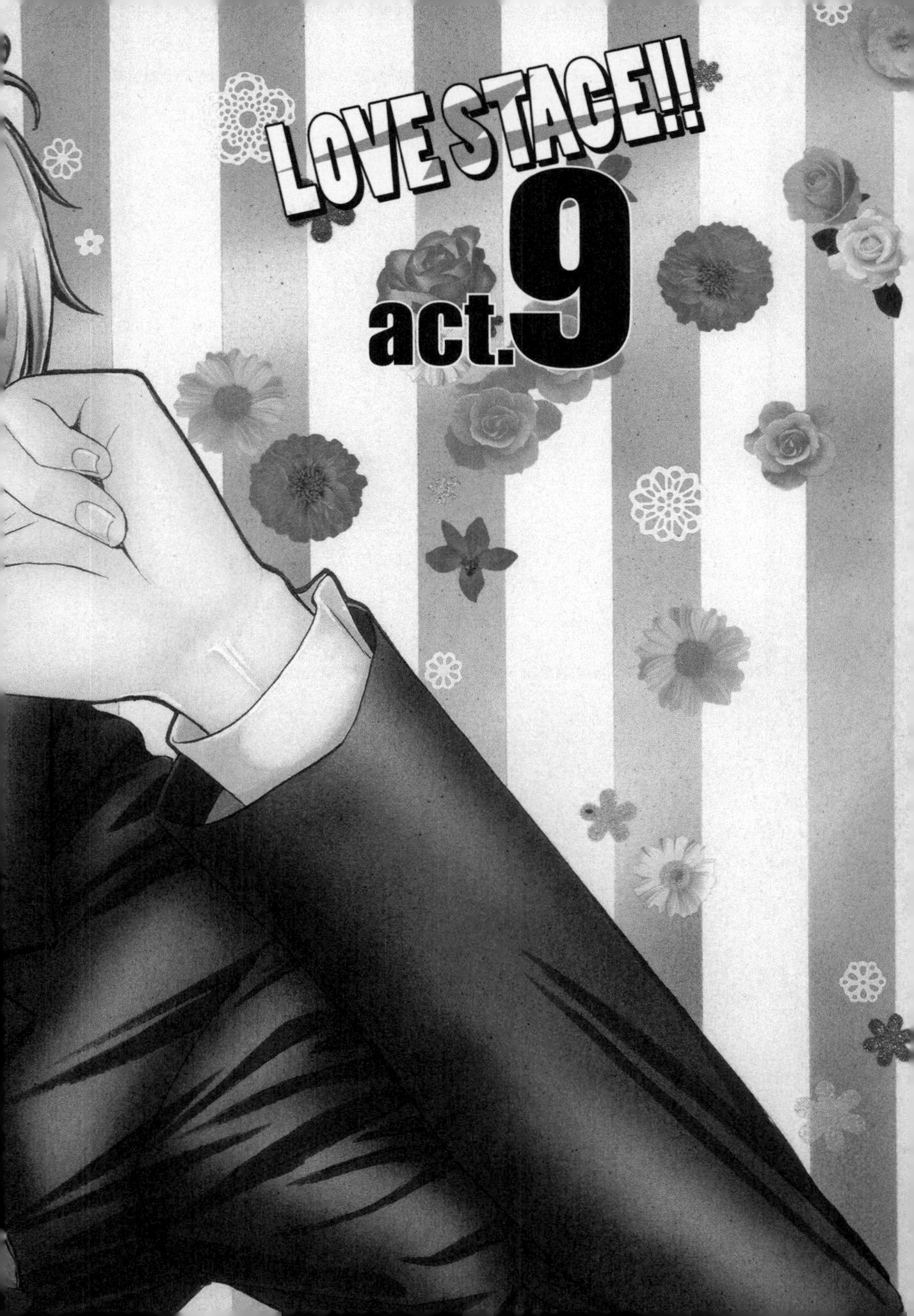
LOVE STAGE!!
act.9

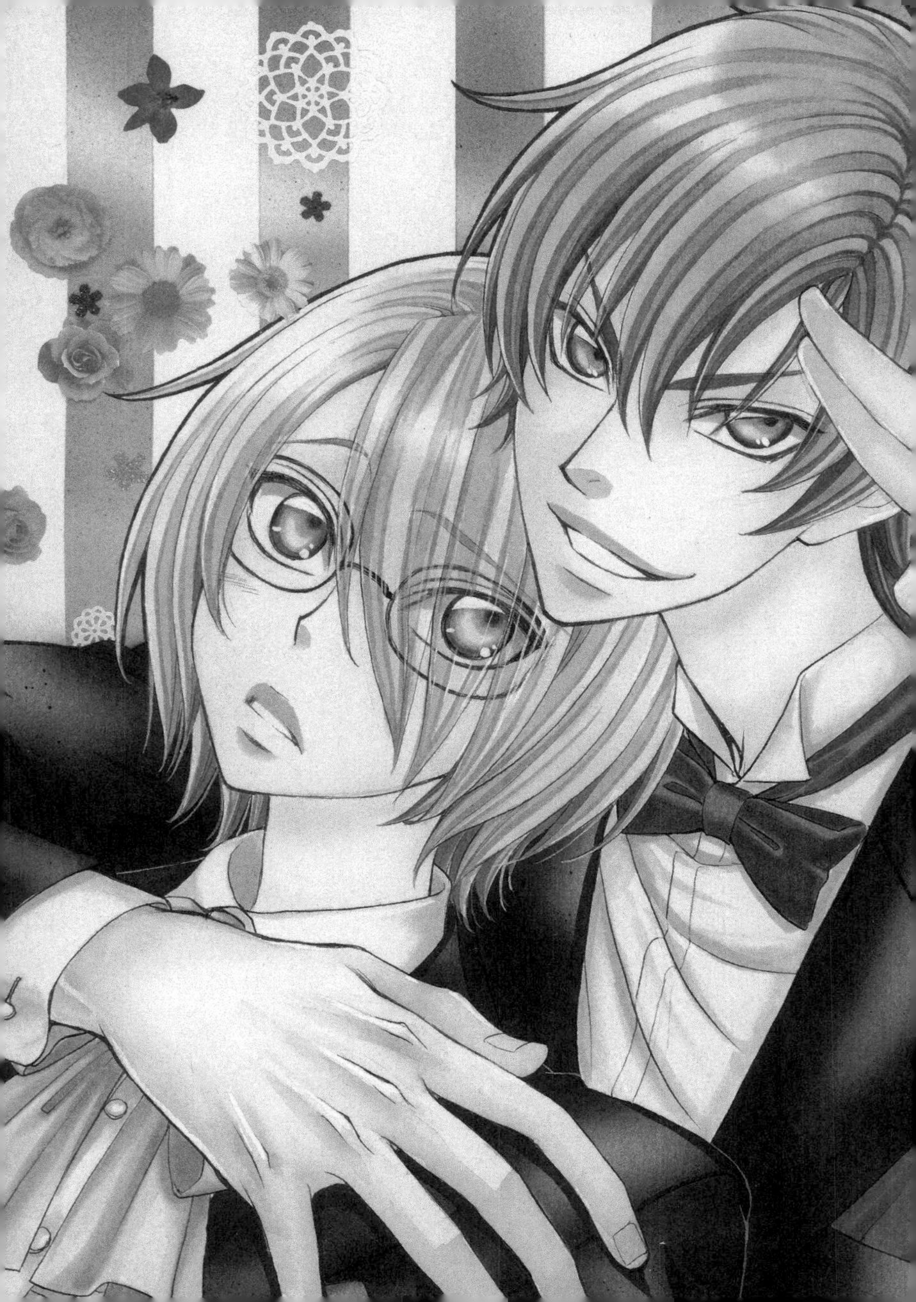

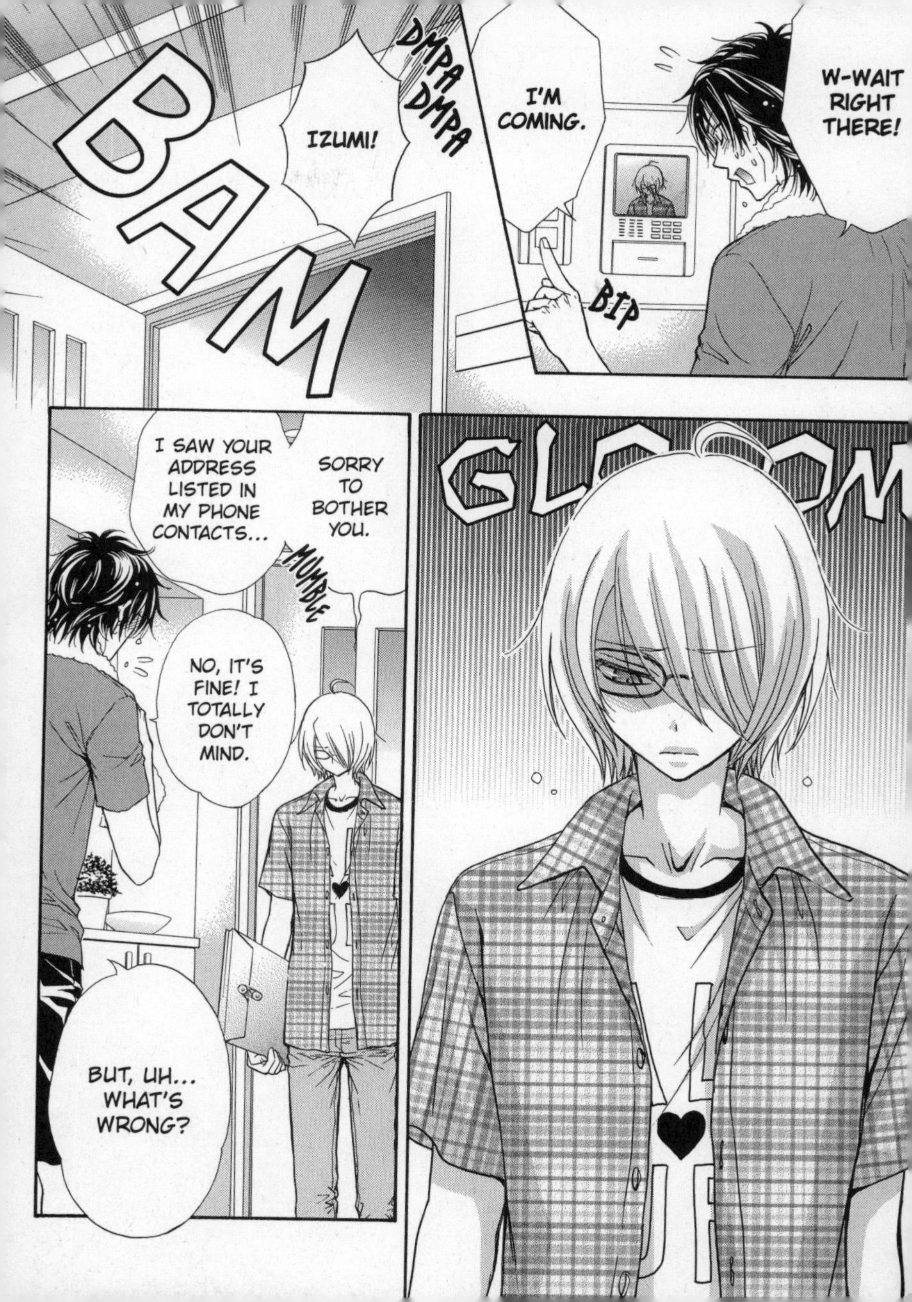
W-WAIT RIGHT THERE!
I'M COMING.
BIP
DMPA DMPA
IZUMI!
BAM
GLO OM
SORRY TO BOTHER YOU.
I SAW YOUR ADDRESS LISTED IN MY PHONE CONTACTS...
MUMBLE
NO, IT'S FINE! I TOTALLY DON'T MIND.
BUT, UH... WHAT'S WRONG?

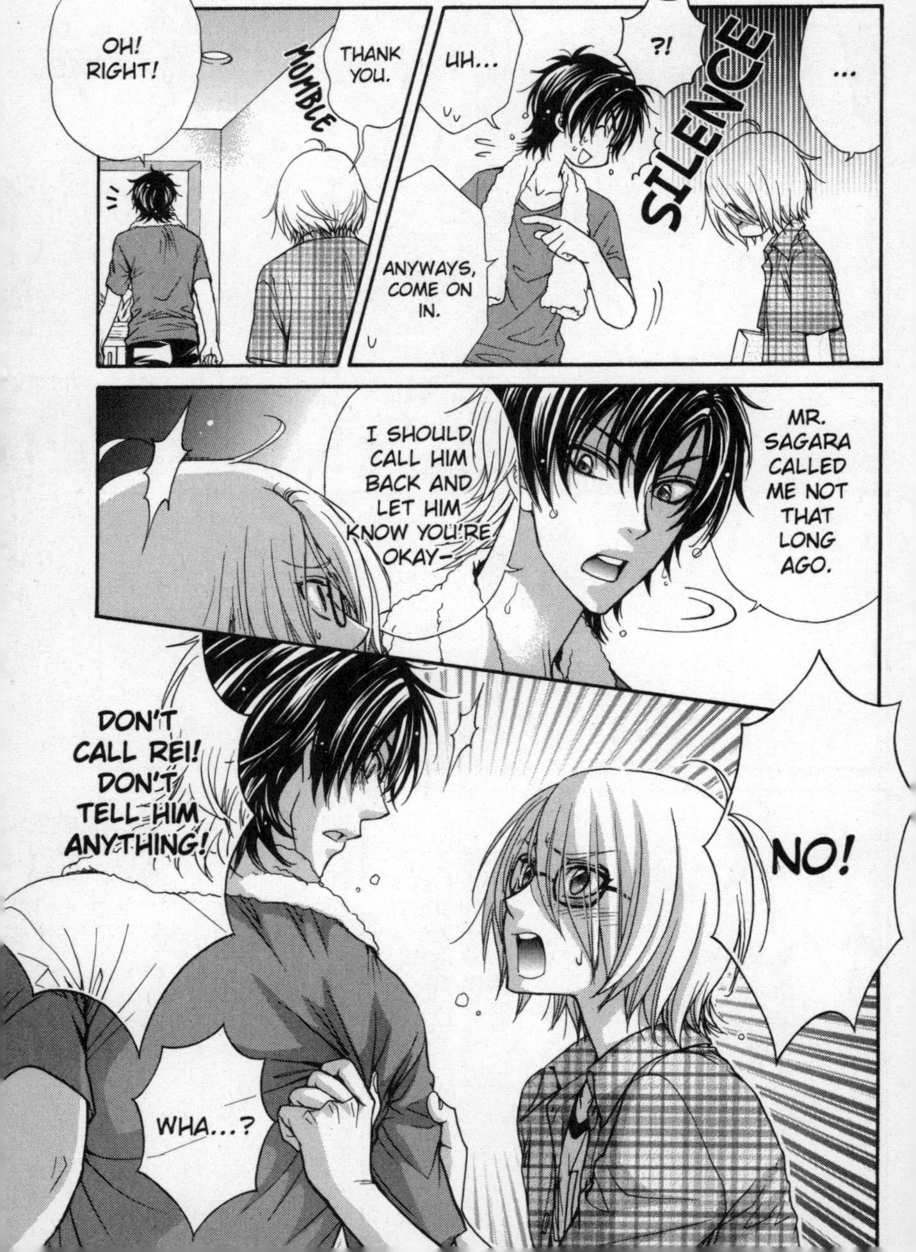
...
?!
SILENCE
UH...
ANYWAYS, COME ON IN.
THANK YOU.
MUMBLE
OH! RIGHT!
MR. SAGARA CALLED ME NOT THAT LONG AGO.
I SHOULD CALL HIM BACK AND LET HIM KNOW YOU'RE OKAY-
NO!
DON'T CALL REI! DON'T TELL HIM ANYTHING!
WHA...?

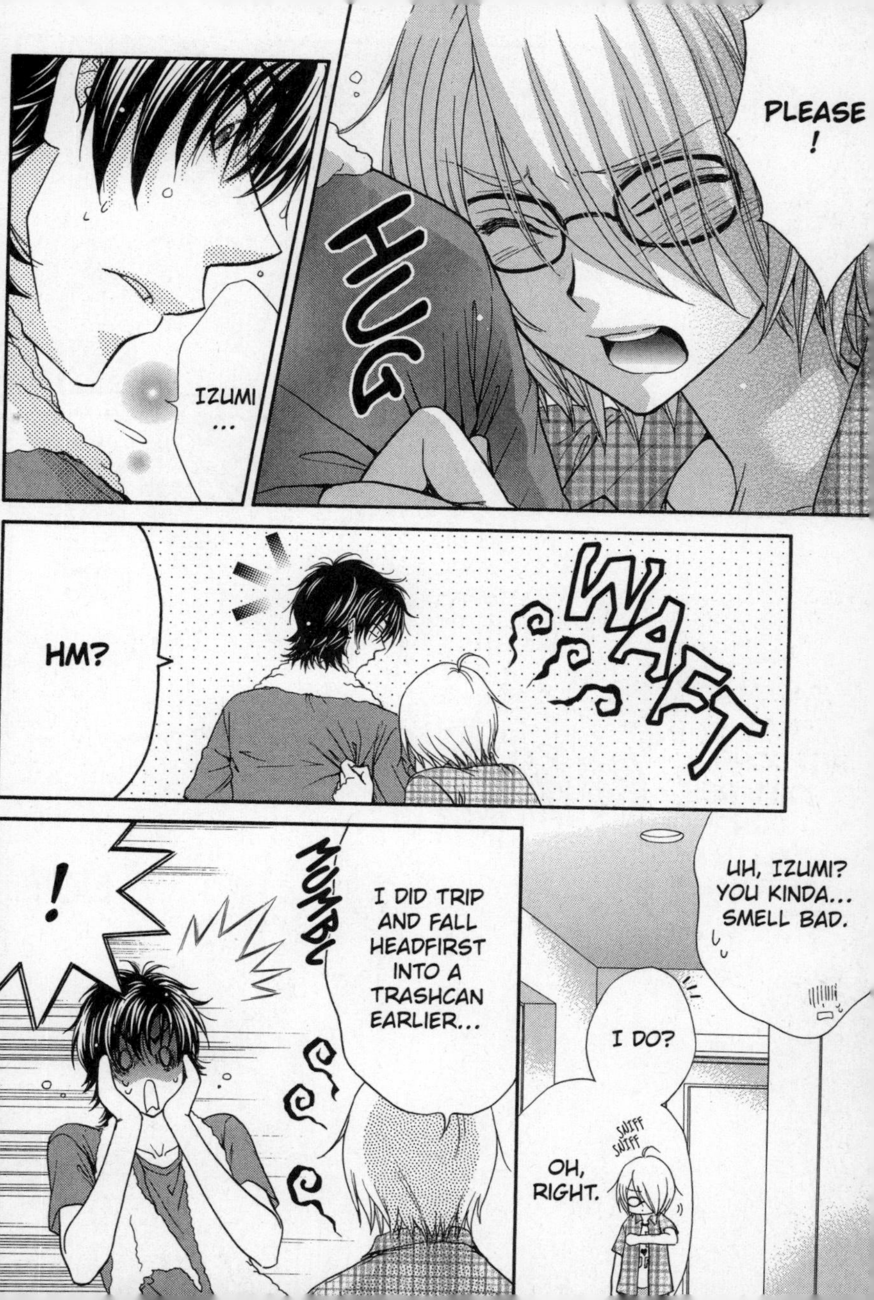
PLEASE !
HUG
IZUMI ...
WAFT
HM?
UH, IZUMI? YOU KINDA... SMELL BAD.
I DO?
SNIFF SNIFF
OH, RIGHT.
I DID TRIP AND FALL HEADFIRST INTO A TRASHCAN EARLIER...
MUMBL
!

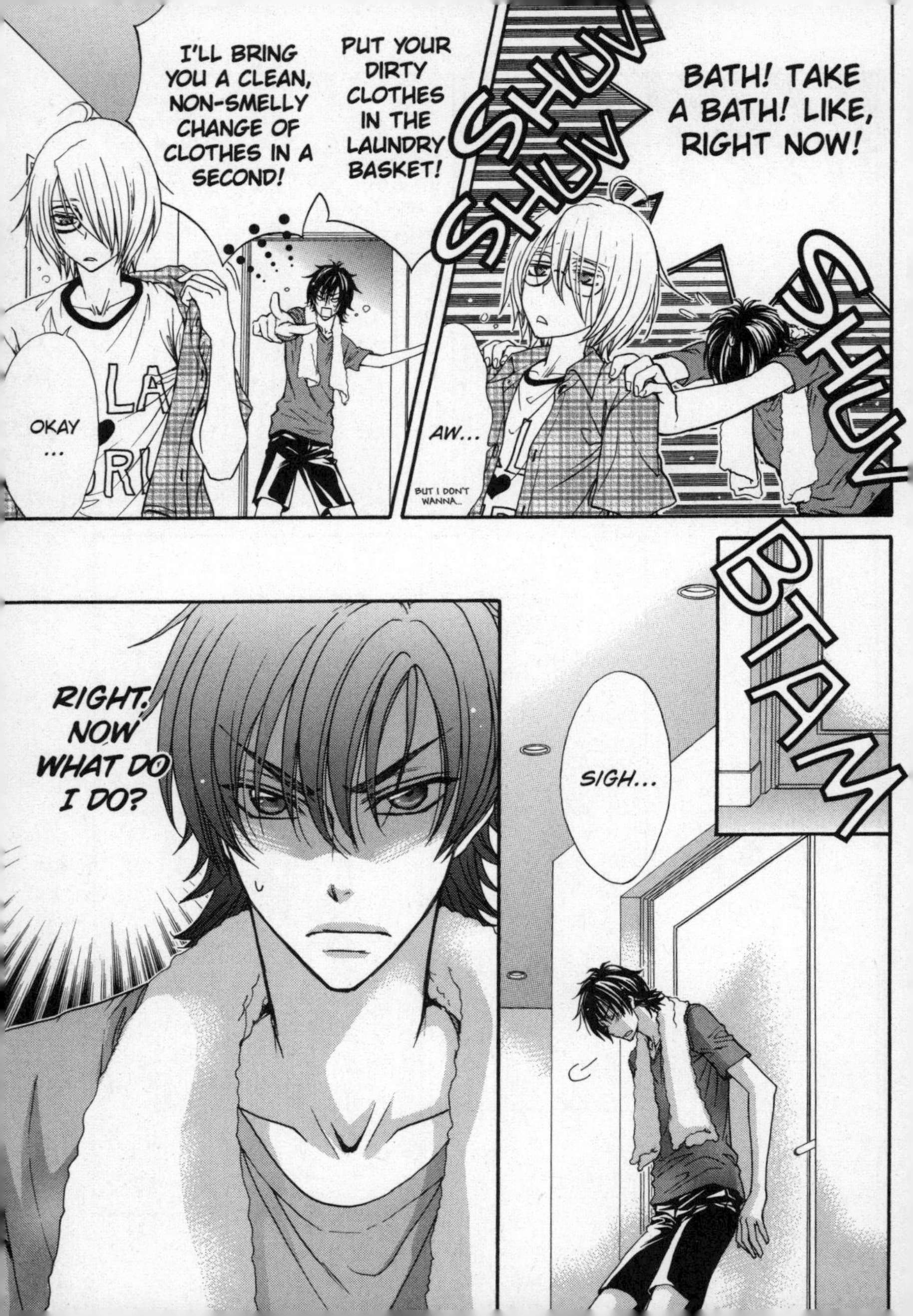
BATH! TAKE A BATH! LIKE, RIGHT NOW!
SHUV SHUV
SHUV
AW...
BUT I DON'T WANNA..
PUT YOUR DIRTY CLOTHES IN THE LAUNDRY BASKET!
I'LL BRING YOU A CLEAN, NON-SMELLY CHANGE OF CLOTHES IN A SECOND!
OKAY ...
BTAM
SIGH...
RIGHT. NOW WHAT DO I DO?

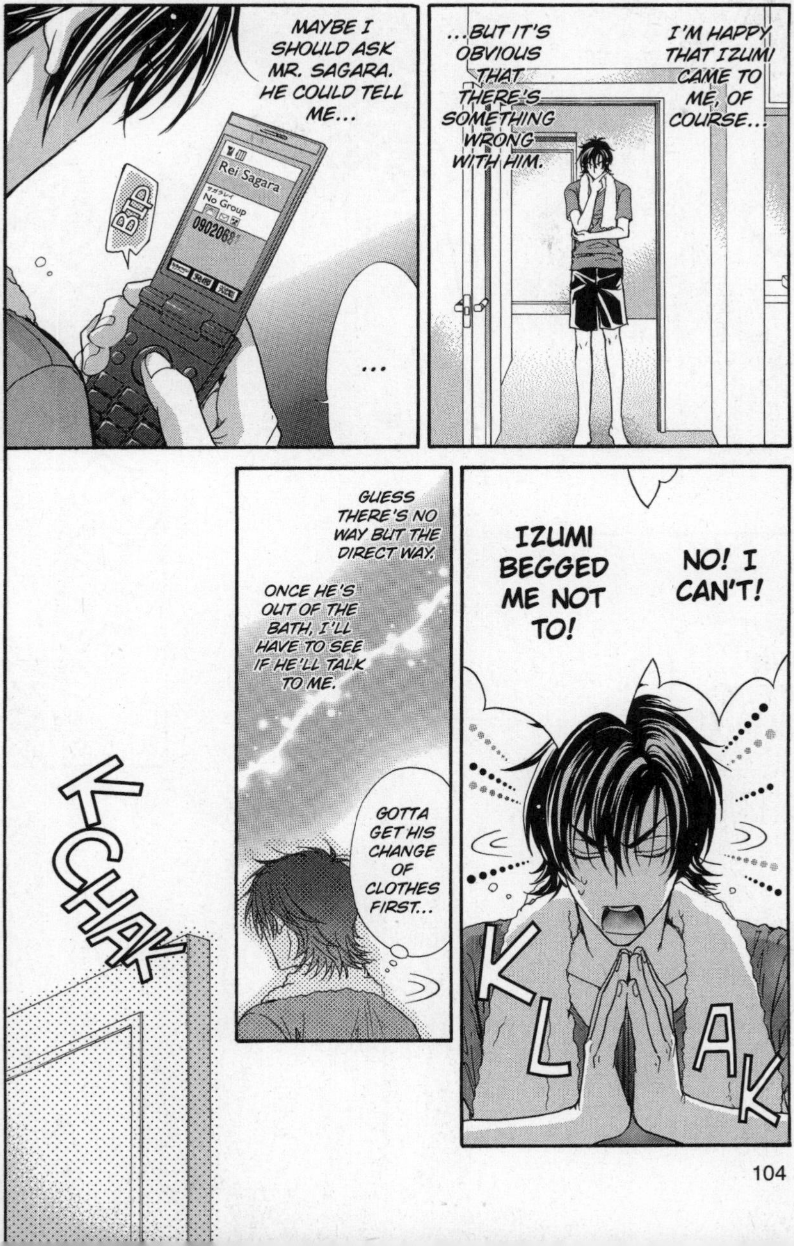
I'M HAPPY THAT IZUMI CAME TO ME, OF COURSE...
...BUT IT'S OBVIOUS THAT THERE'S SOMETHING WRONG WITH HIM.
MAYBE I SHOULD ASK MR. SAGARA. HE COULD TELL ME...
BIP
Rei Sagara
No Group
...
NO! I CAN'T!
IZUMI BEGGED ME NOT TO!
KLAK
GUESS THERE'S NO WAY BUT THE DIRECT WAY.
ONCE HE'S OUT OF THE BATH, I'LL HAVE TO SEE IF HE'LL TALK TO ME.
GOTTA GET HIS CHANGE OF CLOTHES FIRST...
KCHAK

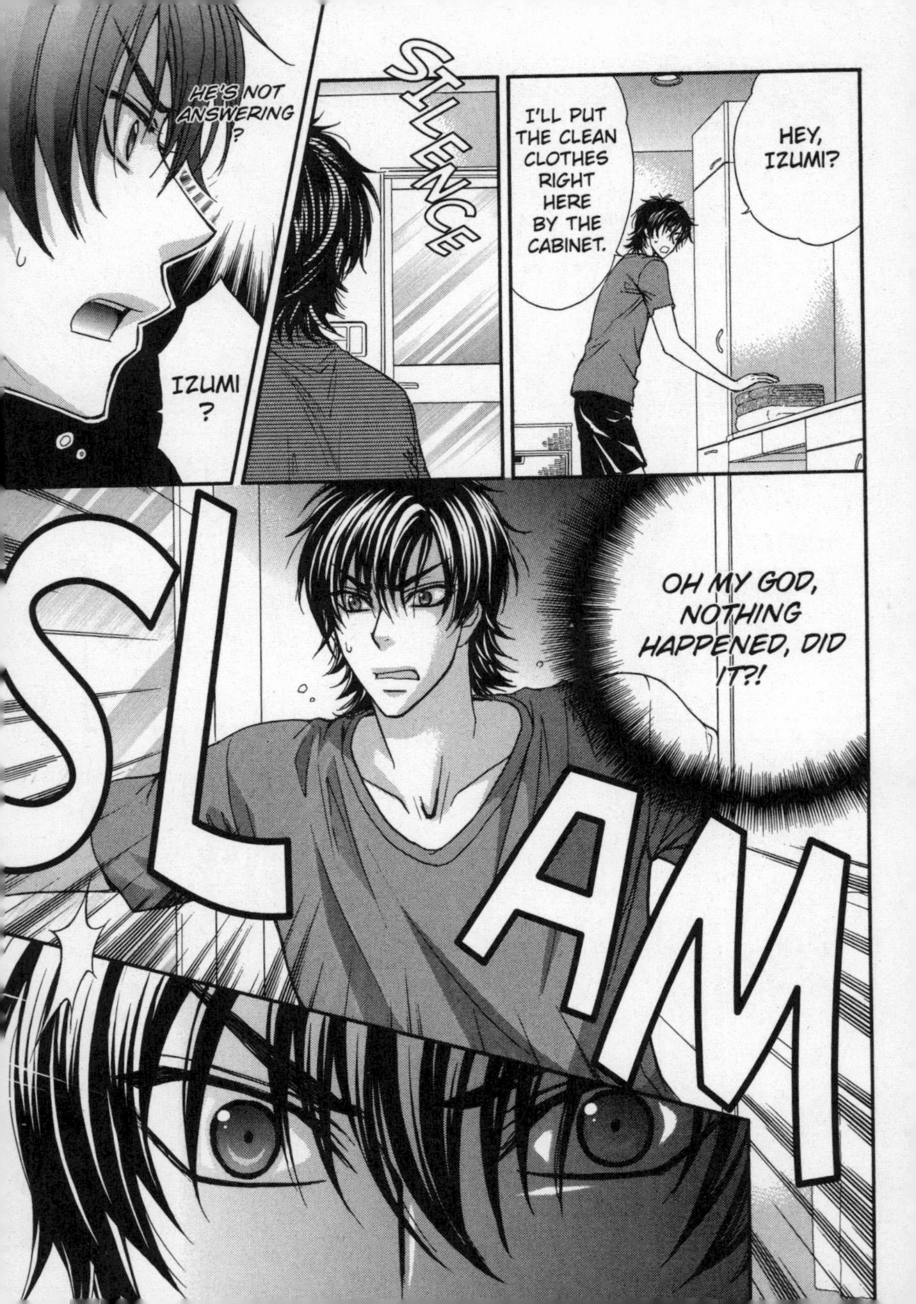
HEY, IZUMI?
I'LL PUT THE CLEAN CLOTHES RIGHT HERE BY THE CABINET.
SILENCE
HE'S NOT ANSWERING?
IZUMI?
OH MY GOD, NOTHING HAPPENED, DID IT?!
SLAM

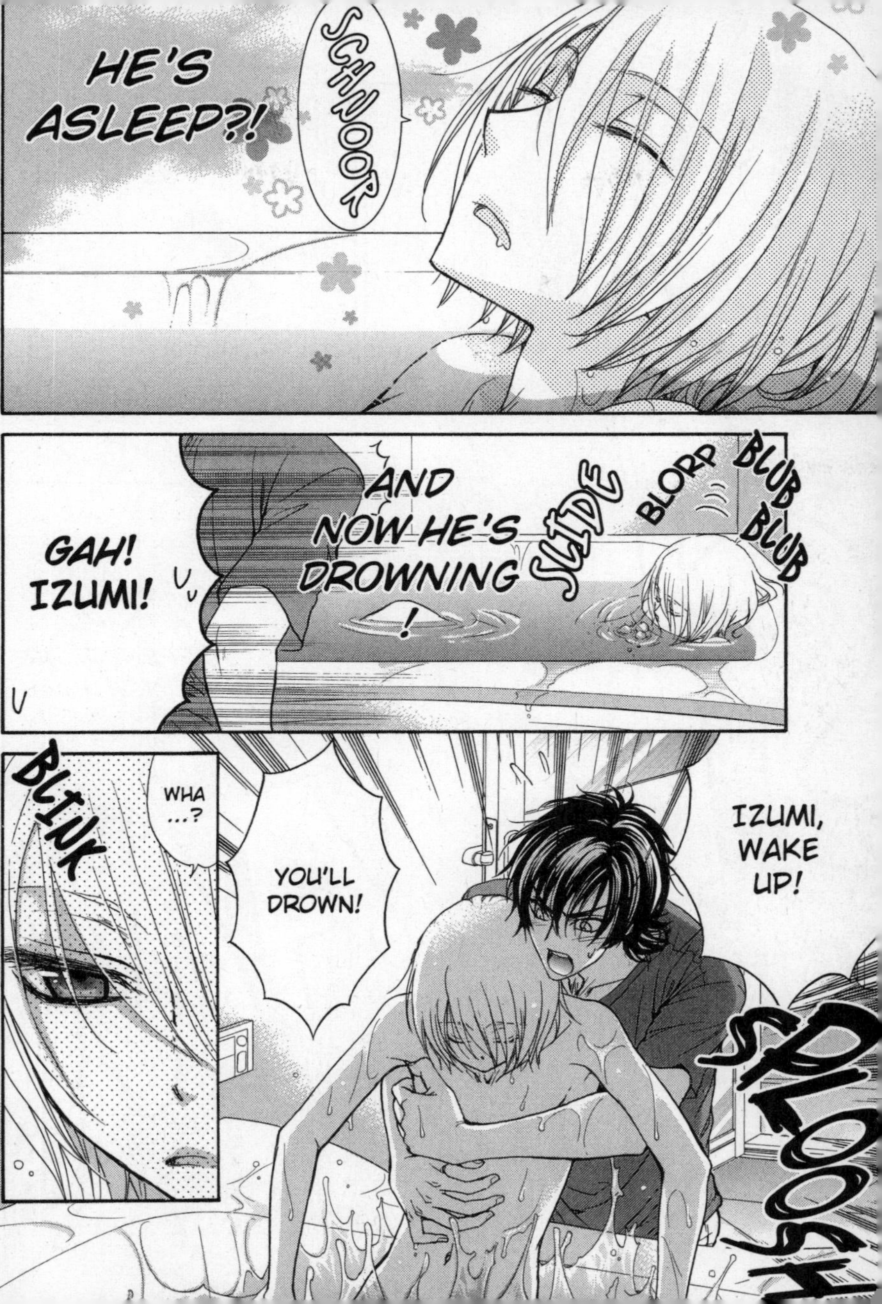
SCHNOOR
HE'S ASLEEP?!
BLUB BLUB
BLORP
SLIDE
AND NOW HE'S DROWNING!
GAH! IZUMI!
IZUMI, WAKE UP!
SPLOOSH
YOU'LL DROWN!
WHA ...?
BLINK

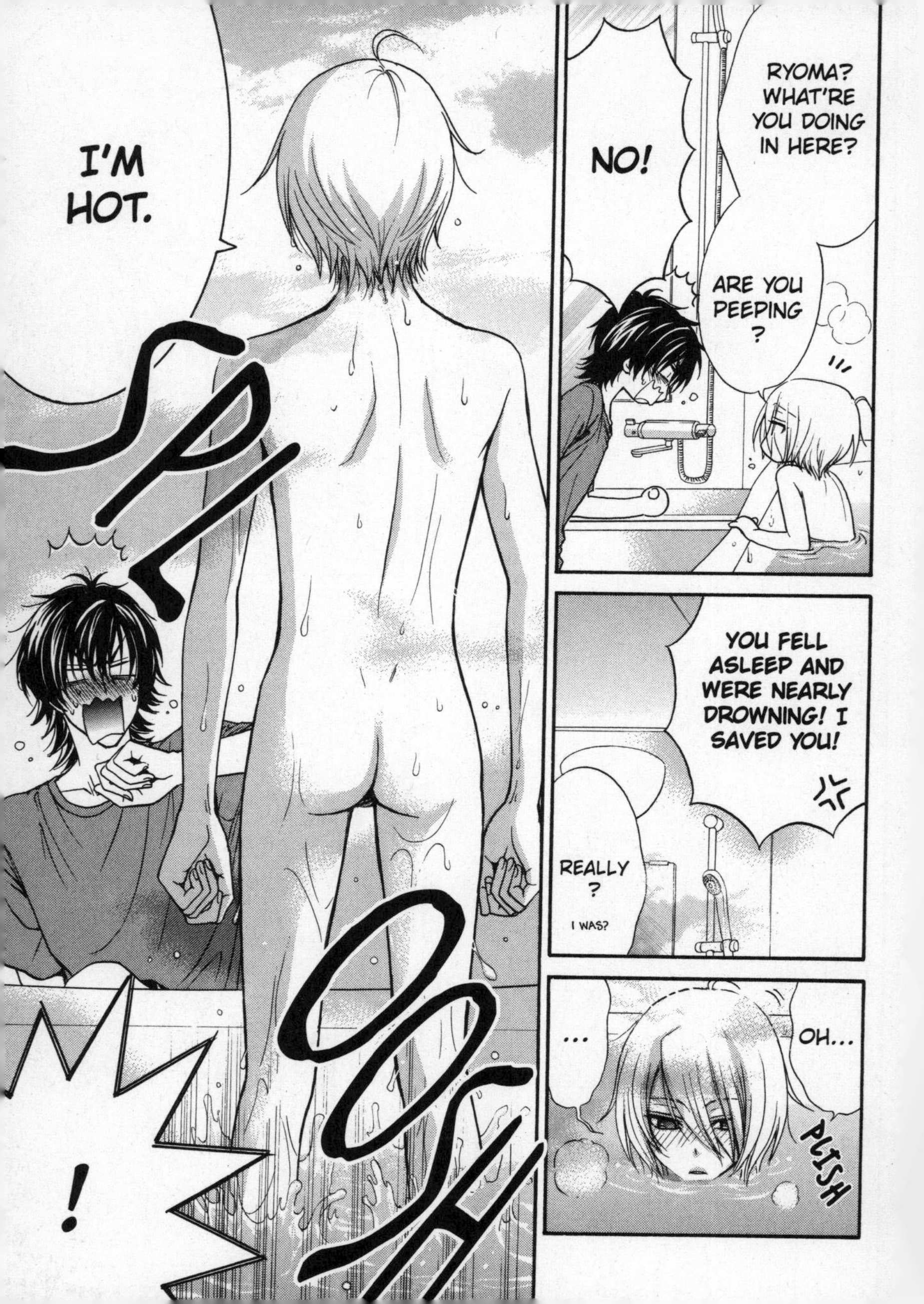
RYOMA? WHAT'RE YOU DOING IN HERE?
NO!
ARE YOU PEEPING?
YOU FELL ASLEEP AND WERE NEARLY DROWNING! I SAVED YOU!
REALLY?
I WAS?
OH...
...
PLISH
I'M HOT.
SPLOOSH
!

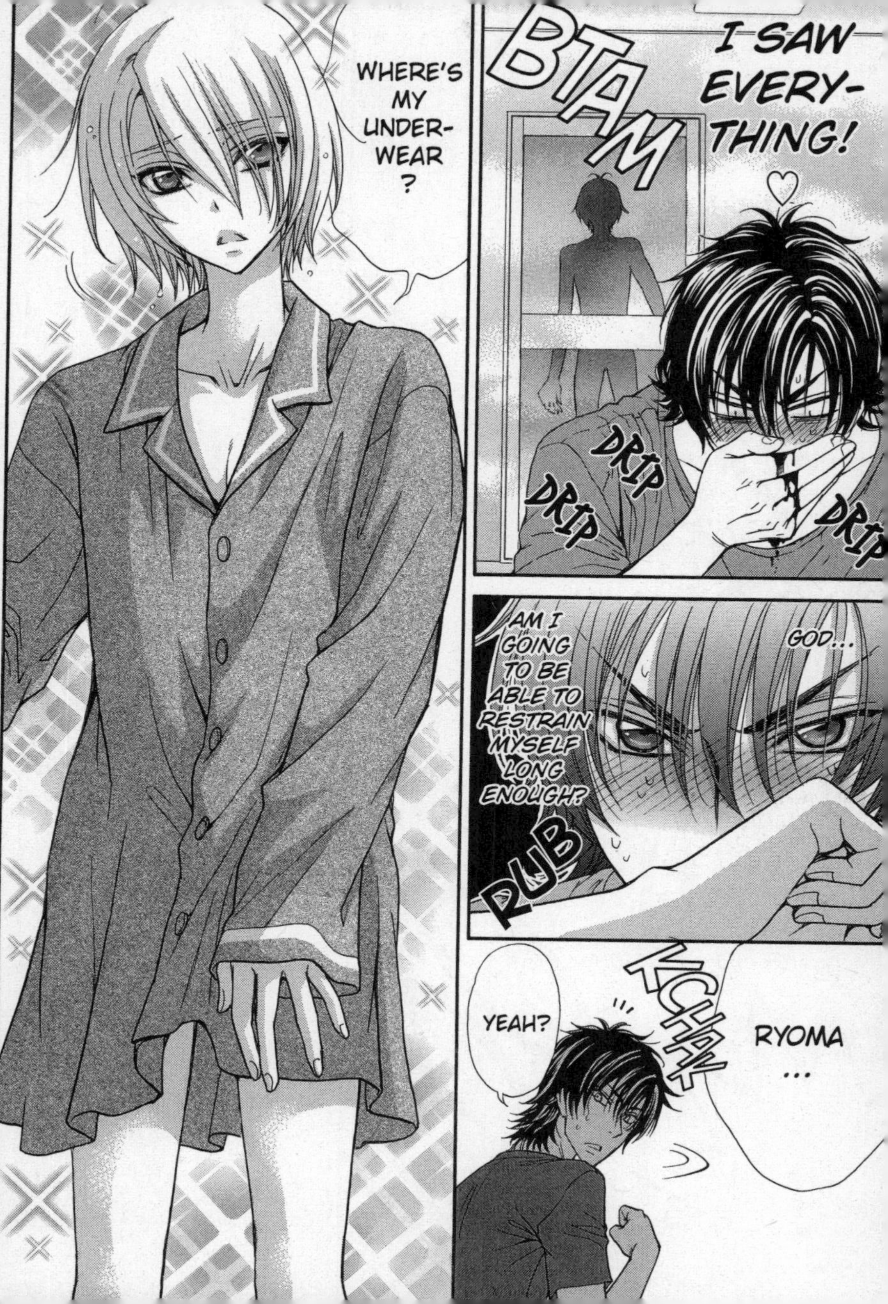
BTAM
I SAW EVERY-THING!
DRIP
DRIP
DRIP
DRIP
GOD...
AM I GOING TO BE ABLE TO RESTRAIN MYSELF LONG ENOUGH?
RUB
RYOMA ...
KCHAK
YEAH?
WHERE'S MY UNDER-WEAR ?

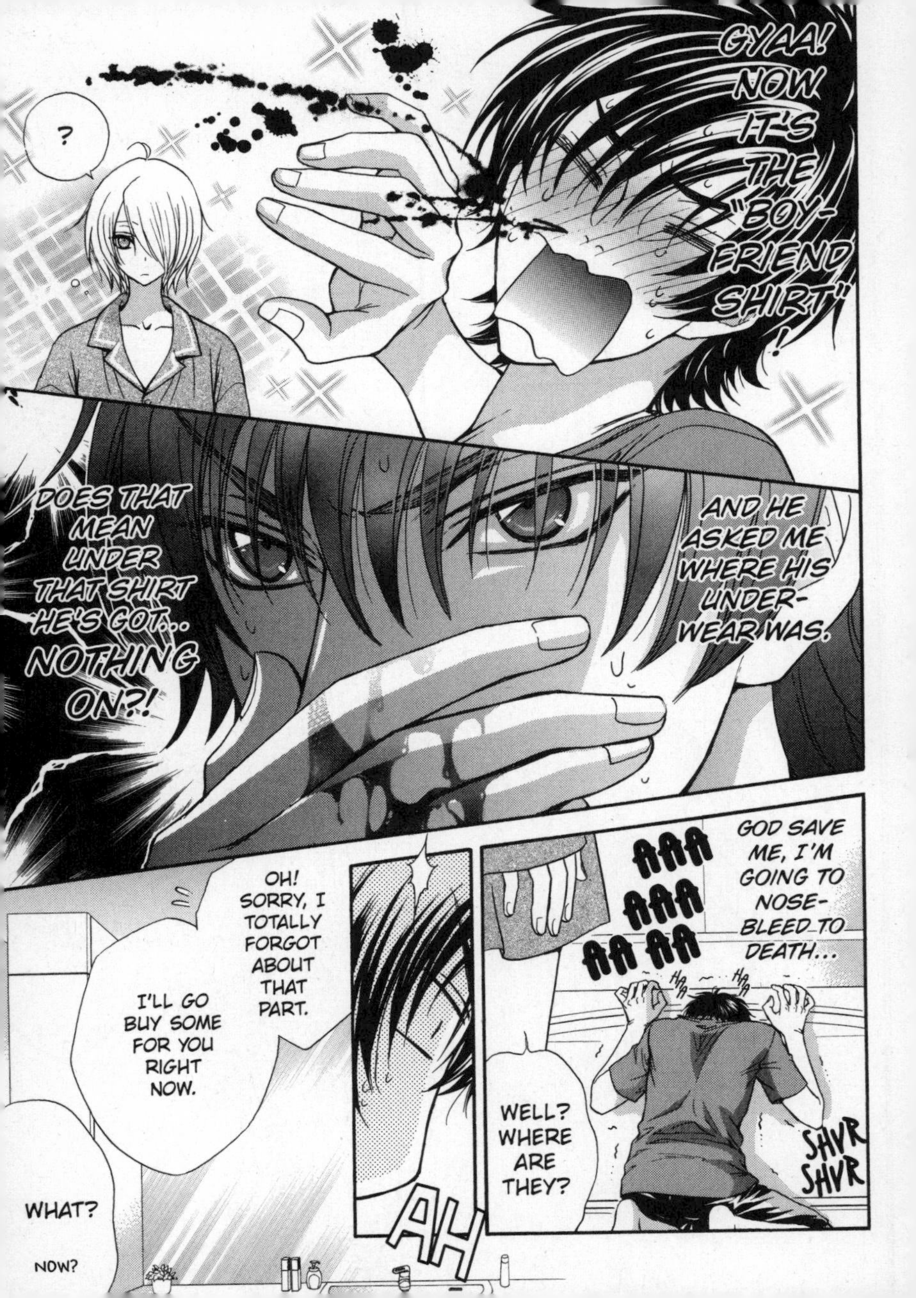
GYAA! NOW IT'S THE "BOY-FRIEND SHIRT"!
?
AND HE ASKED ME WHERE HIS UNDER-WEAR WAS.
DOES THAT MEAN UNDER THAT SHIRT HE'S GOT... NOTHING ON?!
GOD SAVE ME, I'M GOING TO NOSE-BLEED TO DEATH...
AAA AAA AA AA
HAA ~ HAA
WELL? WHERE ARE THEY?
SHVR SHVR
AH
OH! SORRY, I TOTALLY FORGOT ABOUT THAT PART.
I'LL GO BUY SOME FOR YOU RIGHT NOW.
WHAT?
NOW?

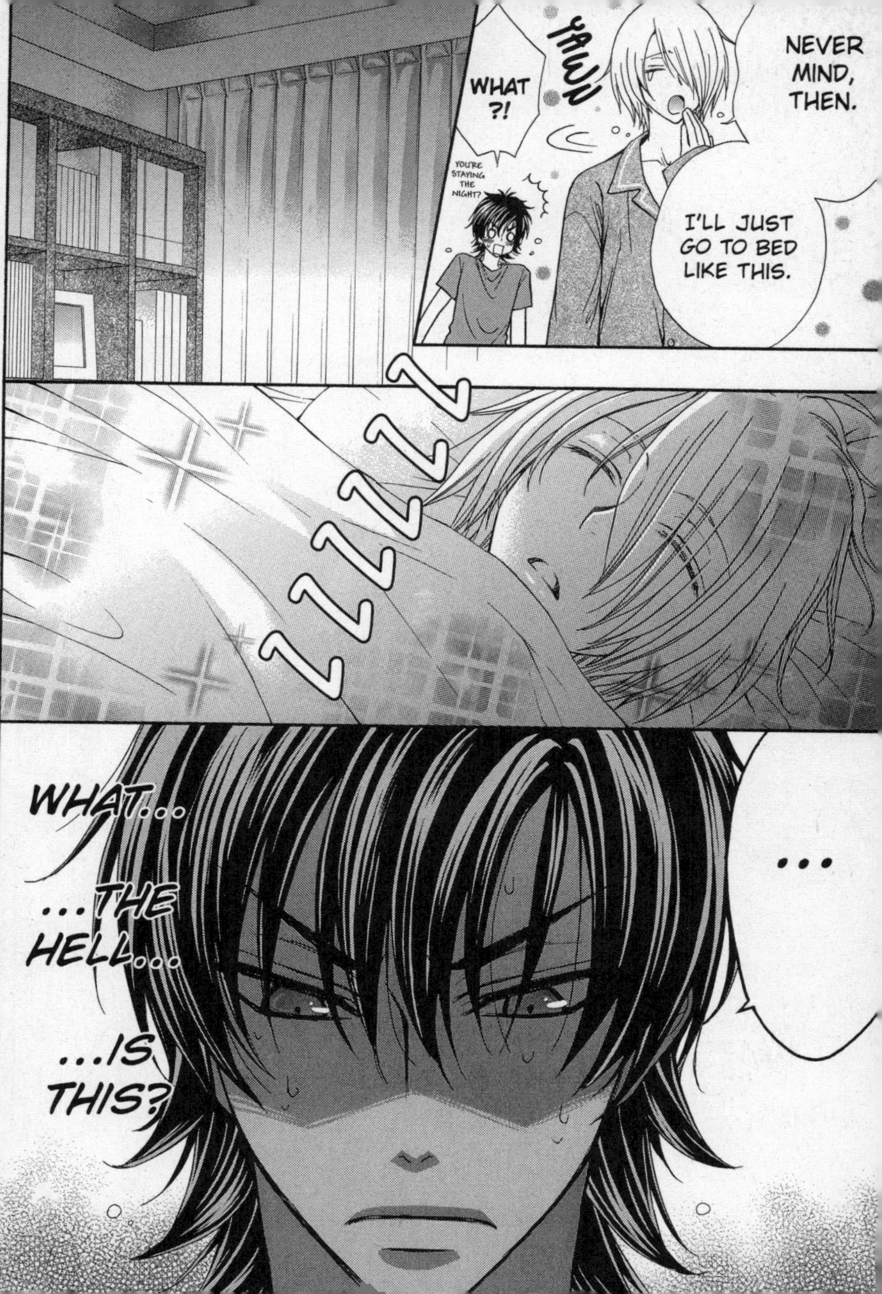
NEVER MIND, THEN.
YAWN
I'LL JUST GO TO BED LIKE THIS.
WHAT?!
YOU'RE STAYING THE NIGHT?
...
WHAT...
...THE HELL...
...IS THIS?

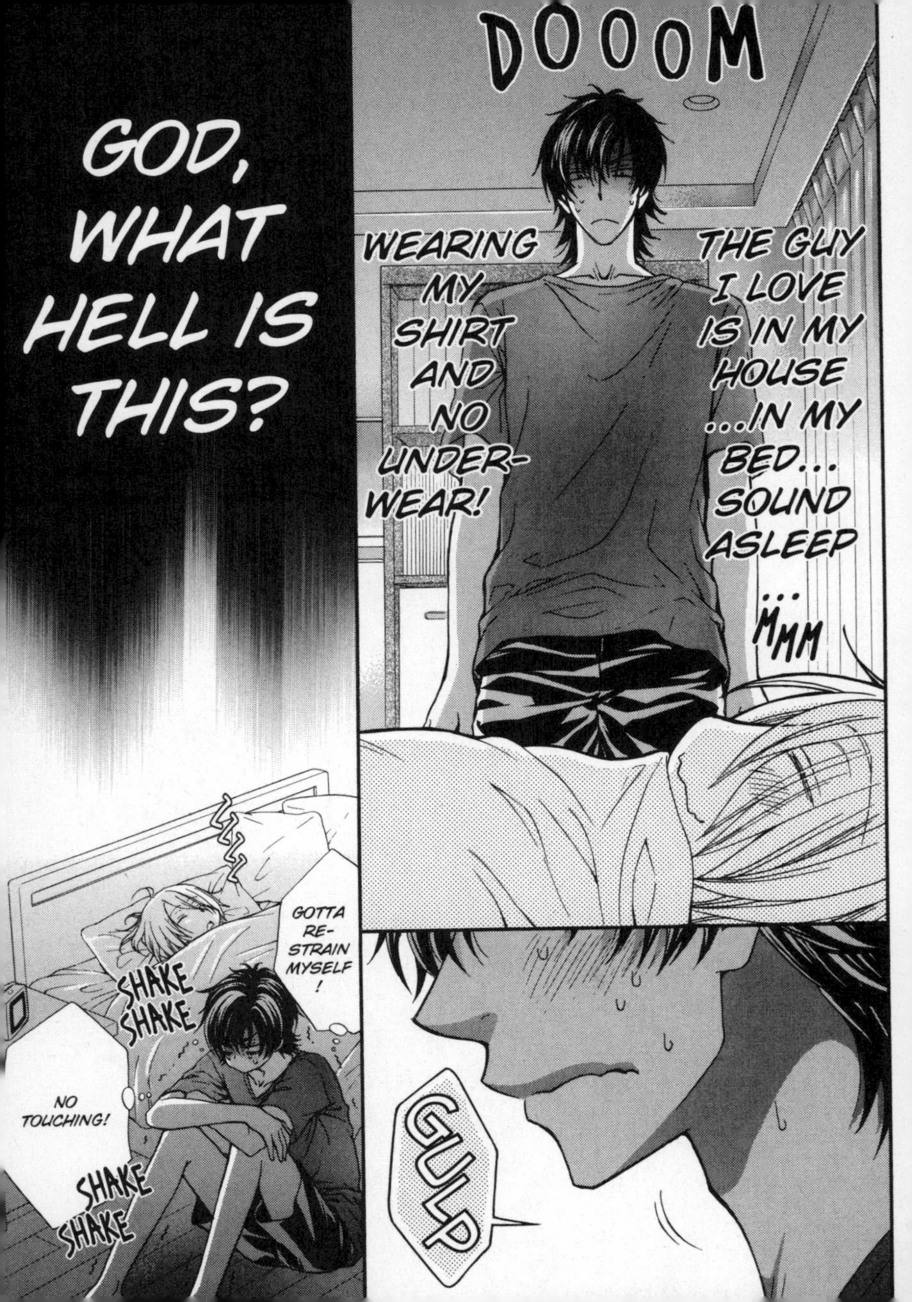
DOOOM
THE GUY I LOVE IS IN MY HOUSE ...IN MY BED... SOUND ASLEEP
WEARING MY SHIRT AND NO UNDER-WEAR!
... MMM
GULP
GOD, WHAT HELL IS THIS?
GOTTA RE-STRAIN MYSELF!
SHAKE SHAKE
NO TOUCHING!
SHAKE SHAKE

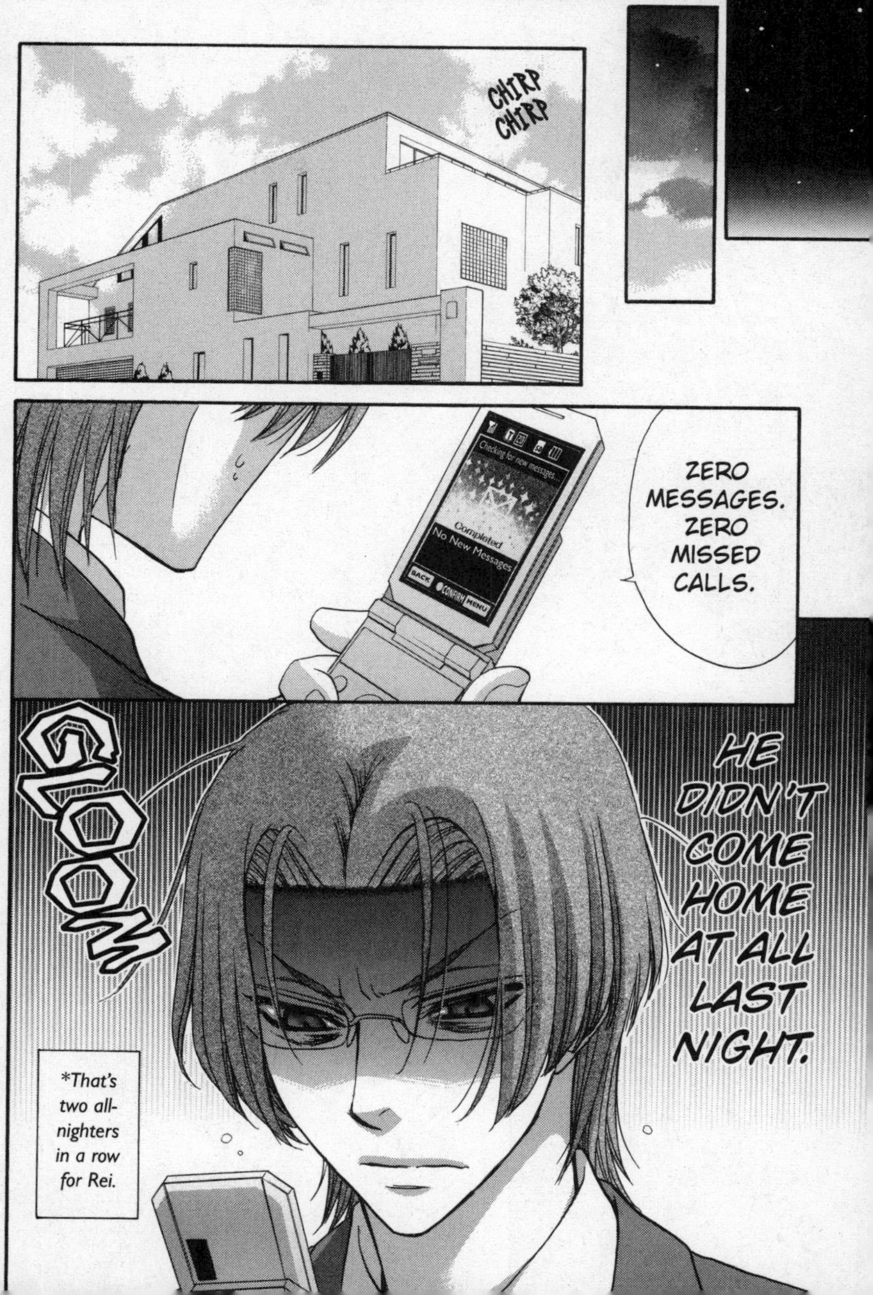
CHIRP CHIRP
Checking for new messages...
Completed
No New Messages
BACK
CONFIRM
MENU
ZERO MESSAGES. ZERO MISSED CALLS.
HE DIDN'T COME HOME AT ALL LAST NIGHT.
GLOOM
*That's two all-nighters in a row for Rei.

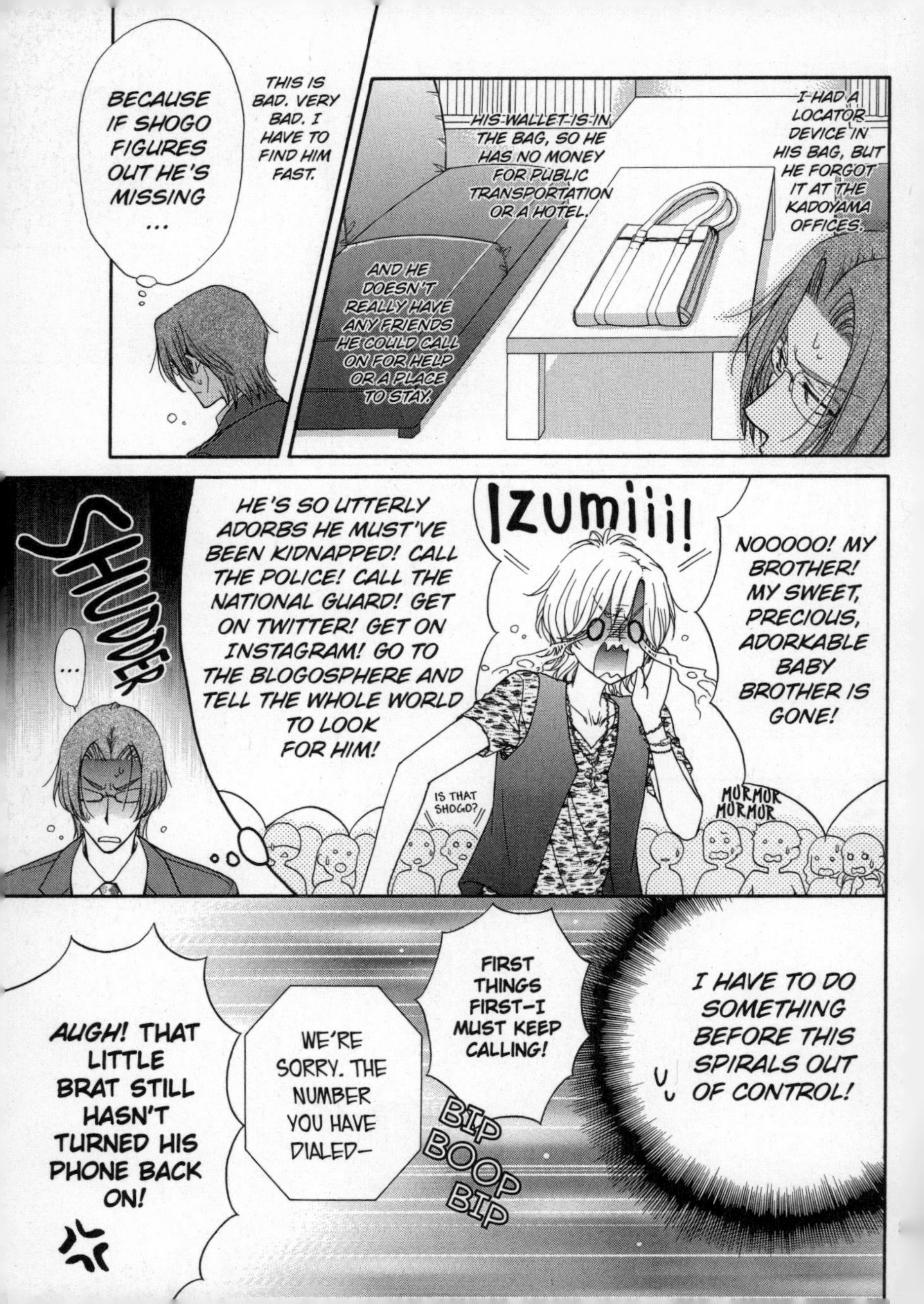
I HAD A LOCATOR DEVICE IN HIS BAG, BUT HE FORGOT IT AT THE KADOYAMA OFFICES.
HIS WALLET IS IN THE BAG, SO HE HAS NO MONEY FOR PUBLIC TRANSPORTATION OR A HOTEL.
AND HE DOESN'T REALLY HAVE ANY FRIENDS HE COULD CALL ON FOR HELP OR A PLACE TO STAY.
THIS IS BAD. VERY BAD. I HAVE TO FIND HIM FAST.
BECAUSE IF SHOGO FIGURES OUT HE'S MISSING ...
NOOOOO! MY BROTHER! MY SWEET, PRECIOUS, ADORKABLE BABY BROTHER IS GONE!
IZUMIIII!
HE'S SO UTTERLY ADORBS HE MUST'VE BEEN KIDNAPPED! CALL THE POLICE! CALL THE NATIONAL GUARD! GET ON TWITTER! GET ON INSTAGRAM! GO TO THE BLOGOSPHERE AND TELL THE WHOLE WORLD TO LOOK FOR HIM!
MURMUR MURMUR
IS THAT SHOGO?
SHUDDER
...
I HAVE TO DO SOMETHING BEFORE THIS SPIRALS OUT OF CONTROL!
FIRST THINGS FIRST—I MUST KEEP CALLING!
BIP BOOP BIP
WE'RE SORRY. THE NUMBER YOU HAVE DIALED—
AUGH! THAT LITTLE BRAT STILL HASN'T TURNED HIS PHONE BACK ON!

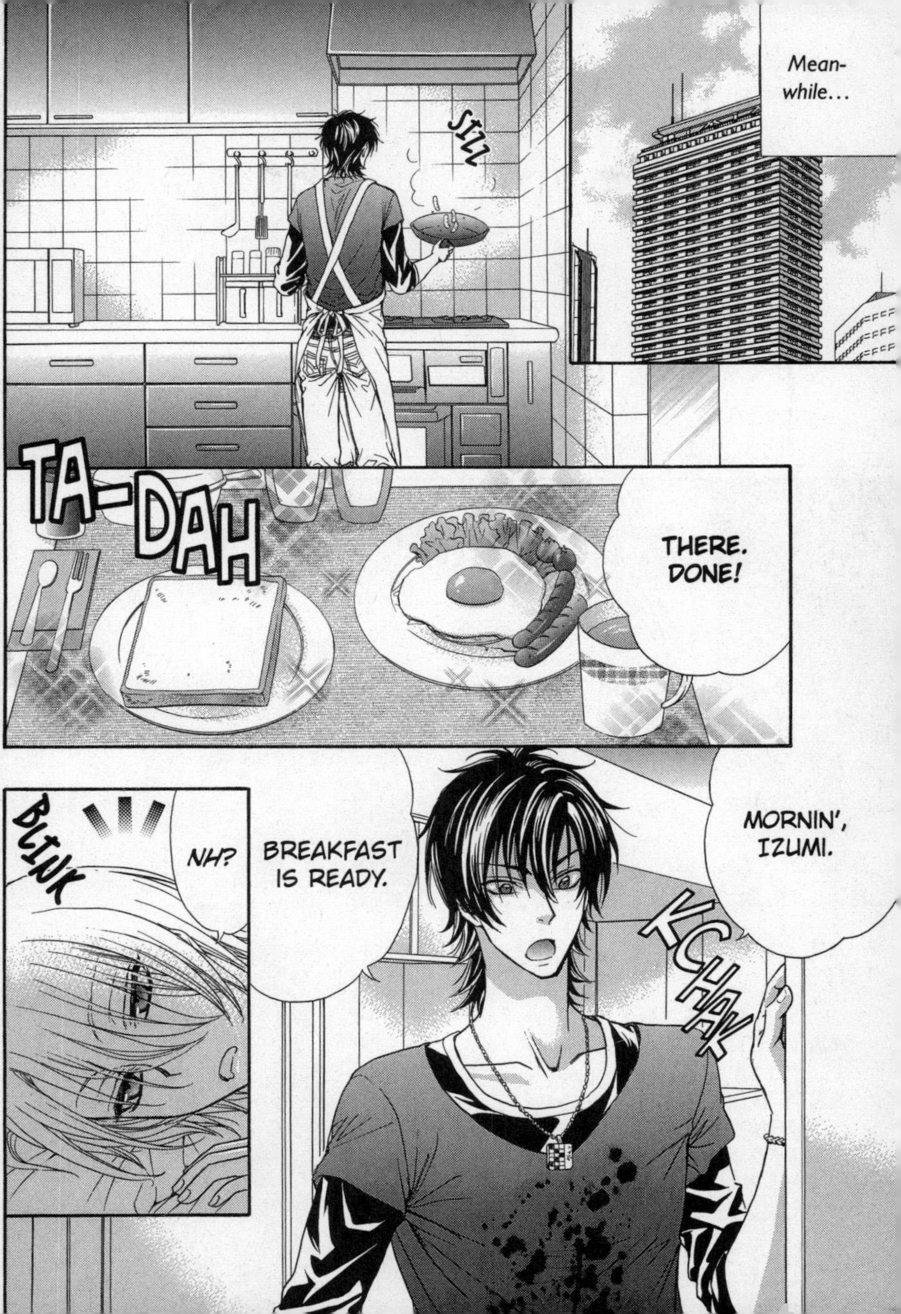

Mean-while…
SIZZ
TA-DAH
THERE. DONE!
MORNIN', IZUMI.
KCHAK
BREAKFAST IS READY.
NH?
BLINK

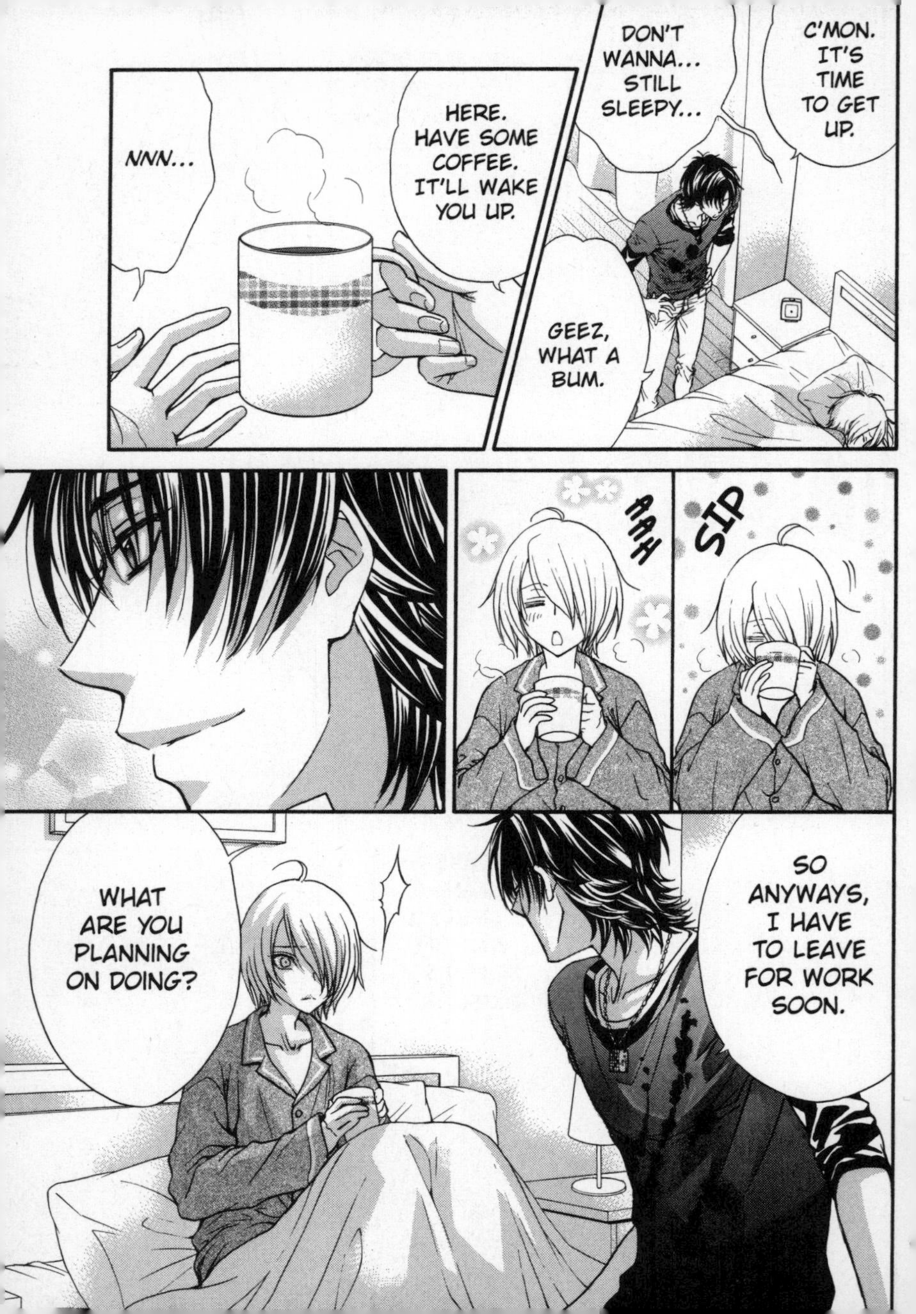
C'MON. IT'S TIME TO GET UP.
DON'T WANNA... STILL SLEEPY...
GEEZ, WHAT A BUM.
HERE. HAVE SOME COFFEE. IT'LL WAKE YOU UP.
NNN...
SIP
AAH
SO ANYWAYS, I HAVE TO LEAVE FOR WORK SOON.
WHAT ARE YOU PLANNING ON DOING?

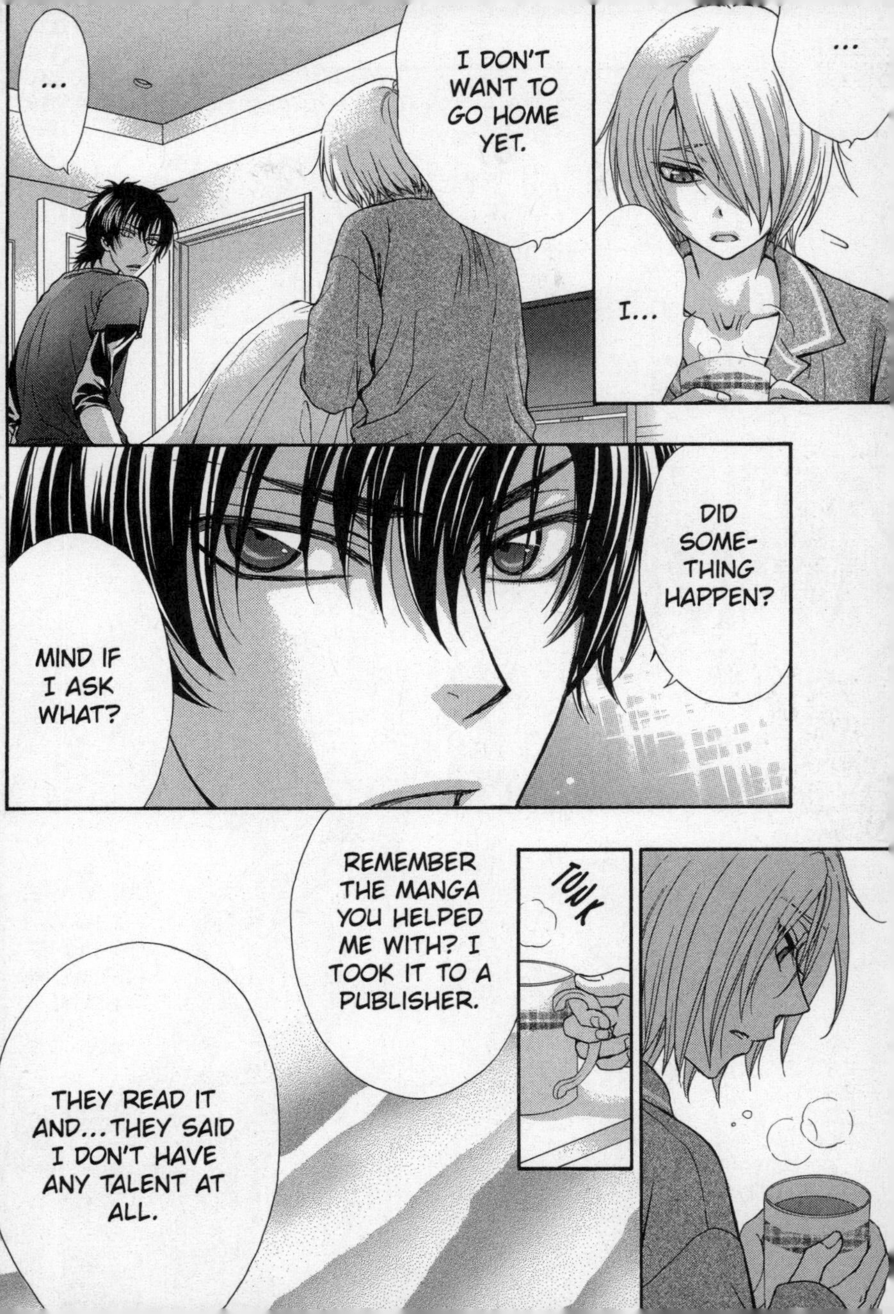
...
I...
I DON'T WANT TO GO HOME YET.
...
DID SOMETHING HAPPEN?
MIND IF I ASK WHAT?
TUNK
REMEMBER THE MANGA YOU HELPED ME WITH? I TOOK IT TO A PUBLISHER.
THEY READ IT AND...THEY SAID I DON'T HAVE ANY TALENT AT ALL.

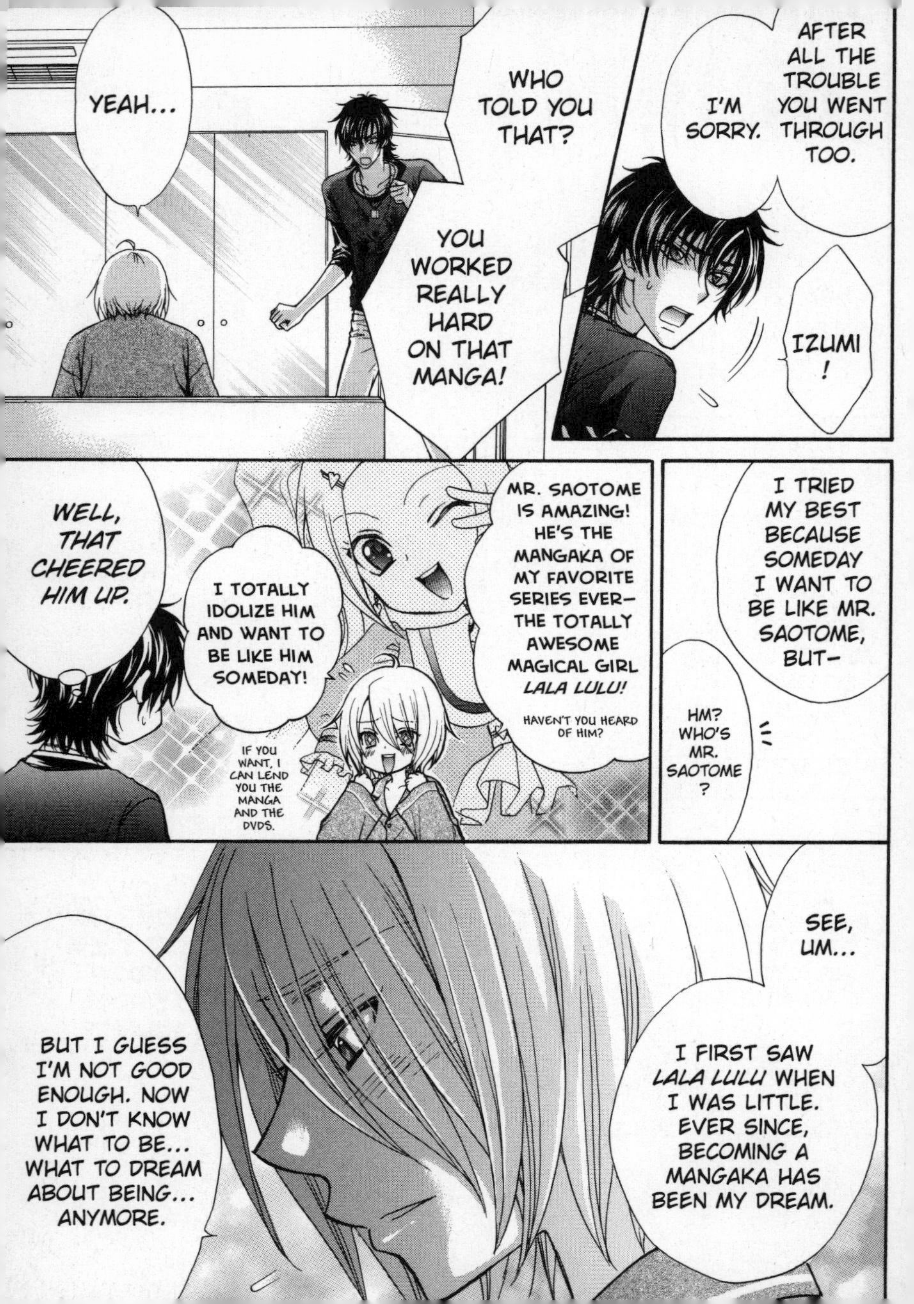

AFTER ALL THE TROUBLE YOU WENT THROUGH TOO.
I'M SORRY.
IZUMI!
WHO TOLD YOU THAT?
YOU WORKED REALLY HARD ON THAT MANGA!
YEAH...
I TRIED MY BEST BECAUSE SOMEDAY I WANT TO BE LIKE MR. SAOTOME, BUT—
HM? WHO'S MR. SAOTOME?
MR. SAOTOME IS AMAZING! HE'S THE MANGAKA OF MY FAVORITE SERIES EVER—THE TOTALLY AWESOME MAGICAL GIRL *LALA LULU*!
HAVEN'T YOU HEARD OF HIM?
I TOTALLY IDOLIZE HIM AND WANT TO BE LIKE HIM SOMEDAY!
IF YOU WANT, I CAN LEND YOU THE MANGA AND THE DVDS.
WELL, THAT CHEERED HIM UP.
SEE, UM...
I FIRST SAW *LALA LULU* WHEN I WAS LITTLE. EVER SINCE, BECOMING A MANGAKA HAS BEEN MY DREAM.
BUT I GUESS I'M NOT GOOD ENOUGH. NOW I DON'T KNOW WHAT TO BE... WHAT TO DREAM ABOUT BEING... ANYMORE.

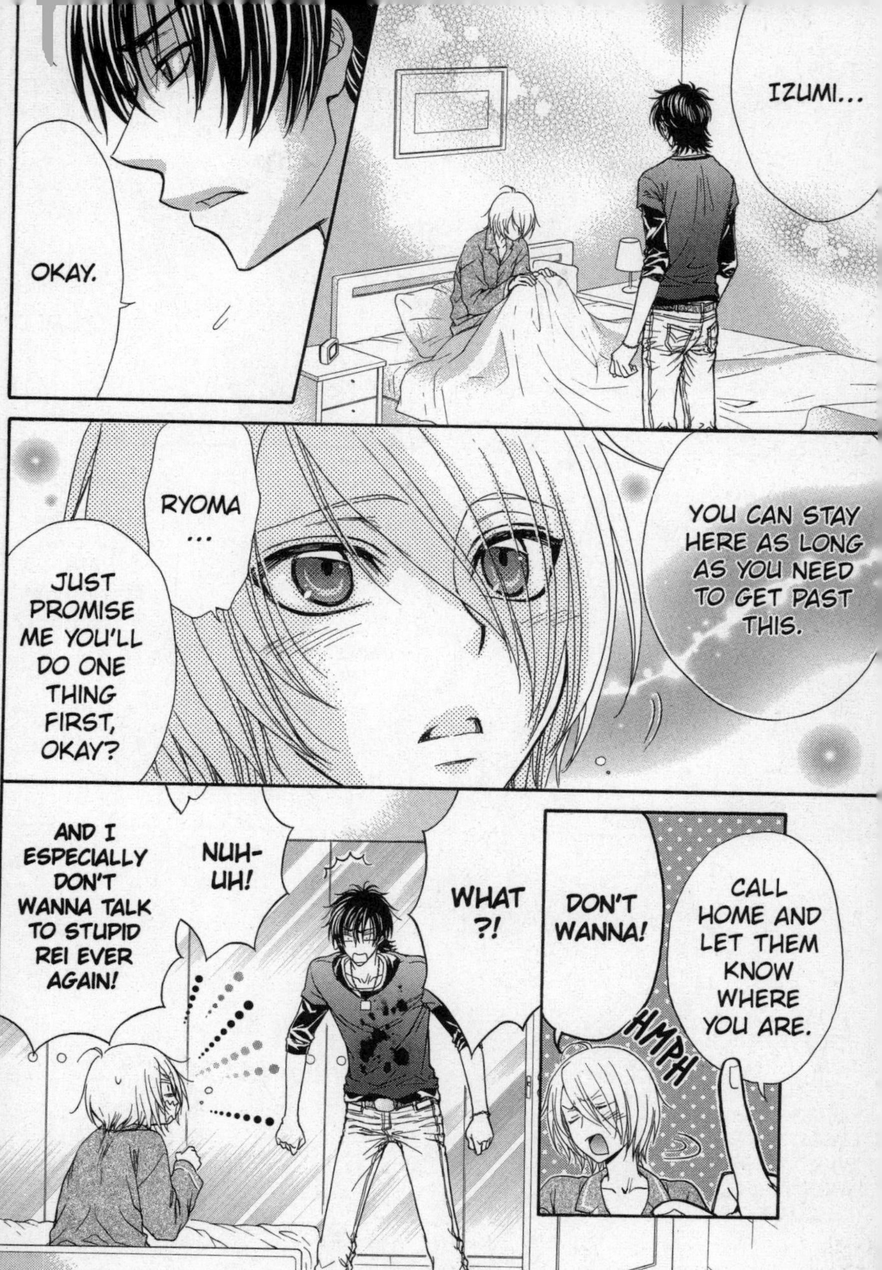
IZUMI...
OKAY.
YOU CAN STAY HERE AS LONG AS YOU NEED TO GET PAST THIS.
RYOMA ...
JUST PROMISE ME YOU'LL DO ONE THING FIRST, OKAY?
CALL HOME AND LET THEM KNOW WHERE YOU ARE.
DON'T WANNA!
HMPH
WHAT ?!
NUH-UH!
AND I ESPECIALLY DON'T WANNA TALK TO STUPID REI EVER AGAIN!

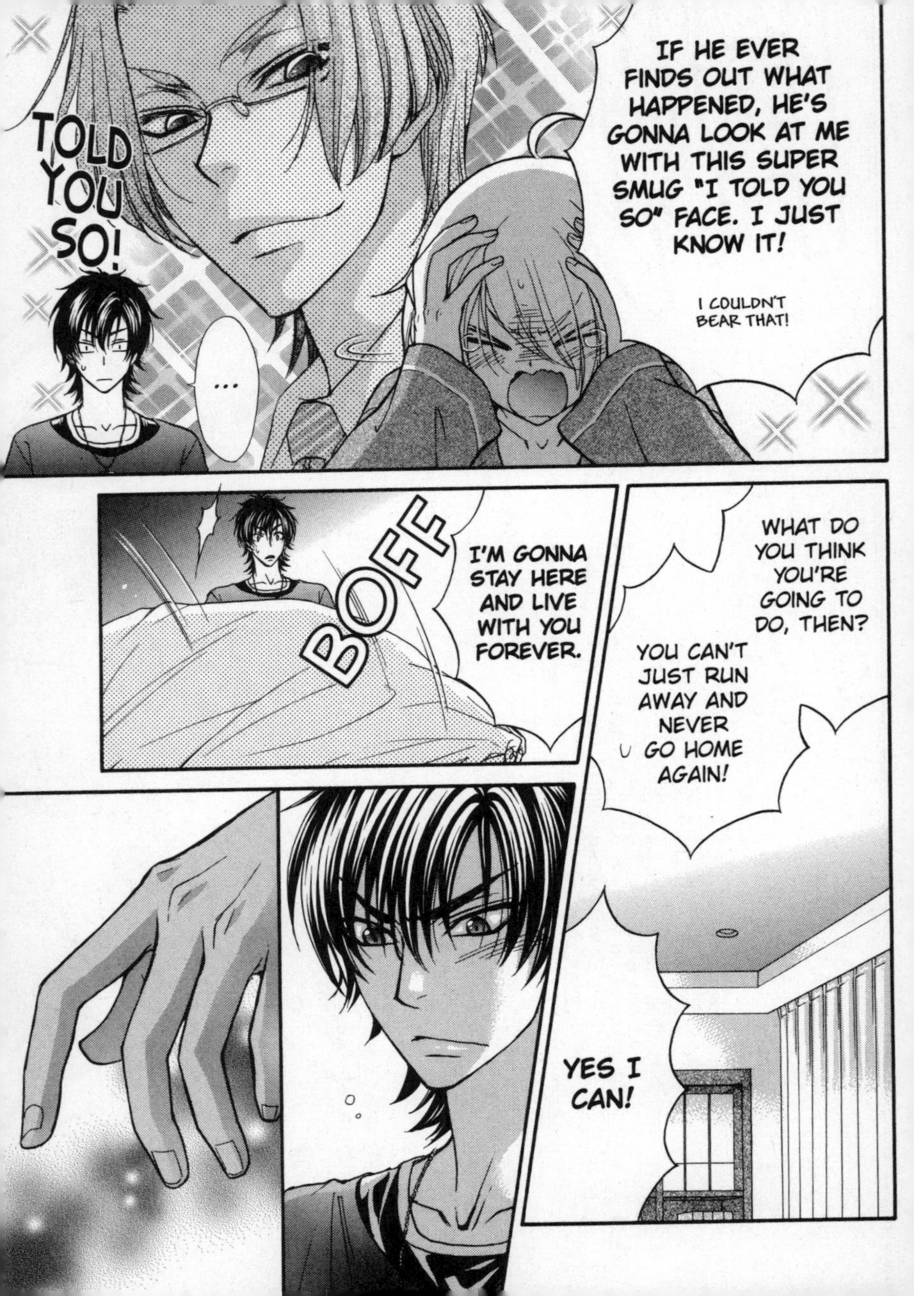
IF HE EVER FINDS OUT WHAT HAPPENED, HE'S GONNA LOOK AT ME WITH THIS SUPER SMUG "I TOLD YOU SO" FACE. I JUST KNOW IT!
I COULDN'T BEAR THAT!
TOLD YOU SO!
...
WHAT DO YOU THINK YOU'RE GOING TO DO, THEN?
YOU CAN'T JUST RUN AWAY AND NEVER GO HOME AGAIN!
YES I CAN!
I'M GONNA STAY HERE AND LIVE WITH YOU FOREVER.
BOFF

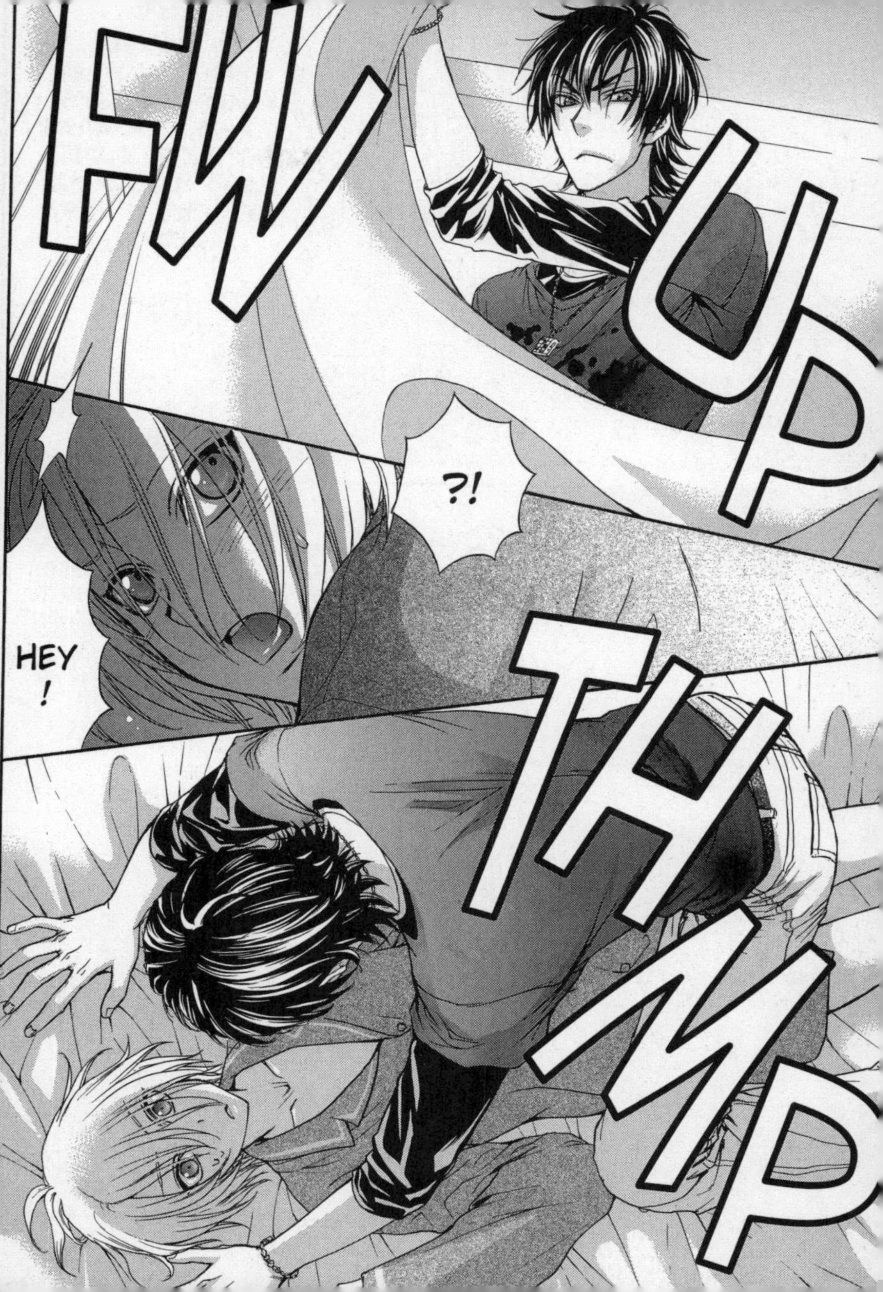
FWUP
?!
HEY !
THMP

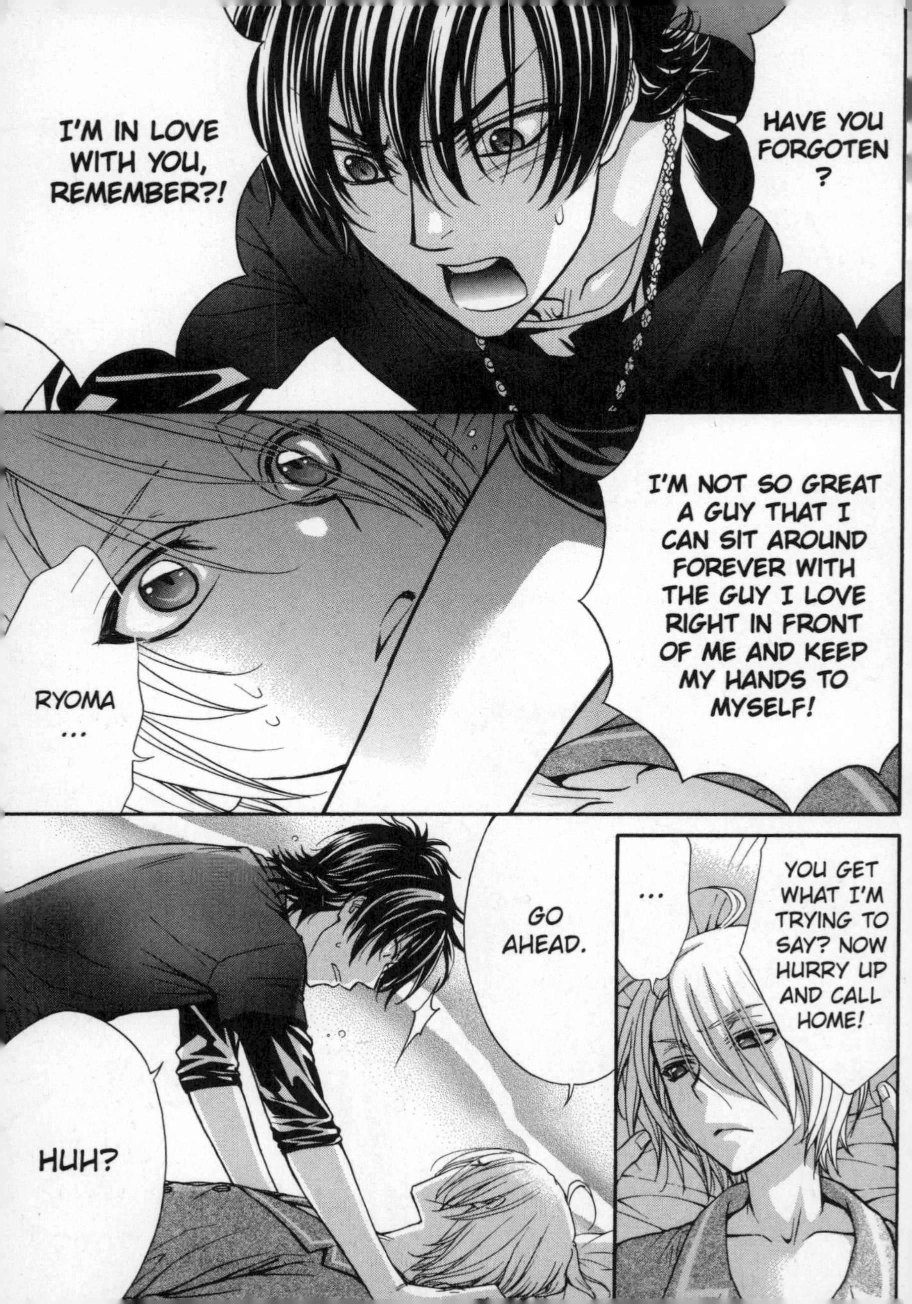
HAVE YOU FORGOTEN ?
I'M IN LOVE WITH YOU, REMEMBER?!
I'M NOT SO GREAT A GUY THAT I CAN SIT AROUND FOREVER WITH THE GUY I LOVE RIGHT IN FRONT OF ME AND KEEP MY HANDS TO MYSELF!
RYOMA ...
YOU GET WHAT I'M TRYING TO SAY? NOW HURRY UP AND CALL HOME!
...
GO AHEAD.
HUH?

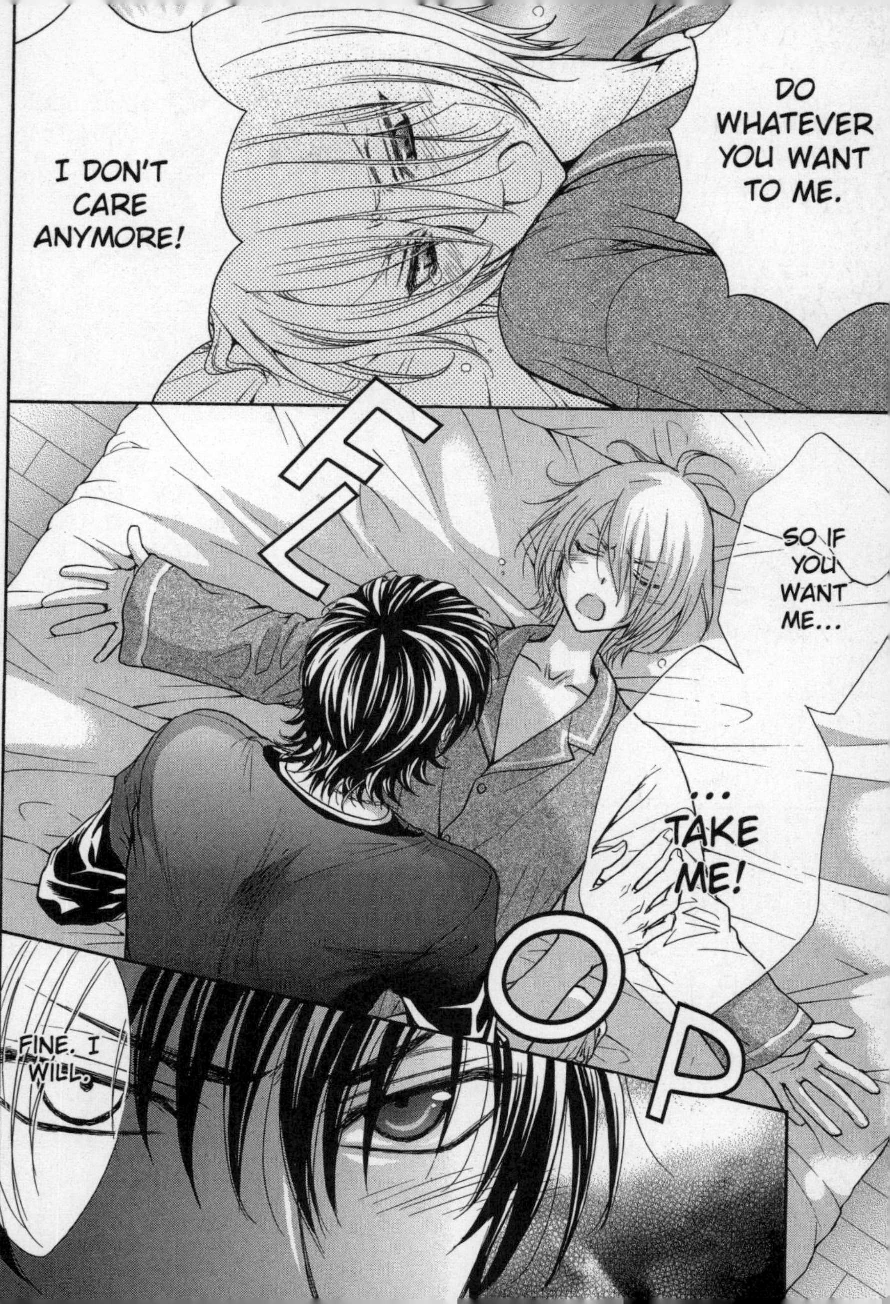
DO WHATEVER YOU WANT TO ME.
I DON'T CARE ANYMORE!
FLOP
SO IF YOU WANT ME...
...TAKE ME!
FINE. I WILL.

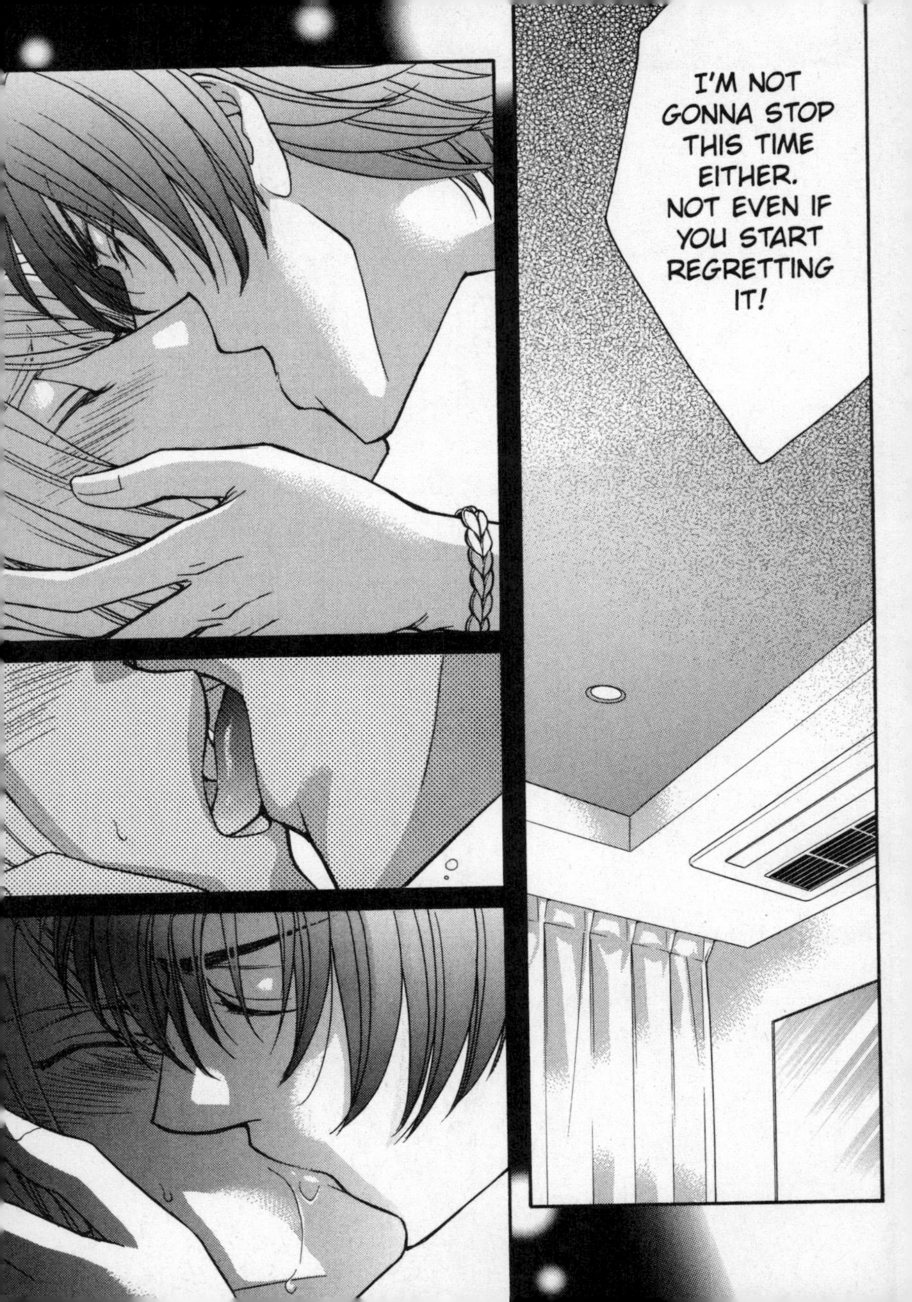
I'M NOT GONNA STOP THIS TIME EITHER. NOT EVEN IF YOU START REGRETTING IT!

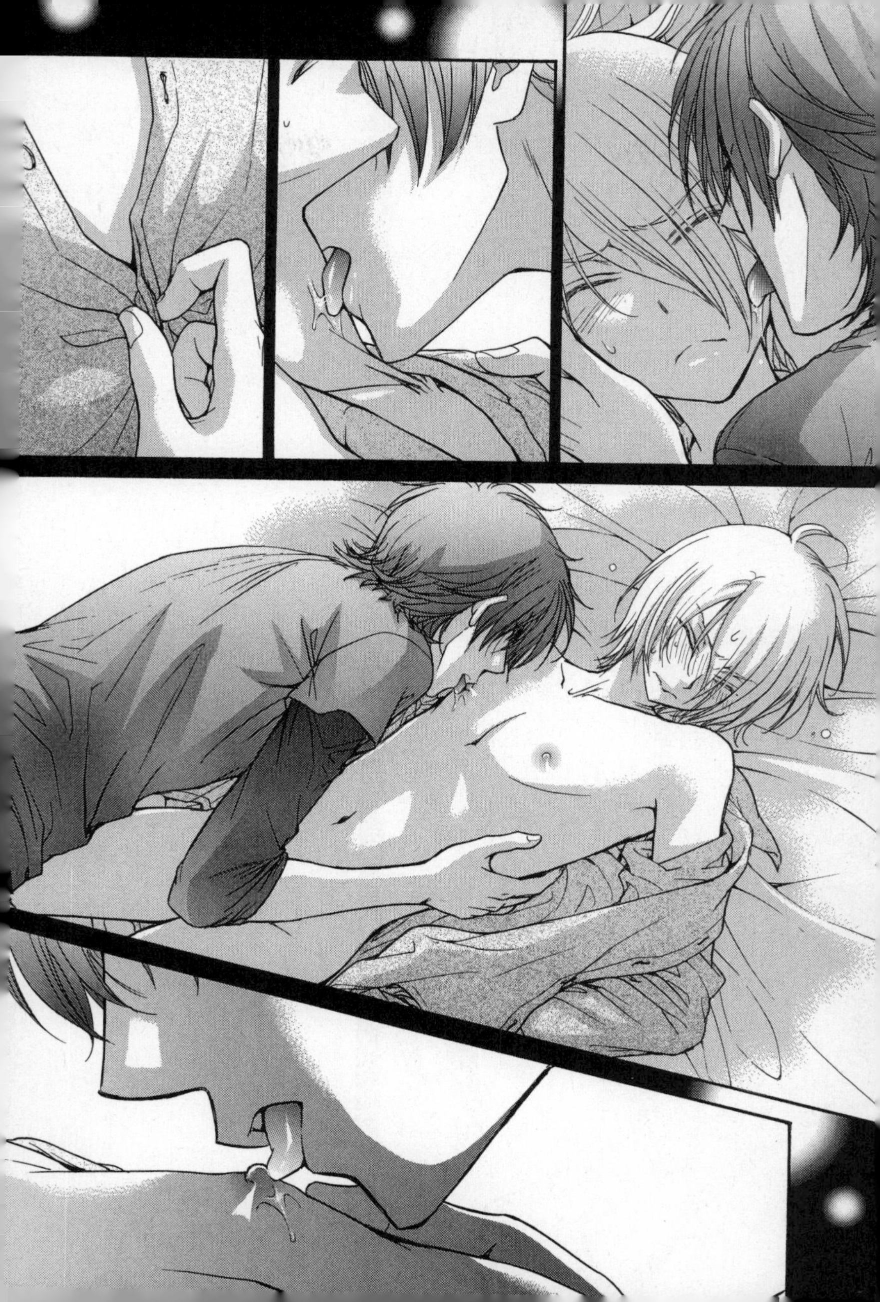

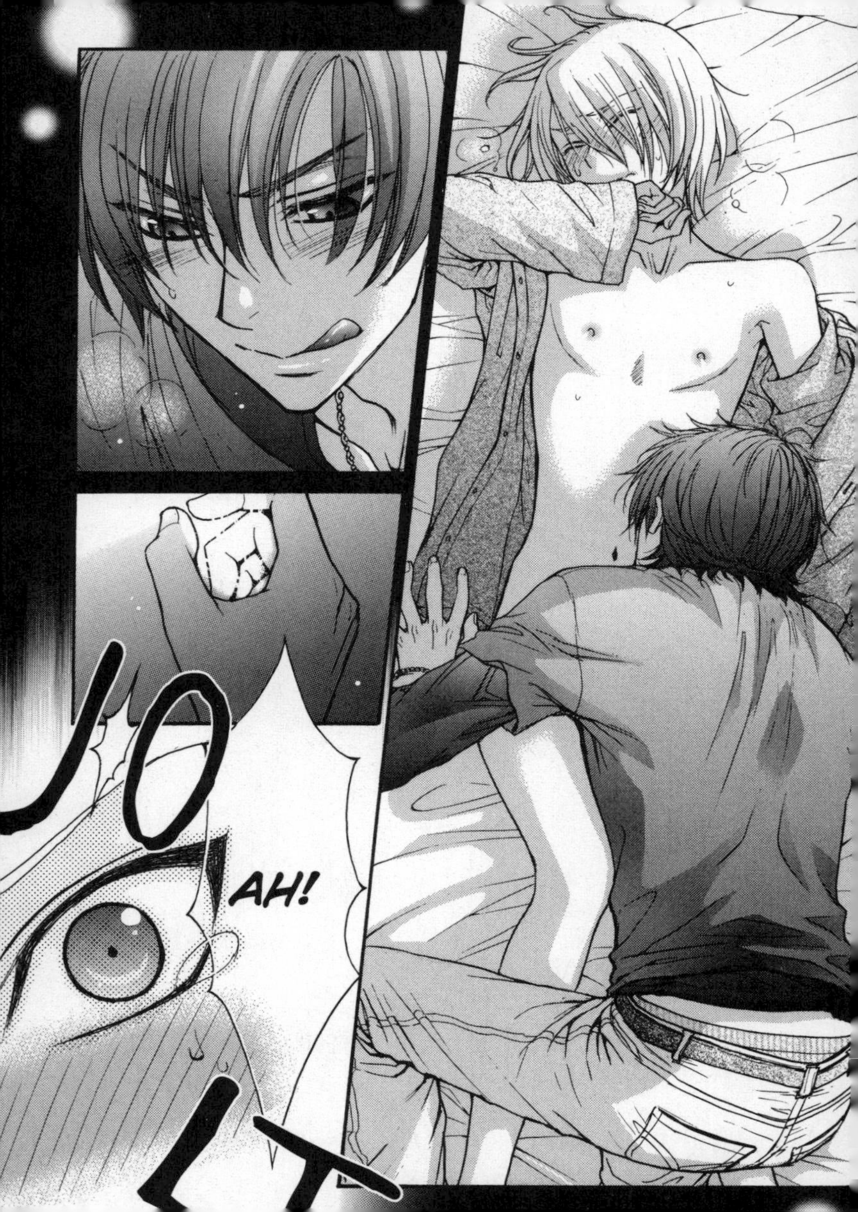
AH!

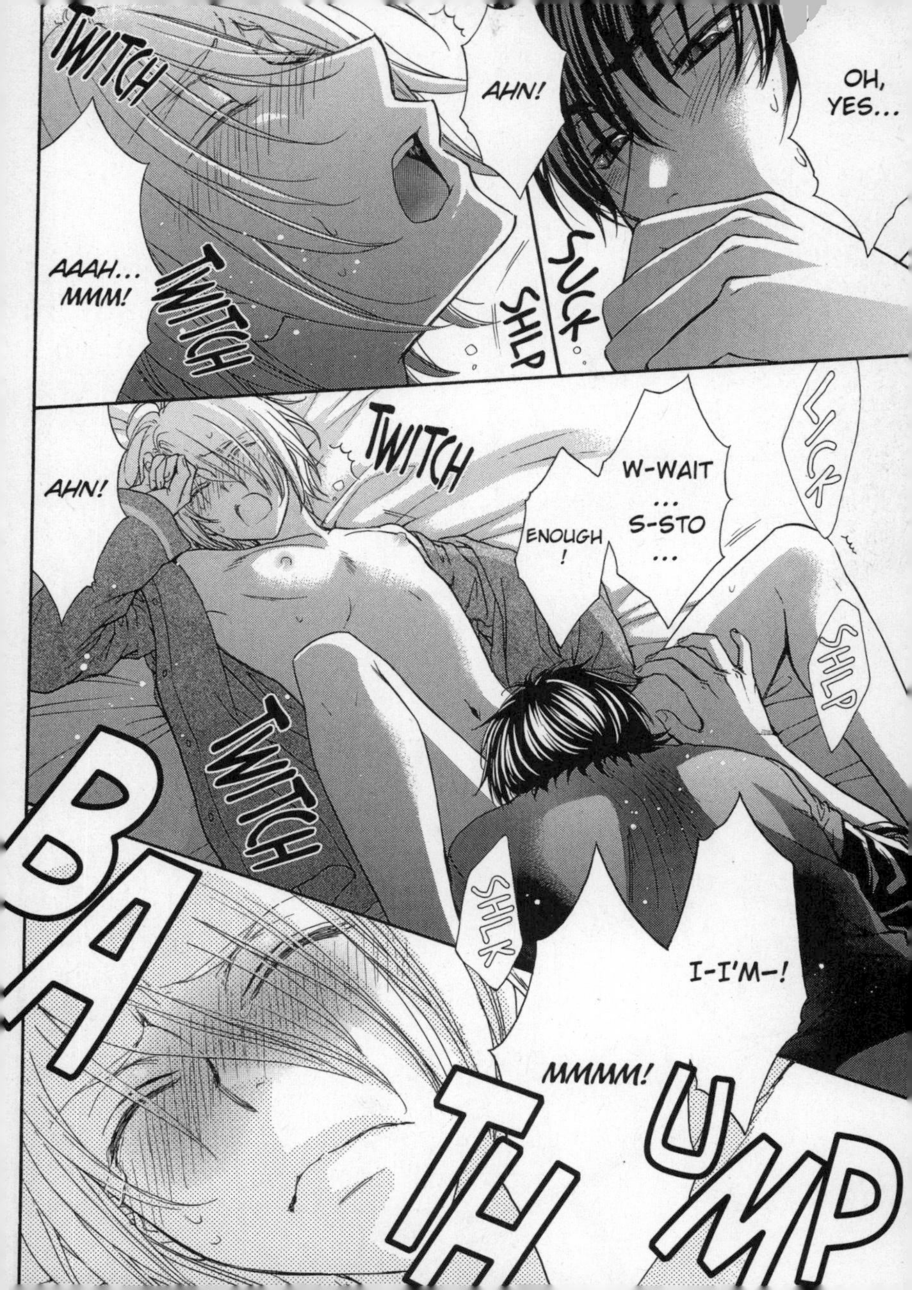
OH, YES...
TWITCH
AHN!
SUCK
SHLP
TWITCH
AAAH... MMM!
LICK
W-WAIT... S-STO...
ENOUGH!
TWITCH
AHN!
SHLP
TWITCH
SHLK
I-I'M-!
MMMM!
BA
THUMP

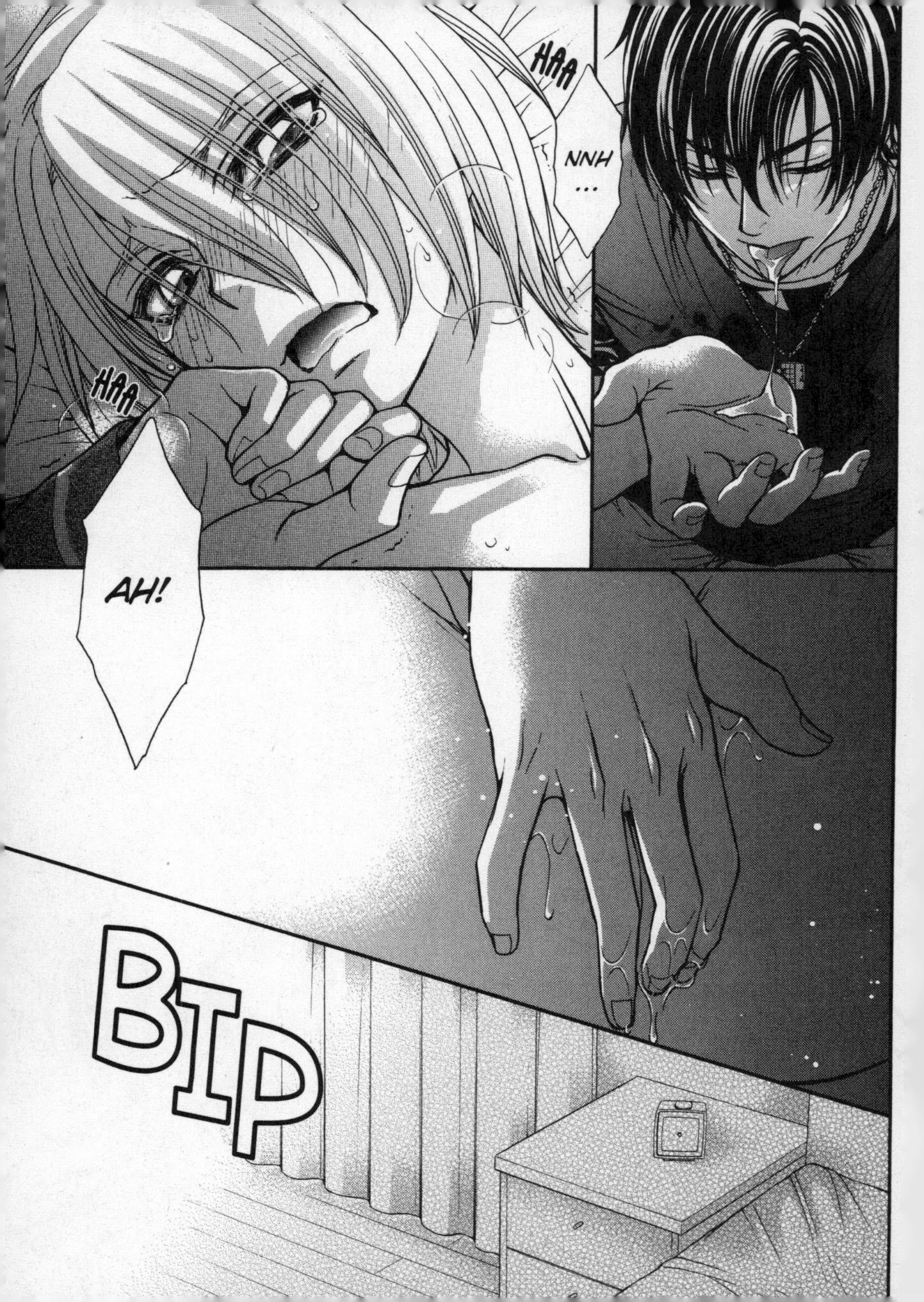
HAA
NNH ...
HAA
AH!
BIP

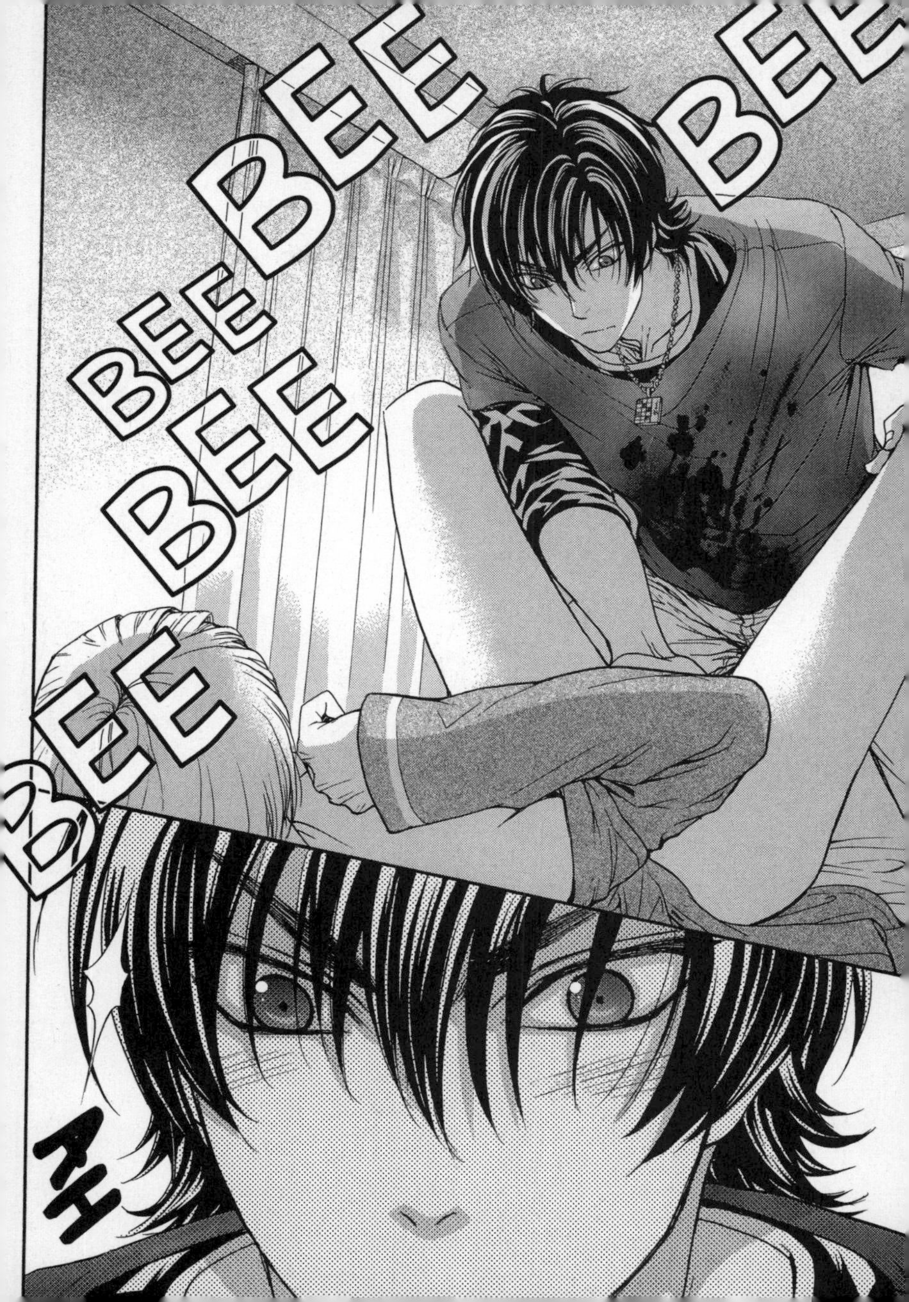
BEE
BEE
BEE
BEE
BEE
BEE
AH

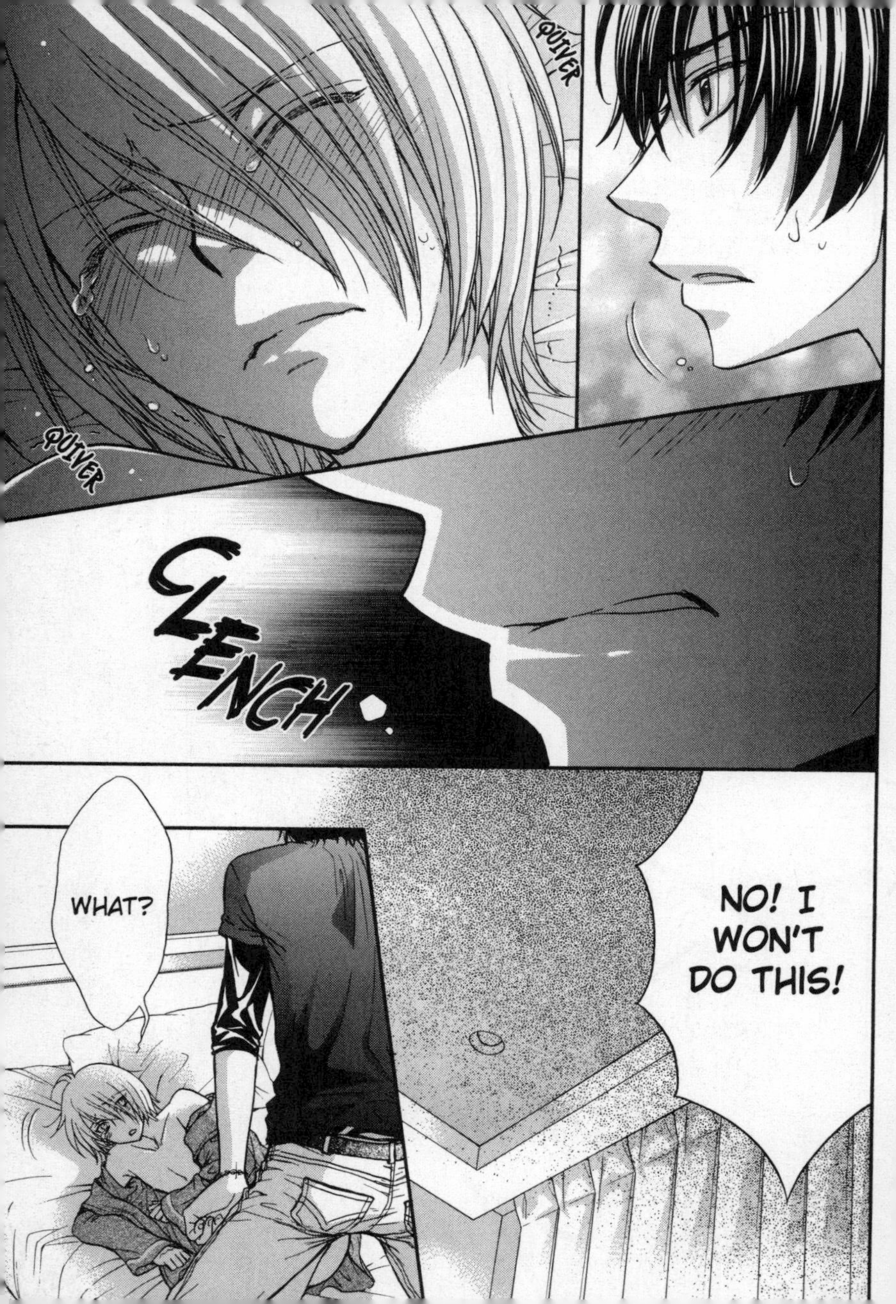
QUIVER
QUIVER
CLENCH
NO! I WON'T DO THIS!
WHAT?

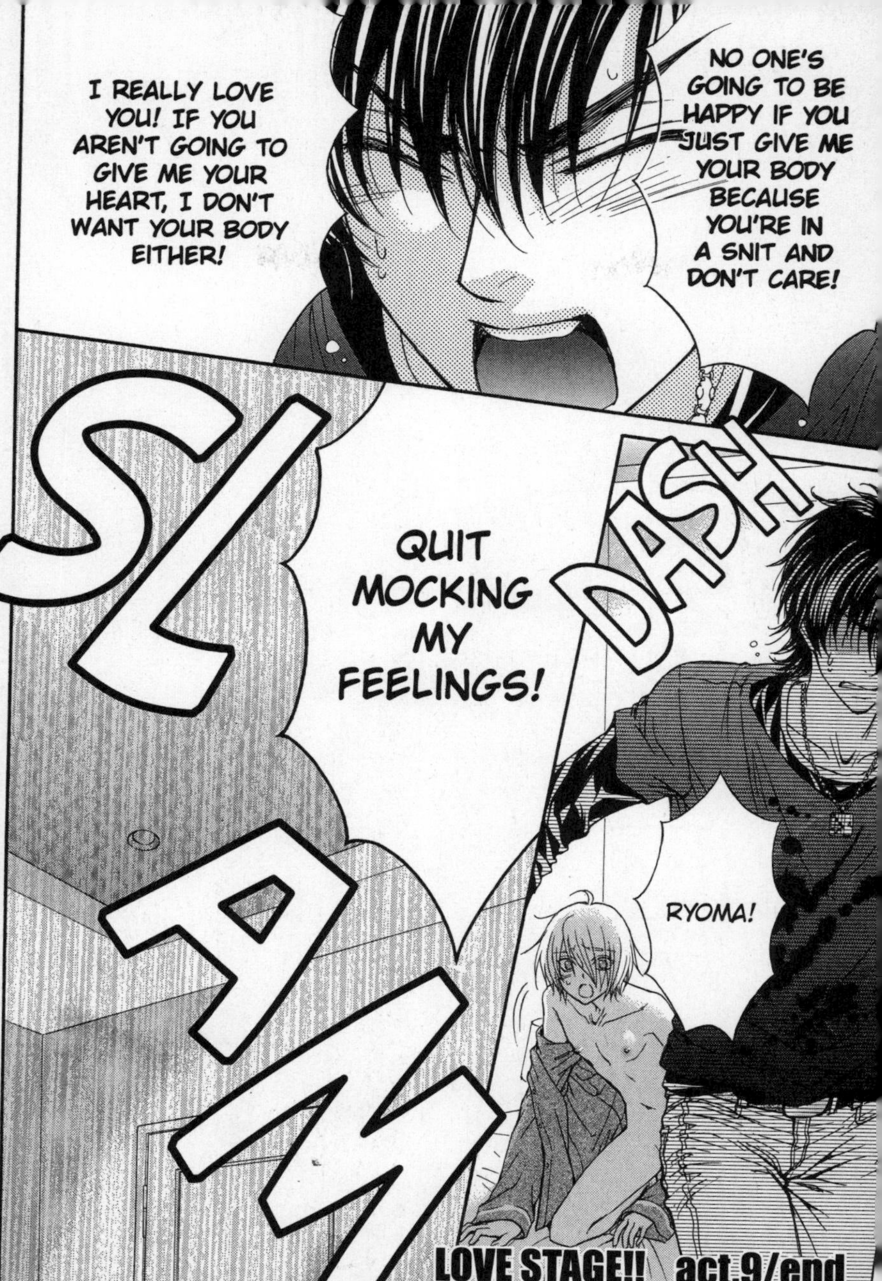
NO ONE'S GOING TO BE HAPPY IF YOU JUST GIVE ME YOUR BODY BECAUSE YOU'RE IN A SNIT AND DON'T CARE!
I REALLY LOVE YOU! IF YOU AREN'T GOING TO GIVE ME YOUR HEART, I DON'T WANT YOUR BODY EITHER!
DASH
RYOMA!
QUIT MOCKING MY FEELINGS!
SLAM
LOVE STAGE!! act.9/end

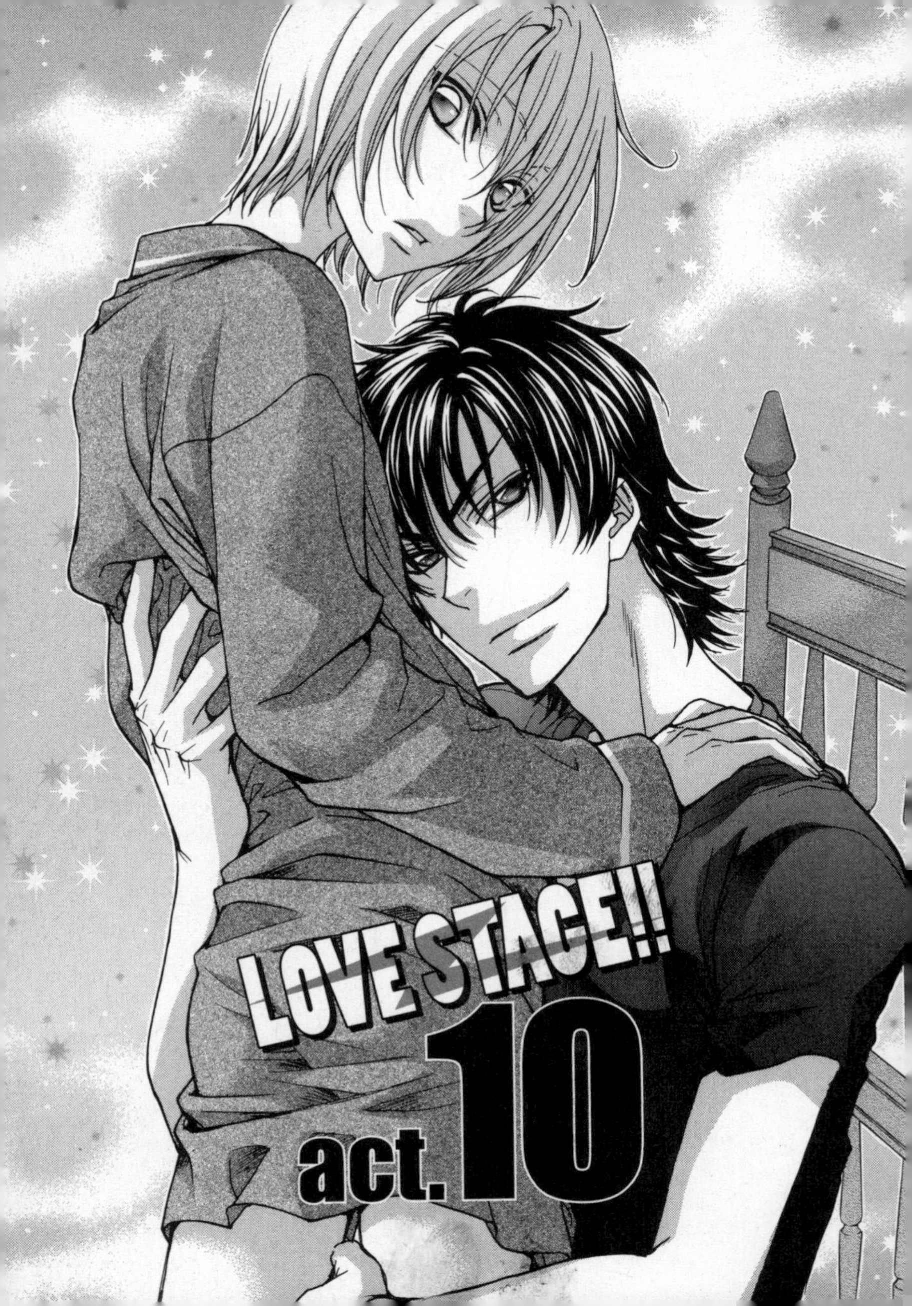
LOVE STAGE!!
act.10

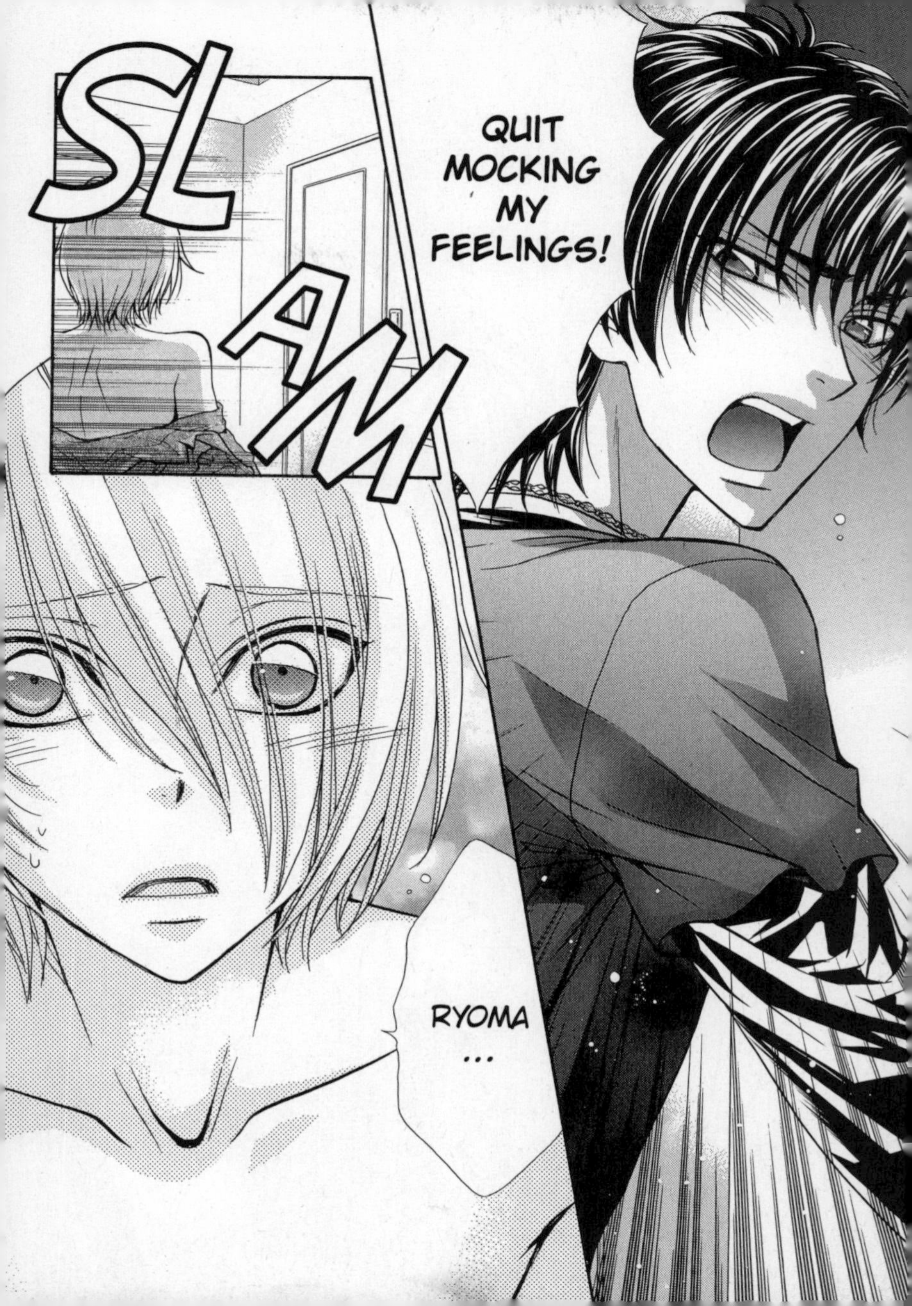
QUIT MOCKING MY FEELINGS!
SLAM
RYOMA ...

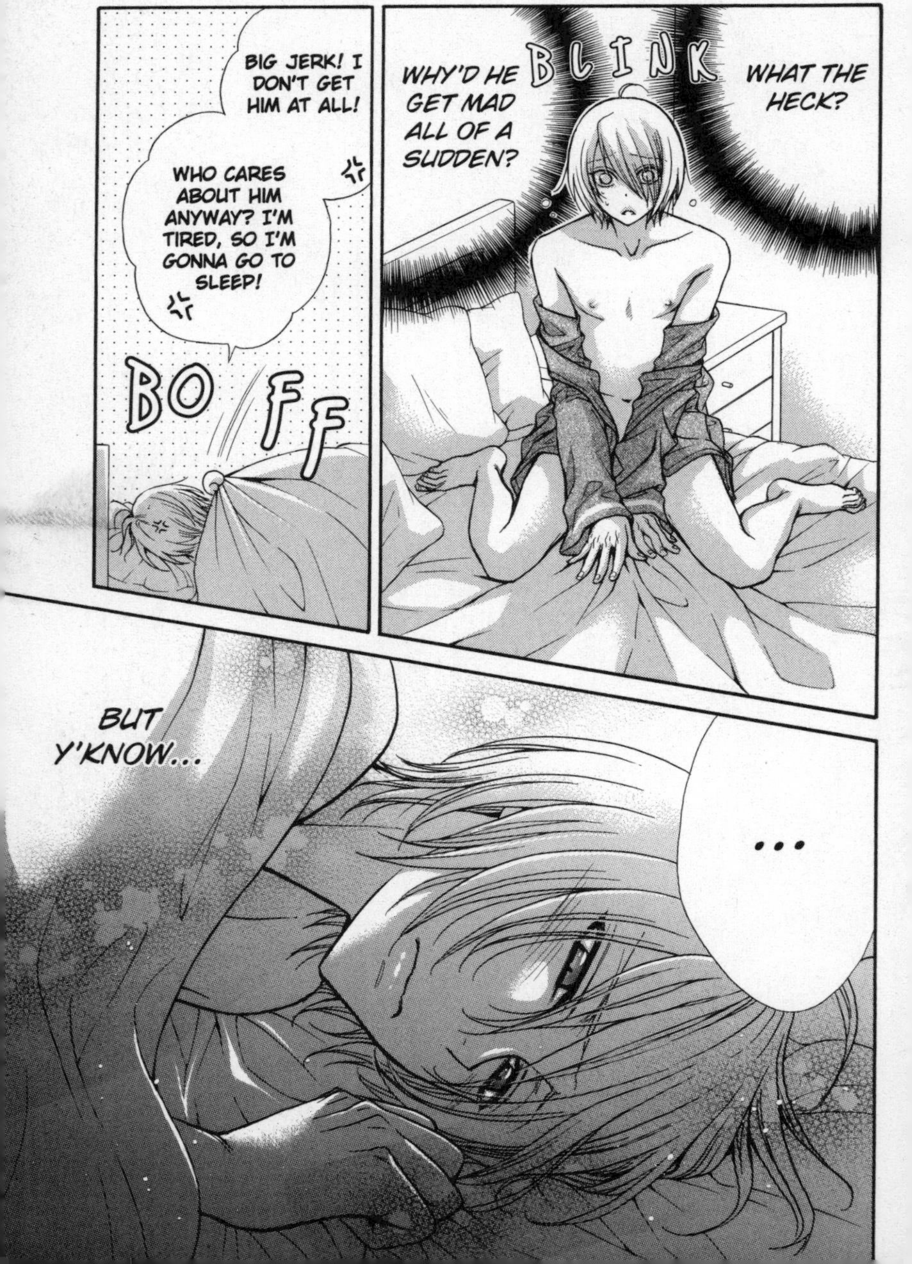
WHAT THE HECK?
BLINK
WHY'D HE GET MAD ALL OF A SUDDEN?
BIG JERK! I DON'T GET HIM AT ALL!
WHO CARES ABOUT HIM ANYWAY? I'M TIRED, SO I'M GONNA GO TO SLEEP!
BOFF
BUT Y'KNOW...
...

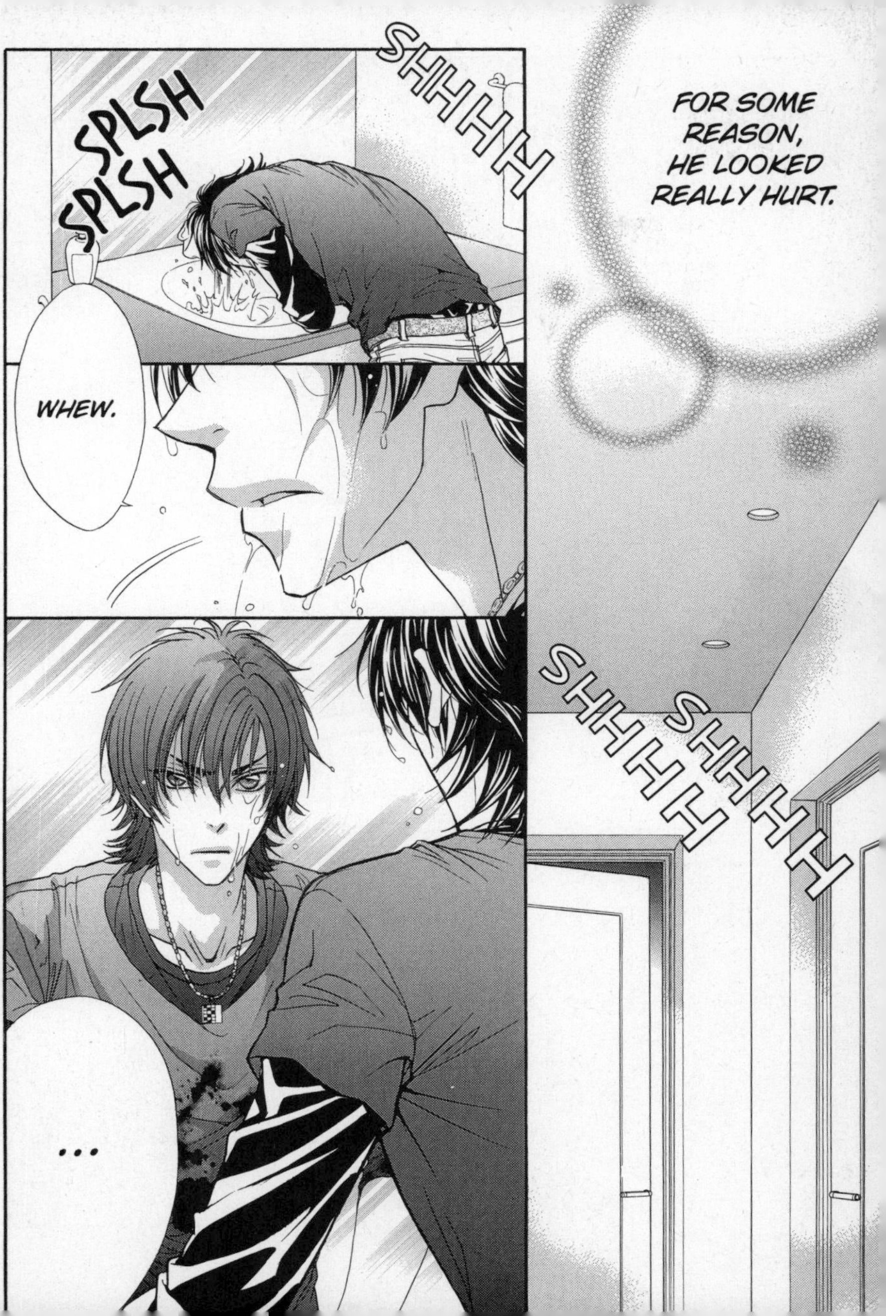
FOR SOME REASON, HE LOOKED REALLY HURT.
SHHHHH
SHHHHH
SHHHHH
SPLSH SPLSH
WHEW.
...

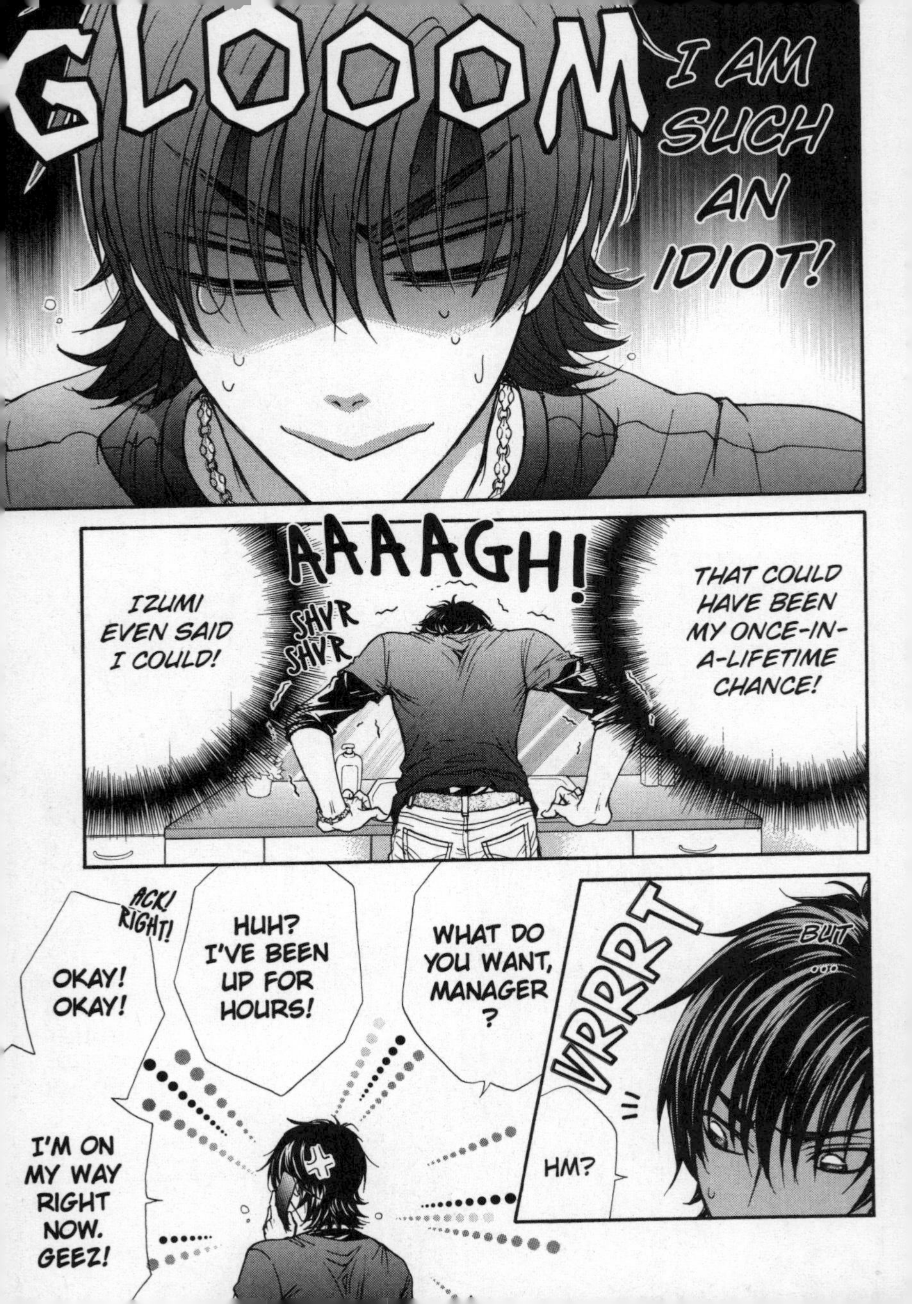
GLOOOM
I AM SUCH AN IDIOT!
AAAAGH!
SHVR SHVR
THAT COULD HAVE BEEN MY ONCE-IN-A-LIFETIME CHANCE!
IZUMI EVEN SAID I COULD!
BUT...
VRRRT
HM?
WHAT DO YOU WANT, MANAGER?
HUH? I'VE BEEN UP FOR HOURS!
ACK! RIGHT!
OKAY! OKAY!
I'M ON MY WAY RIGHT NOW. GEEZ!

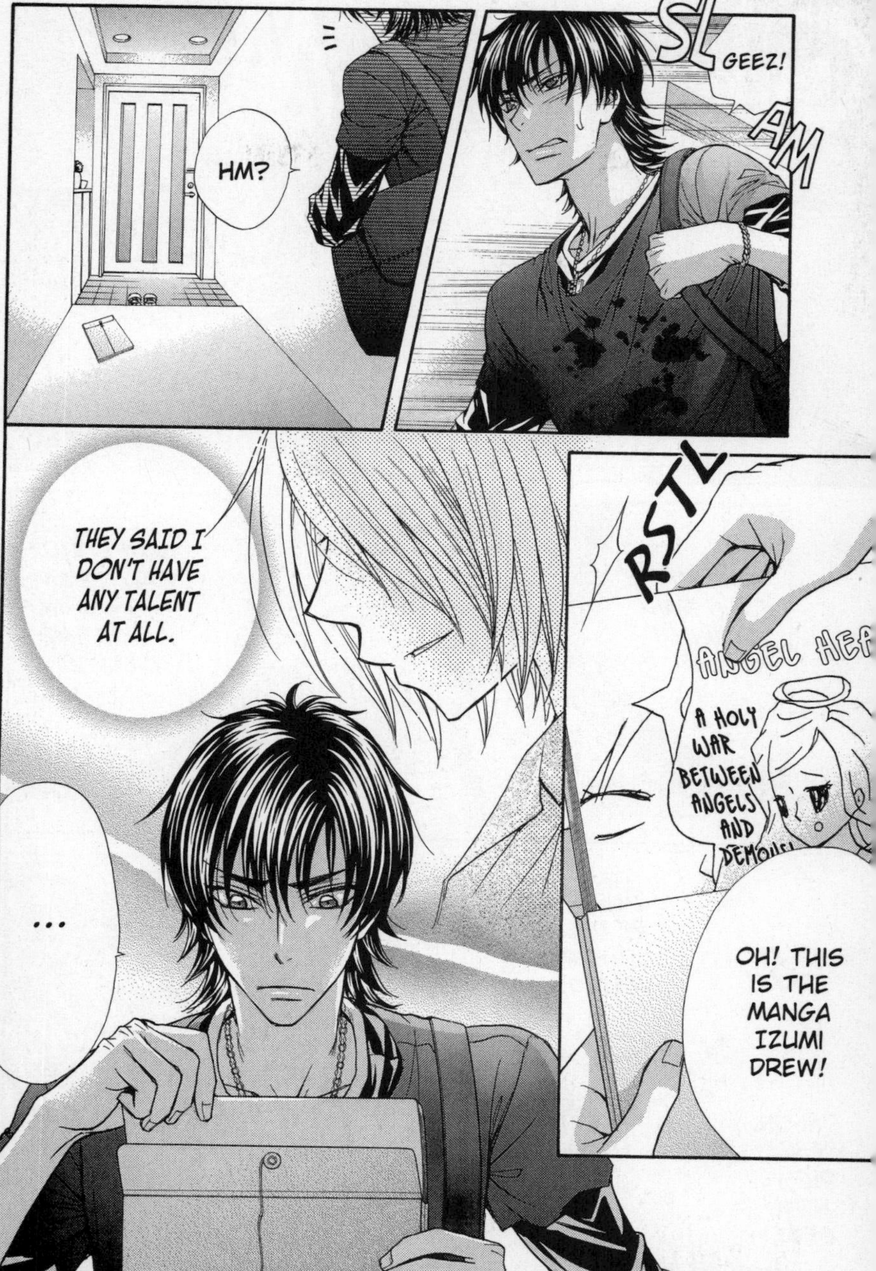
SLAM
GEEZ!
HM?
RSTL
ANGEL HEA
A HOLY WAR BETWEEN ANGELS AND DEMONS!
OH! THIS IS THE MANGA IZUMI DREW!
THEY SAID I DON'T HAVE ANY TALENT AT ALL.
...

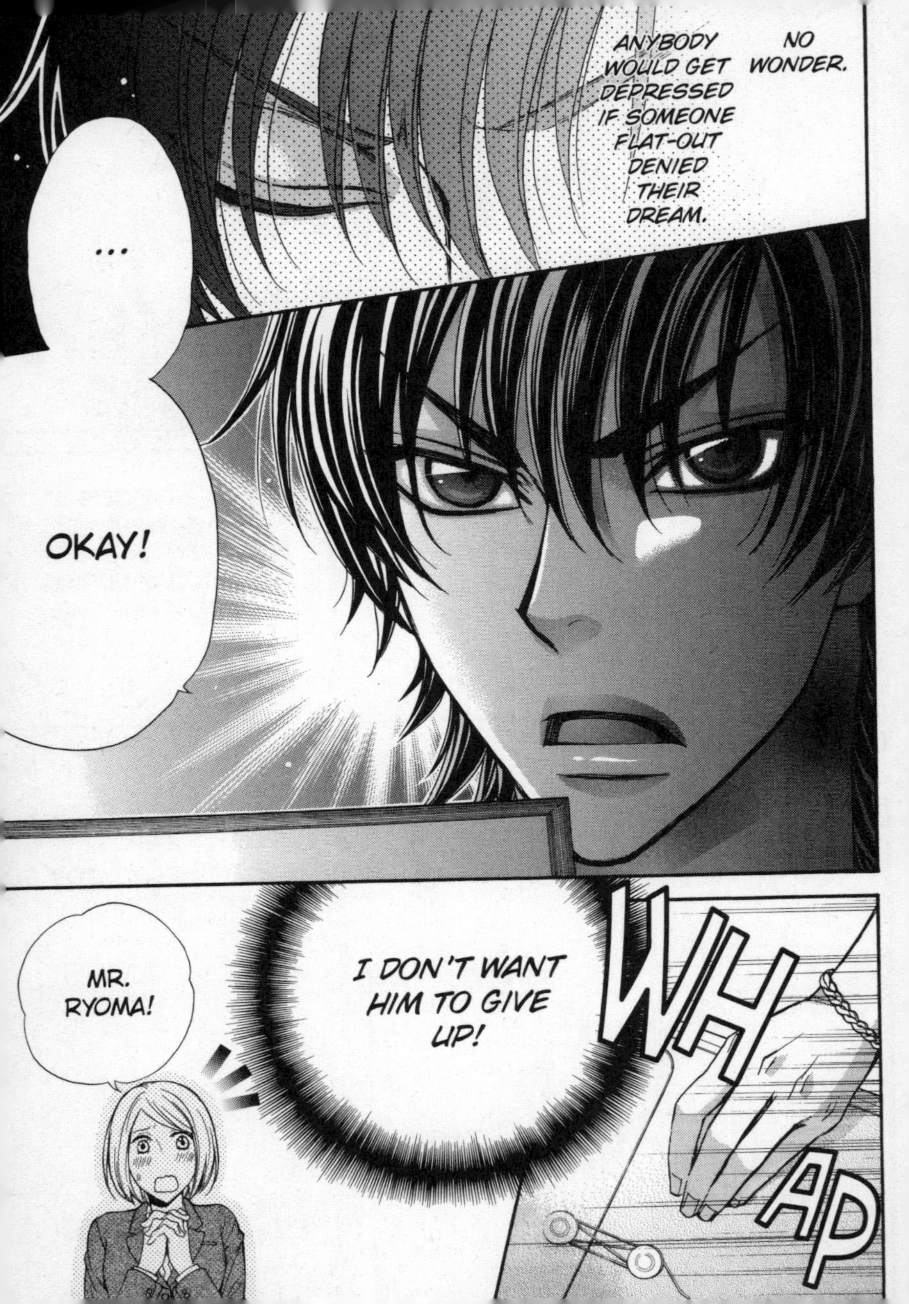
NO WONDER.
ANYBODY WOULD GET DEPRESSED IF SOMEONE FLAT-OUT DENIED THEIR DREAM.
...
OKAY!
WHAP
I DON'T WANT HIM TO GIVE UP!
MR. RYOMA!

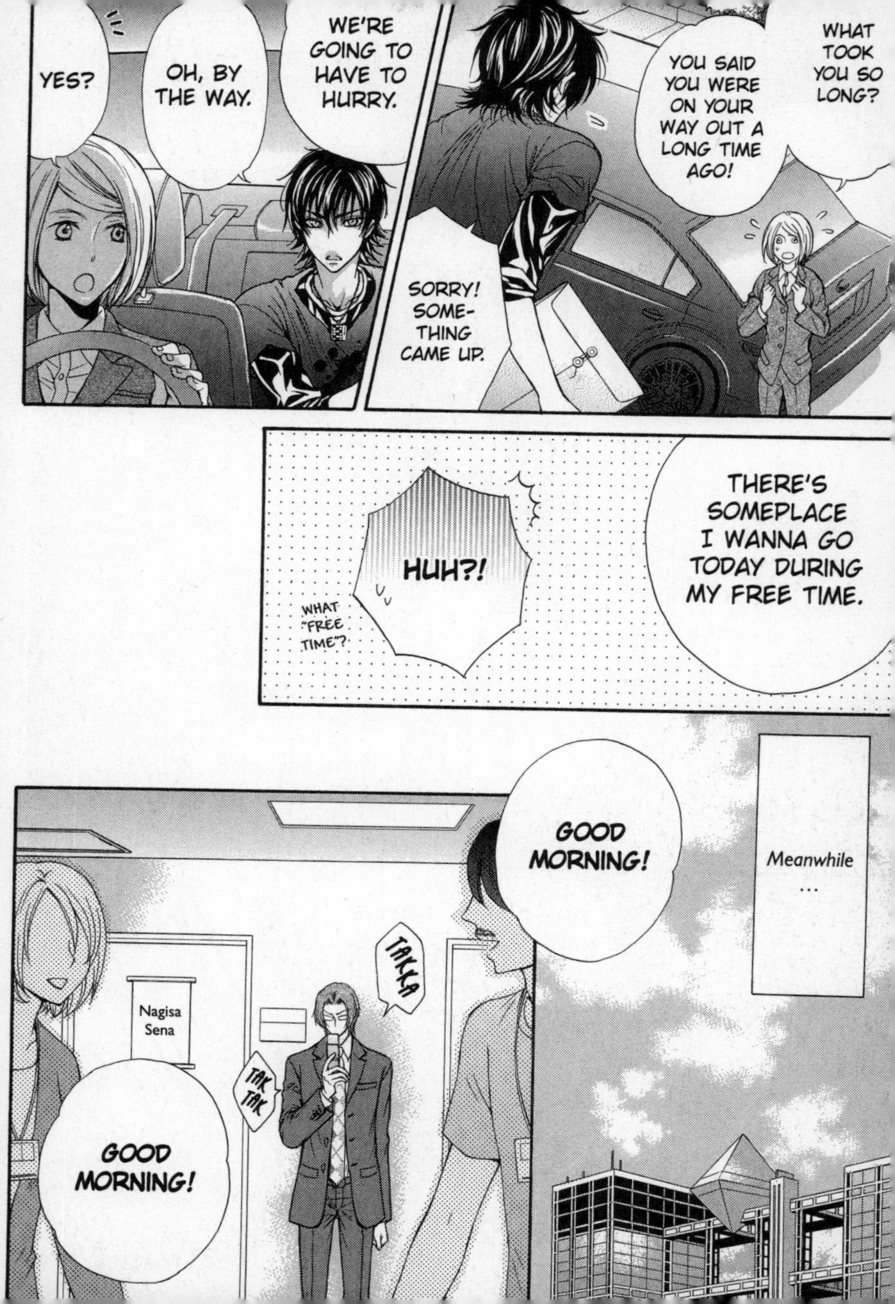
WHAT TOOK YOU SO LONG?
YOU SAID YOU WERE ON YOUR WAY OUT A LONG TIME AGO!
SORRY! SOME-THING CAME UP.
WE'RE GOING TO HAVE TO HURRY.
OH, BY THE WAY.
YES?
THERE'S SOMEPLACE I WANNA GO TODAY DURING MY FREE TIME.
HUH?!
WHAT "FREE TIME"?
Meanwhile ...
GOOD MORNING!
TAKKA
Nagisa Sena
TAK TAK
GOOD MORNING!

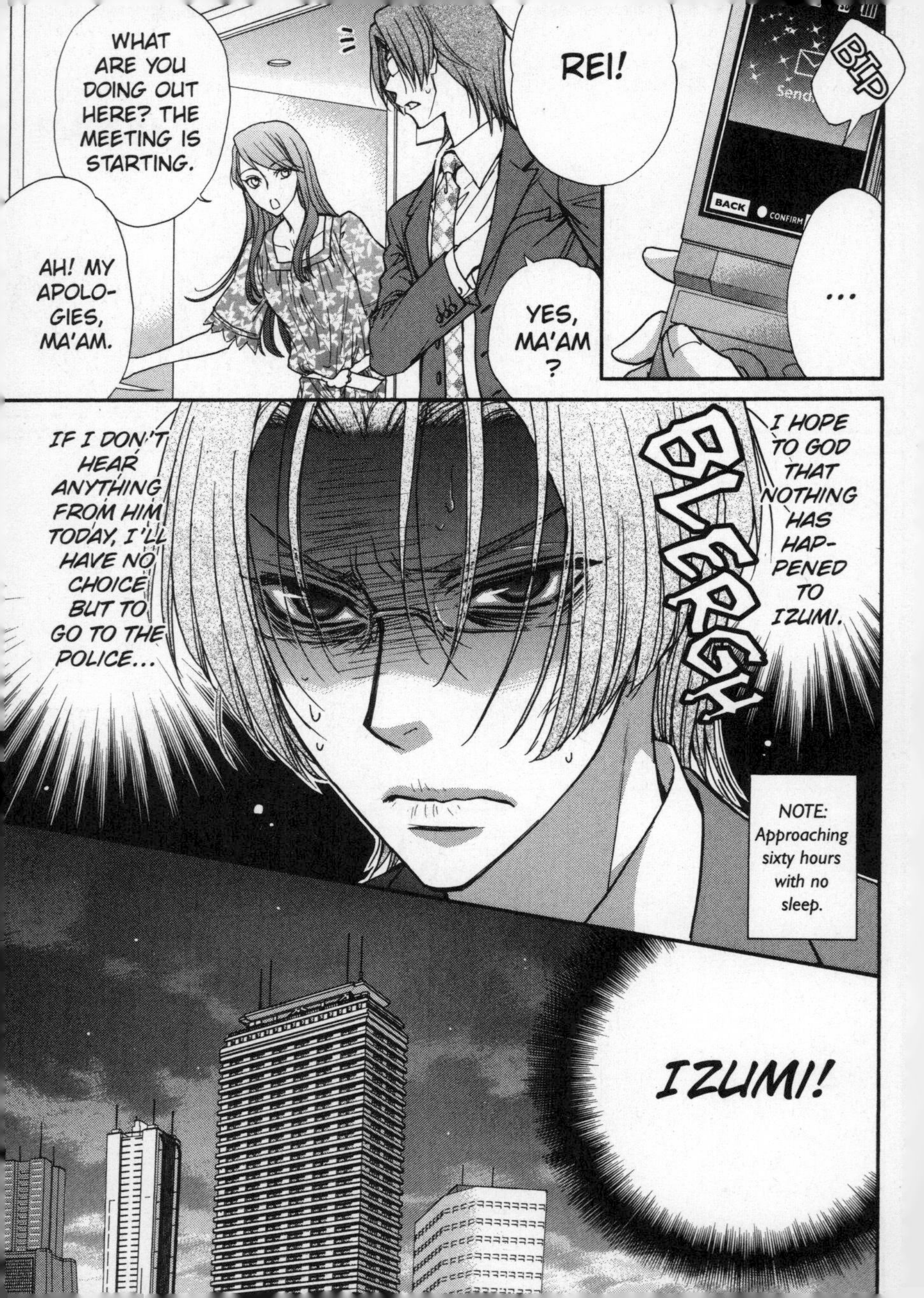
BIP
Send
BACK
CONFIRM
...
REI!
WHAT ARE YOU DOING OUT HERE? THE MEETING IS STARTING.
YES, MA'AM?
AH! MY APOLOGIES, MA'AM.
I HOPE TO GOD THAT NOTHING HAS HAPPENED TO IZUMI.
BLEEGH
IF I DON'T HEAR ANYTHING FROM HIM TODAY, I'LL HAVE NO CHOICE BUT TO GO TO THE POLICE...
NOTE: Approaching sixty hours with no sleep.
IZUMI!

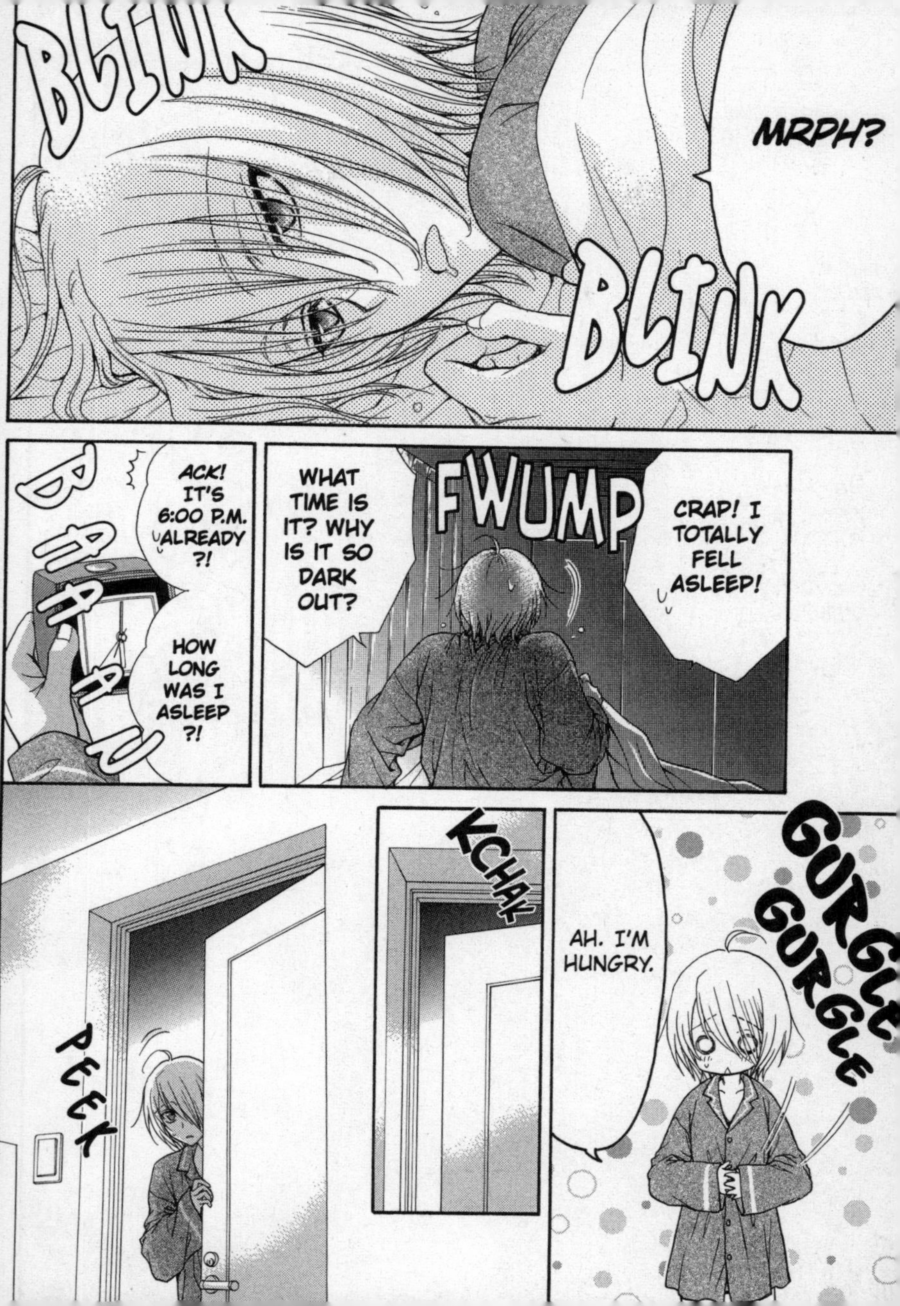
MRPH?
BLINK
BLINK
CRAP! I TOTALLY FELL ASLEEP!
FWUMP
WHAT TIME IS IT? WHY IS IT SO DARK OUT?
ACK! IT'S 6:00 P.M. ALREADY ?!
HOW LONG WAS I ASLEEP ?!
BAAAN
GURGLE GURGLE
AH. I'M HUNGRY.
KCHAK
PEEK

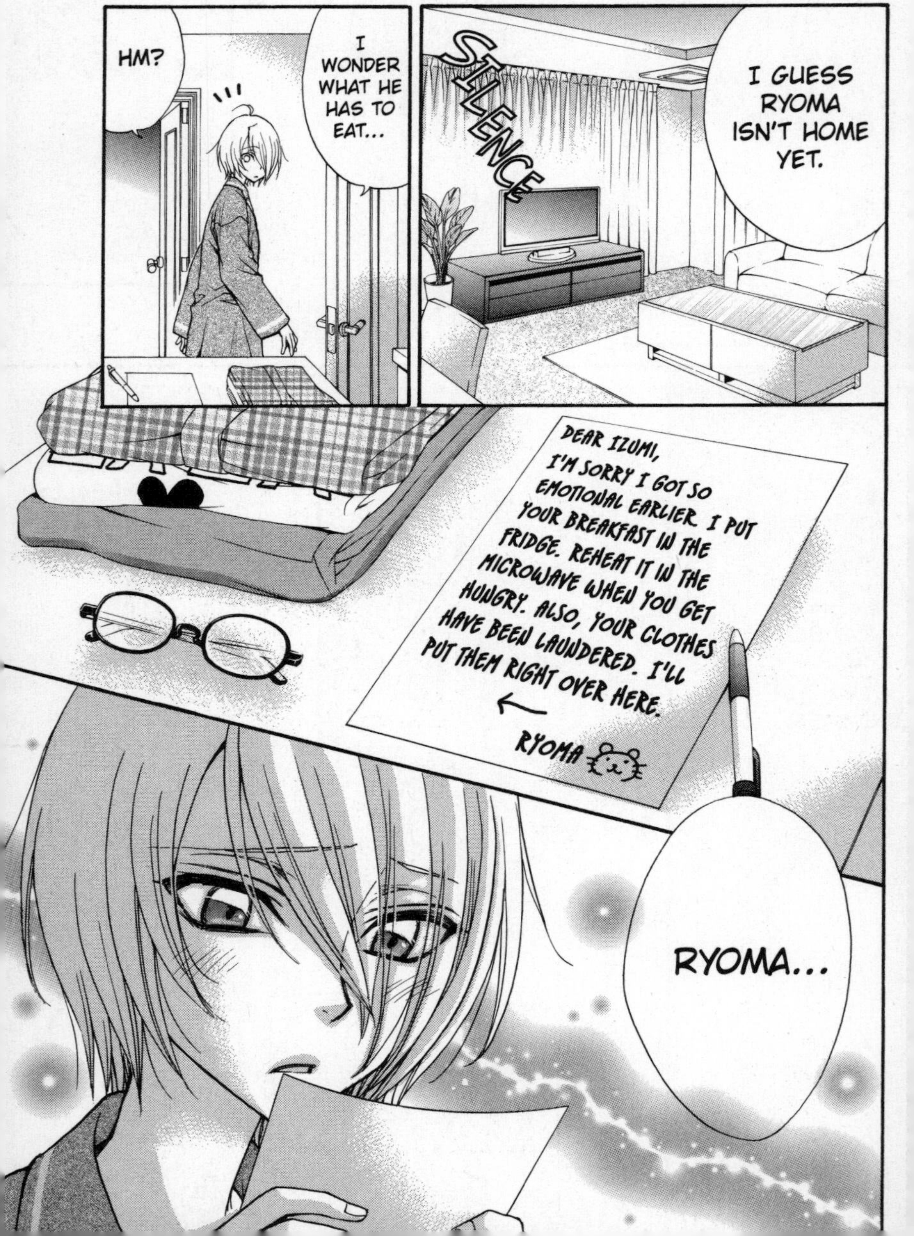
I GUESS RYOMA ISN'T HOME YET.
SILENCE
I WONDER WHAT HE HAS TO EAT...
HM?
DEAR IZUMI,
I'M SORRY I GOT SO EMOTIONAL EARLIER. I PUT YOUR BREAKFAST IN THE FRIDGE. REHEAT IT IN THE MICROWAVE WHEN YOU GET HUNGRY. ALSO, YOUR CLOTHES HAVE BEEN LAUNDERED. I'LL PUT THEM RIGHT OVER HERE.
←
RYOMA
RYOMA...

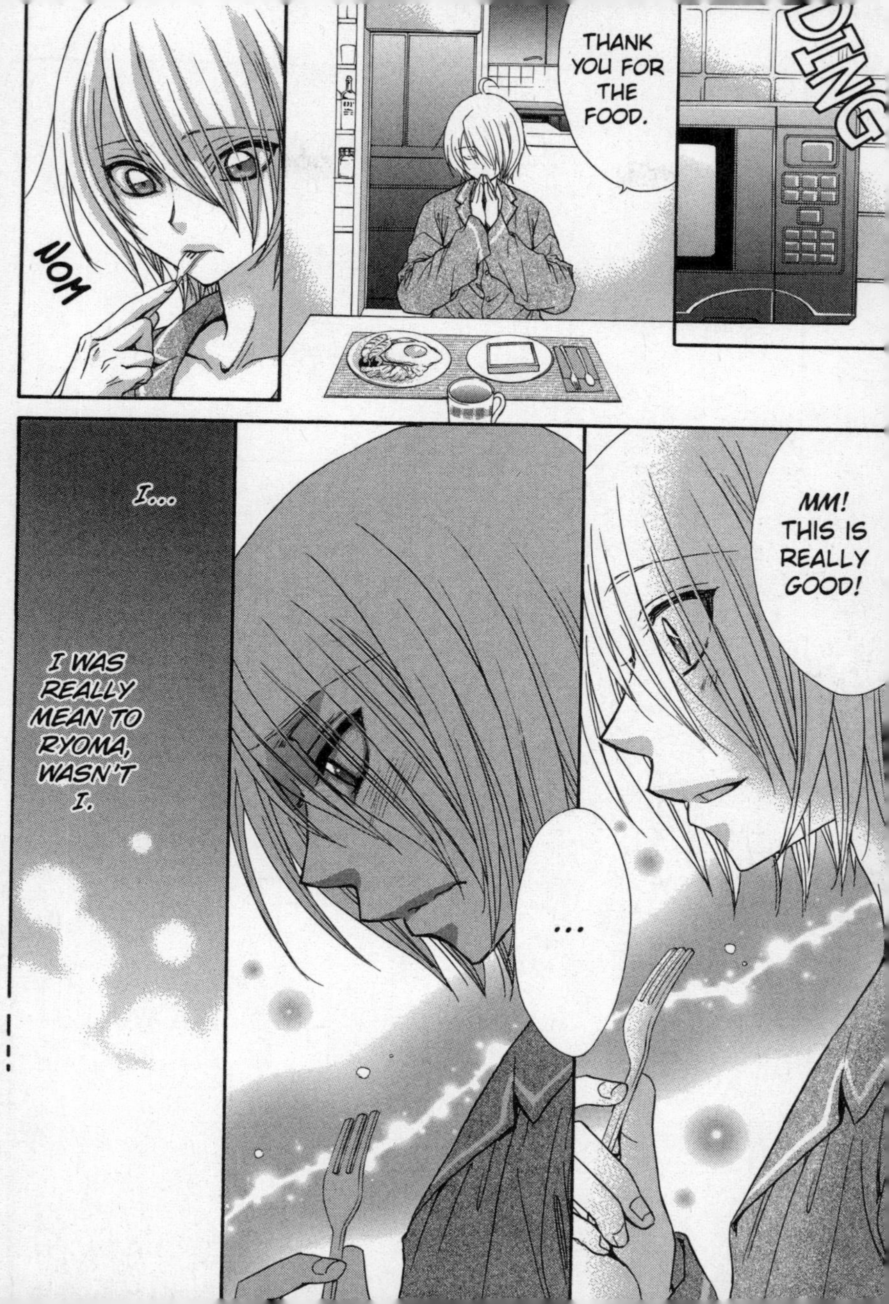
DING
THANK YOU FOR THE FOOD.
NOM
MM! THIS IS REALLY GOOD!
...
I...
I WAS REALLY MEAN TO RYOMA, WASN'T I.

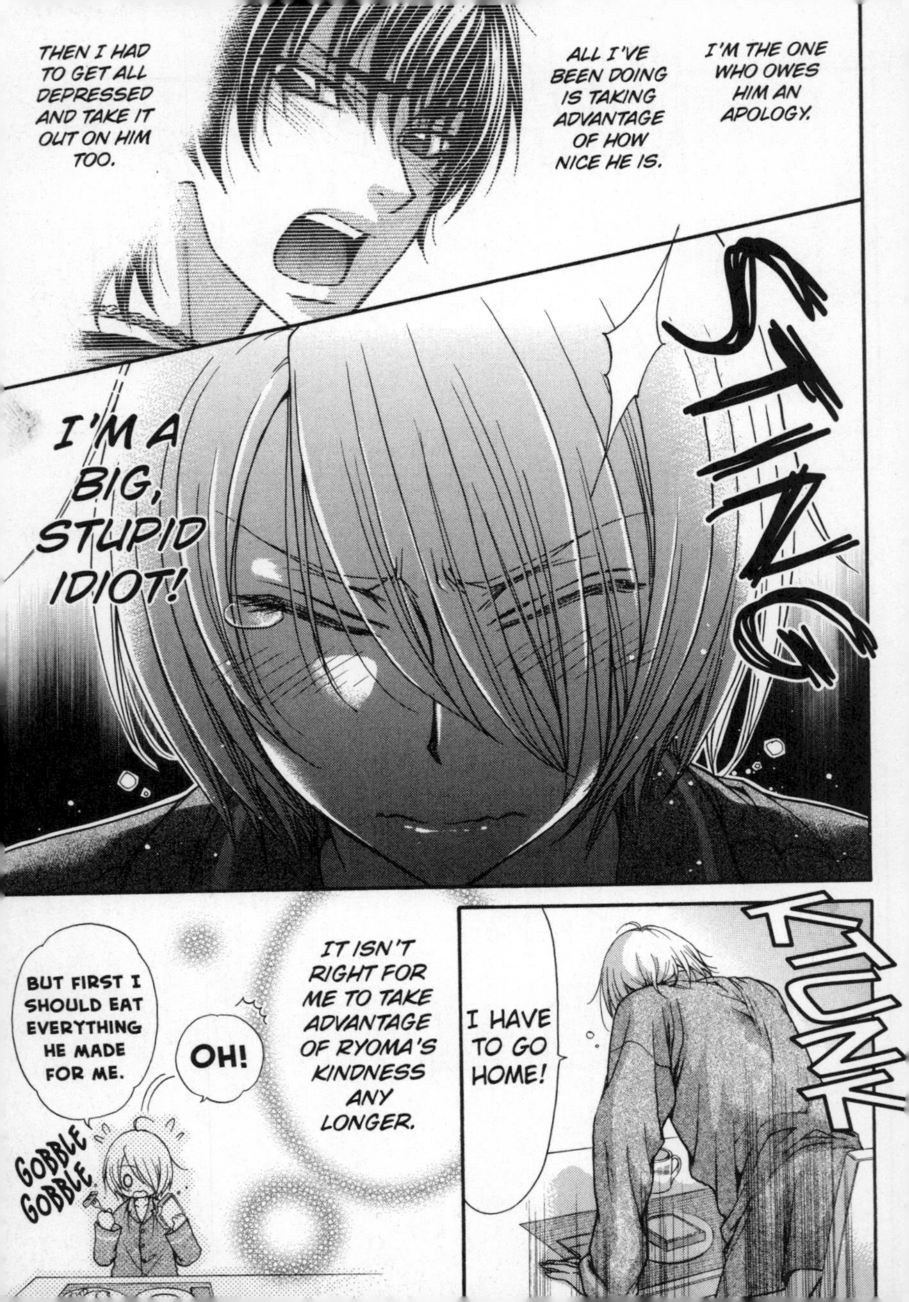
I'M THE ONE WHO OWES HIM AN APOLOGY.
ALL I'VE BEEN DOING IS TAKING ADVANTAGE OF HOW NICE HE IS.
THEN I HAD TO GET ALL DEPRESSED AND TAKE IT OUT ON HIM TOO.
STING
I'M A BIG, STUPID IDIOT!
KTUNK
I HAVE TO GO HOME!
IT ISN'T RIGHT FOR ME TO TAKE ADVANTAGE OF RYOMA'S KINDNESS ANY LONGER.
OH!
BUT FIRST I SHOULD EAT EVERYTHING HE MADE FOR ME.
GOBBLE GOBBLE

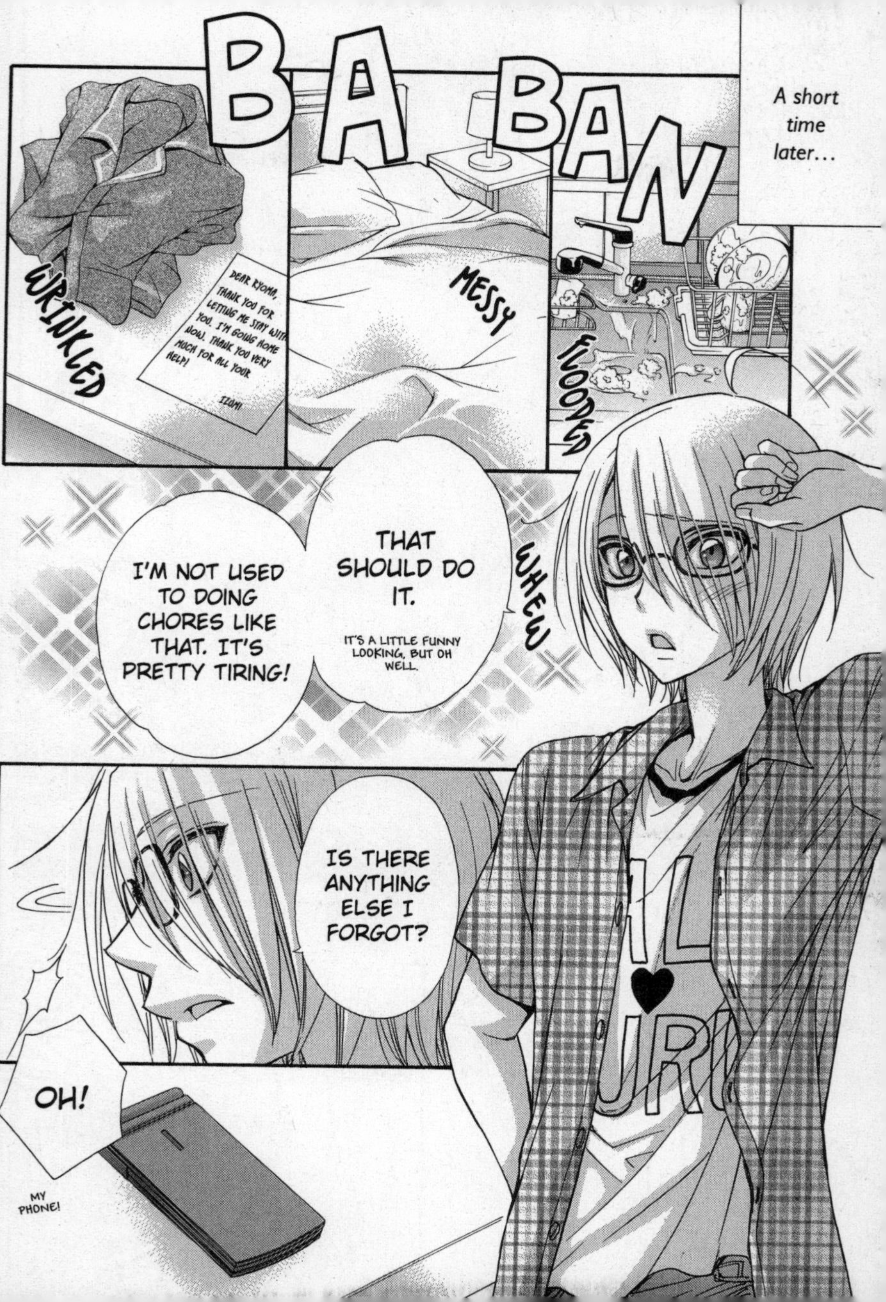
A short time later...
BA BAN
FLOODED
MESSY
DEAR RYOMA, THANK YOU FOR LETTING ME STAY WITH YOU. I'M GOING HOME NOW. THANK YOU VERY MUCH FOR ALL YOUR HELP! IZUMI
WRINKLED
WHEW
THAT SHOULD DO IT.
IT'S A LITTLE FUNNY LOOKING, BUT OH WELL.
I'M NOT USED TO DOING CHORES LIKE THAT. IT'S PRETTY TIRING!
IS THERE ANYTHING ELSE I FORGOT?
OH!
MY PHONE!

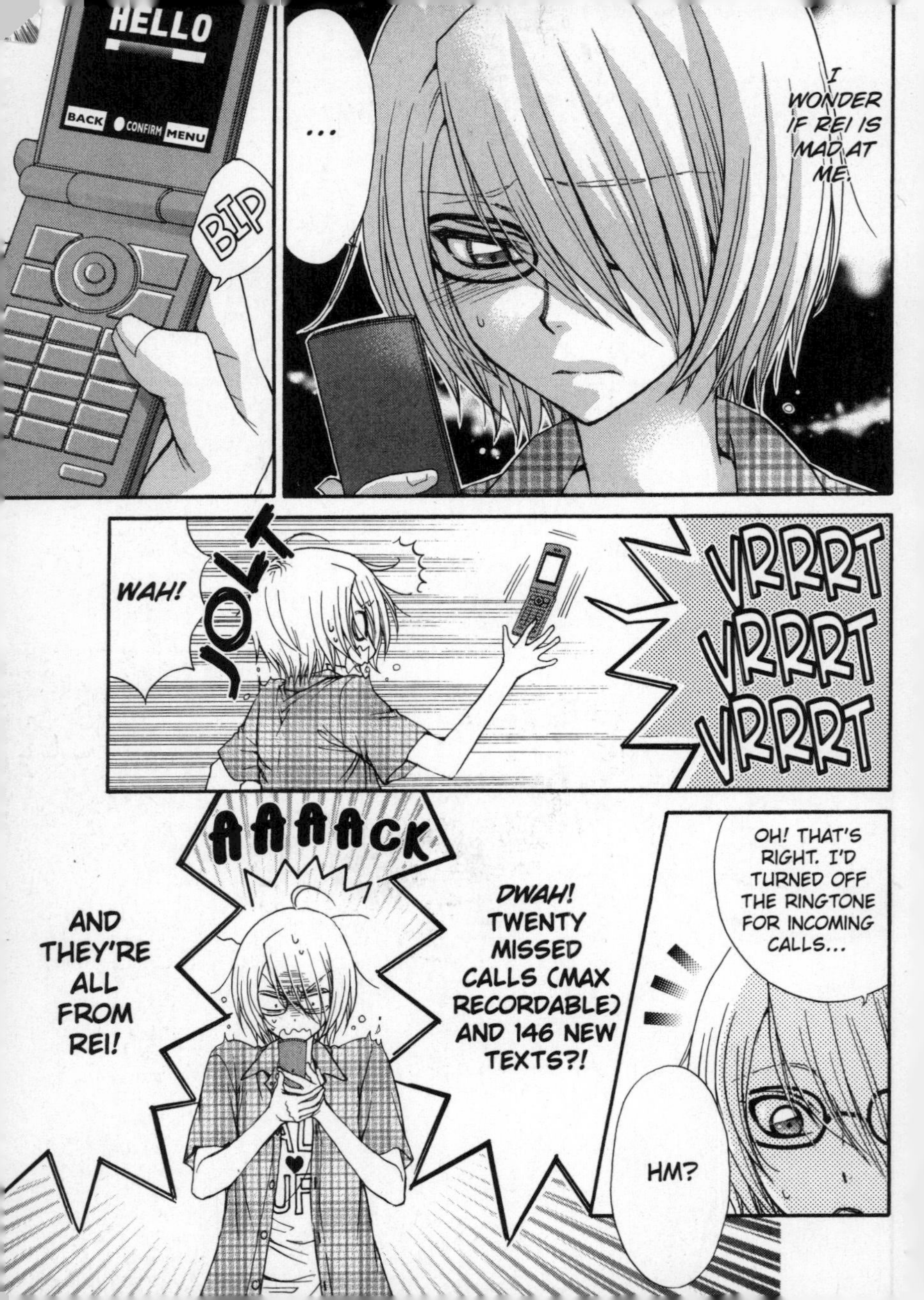
I WONDER IF REI IS MAD AT ME.
...
HELLO
BACK
CONFIRM
MENU
BIP
VRRRT
VRRRT
VRRRT
JOLT
WAH!
OH! THAT'S RIGHT. I'D TURNED OFF THE RINGTONE FOR INCOMING CALLS...
HM?
AAAACK
DWAH! TWENTY MISSED CALLS (MAX RECORDABLE) AND 146 NEW TEXTS?!
AND THEY'RE ALL FROM REI!

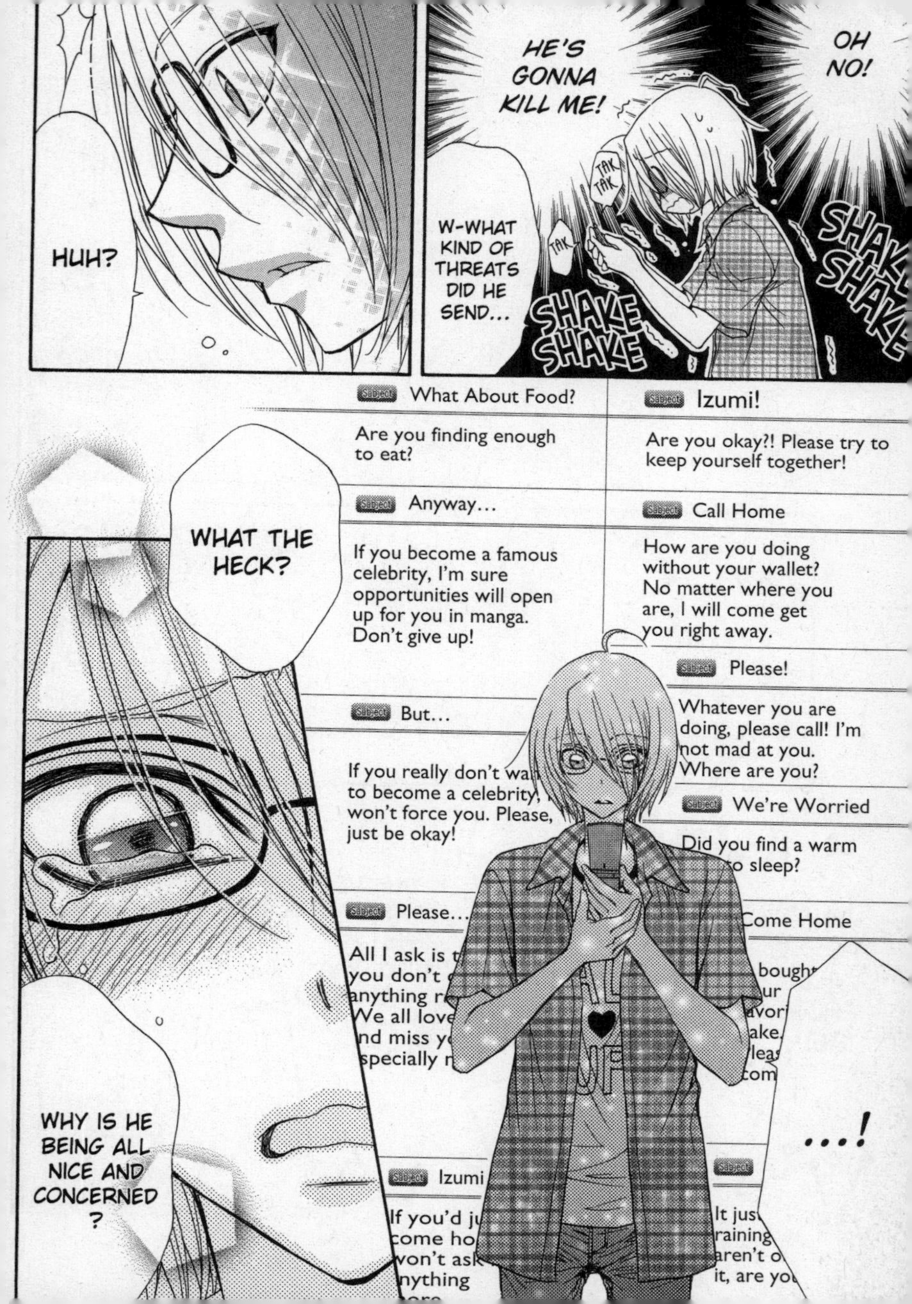
OH NO!
HE'S GONNA KILL ME!
TAK TAK
TAK
W-WHAT KIND OF THREATS DID HE SEND...
SHAKE SHAKE
SHAKE SHAKE
HUH?
Subject Izumi!
Are you okay?! Please try to keep yourself together!
Subject What About Food?
Are you finding enough to eat?
Subject Call Home
How are you doing without your wallet? No matter where you are, I will come get you right away.
Subject Anyway...
If you become a famous celebrity, I'm sure opportunities will open up for you in manga. Don't give up!
Subject Please!
Whatever you are doing, please call! I'm not mad at you. Where are you?
Subject But...
won't force you. Please, just be okay!
Subject We're Worried
Did you find a warm
Subject Please...
Come Home
Subject Izumi
Subject
...!
WHAT THE HECK?
WHY IS HE BEING ALL NICE AND CONCERNED?

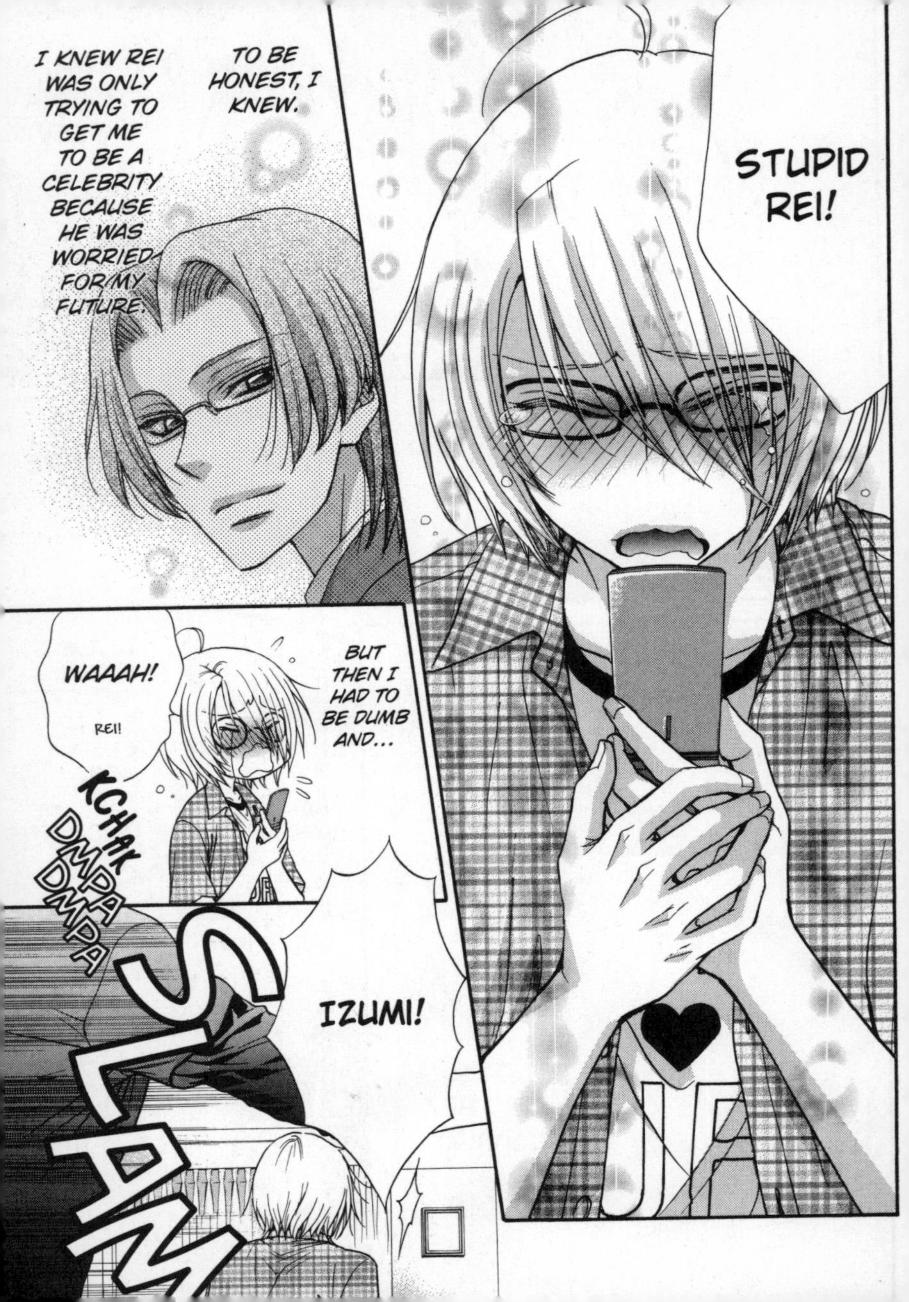
STUPID REI!
TO BE HONEST, I KNEW.
I KNEW REI WAS ONLY TRYING TO GET ME TO BE A CELEBRITY BECAUSE HE WAS WORRIED FOR MY FUTURE.
BUT THEN I HAD TO BE DUMB AND...
WAAAH!
REI!
KCHAK
DMPA DMPA
IZUMI!
SLAM

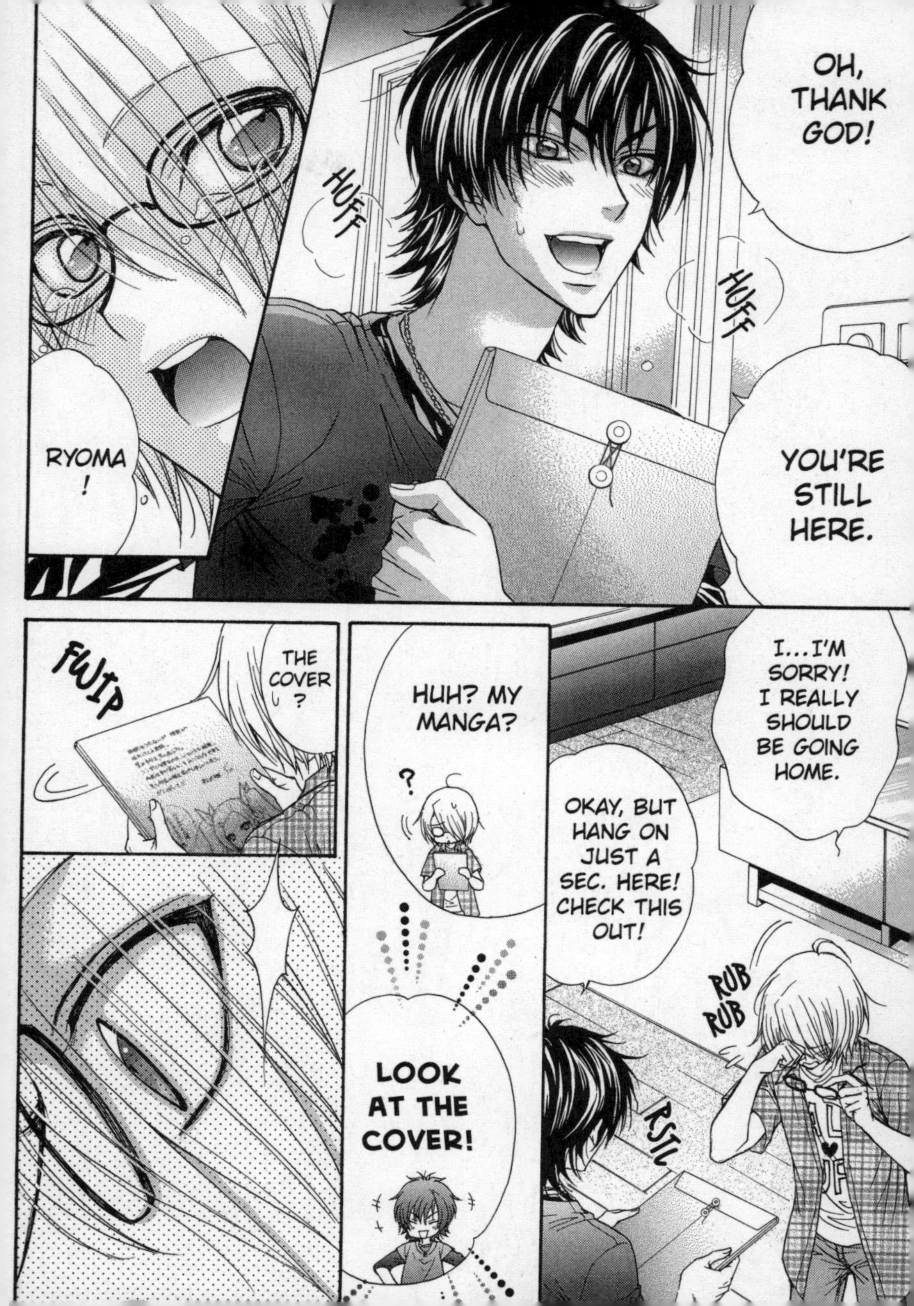
OH, THANK GOD!
HUFF
HUFF
YOU'RE STILL HERE.
RYOMA!
I...I'M SORRY! I REALLY SHOULD BE GOING HOME.
OKAY, BUT HANG ON JUST A SEC. HERE! CHECK THIS OUT!
RUB RUB
RSTL
HUH? MY MANGA?
?
LOOK AT THE COVER!
THE COVER?
FWIP

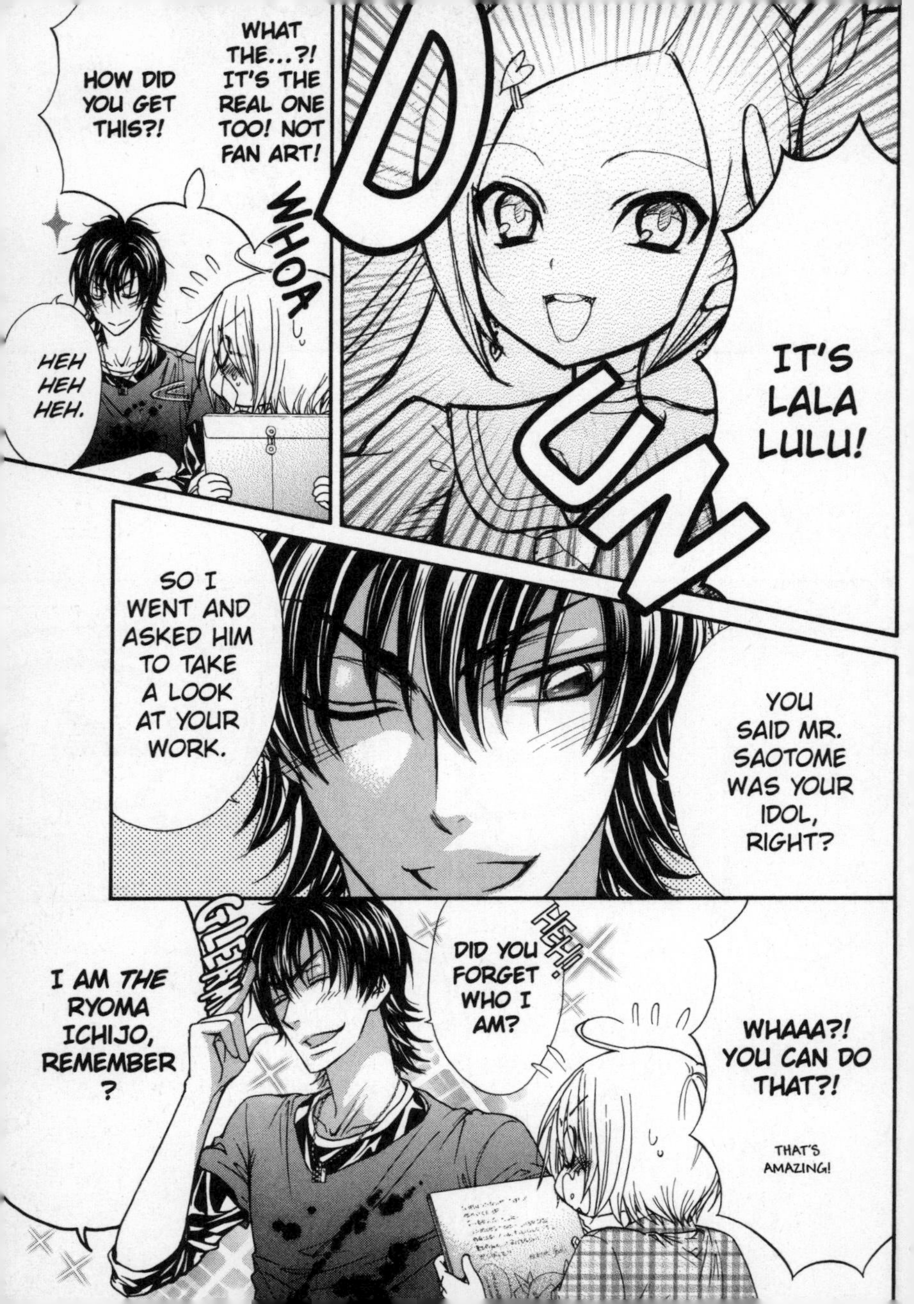
DUN
IT'S LALA LULU!
WHAT THE...?! IT'S THE REAL ONE TOO! NOT FAN ART!
HOW DID YOU GET THIS?!
WHOA
HEH HEH HEH.
YOU SAID MR. SAOTOME WAS YOUR IDOL, RIGHT?
SO I WENT AND ASKED HIM TO TAKE A LOOK AT YOUR WORK.
WHAAA?! YOU CAN DO THAT?!
THAT'S AMAZING!
HEH!
DID YOU FORGET WHO I AM?
GLEAM
I AM *THE* RYOMA ICHIJO, REMEMBER?

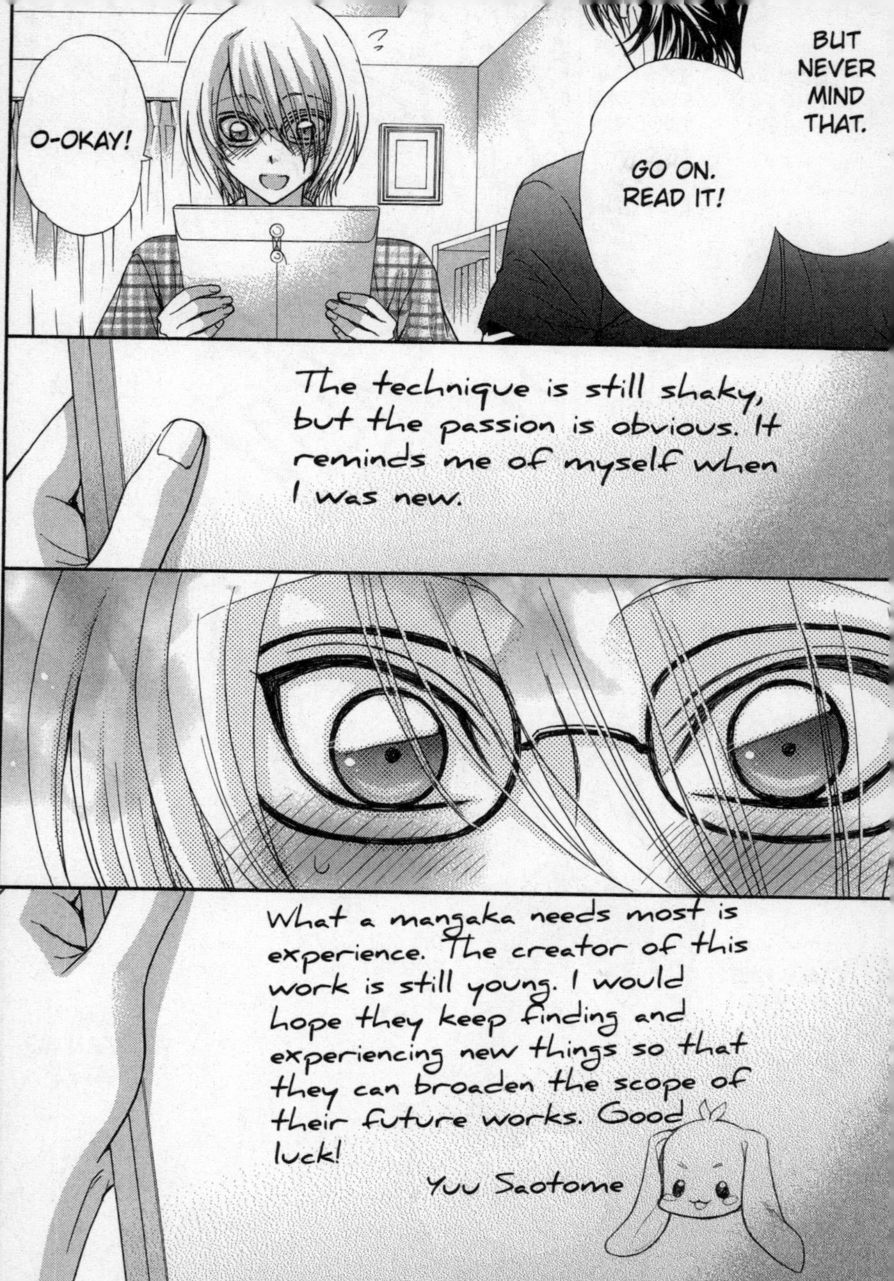
BUT NEVER MIND THAT.
GO ON. READ IT!
O-OKAY!
The technique is still shaky, but the passion is obvious. It reminds me of myself when I was new.
What a mangaka needs most is experience. The creator of this work is still young. I would hope they keep finding and experiencing new things so that they can broaden the scope of their future works. Good luck!
Yuu Saotome

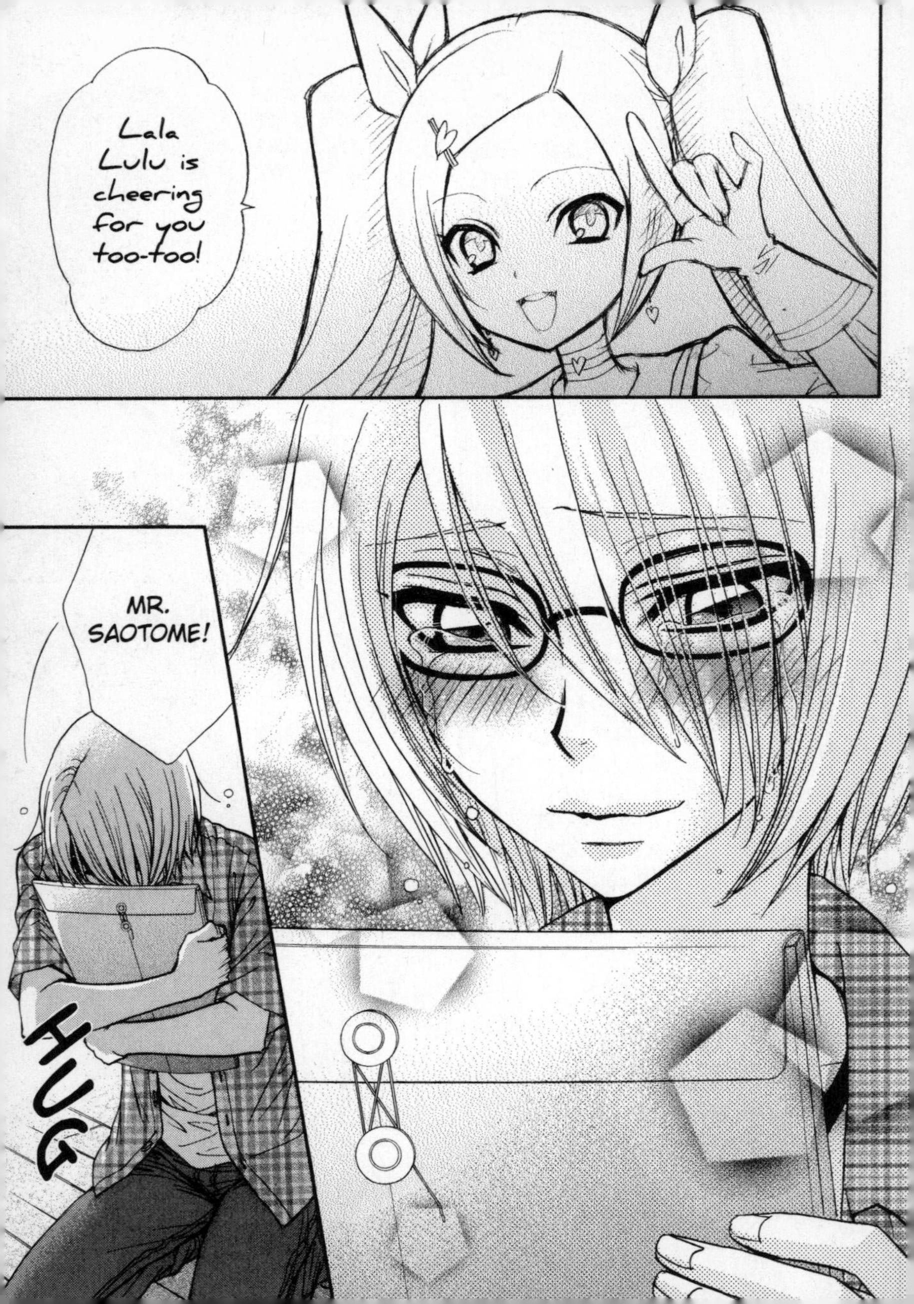
Lala Lulu is cheering for you too-too!
MR. SAOTOME!
HUG

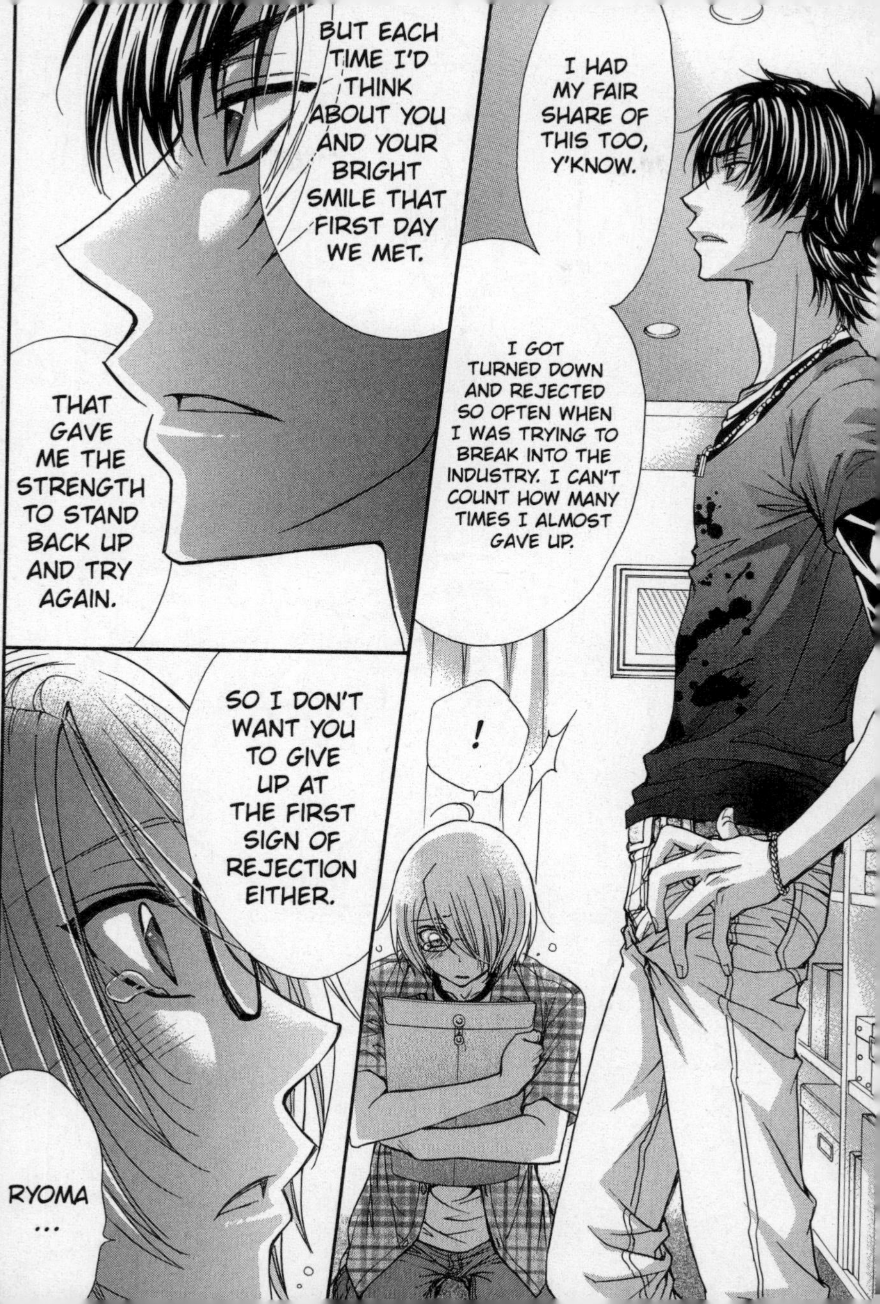
I HAD MY FAIR SHARE OF THIS TOO, Y'KNOW.
I GOT TURNED DOWN AND REJECTED SO OFTEN WHEN I WAS TRYING TO BREAK INTO THE INDUSTRY. I CAN'T COUNT HOW MANY TIMES I ALMOST GAVE UP.
!
BUT EACH TIME I'D THINK ABOUT YOU AND YOUR BRIGHT SMILE THAT FIRST DAY WE MET.
THAT GAVE ME THE STRENGTH TO STAND BACK UP AND TRY AGAIN.
SO I DON'T WANT YOU TO GIVE UP AT THE FIRST SIGN OF REJECTION EITHER.
RYOMA ...

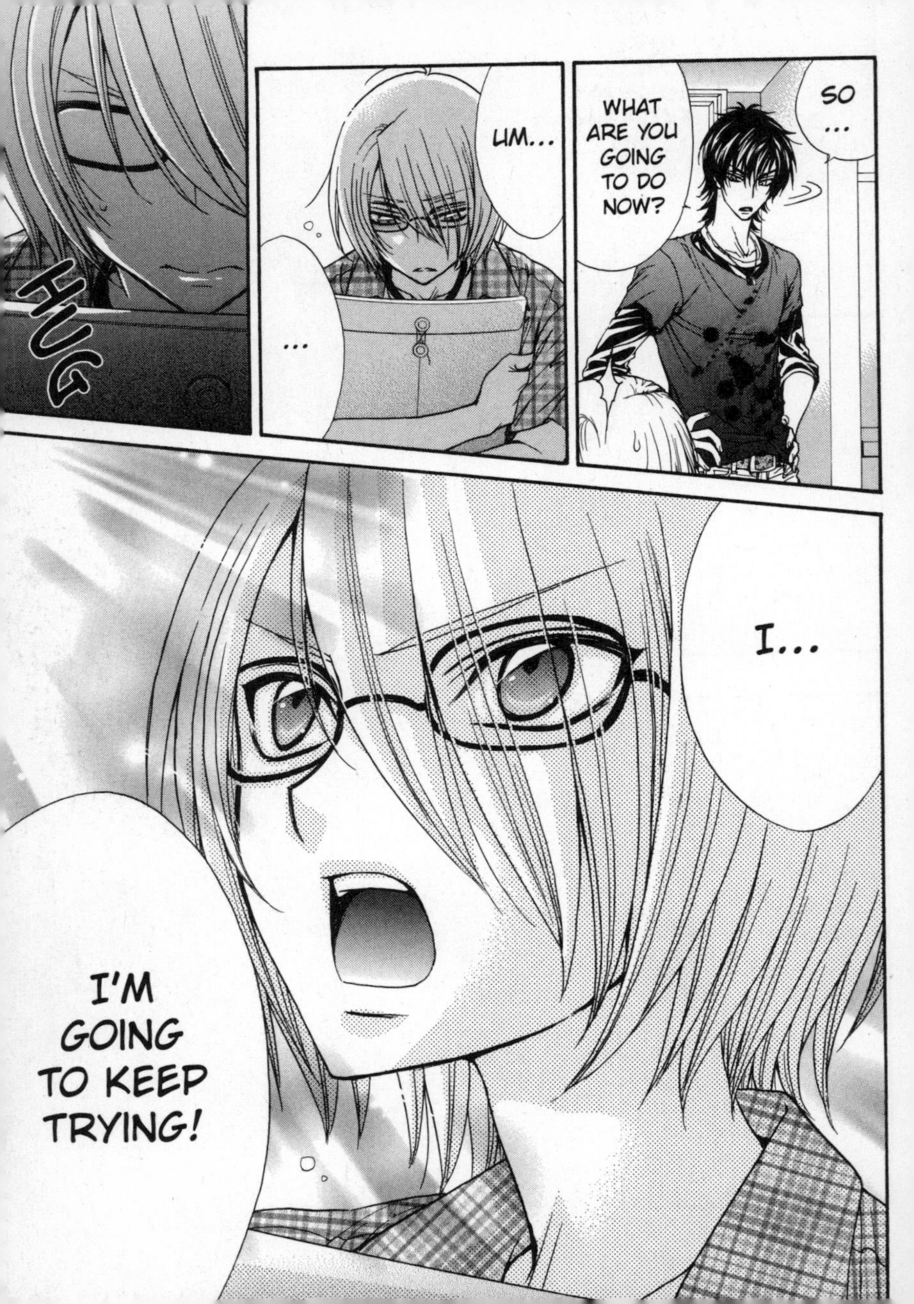
SO ...
WHAT ARE YOU GOING TO DO NOW?
UM...
...
HUG
I...
I'M GOING TO KEEP TRYING!

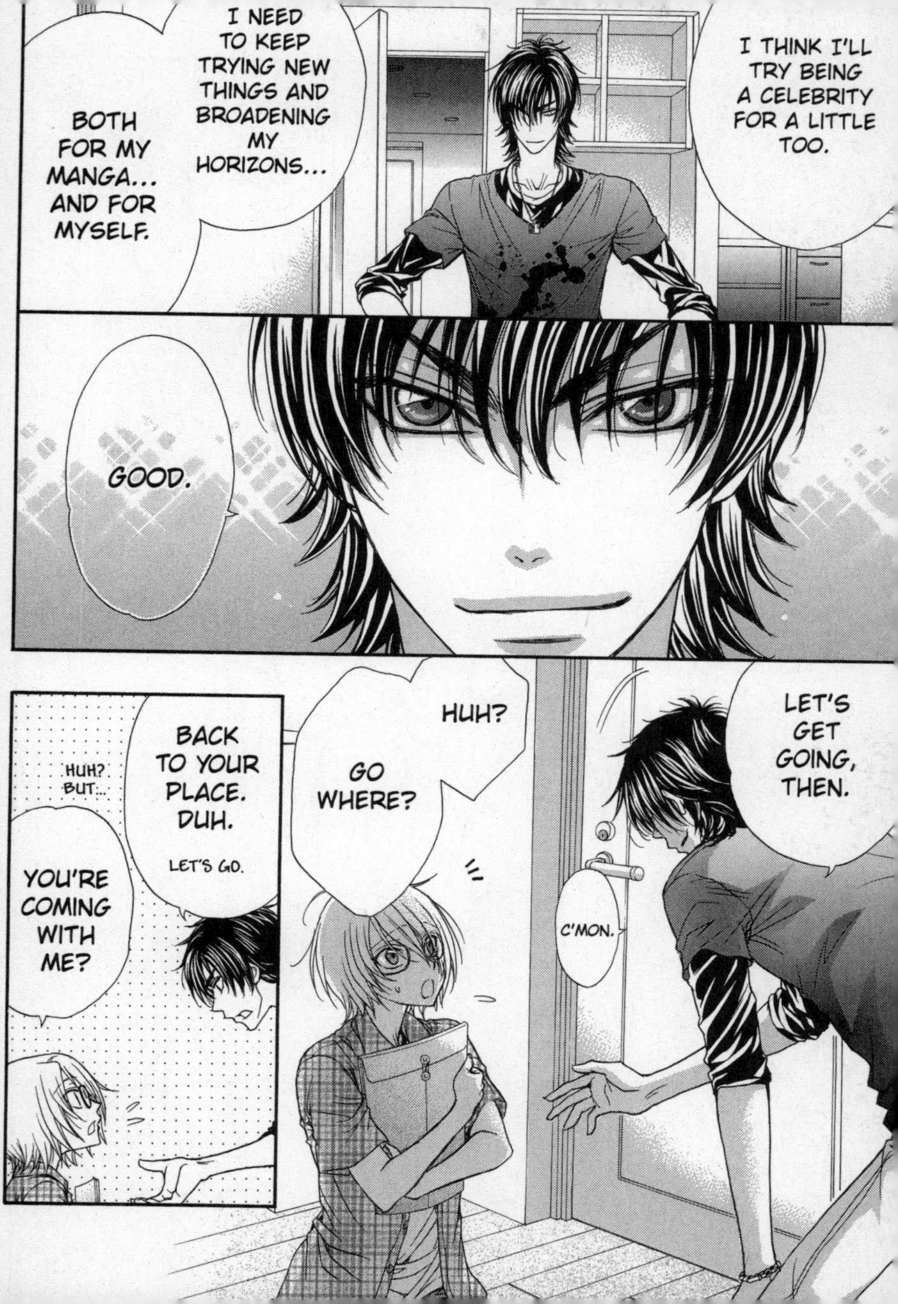

I THINK I'LL TRY BEING A CELEBRITY FOR A LITTLE TOO.
I NEED TO KEEP TRYING NEW THINGS AND BROADENING MY HORIZONS...
BOTH FOR MY MANGA... AND FOR MYSELF.
GOOD.
LET'S GET GOING, THEN.
C'MON.
HUH?
GO WHERE?
BACK TO YOUR PLACE. DUH.
HUH? BUT...
LET'S GO.
YOU'RE COMING WITH ME?

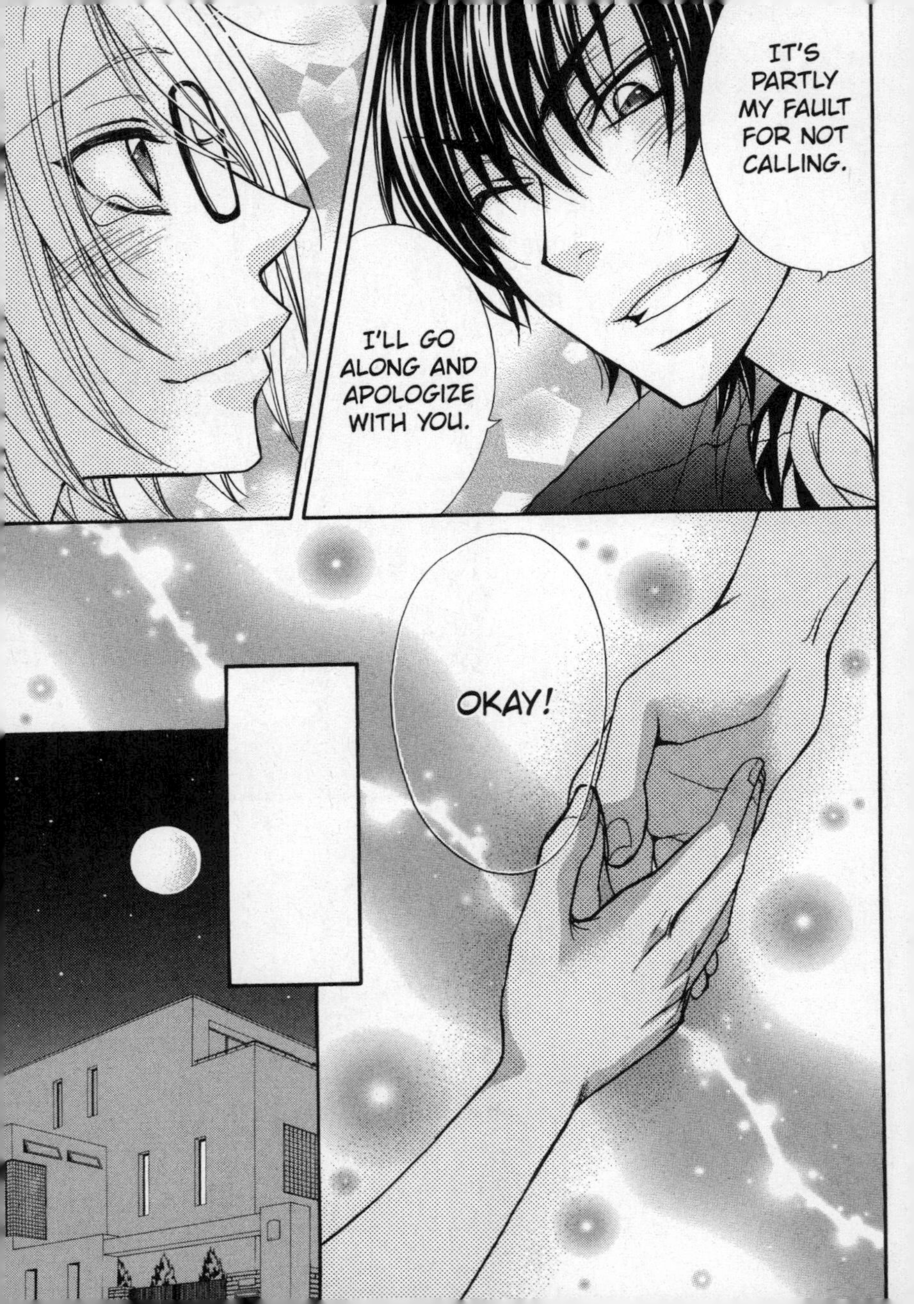
IT'S PARTLY MY FAULT FOR NOT CALLING.
I'LL GO ALONG AND APOLOGIZE WITH YOU.
OKAY!

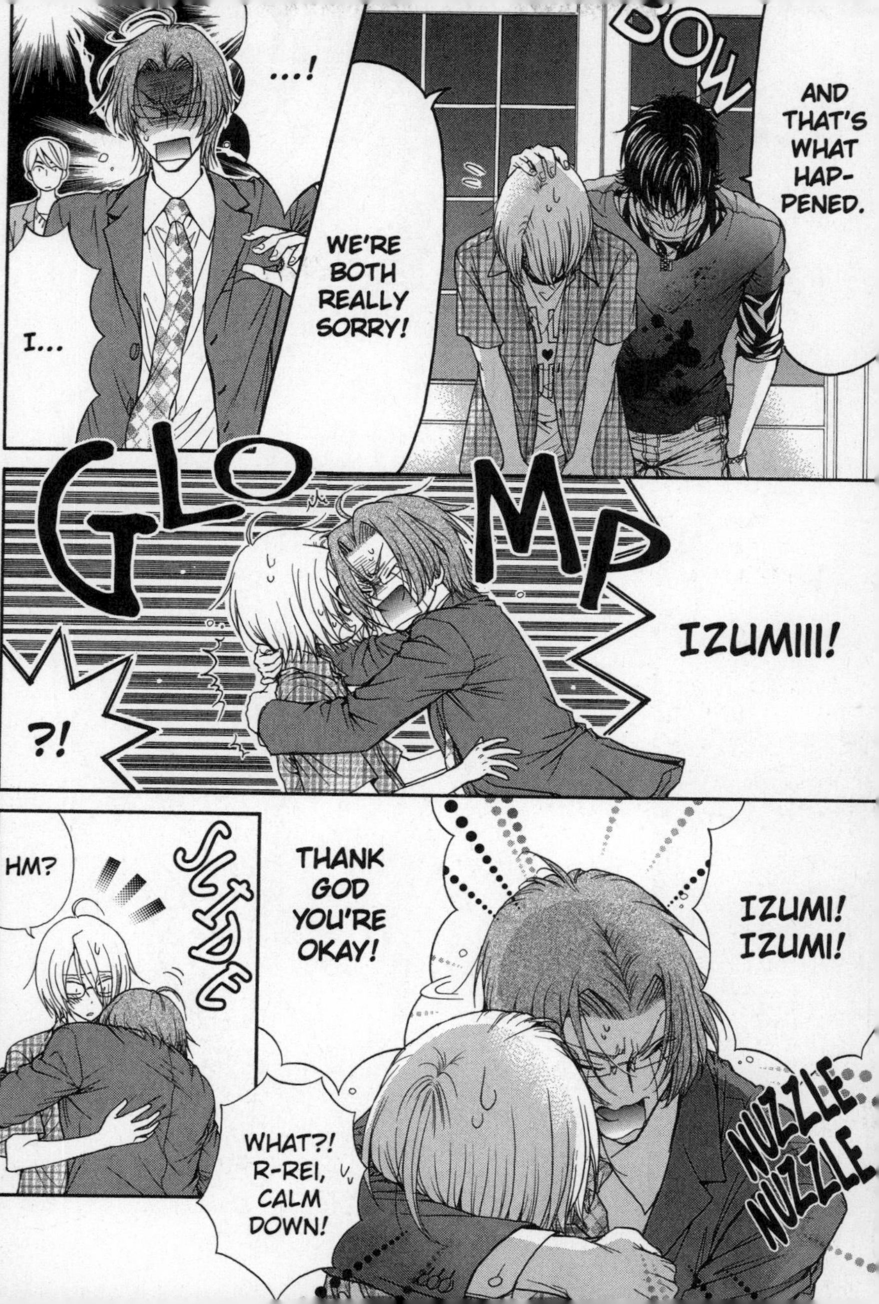
BOW
AND THAT'S WHAT HAP-PENED.
WE'RE BOTH REALLY SORRY!
...!
I...
GLOMP
IZUMIII!
?!
IZUMI! IZUMI!
THANK GOD YOU'RE OKAY!
NUZZLE NUZZLE
WHAT?! R-REI, CALM DOWN!
HM?
SLIDE

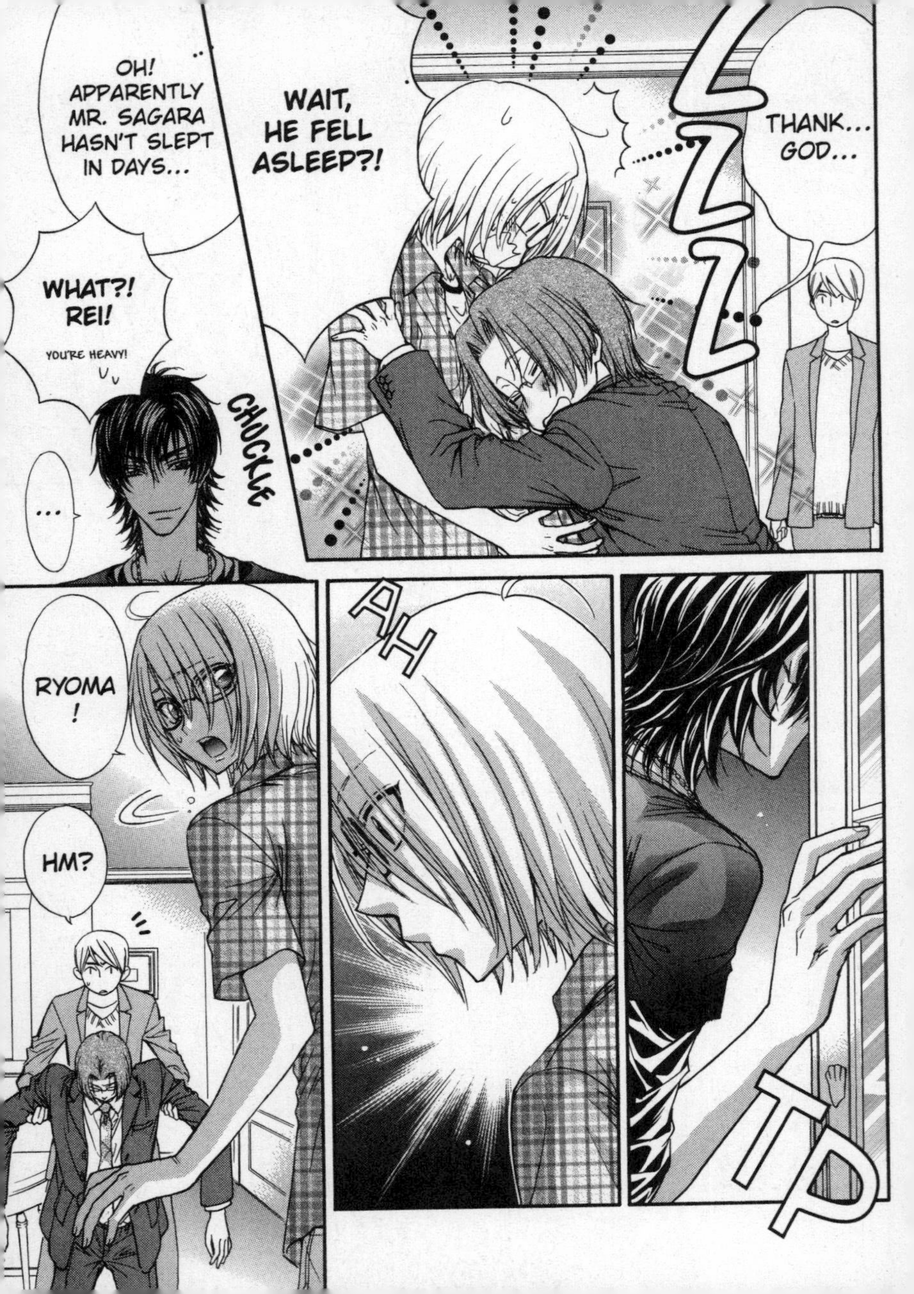
THANK... GOD...
ZZZ
WAIT, HE FELL ASLEEP?!
OH! APPARENTLY MR. SAGARA HASN'T SLEPT IN DAYS...
WHAT?! REI!
YOU'RE HEAVY!
CHUCKLE
...
TP
AH
RYOMA!
HM?

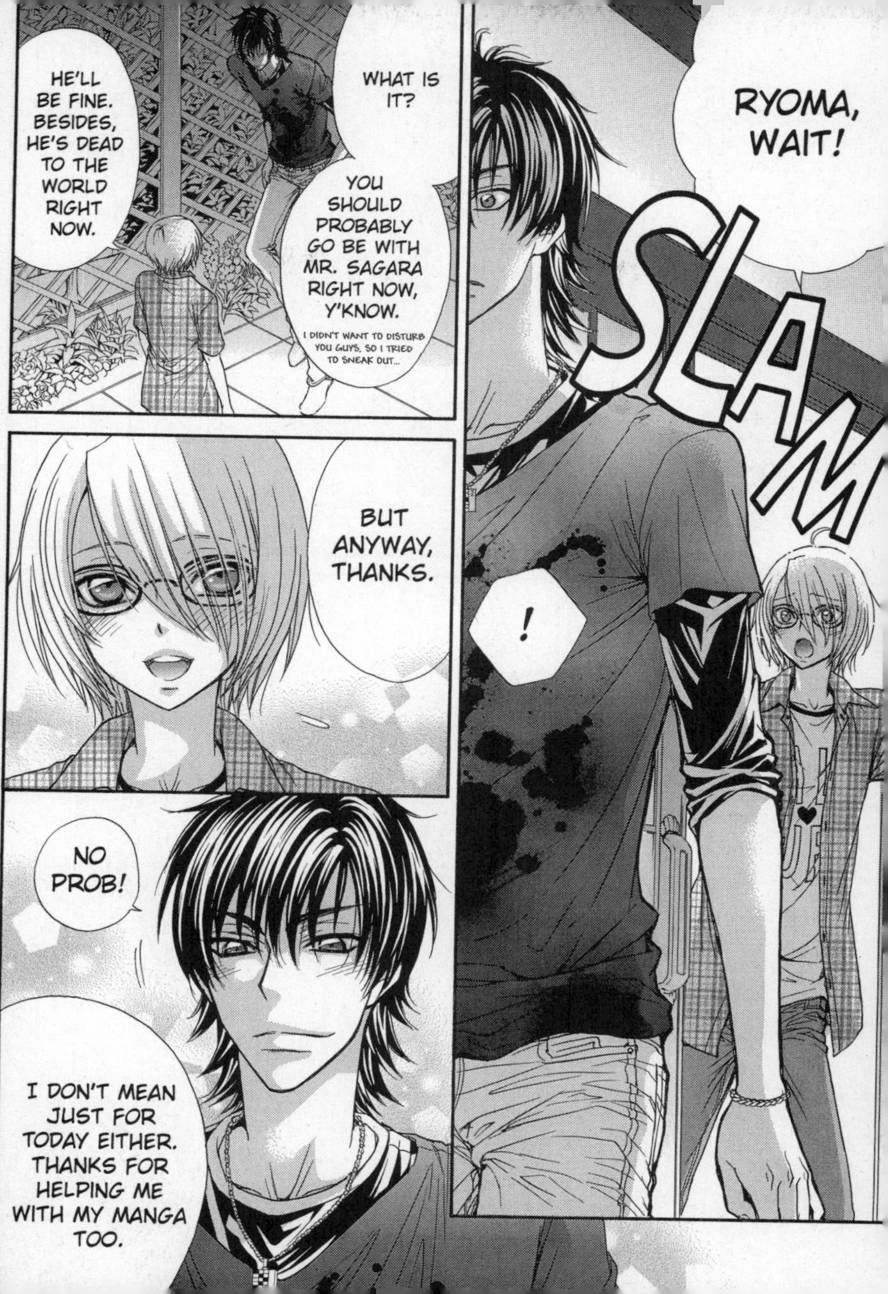
RYOMA, WAIT!
SLAM
!
WHAT IS IT?
YOU SHOULD PROBABLY GO BE WITH MR. SAGARA RIGHT NOW, Y'KNOW.
I DIDN'T WANT TO DISTURB YOU GUYS, SO I TRIED TO SNEAK OUT...
HE'LL BE FINE. BESIDES, HE'S DEAD TO THE WORLD RIGHT NOW.
BUT ANYWAY, THANKS.
NO PROB!
I DON'T MEAN JUST FOR TODAY EITHER. THANKS FOR HELPING ME WITH MY MANGA TOO.

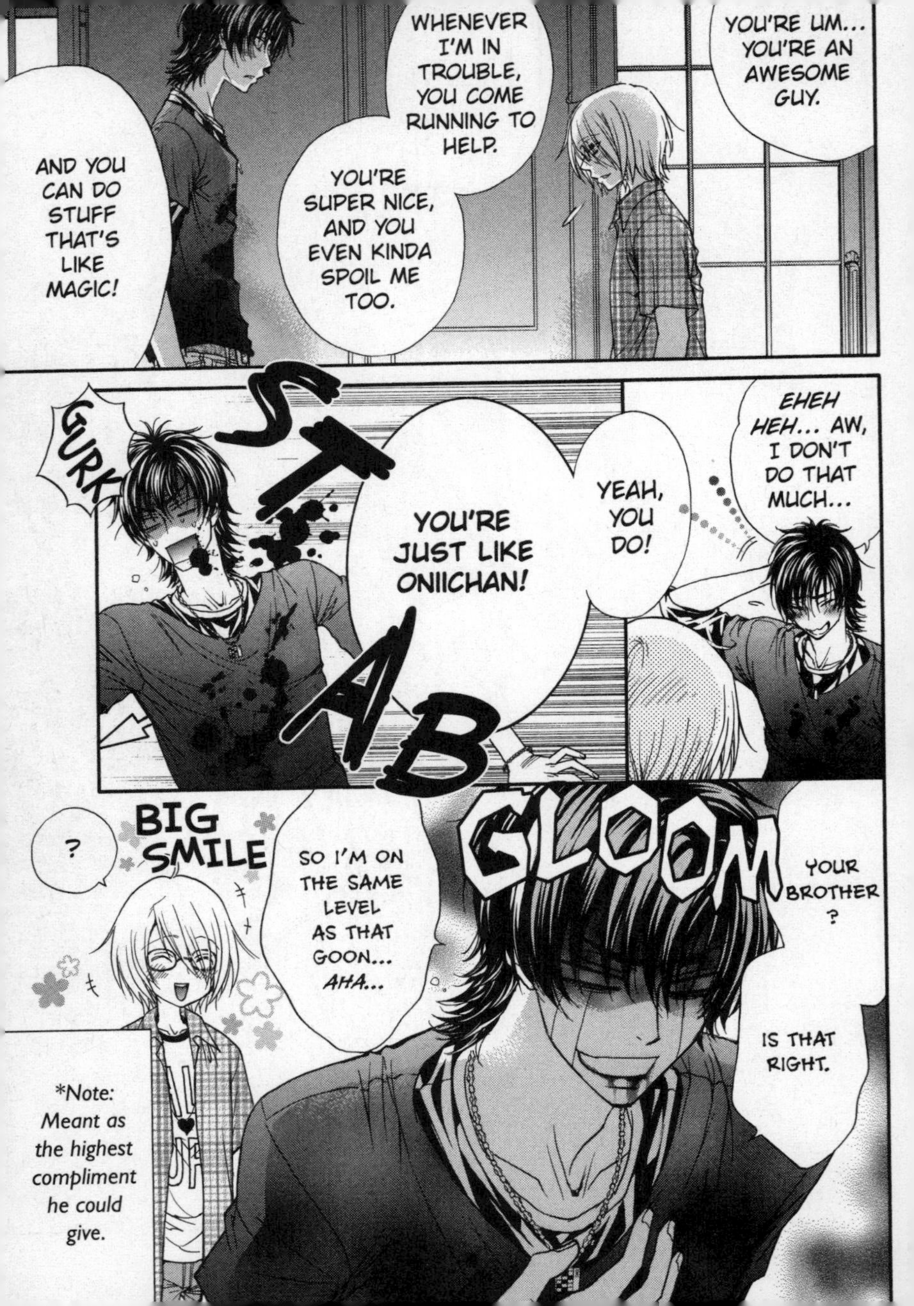
YOU'RE UM... YOU'RE AN AWESOME GUY.
WHENEVER I'M IN TROUBLE, YOU COME RUNNING TO HELP.
YOU'RE SUPER NICE, AND YOU EVEN KINDA SPOIL ME TOO.
AND YOU CAN DO STUFF THAT'S LIKE MAGIC!
EHEH HEH... AW, I DON'T DO THAT MUCH...
YEAH, YOU DO!
YOU'RE JUST LIKE ONIICHAN!
STAB
GURK
GLOOM
YOUR BROTHER?
IS THAT RIGHT.
SO I'M ON THE SAME LEVEL AS THAT GOON... AHA...
BIG SMILE
?
*Note: Meant as the highest compliment he could give.

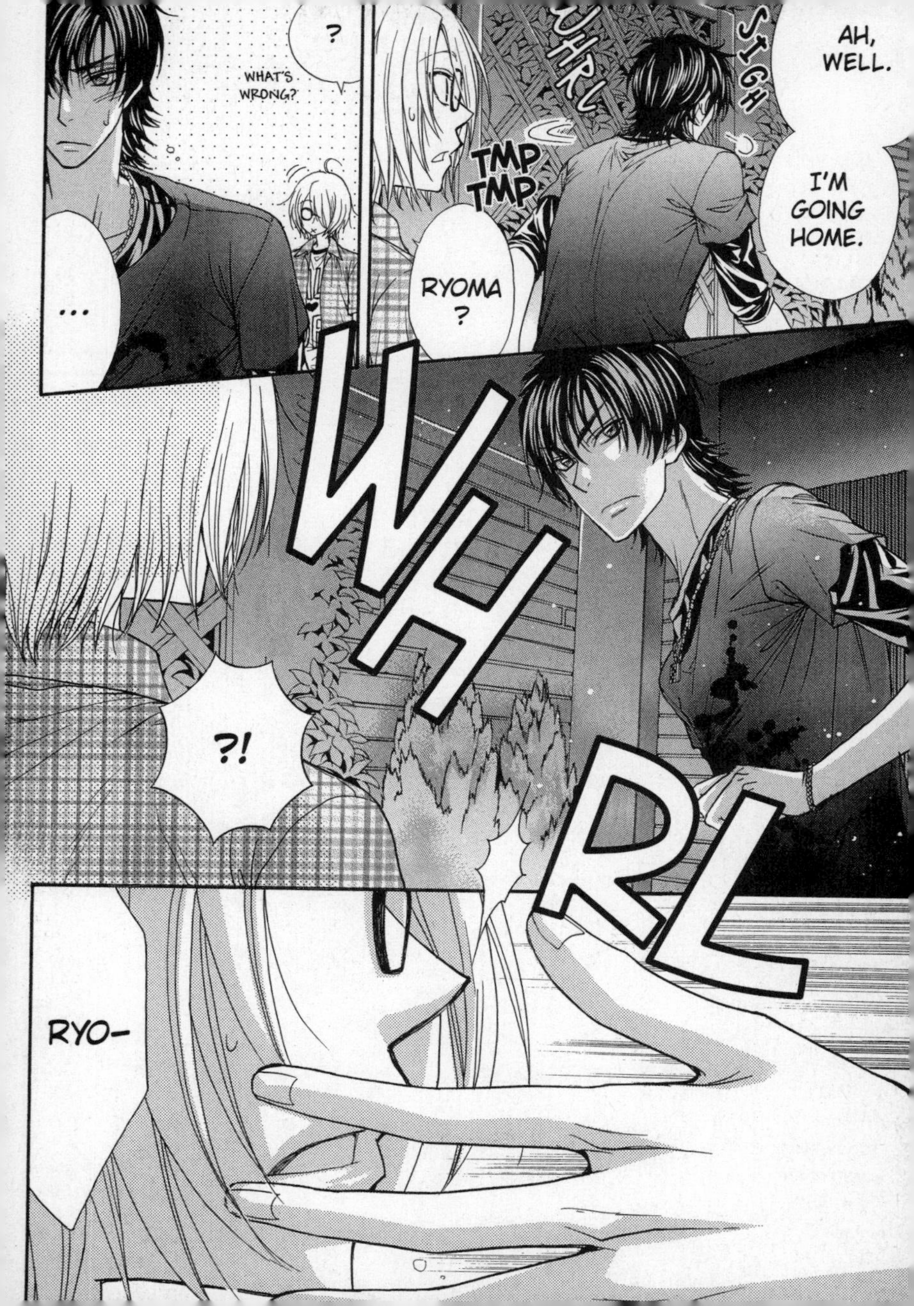
SIGH
AH, WELL.
I'M GOING HOME.
TMP TMP
RYOMA ?
?
WHAT'S WRONG?
...
WHRL
?!
RYO-

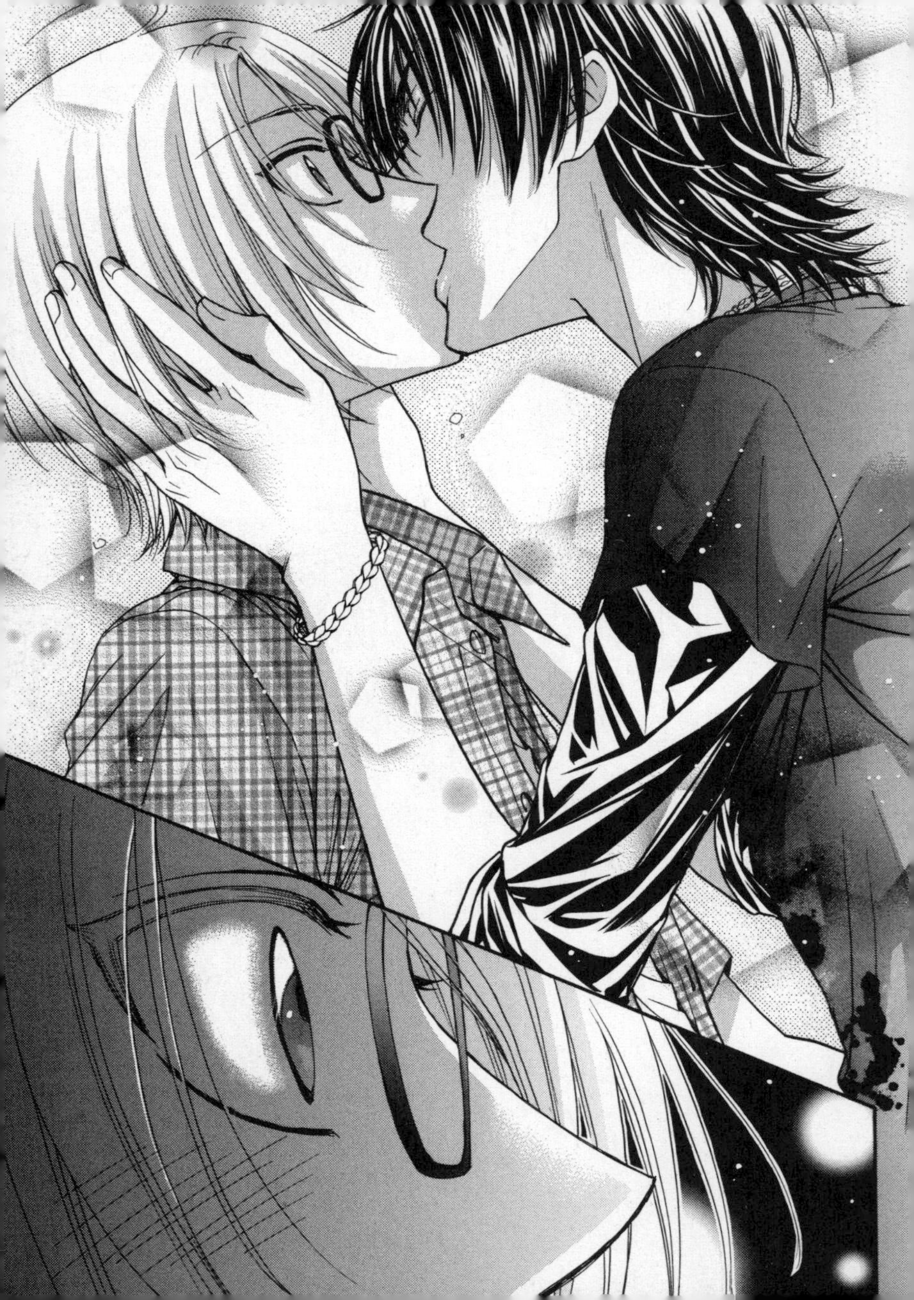

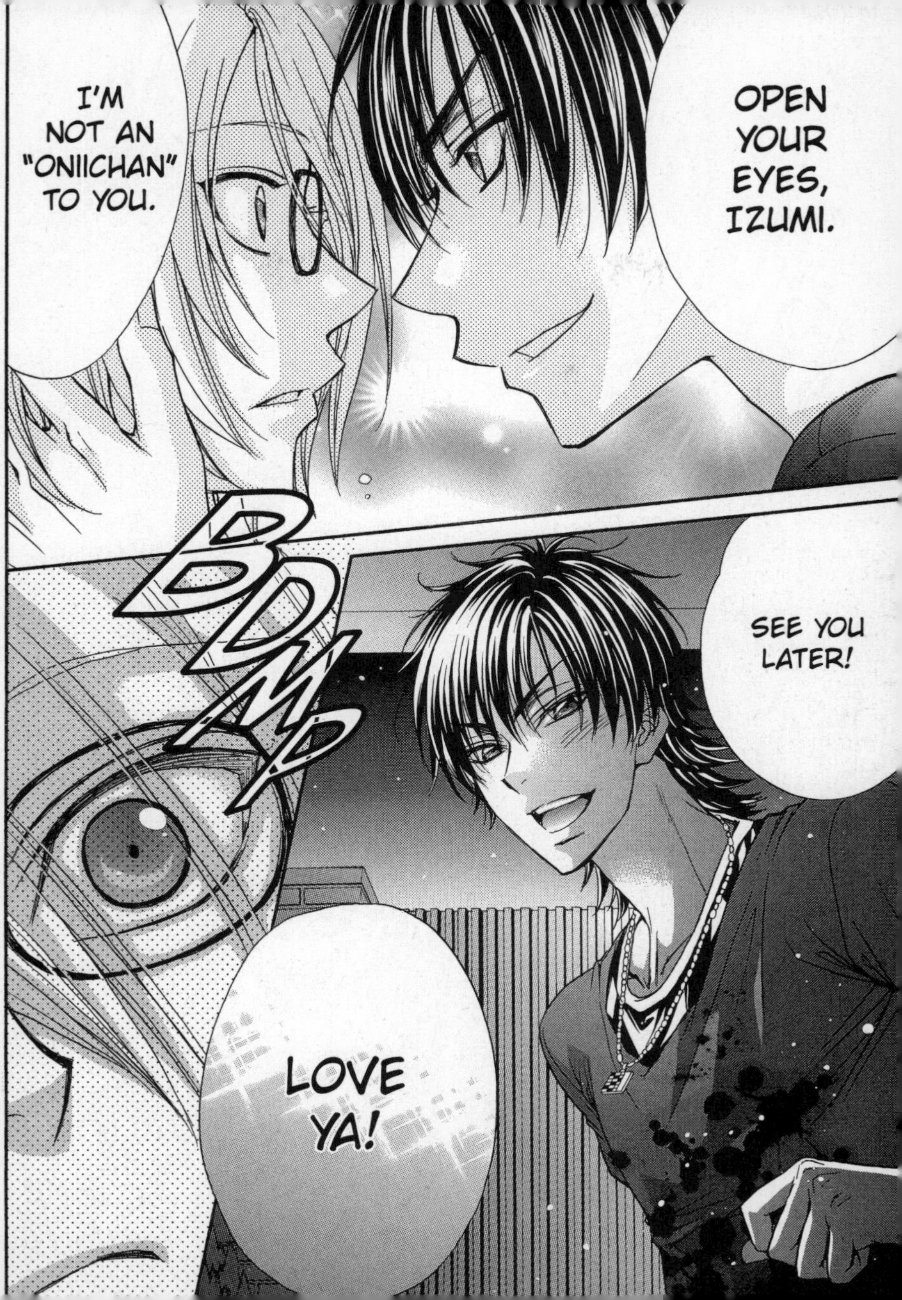
OPEN YOUR EYES, IZUMI.
I'M NOT AN "ONIICHAN" TO YOU.
SEE YOU LATER!
BDMP!
LOVE YA!

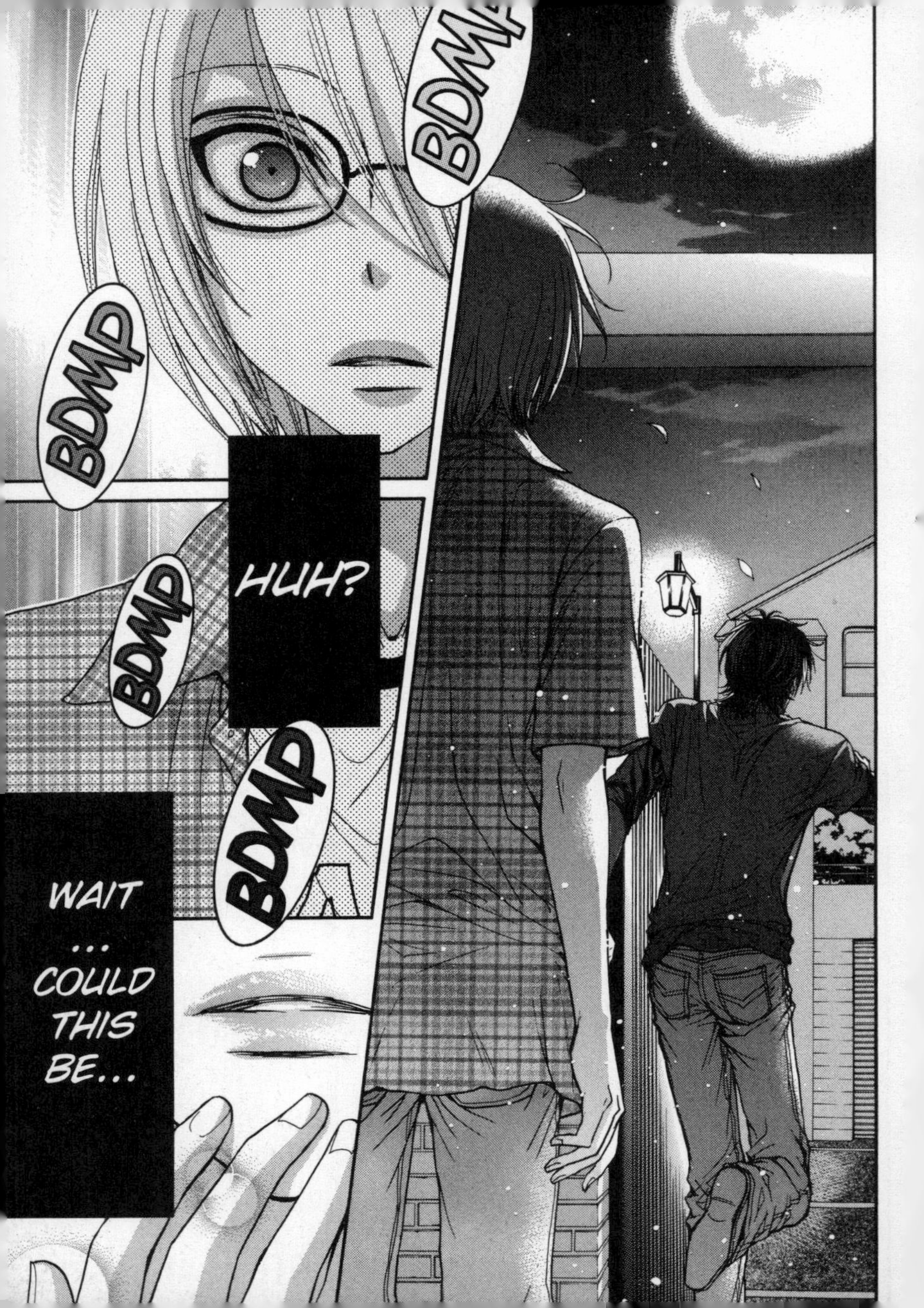
BDMP
BDMP
HUH?
BDMP
BDMP
WAIT ... COULD THIS BE...

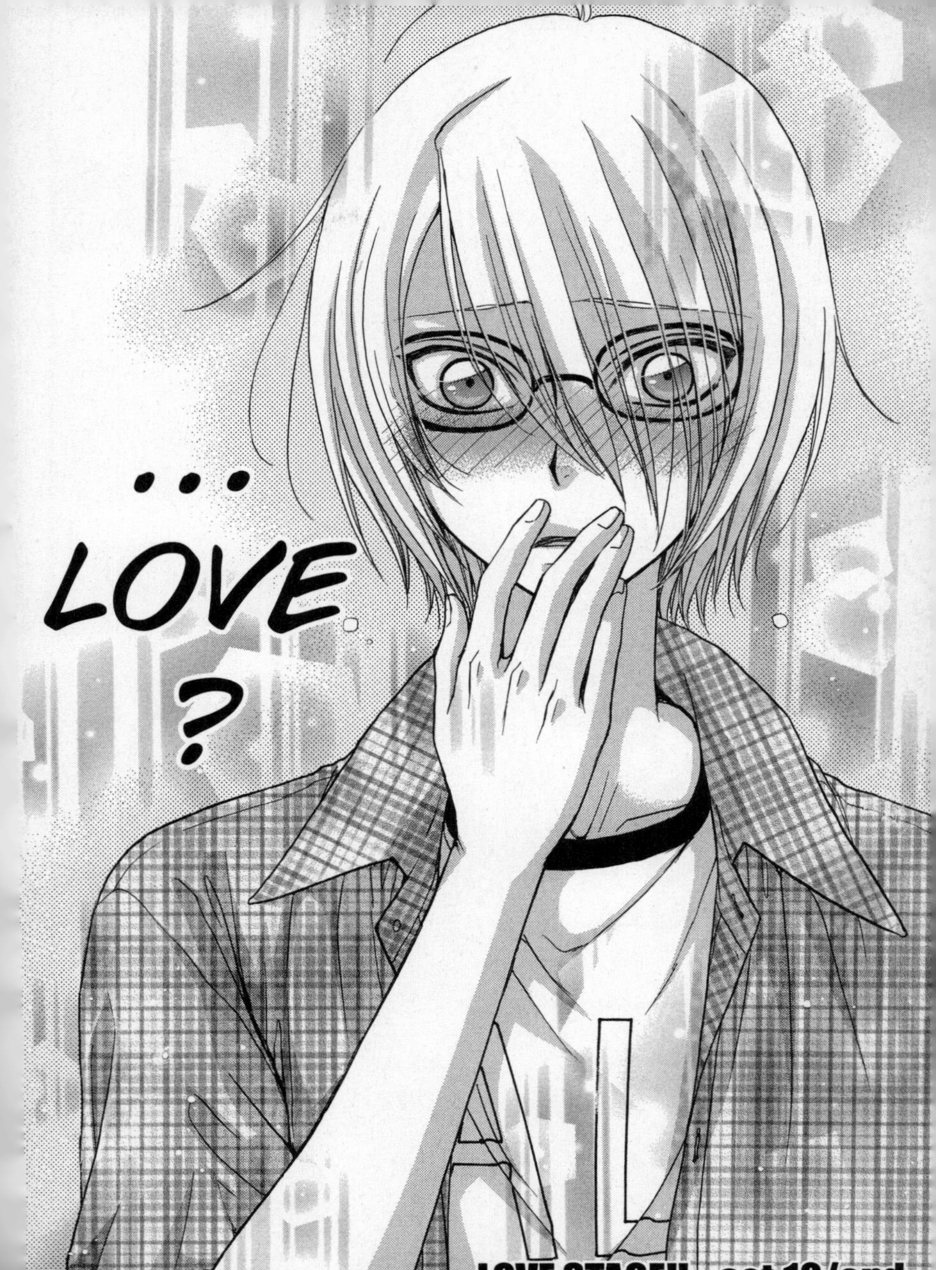
...LOVE?

LOVE STAGE!! act.10/end

LOVE STAGE!!

LOVE STAGE!!

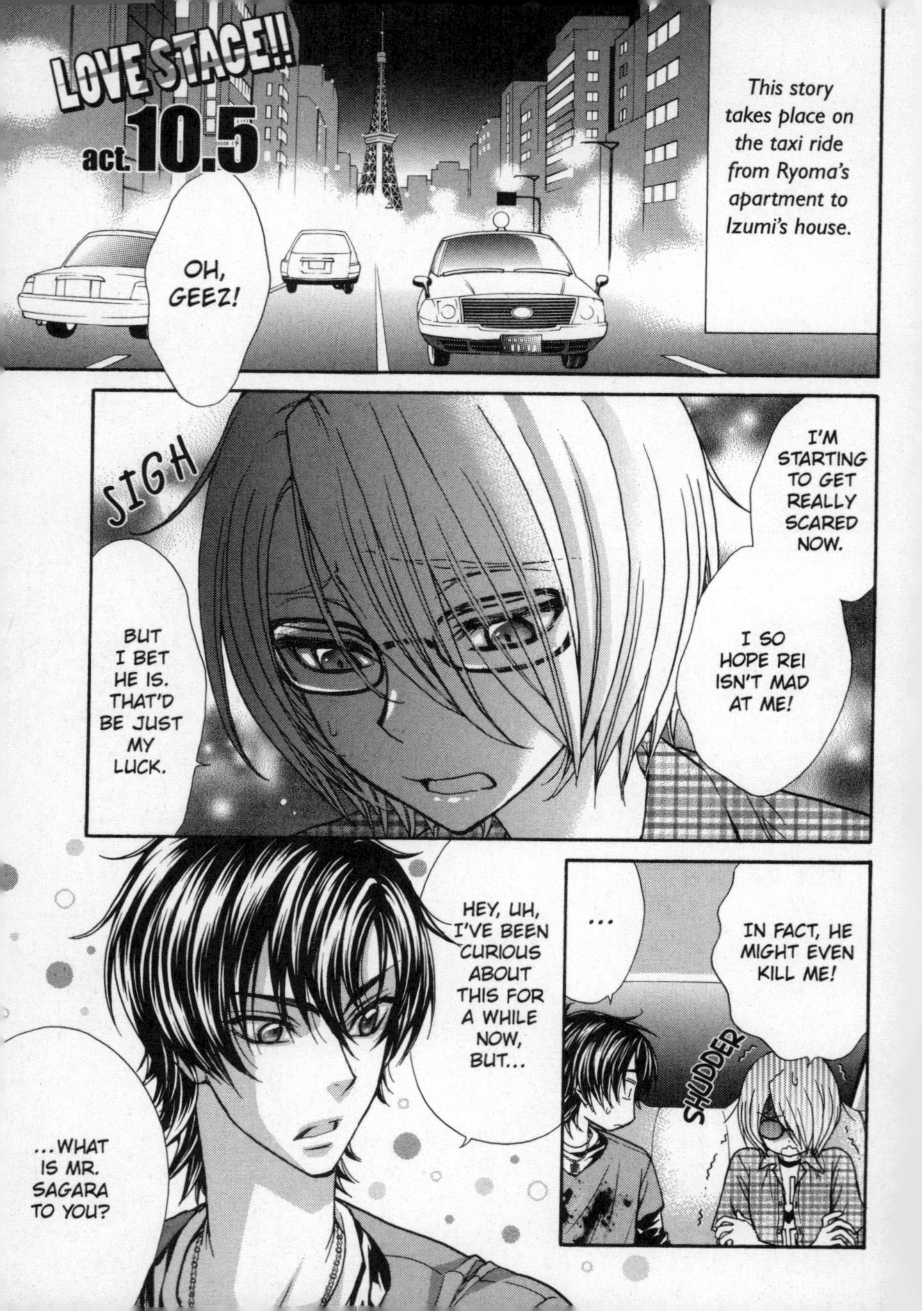
This story takes place on the taxi ride from Ryoma's apartment to Izumi's house.
LOVE STAGE!!
act.10.5
OH, GEEZ!
I'M STARTING TO GET REALLY SCARED NOW.
SIGH
I SO HOPE REI ISN'T MAD AT ME!
BUT I BET HE IS. THAT'D BE JUST MY LUCK.
IN FACT, HE MIGHT EVEN KILL ME!
...
SHUDDER
HEY, UH, I'VE BEEN CURIOUS ABOUT THIS FOR A WHILE NOW, BUT...
...WHAT IS MR. SAGARA TO YOU?

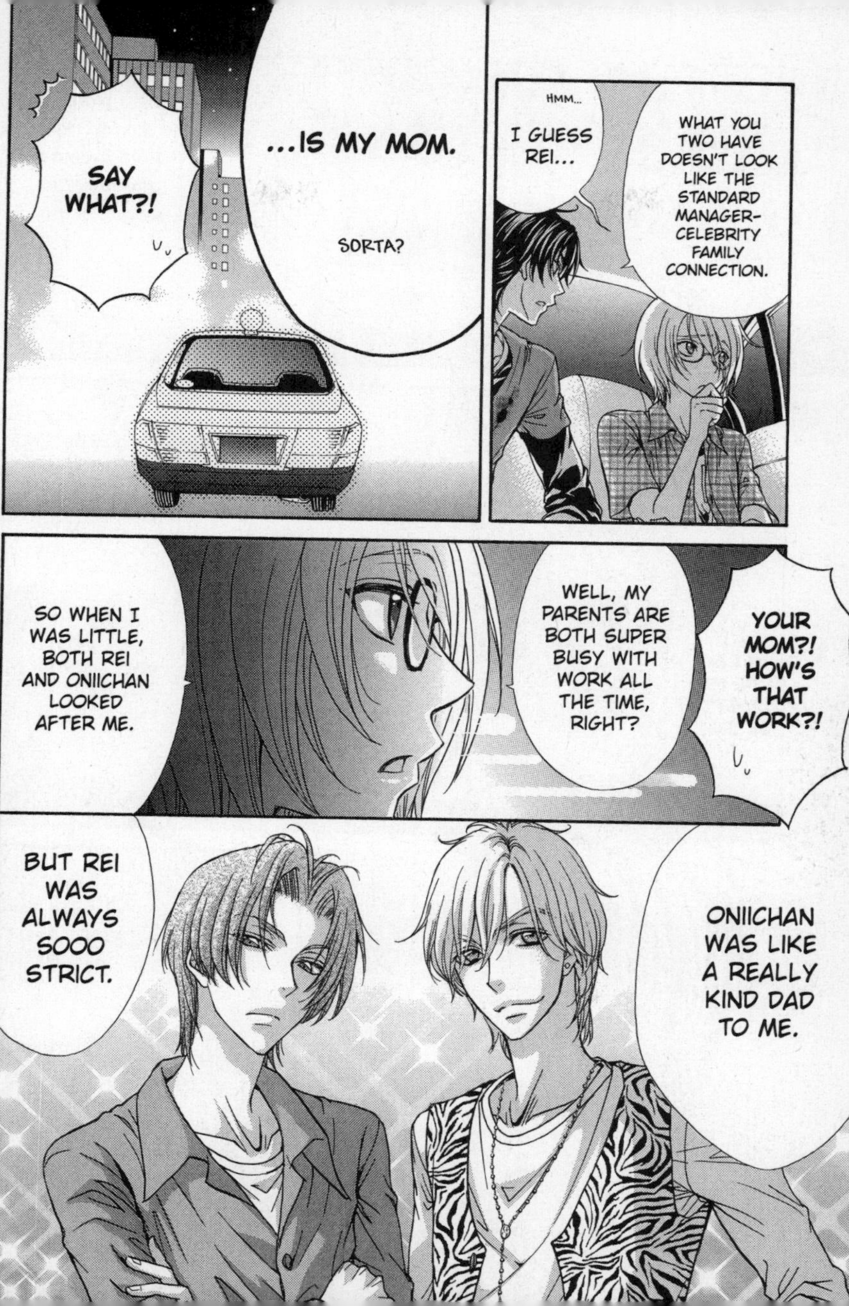
WHAT YOU TWO HAVE DOESN'T LOOK LIKE THE STANDARD MANAGER-CELEBRITY FAMILY CONNECTION.
HMM...
I GUESS REI...
...IS MY MOM.
SORTA?
SAY WHAT?!
YOUR MOM?! HOW'S THAT WORK?!
WELL, MY PARENTS ARE BOTH SUPER BUSY WITH WORK ALL THE TIME, RIGHT?
SO WHEN I WAS LITTLE, BOTH REI AND ONIICHAN LOOKED AFTER ME.
ONIICHAN WAS LIKE A REALLY KIND DAD TO ME.
BUT REI WAS ALWAYS SOOO STRICT.

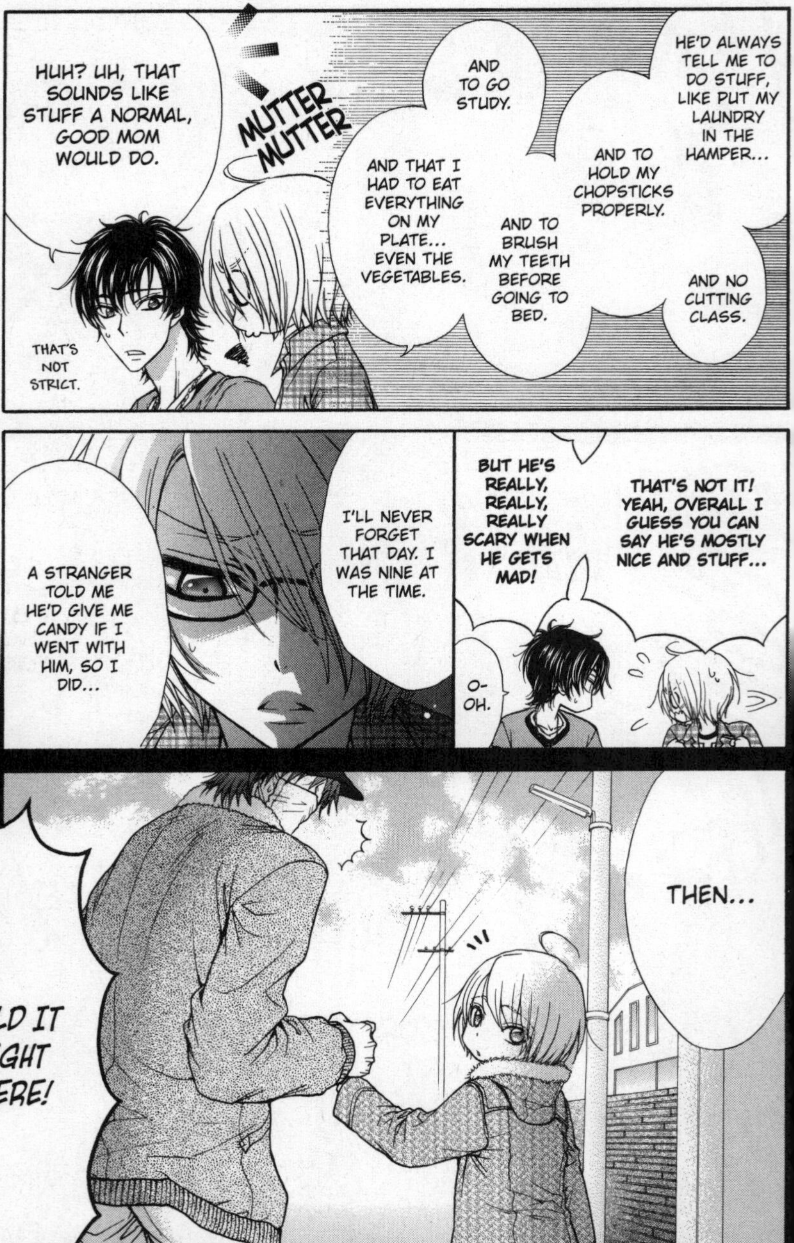
HE'D ALWAYS TELL ME TO DO STUFF, LIKE PUT MY LAUNDRY IN THE HAMPER...
AND TO HOLD MY CHOPSTICKS PROPERLY.
AND NO CUTTING CLASS.
AND TO GO STUDY.
AND TO BRUSH MY TEETH BEFORE GOING TO BED.
AND THAT I HAD TO EAT EVERYTHING ON MY PLATE... EVEN THE VEGETABLES.
MUTTER MUTTER
HUH? UH, THAT SOUNDS LIKE STUFF A NORMAL, GOOD MOM WOULD DO.
THAT'S NOT STRICT.
THAT'S NOT IT! YEAH, OVERALL I GUESS YOU CAN SAY HE'S MOSTLY NICE AND STUFF...
BUT HE'S REALLY, REALLY, REALLY SCARY WHEN HE GETS MAD!
O-OH.
I'LL NEVER FORGET THAT DAY. I WAS NINE AT THE TIME.
A STRANGER TOLD ME HE'D GIVE ME CANDY IF I WENT WITH HIM, SO I DID...
THEN...
HOLD IT RIGHT THERE!

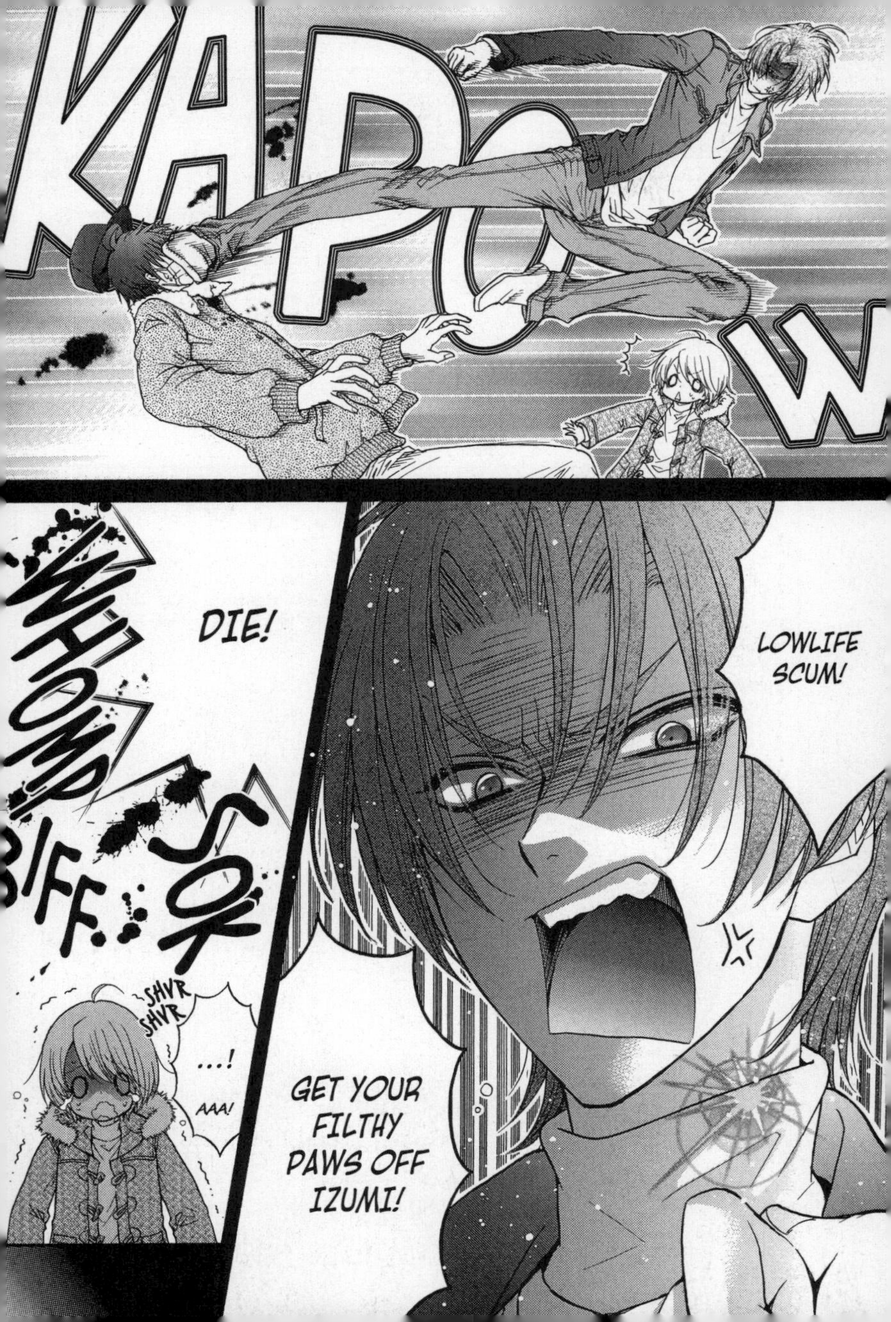
KAPOW
LOWLIFE SCUM!
GET YOUR FILTHY PAWS OFF IZUMI!
WHOMP!
SOK
BIFF
DIE!
SHVR SHVR
...!
AAA!

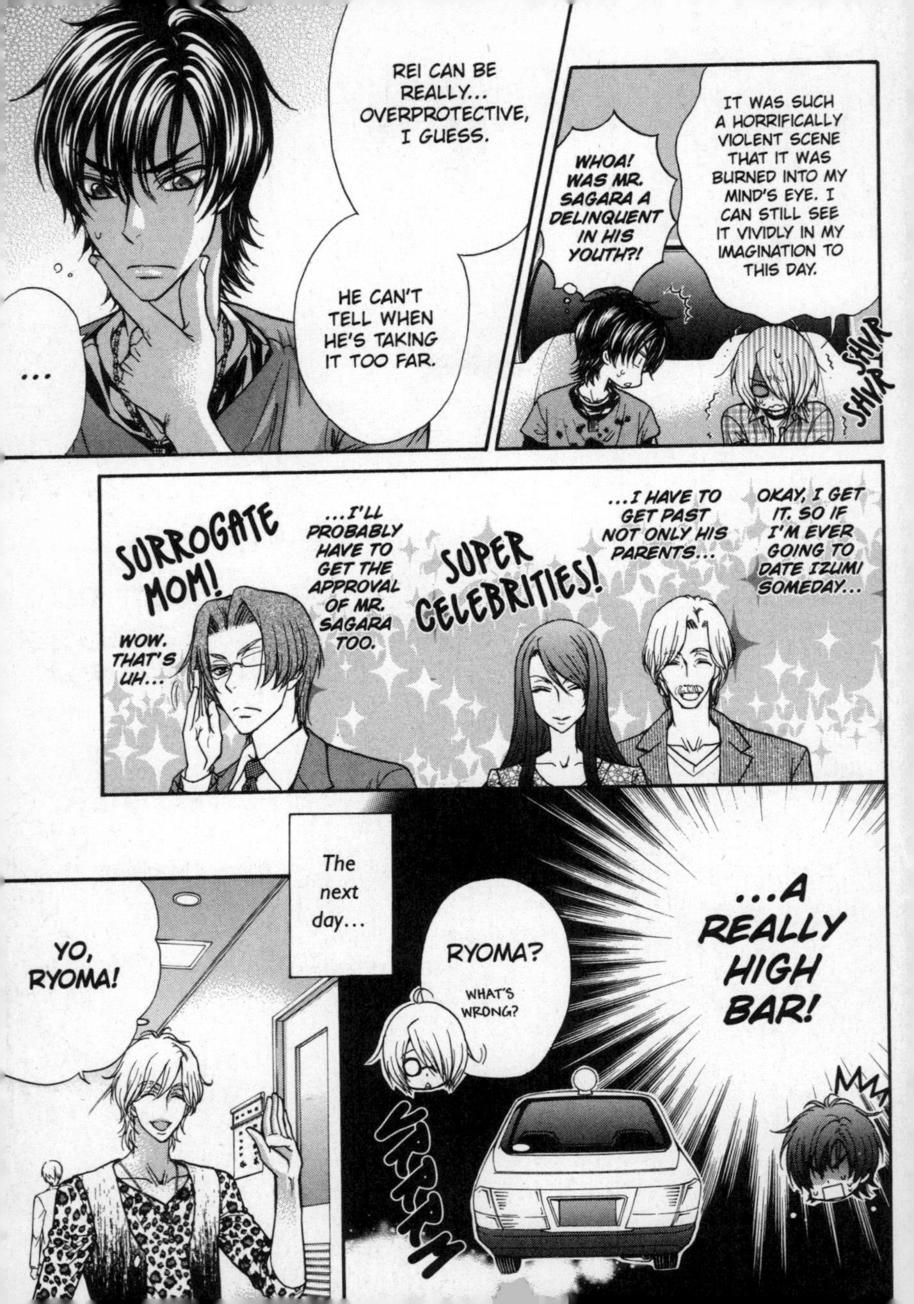
IT WAS SUCH A HORRIFICALLY VIOLENT SCENE THAT IT WAS BURNED INTO MY MIND'S EYE. I CAN STILL SEE IT VIVIDLY IN MY IMAGINATION TO THIS DAY.
WHOA! WAS MR. SAGARA A DELINQUENT IN HIS YOUTH?!
SHVR SHVR
REI CAN BE REALLY... OVERPROTECTIVE, I GUESS.
HE CAN'T TELL WHEN HE'S TAKING IT TOO FAR.
...
OKAY, I GET IT. SO IF I'M EVER GOING TO DATE IZUMI SOMEDAY...
...I HAVE TO GET PAST NOT ONLY HIS PARENTS...
SUPER CELEBRITIES!
...I'LL PROBABLY HAVE TO GET THE APPROVAL OF MR. SAGARA TOO.
SURROGATE MOM!
WOW. THAT'S UH...
...A REALLY HIGH BAR!
RYOMA?
WHAT'S WRONG?
VRRRRM
The next day...
YO, RYOMA!

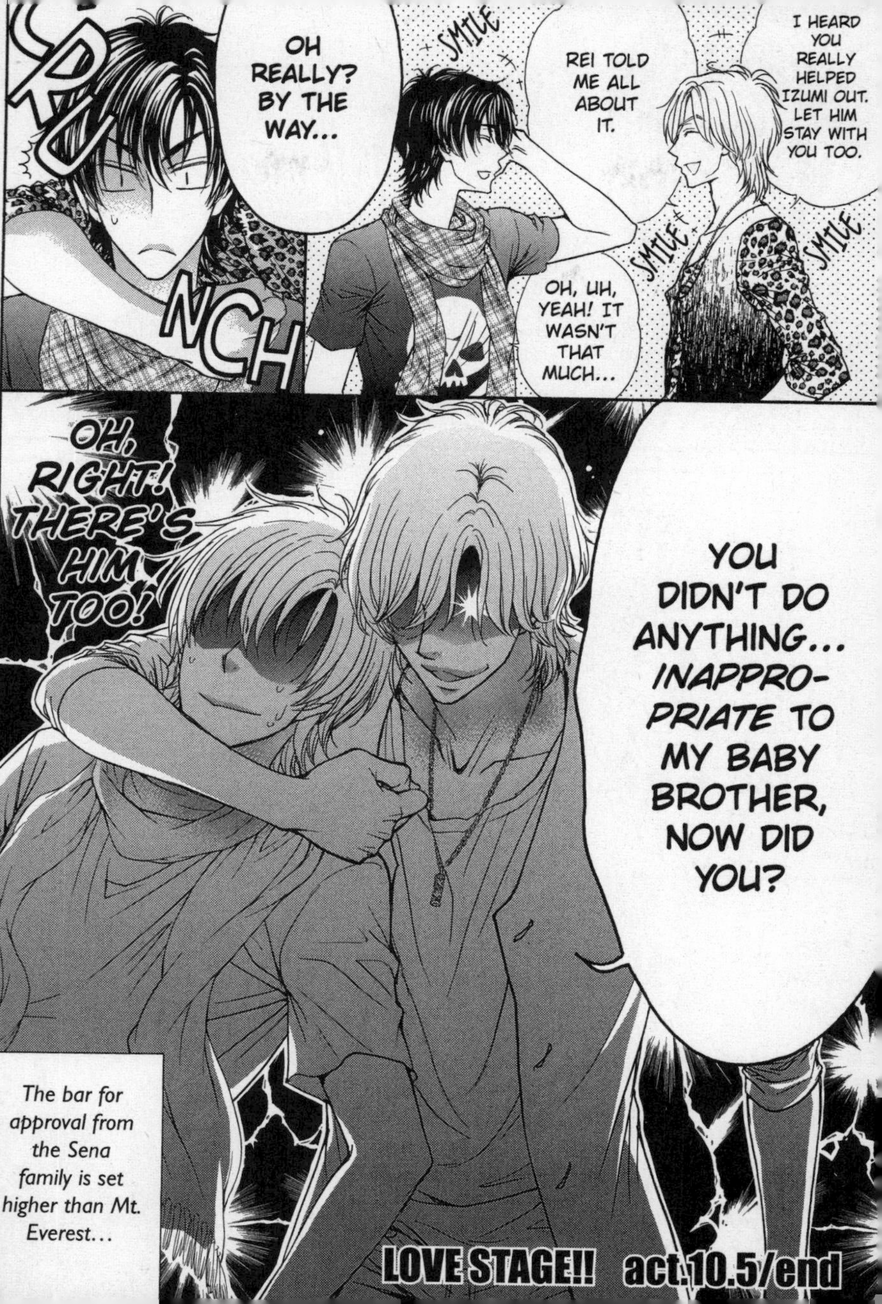
I HEARD YOU REALLY HELPED IZUMI OUT. LET HIM STAY WITH YOU TOO.
SMILE
SMILE
REI TOLD ME ALL ABOUT IT.
SMILE
OH, UH, YEAH! IT WASN'T THAT MUCH...
OH REALLY? BY THE WAY...
CRUNCH
YOU DIDN'T DO ANYTHING... *INAPPROPRIATE* TO MY BABY BROTHER, NOW DID YOU?
OH, RIGHT! THERE'S HIM TOO!
The bar for approval from the Sena family is set higher than Mt. Everest...
LOVE STAGE!! act.10.5/end

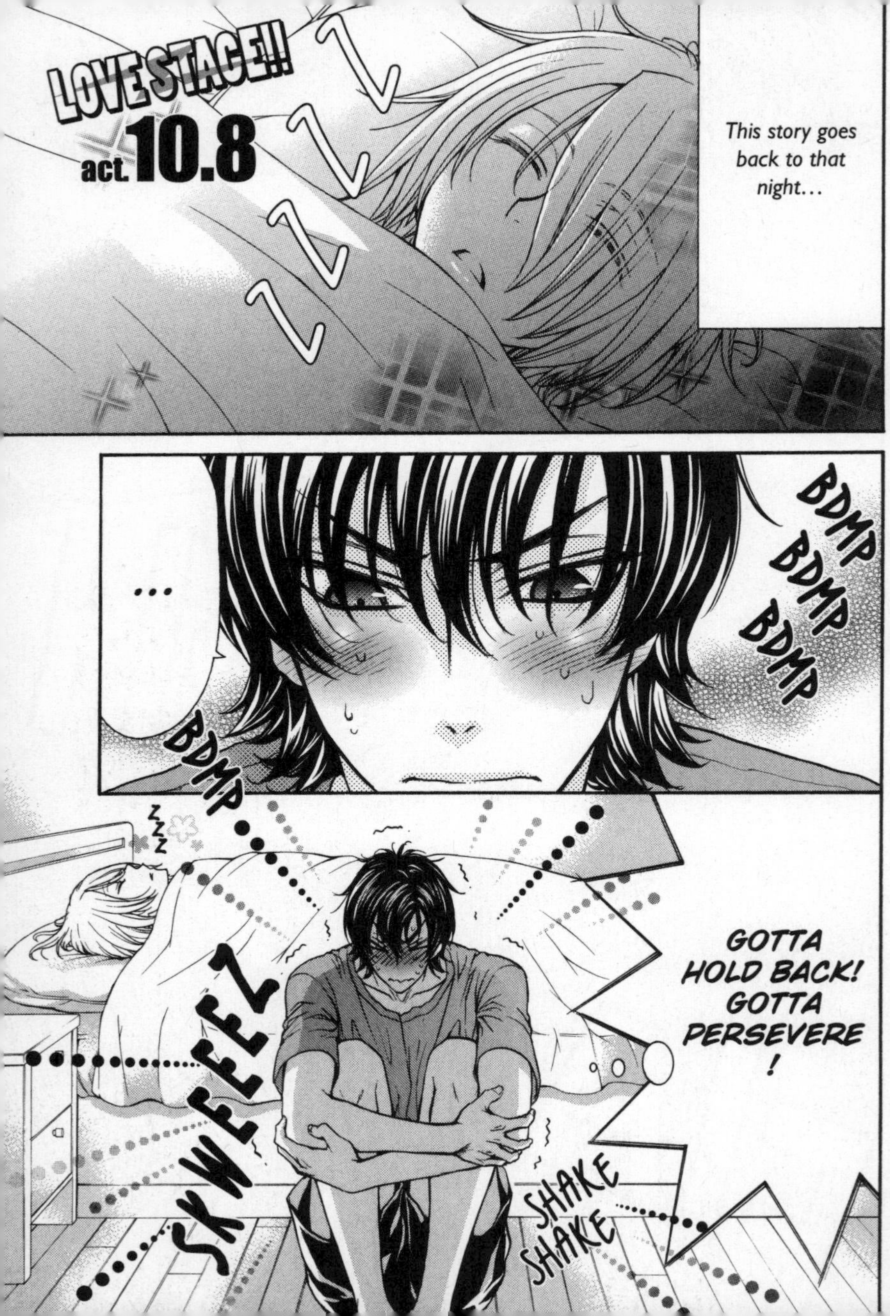
This story goes back to that night…
LOVE STAGE!!
act. 10.8
ZZZZZ
BDMP BDMP BDMP
…
BDMP
GOTTA HOLD BACK! GOTTA PERSEVERE!
SHAKE SHAKE
SKWEEZ
ZZZ

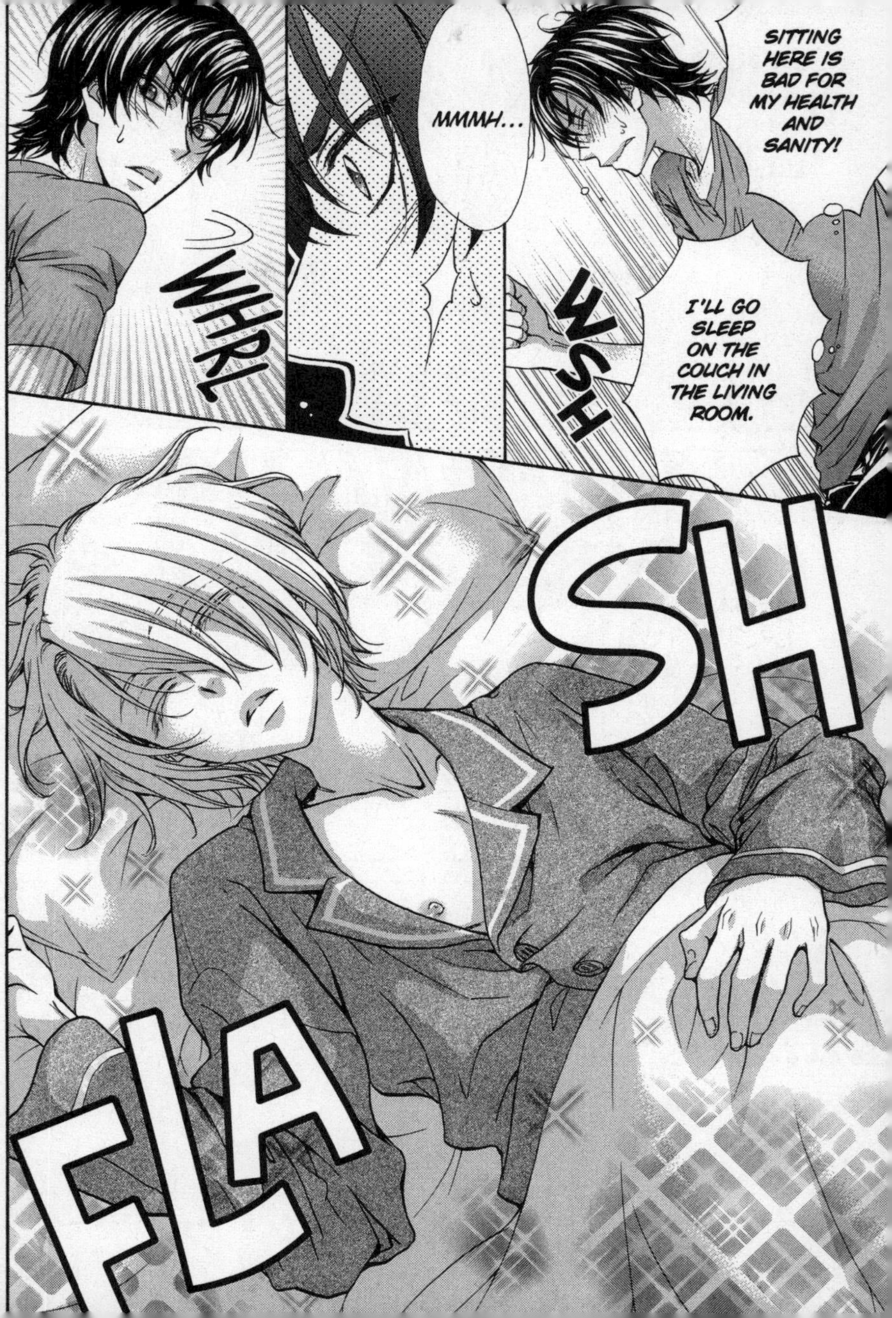
SITTING HERE IS BAD FOR MY HEALTH AND SANITY!
I'LL GO SLEEP ON THE COUCH IN THE LIVING ROOM.
WSH
MMMH...
WHIRL
FLASH

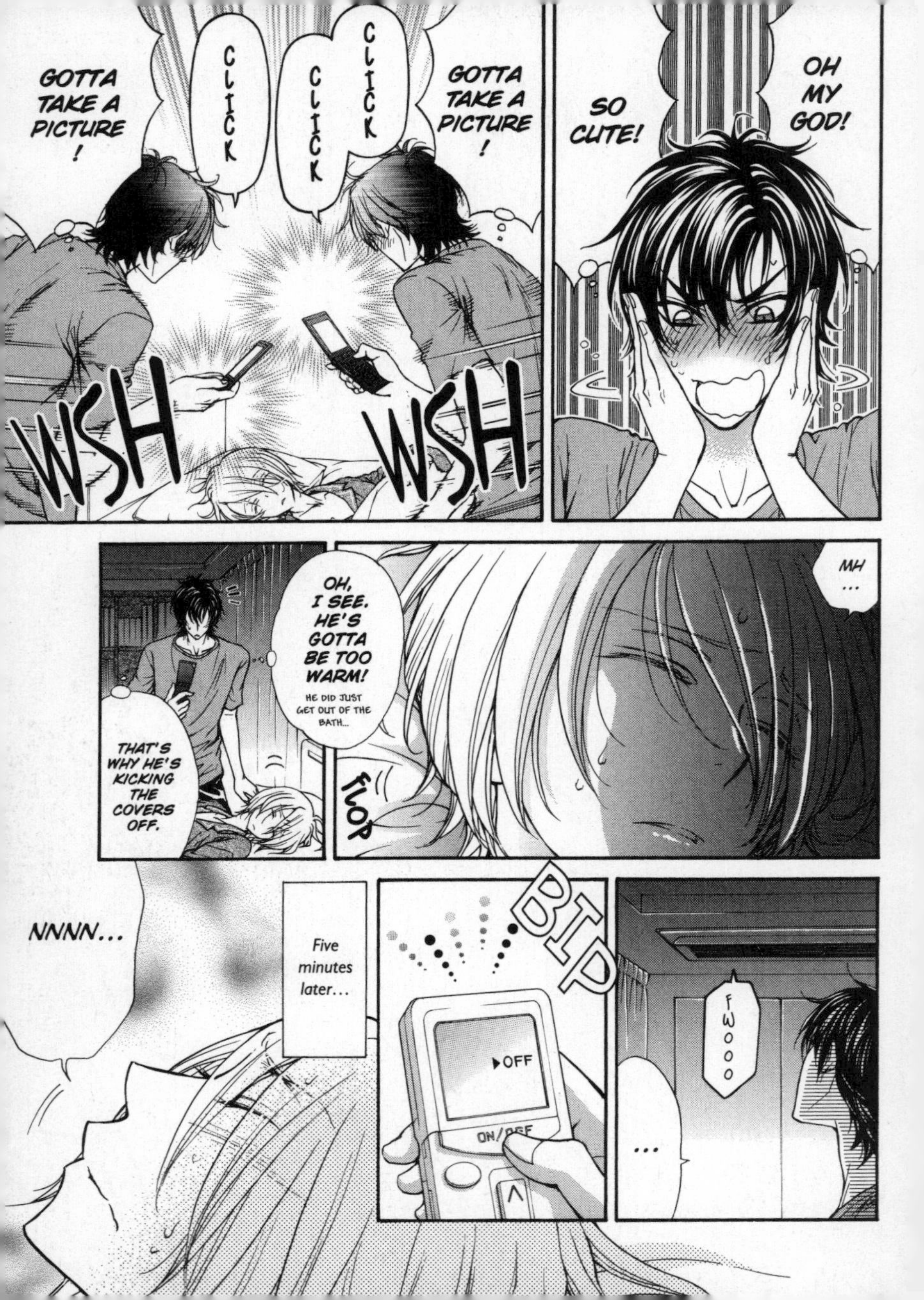
OH MY GOD!
SO CUTE!
GOTTA TAKE A PICTURE!
CLICK CLICK
CLICK CLICK
GOTTA TAKE A PICTURE!
WSH
WSH
MH...
FLOP
OH, I SEE. HE'S GOTTA BE TOO WARM!
HE DID JUST GET OUT OF THE BATH...
THAT'S WHY HE'S KICKING THE COVERS OFF.
FWOOO
...
BIP
▶OFF
ON/OFF
Five minutes later...
NNNN...

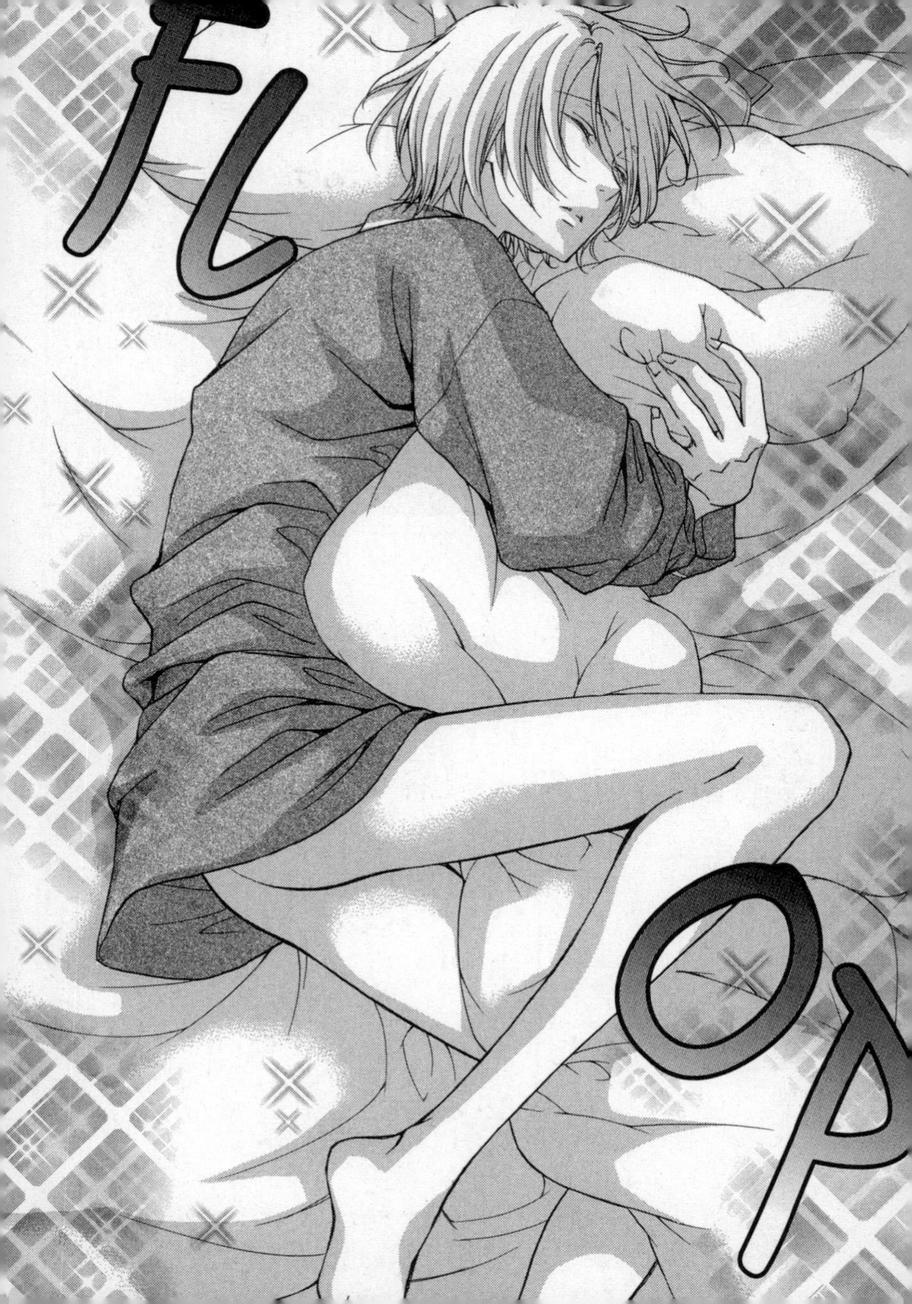
FLOP

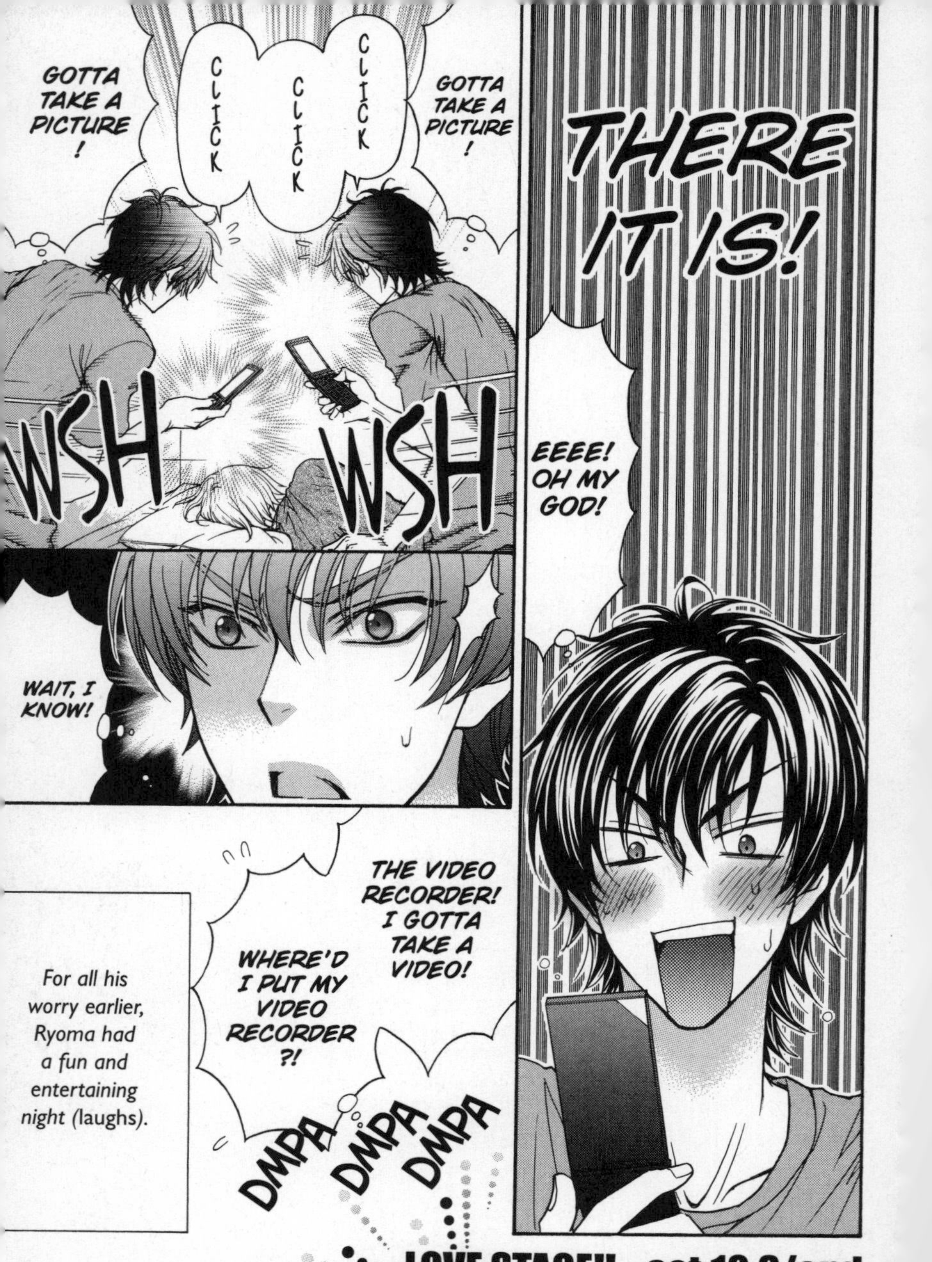
THERE IT IS!
EEEE! OH MY GOD!
GOTTA TAKE A PICTURE!
CLICK
CLICK
CLICK
GOTTA TAKE A PICTURE!
WSH
WSH
WAIT, I KNOW!
THE VIDEO RECORDER! I GOTTA TAKE A VIDEO!
WHERE'D I PUT MY VIDEO RECORDER?!
DMPA
DMPA
DMPA
For all his worry earlier, Ryoma had a fun and entertaining night (laughs).

LOVE STAGE!! act.10.8/end

Eiki Eiki is the creator of numerous yaoi and shojo manga. Her previous English-language releases include *Train ★ Train*, *Millennium Prime Minister*, and *The Art of Loving*. Born on December 6th, she is a Sagittarius with an A blood type.

Taishi Zaou's works have been published in English, French, and German. Her previous English-language releases include *Green Light*, *Fevered Kiss*, *Living For Tomorrow*, *Mysterious Love*, and *Electric Hands*. She was born a Capricorn on January 10th and has an O blood type.

About the Creators

Their hit series *Love Stage!!* has been adapted into a drama CD and a television anime series. Eiki Eiki and Taishi Zaou also publish *doujinshi* (independent comics) under the name "Kozouya." You can find out more about them at their website, http://www.kozouya.com/.

Love Stage!!
Volume 2
SuBLime Manga Edition

Story by **Eiki Eiki**
Art by **Taishi Zaou**

Translation—**Adrienne Beck**
Touch-up Art and Lettering—**Wally**
Cover and Graphic Design—**Yukiko Whitley**
Editor—**Jennifer LeBlanc**

LOVE STAGE!! Volume 2
©Eiki EIKI 2012
©Taishi ZAOU 2012
Edited by KADOKAWA SHOTEN
First published in Japan in 2012
by KADOKAWA CORPORATION, Tokyo.
English translation rights arranged
with KADOKAWA CORPORATION, Tokyo.

**ASUKA
COMICS
CLX^D**

Printed in the U.S.A.

Published by SuBLime Manga
P.O. Box 77010
San Francisco, CA 94107

10 9 8 7 6 5 4 3 2 1
First printing, July 2015

PARENTAL ADVISORY
LOVE STAGE!! is rated M for Mature and is recommended for mature
readers. This volume contains graphic imagery and mature themes.
MATURE

www.SuBLimeManga.com

For more information

on all our products, along with the most up-to-date news on releases, series announcements, and contests, please visit us at:

 SuBLimeManga.com

 twitter.com/**SuBLimeManga**

 facebook.com/**SuBLimeManga**

 SuBLimeManga.tumblr.com

SUBLIME
MANGA

More of the best digital BL manga from

SUBLIME

Sweet Monster
by Tsubaki Mikage

**Pretty Men
Fighting Dirty**
by Sakira

Perfect Training
by Yuiji Aniya

Available **Worldwide** in
Download-To-Own Format

Get them now for only **$5.99** each at **SuBLimeManga.com!**

Downloading is as easy as:

1

Login/Email

Password

LOGIN
REGISTER NOW
Forgot Password

2

PAY with **PayPal**

— OR —

Pay Now with **amazon** ▶

The Simple, Trusted Way to Pay

Digital Edition includes **BOTH**
Download-to-own PDF and
online viewing option.

3

View your purchase as:

DOWNLOAD-TO-OWN PDF